TALLEYRAND
Statesman Priest

The Agent-General of the Clergy

And the Church of France at the End of the Old Regime

by

Louis S. Greenbaum

THE CATHOLIC UNIVERSITY OF AMERICA PRESS, INC.

Washington, D. C. 20017

1970

227932

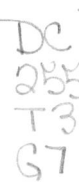

Copyright © 1970 by
The Catholic University of America Press, Inc.
All rights reserved

Library of Congress Catalog Card No.: 76-101408
S.B.N. 8132-0497-8

TO MY PARENTS

AND

TO THE MEMORY OF MY GRANDMOTHER,
Mary Goldgut Koppel, 1877-1955

TABLE OF CONTENTS

page

PREFACE vii

INTRODUCTION 1

CHAPTER I

The Genesis of a Clerical Career..................... 7

CHAPTER II

The General Assembly of the Clergy of France............ 24

CHAPTER III

The Agent-General of the Clergy of France:
the Office and the Man 57

CHAPTER IV

The Agent-General and the Inviolability of the
Church Temporal 79

CHAPTER V

The Agent-General and the Maintenance of
Ecclesiastical Jurisdiction 107

CHAPTER VI

The Agent-General as Servant of the Clergy............ 145

CHAPTER VII

The Agent-General and the Administrative Machinery
of the Clergy 174

CHAPTER VIII

Talleyrand's Legacy to the Church.................... 203

Notes 217

Bibliography 258

Preface

The purpose of this book is explained in the pages which follow. Here I should like to acknowledge a debt of gratitude owed to many people who contributed in various ways to the preparation of my work. Foremost among them are the late Professor Chester Penn Higby of the University of Wisconsin, whose seminar won scores of students to careers in European history; the late Professor Crane Brinton of Harvard, who so effectively demonstrated the central bearing of religion in history; and Professor George H. Williams of the Harvard Divinity School in whose exciting classroom I began the study of Church history. It is a pleasure to acknowledge the interest and helpfulness of Professor Joseph N. Moody of The Catholic University of America and the Reverend Robert Trisco, able Managing Editor of *The Catholic Historical Review*. All these men have furnished years of generous assistance and encouragement which these expressions of gratefulness could never hope to repay.

Grants from the Fulbright Commission, the French Government, the American Philosophical Society and the Research Council of the University of Massachusetts enabled me to gain access to the archival material in France which provides the basis for this book. Research was immeasurably facilitated by archivists and librarians abroad, too numerous to name, who lightened my burdens in the national, departmental, municipal, ecclesiastical, and private archives and libraries listed in the bibliography.

Particular appreciation is extended to the Broglie family and its present head, the eminent scientist, Duke Louis de Broglie, and his sister, Countess Jean de Pange, Count Bernard de Lacombe, and M. Robert Lacour-Gayet—Talleyrand enthusiasts all—who graciously shared their papers with me. I am indebted finally to the suggestions of Professor Jean Leflon of the Institut Catholique of Paris, to the stimulating discussions with colleagues in the History Department of the University of Massachusetts, and to the kindness of the editors of the *Journal of Modern History, French Historical Studies,* and *The Catholic Historical Review* for permission to quote from articles published in their journals.

To all these teachers, friends, benefactors, colleagues, and institutions I wish to express my thanks.

Introduction

This book which deals with the history of the Catholic Church of France in the decade before the Revolution has a two-fold aim. First, it wishes to explain the work of the executive administrative officer of the First Estate in the Old Regime, the Agent-General of the Clergy, occupied between 1780 and 1785 by the legendary statesman and diplomat, Charles-Maurice de Talleyrand-Périgord (1754-1838). Second, it seeks to weigh the influence of this ecclesiastical ministry in the forging of a political genius whose life was intimately linked with the fortunes of the French nation from Louis XVI to Louis-Philippe.

The history of the Church of France which Talleyrand served after the third quarter of the eighteenth century reveals a dramatic change in emphasis from matters of faith and doctrine to an almost exclusive preoccupation with temporal affairs. The Church had already composed the Protestant issue, by might rather than by prudence or clemency. It weathered the divisive and acrimonious theologico-political squabbles between Jesuits and Jansenists which more effectively than the freethinkers rent the internal harmony of the clergy and weakened the appeal of religion in the Age of Reason. It repaired the worst excesses of the moribund religious communities in the kingdom and beat back the challenges of the Parlements to its temporal and even spiritual jurisdiction. Finally, it parried, valiantly if somewhat futilely, the onslaughts of the Philosophers against religious orthodoxy commenced more than a quarter-century before. In the twilight of the Old Regime the Church was faced with another, and in some ways, more elemental question. At stake was the inviolability of the clergy's landed wealth and corporate privileges, symbols which brought into question the whole matter of its existence as an autonomous Estate.

For more than two hundred years before 1789 the Church had been threatened with the secularization of its temporal property. These threats, initiated by political groups jealous of clerical power and opulence or convinced that the State could make better use of ecclesiastical revenues and domains, had begun as early as the Wars of Religion when the Estates-General of Orleans in 1560 proposed that the clergy should be forced to deliver up to the nation the enormous riches in its store. While none of these menaces, however vocal or widespread, actually materialized during the Old Regime, thanks largely to a monarchy which to the last remained solemnly devoted to the established Church even after important segments of its subjects ceased to be, the successful one was launched in the early Revolution (October 10, 1789) in form of a motion before the National Assembly by a Catholic prelate, the same Charles-Maurice de Talleyrand-Périgord, Bishop of Autun since 1788. It was this motion, familiar to every student of French history, which fathered the sequestration law of November 2, whose provisions resulted in the dissolution of the Church's ancient patrimony, its autonomous governing bodies, its fiscal-corporate privileges, and its national-diocesan administration.

Thanks to his five-year service as Agent-General, into whose hands the Church's temporal and corporate privileges were entrusted, the youthful bishop of thirty-five who mounted the tribune of the Assembly was qualified as few others in France to talk about the clergy's organization, administration, and finances. With one stroke the legislation he helped inaugurate decreed the destruction of a proud and ancient institution whose divine origins only a handful of unbelievers disputed, whose spiritual vitality and intellectual vigor placed it in the forefront of the churches of the West, and whose eminence, wealth, and political power survived the exigencies and upheavals of a thousand years of French history. It also marked the rupture of the historic union between throne and altar, signalized, on the one hand, by the Church's age-old monarchism and coronation of the king and, on the other, by the ecclesiastical paternalism of the sovereigns of France whose royal edicts betrayed no discriminatory separation between Church and State in legal and judicial matters of common concern to both.

Alone among the three orders of the kingdom, the clergy could boast of being a true Estate, that is, a distinct legal, corporate, structural entity, with an elaborate and effective central administration and personnel responsible to it alone. More powerful and respected than the provincial estates, and in marked contrast to the Second Estate whose corporate privileges boiled down to the *taille* exemption and favors in the payment of taxes determined by the State, the clergy enjoyed almost complete financial autonomy and constituted a body separate from all others by its organization and prerogatives. Its permanent General Assembly, which met regularly since the time of Henry III, exercised not only doctrinal, jurisdictional, and disciplinary powers, but also broad legislative, temporal, and financial authority, rivalling that of the State itself, over a clerical society variously estimated at between 130,000 and 200,000 members. And like the State its broad avenues of autonomous government extended beyond the national level to the provinces, dioceses, and 40,000 parishes. Despite huge reservoirs of corporate wealth in lands, buildings, and revenues, long the envy of the other orders of the realm, the clergy could not be taxed like the other estates. Throughout the course of the Old Monarchy, the kings of France never formally put an end to the Church's pretensions at once of absolute corporate immunity, of the divine character of its property and privileges (which Bossuet claimed were an integral part of the Catholic religion), and of the illegality of being taxed by the State except by its own consent. Indeed, until the very end, the clergy never relinquished the precious power of bargaining and setting conditions on the payment of its royal subsidies. In return for these it got solemn governmental recognition of its immunities; it remained sovereign in the levy and collection of these monies by its own machinery; and it reduced the whole burden of its fiscal contributions, which most students of French national finance agree was the lowest of the three Estates and far below its wealth and ability to pay, to the *dons gratuits* or voluntary gifts.

Secure in its spiritual monopoly of the realm, being the only legally recognized cult, with the exclusive right to define theological truth and religious-moral values, the Church of France was invested with still other awesome powers. To it was given the exercise of public worship, the right of public education, the supervision of public assistance and hospitals, and the care of the poor. As the representative of the State it touched the lives of Frenchmen from cradle to grave: it maintained the civil register of births and deaths, celebrated marriages, and with public officials received wills. It wielded considerable power in shaping public opinion and conscience through its control of religion on the parish level, through its maintenance of the schools and universities of the land, and through the work of its intellectual leaders and literary organs. It assured the diffusion of the government's laws to the farthest corners of the kingdom through the tribunes of the parish churches and contributed powerfully to the maintenance of justice. Nor was it an inconsiderable force in determining the course of royal policy through the nationwide publicity the well known and respected General Assemblies of the Clergy gave its ecclesiastical judgments and its opinions on crucial issues affecting Church and State. Its autonomy as a closed corporation was repeatedly acknowledged by the kings of France right up to the close of the monarchy. Indeed, insofar as the crown recognized it as the custodian of the national religious conscience, the Church was an institution of public law, a legal and moral unity which linked the king's subjects into a common bond. The need to insure the efficacy of its spiritual mission explains the receipt of the tithes from all classes, including the nobility, whose collection was guaranteed by the State. Similarly it assured the Church the retention of its patrimonial property and the benefices which sustained the clergy, the permanence of its organs of central and provincial government, the jurisdiction of separate ecclesiastical tribunals to try clerical personnel, and its ability to act before the king's councils and courts. To permit the pursuit of the ecclesiastical ministry, the crown accorded the clergy personal exemptions from military service and municipal charges and conferred special rights of trusteeship and guardianship. This situation is of course explicable not only within a context where Church and State were not separated but also where the Catholic sovereigns of the realm were personally committed to the interests of religion.

The key to the First Estate's success as a privileged order lay in the fact that alone among the three it secured and maintained independence in regularizing its fiscal obligations to the State. Its financial strength, based on landed wealth and "voluntary" taxes, made it a power to reckon with. As an equal it negotiated its monetary gifts with the king each five years. This envied prerogative of giving voluntarily, maintained by unwritten agreement since the Middle Ages and contractually for well over two hundred years, ended only with the fall of the ecclesiastical temporal. Another significant factor which explains the clergy's unique corporate success was the effectiveness of its ministers, the Agents-General, who constituted an instrument of perpetual surveillance of the rights and authority of the First Estate and acted as permanent representatives of its interests before the king and government. Like the General Assembly of the Clergy itself, they had no parallel among the other two orders.

In a very real sense, then, the clergy can be likened to a small nation living apart. It had its own popularly acknowledged constitution, its own representative system, its own national administration and courts. It clung jealously to its privileges and divided its taxes by an independent scheme approved by the government. It guarded its group liberties through national meetings, which were forbidden to the other orders in the nation, for two centuries. Secure in its relations with the sovereign, it addressed the king in words of freedom which the rest of the nation dared not speak. In the words of one contemporary, "[France] is today the only kingdom of Europe where the ministers of the Church have retained the republican form [of government] . . . joined to their other prerogatives this tends to give them great political influence."[1]

The period under examination, an era of severe financial crisis, threatening national bankruptcy, and widening popular hostility to the opulent clerical leadership, saw the property and immunities of the First Estate under bombardment. If the Church could not face its critics with united ranks in the decade before 1789, it was because the Catholic clergy, some of whom were in open rebellion against their ecclesiastical superiors, was divided by class lines closely akin to those which separated the Third Estate from the other two. The secularization of religious ideals and the mocking of spiritual institutions and beliefs by the new Philosophy (contemptuously referred to by the Church as the "evil books") made inroads in the opinions of the clergy, as they had on the laity, all over the kingdom. Indeed *philosophe* priests, like the Abbés Mably, Meslier, Marmontel, de Prades, Morellet, Raynal, Yvon, Condillac, Audra, Prévost, Mallet and Terrasson, successors of the libertine priests of the Temple earlier in the century, contributed to the success of irreligion by their own popular works. The new ideas, combined with the unwillingness of the hierarchical Church to accommodate the genuine economic and social grievances of the plebeian parish clergy, and considering the leadership it gradually forfeited by indifference and impiety, unfastened the bonds of allegiance to a society founded on tradition, aristocratic privilege, and outmoded social beliefs. As defender of the clergy's interests between 1780 and 1785 Agent-General Talleyrand held a place of creative responsibility in the temporal issues of concern to his estate and, as will be shown, left his imprint on the serious ecclesiastical decisions of the period.

The second theme of this book is that the office occupied by Talleyrand, for the most part neglected by his fecund biographers, was a capital episode in the life of one of modern Europe's dominant political figures. It is frequently forgotten that the controversial minister of seven governments and a half-century of national leadership, traditionally studied in the context of diplomacy, politics, and statecraft, spent the first thirty-seven years of his life as a priest. The reasons for this neglect are not hard to explain—a large part of the blame can be laid to Talleyrand himself. Though the famed statesman repeatedly acknowledged that it was in the period of his ecclesiastical formation that he developed his flexibility of mind *(souplesse de raisonnement)* and the other skills and attainments of his later political career, he was not proud of the clerical profession. As a defrocked priest, an apostate bishop, and excommunicated Catholic; as the villain of the Church's sequestration and the founding father of the Civil Constitutional Clergy, he understandably avoided all discussions, oral or written. In the absence at once of reliable documentation and serious monographs covering these formative years, historians have summarily dismissed his pre-episcopal career in two ways. If they were favorable, they repeated the platitudes of early hagiographers and the banal confessions of his memoirs. If they were hostile, as most were, they reproduced the fabulous allegations of unprincipled publicists and the bitter denunciations of polemicists. The documents of the Church have not been systematically exploited in evaluating this unvisited portion of his life.

The hope of the present work is to fill this gap by examining the one abandoned segment of Talleyrand's public service. For it was as Agent-General of the Clergy that a journeyman priest, hard at work in the company of some of the nation's most accomplished leaders and tested administrators, was first exposed to broad and difficult questions of crucial bearing to both Church and State. It was here, too, that Talleyrand earned his apprenticeship, and first laurels, in finance, legislation, administration, law, diplomacy, and politics, far from the breath of scandal and class treason which after 1789 were to ruin his reputation and cast a pall over his entire public career. Without the Agency-General which prepared its occupant for a bishopric, there would never have been the school for statesmanship nor the introduction to national office, without which, in turn, there might never have been the notorious politician of the history books.

I

The Genesis of a Clerical Career

Had the right leg of Talleyrand—like the legendary nose of Cleopatra—been just a little longer, his destiny, and France's, might have been very different. But a fall incurred shortly after birth in February, 1754, in a suburb of Paris where the son of courtier parents had been left to be nursed out,[1] caused an atrophy of the right leg by three inches. This affliction, which resulted in permanent lameness, rendered Talleyrand unfit for the career of arms and the leadership of the family assured him by the rights of primogeniture.[2] For the rest of his life it would remain a barrier to success and a trademark of humiliation and pain. The future Prince de Bénévent was not to become the Count de Talleyrand. The scion of the ancient Counts of Périgord and Grignols and the Princes of Chalais[3] could no longer aspire to his father's title and property nor to the glorious military tradition of a family whose nobility went back to Hugh Capet and whose generations provided a long succession of generals who gave up their lives heroically in the service of the sovereigns of France.

But for this misfortune, he too might have become a general, a minister, or a governor, like the rest of his Talleyrand and d'Antigny ancestors.[4] Instead, as a younger son of the nobility (for he lost his inheritance to his second brother Archambault, "whose faculties," Lord Brougham righteously proclaimed, "were far more crippled by nature than his bodily frame had been from mischance")[5] it was decided that, however lacking in vocation or inclination, he would seek his fortune in the Church. By its wealth, abundant offices, and opportunity for rapid advancement, the Church was at once a worthy dumping grounds and a generous system of outdoor relief for the superfluous sons of the Second Estate. The decision to enter young Talleyrand into the ranks of the priesthood instead of allowing him to perpetuate the chivalric cult of his ancestors was, as has been aptly suggested, "the first of his misfortunes, and the source of all others."[6]

Generations of historians have followed the lead of the Orleanist scholar François Mignet who concluded that Talleyrand became a priest by "social predestination."[7] The genesis of Talleyrand's sacerdotal career, he explained, was to be found in the remorseless social conventions of the Old Regime by which the professions of children were determined by their parents in the best interests of the family without regard to their wishes, temperament, or particular attributes. Eldest sons were sent to the army to perpetuate the glory of the family and from there were channeled to worthy dignities at court, in the provincial government, or in the king's magistracy. Cadets were sent, or pushed, into the Church to lighten the load on the head of the family and to maintain the integrity of the family patrimony. Tonsured early to secure benefices, they obtained incomes and abbeys which assured financial independence. For the highest nobility the road to success led straight to the episcopate.[8] As Talleyrand put it, "It was the family that one loved much more than individuals who were not yet recognized, . . . it was generally considered enough to prepare for their advancement . . . to marry them off, or to augment their fortune."[9]

The parents responsible for this unkind, but not uncommon, decision were both servants of the monarchy. Talleyrand *père* was lieutenant-general of Louis XV's armies with *cordon bleu;* and though he had no time to instruct his own sons, he served as tutor to the future Louis XVI. Mme de Talleyrand was *dame d'honneur* of Louis XVI's mother and *dame du palais* of his wife. Their responsibilities at court left little time to raise their children, to supervise their adolescence, or to guide their education. Despite choicest birth and envied places at court, the Talleyrands suffered, like many members of their class, from relative poverty. Their fortune, like that of other first families of the Sword, had drastically waned by the latter part of the eighteenth century.[10] Married to a valiant but impecunious Count, Mme de Talleyrand had early in the marriage brought an annual annuity of 15,000 *livres* from her dowry as the main and, for some time, the sole income of the family.[11] The young *ménage* were tenants of simple quarters on the rue Garancière in Paris, in the shadows of Servandoni's twin towers of the Church of Saint-Sulpice, close by the Sorbonne, the religious and intellectual

Genesis of a Clerical Career

heart of eighteenth-century Paris.[12] The mother of Mme de Talleyrand, probably in place of servants, kept house. Their income was scarcely enough to maintain a residence in one of Paris' fashionable pre-Revolution neighborhoods and to meet the high costs of living at Versailles. A contemporary memorialist wrote that the Talleyrands "lived from the buffets of the court at public expense" and that young Charles-Maurice had, in effect, been nourished "by crumbs that fell from the banquet tables of Versailles."[13] There are suggestions that at one time the Talleyrands had been hard pressed enough to consider pawning the family Bible.[14] Talleyrand admitted that his first obligation upon receipt of the lucrative Abbey of St. Denis, as a young priest of twenty-one, was to pay off his school debts which his parents had not been able to discharge.[15]

The inventories of Count Charles-Daniel de Talleyrand's property, revenues, and expenses made at the time of his death, on November 6, 1788, reinforce the image of the family's mediocre means.[16] The Count owed 65,166 *l*. His revenues from government and court had amounted to 13,541 *l*.; similar income of his wife was 5,400 *l*. This made a total of 18,941 *l*. or one-third of what his brother, the Archbishop of Reims, spent annually on his kitchen and stables alone.[17] To cover the Count's obligations at his death, 18,000 *l*. were forthcoming from funds connected with Mme de Talleyrand's dowry, an equal amount from the Talleyrands' combined court revenues, 4,112 *l*. from their son Archambault, who made an exceptionally good marriage,[18] and the remaining 24,000 *l*. from the prelate of Reims.

With family indigence added to his dread infirmity, it was all the more necessary that Talleyrand should enter the service of God at once to provide for his future and to exempt his parents from his support. And for one of the great nobles of the kingdom there was either the army or the Church. "A man of my name scarcely had any other career . . . I understood . . . that my parents were determined according to what they regarded as family interest to lead me to a profession for which I showed no disposition whatever."[19] The Church was Talleyrand's fortune and fatality. Though furnishing the means for power, fame, and wealth, it also demanded conformity to a rigorous sacerdotal code which he loathed and resented.[20] The tragedy of Talleyrand's impressment into ecclesiastical service was not only that he had none of the spiritual qualities required for the priesthood, but also that he openly abjured his forced profession until his death.[21] Born without spiritual conviction, he could not look to his parents to induce or encourage it. To as sober a critic as Lord Acton it was the Talleyrands who were responsible for their son's baleful future: "If by taking orders without vocation he became a sacrilegious priest, destined in his long life never to know the security of a tranquil conscience, the crime was theirs."[22]

Mignet's long standing hypothesis is in need of revision, because the decision to bring Talleyrand into the Church was founded, to a far greater extent than has been previously understood, on ecclesiastical rather than purely social considerations. Talleyrand's clerical career cannot be explained, as it has been, simply as the result of the decision of his parents, for whom ecclesiastical offices existed as just another vehicle of social convenience and as a way to avoid the financial responsibilities of their children's future. Rather it is to be ascribed in large measure to the personal ambitions of the boy's uncle, Alexandre-Angélique de Talleyrand-Périgord (1736-1821), Archbishop of pre-Revolution Reims and later Cardinal-Archbishop of Restoration Paris.[23] These ambitions derived at once from the character of the French Church of the latter eighteenth century in which, as archbishop and First Peer of France, the elder Talleyrand spoke with preeminent authority, and from the peculiar organization and practices of a tightly knit episcopate, in which he was one of the prime policy-makers. This man, who received as a lame acolyte the eldest son of his only brother, the natural heir of an ancient but straitened family, intended to do what all his episcopal colleagues were doing during this period—to magnify the riches and power of his family by establishing a dynasty of Talleyrands in the most lucrative ecclesiastical offices, the bishoprics. In order to carry this out, he needed a successor. The French Church of the later Old Regime was no different from the army, the Parlements, and the magistracy, insofar as its benefices and higher offices were construed not as public charges but as the exclusive, quasi-feudal preserve, the "apanage" of the nobility, and the private hereditary patrimony of their families.[24] As the Abbé Morellet cogently observed, the first thought of the young patrician bishop-to-be was to enrich himself, as his cousins of the lay nobility had, by "a proper marriage . . . to a well dowered see."[25]

Although it was this uncle who introduced the future diplomat into the Church and provided for his sacerdotal and episcopal promotion, little has survived of their ties. Clerical biographers of the pious prelate, chagrined at the blood relationship between saint and apostate, have understandably attempted to draw the connecting lines as casually as possible.[26] Even the biographers of Talleyrand have accorded the Archbishop scant reference, usually dismissing him as a mere accessory to the plot of the Talleyrand clan to ensnare the free-thinking Charles-Maurice, against his will, into the Church.[27] It is not, however, as a peripheral figure, as he is consistently represented, but as the key influence in his nephew's clerical career that the Cardinal's true role becomes clear. For it is certain that without his repeated favors and intercessions, Talleyrand, regardless of what his parents wanted, would never have been received into the priesthood nor would he have risen so quickly and effortlessly to its highest offices. Moreover, it is only in understanding the Archbishop's passion to establish a successor that it is possible to explain why a prelate who was revered as a saint in his own lifetime tolerated the commonly asserted unecclesiastical deportment of his nephew, and why he braved the remorseless opposition of the "priest in spite of himself" in order to reconcile him to his forced profession. Talleyrand-Périgord's actions are comprehensible not because he wished above everything else to facilitate the plans of his brother and sister-in-law—as will be shown, he more than fulfilled ordinary family obligations—but because he had personal motives for bringing his kinsman into the ministry.

The French episcopate on the eve of the French Revolution was not only a hermetically sealed corporation of highest-born nobles but a tight clique of a few episcopal families. Of France's 130 bishoprics nearly one-quarter of the offices were controlled by thirteen families: the Castellane family controlled four dioceses; the La Rochefoucauld and the Cortois families, three each; and the Rohan, Talleyrand-Périgord, Champion de Cicé, Brienne, Bernis, Conzié, Du Plessis d'Argentré, Nicolaï, Barral, and Lastic families, two each.[28] Several episcopal seats had become the almost exclusive patrimony of certain families whose only obligation was to furnish these offices with titularies at each generation.[29] The aristocratic prelacy that monopolized the bishoprics extended their patronage to the collateral prizes of the Church: the abbeys, priories, collegiates, canonries, and prebends; and to the ecclesiastical charges of the crown, the almoners, chaplains, preceptors, and readers of the royal family.[30] Talleyrand's observation, that ". . . within the Church and the episcopate the most lucrative dignities had become the almost exclusive property of the noble class"[31] is accurate in every respect. The monarchy, which for centuries had done so much to deracinate and domesticate the recently predatory nobility, could not oppose a situation in the Church which was, in large part, of its own making. As with the lay nobility the king was also responsible for supporting the patrician members of the priesthood, who were compensated by rich ecclesiastical offices for their loss of political power.[32]

In order that these lucrative holdings should not escape the family, many sons like Talleyrand, regardless of their qualifications and oftentimes against their will, were conscripted into clerical service. It is no accident that among these forced clerics should have figured the four founding bishops of the Constitutional Church: Talleyrand, Loménie de Brienne, Jarente, and Lafont de Savines.[33] Talleyrand's friend, Charles-Antoine Osmond de Médavy, who succeeded his uncle as Bishop of Comminges, was also forced into the Church as a result of a similar deformation of his leg.[34] Turgot, according to his intimate the Abbé Morellet, had been sent into the Church by his parents, who rejected him as savage and taciturn.[35] The sons of Latour d'Auvergne Lauragais, the Duke of Beauvillier, and even Chateaubriand were victims of this system.[36] Spiritual attributes, which Talleyrand abjured throughout his lifetime, were by no means regarded as indispensable. When the Abbé Turgot announced to his fellow seminarists (the future leaders of the French episcopate, Loménie de Brienne, Champion de Cicé, and Boisgelin de Cucé) that for lack of faith he could not embark on the priesthood, they urged him not to trouble himself with "this scruple."[37] Talleyrand's aversion for these conventions which created forced priests (among whom he was perhaps the most notorious) was manifested when, as Bishop of Autun, and in a position to do something about them, he ordered his Episcopal Council to admit no candidates to sacerdotal orders without first having given evidence of a "proven vocation."[38]

The determination of the Archbishop of Reims to magnify the grandeur of the House of Talleyrand by accepting his nephew as his prospective heir was based on the solid precedents of his contemporaries, who rivalled each other in influence and intrigue to capture the limited number of opulent and prestigious episcopal offices for members of their family.[39] Four Rohans, uncles and nephews, had ruled Strasbourg for over a century.[40] The office of Grand Almoner (reputedly the most prestigious office of the clergy, whose occupant, usually a cardinal or soon to be made one, was nominally responsible for the king's religion and religious policy,

Genesis of a Clerical Career

discussed all ecclesiastical appointments with the king, directed his charities, said grace at his meals, recited his prayers, gave him his prayer book, and held his hat during important Church ceremonies) like the bishopric of Strasbourg, was for generations in the hands of this family.[41] Cardinal de La Rochefoucauld, Archbishop of Rouen, himself introduced into the priesthood and named vicar-general by his uncle, Cardinal-Archbishop of Bourges, made one of his nephews Agent-General of the Clergy and Bishop of Saintes and a second nephew Bishop of Beauvais.[42] The familiar pattern of episcopal patronage by which bishop-uncles introduced their nephews into the clergy, had them appointed to executive offices in the clergy's General Assembly, named them their own or close colleagues' vicars-general or coadjutors, and finally secured their elevation to the episcopate is exemplified by virtually all the leading members of the hierarchy and by minor ones as well: Cardinal Bernis, Archbishop of Albi; Cardinal Montmorency, Bishop of Metz; Archbishops Boisgelin of Aix, Dillon of Narbonne, Dulau of Arles, and Loménie de Brienne of Sens; and Bishops Jarente of Orleans, Barral of Troyes, Lubersac of Chartres, Vintimille of Toulon, and Osmond de Médavy of Comminges.[43] This system was operative not only between uncles and nephews but as well between brothers (one Champion de Cicé was Archbishop of Bordeaux, while his brother was Bishop of Auxerre;[44] the brother of Gabriel Cortois de Pressigny, Bishop of Saint-Malo, was Bishop of Nîmes; their uncle was Bishop of Belley) and even cousins (as in the case of the Du Plessis d'Argentré, Bishops of Tulle and Limoges), who in turn procured the succession of their seats for their nephews.[45]

The first significant encounter between the two Talleyrands occurred in 1769 at Reims. Charles-Maurice, then fifteen, had passed the first four years of Périgord, learning his ABC's and the sweetness of family affections from his paternal great-grandmother, the Princess de Chalais. A woman of noble character and great heart, probably the only Talleyrand who ever loved the unfortunate cripple, she was memorialized long after, lovingly and gratefully, as "a fervent Christian, but a little Jansenist."[46] The next seven years were spent as an undistinguished scholar at the Collège d'Harcourt in Paris, a preparatory school favored by the nobility for the education of their sons, particularly those destined for the priesthood.[47] Before being sent to a seminary, it was fitting that the boy should visit his uncle who had already made a distinguished name for himself among the clergy for his ability, piety, and diligence. Alexandre-Angélique was then only thirty-three years old but for three years had been Archbishop of Trajanopolis and trusted Coadjutor of Cardinal-Archbishop La Roche-Aymon, one-time Minister of the *feuille des bénéfices* (held by a ranking prelate who, as a sort of minister of the cult, designated ecclesiastical candidates to the king for vacant episcopal sees and benefices)[48] and incumbent Grand-Almoner of France, with promised rights of succession to the ancient primatial see of the Gauls and the First Peerage of France.[49]

Talleyrand correctly surmised that the one-year sojourn in Reims was meant to give him an "advantageous and even tempting idea of the state for which [he] was destined."[50] There is no reason to doubt that the Coadjutor, by passing on to him the biographies of the great prelate-diplomats, Hincmar of Reims, Ximenes and de Retz, fired the imagination of the unhappy youth of fifteen, who, despite his acolyte's soutane, like most boys his age, dreamt not of saints and martyrs but of soldiers and statesmen.[51] In this connection, as most Talleyrand biographers have held, by making the priesthood an inviting profession, the prelate was supporting the plans of the Talleyrands for their son's career.

But it is even more likely that the Archbishop was seeking a younger relative upon whom to place his episcopal mantle and so was acting in his own interest. Precisely for this reason it is inconceivable that Talleyrand would not have tempted his intractable nephew with stories which had a truer, more immediate ring, because they described conditions prevailing in the Church of their own day, namely, the accounts of the luxury and power, the broad avenues of administrative and political positions within the State as well as the Church which were easily accessible to *prélats politiques et administrateurs,* "half sacred, half profane . . . interested in everything except theology."[52] He did not have to stop with the Cardinal-Ministers Richelieu, Mazarin, Dubois, Tencin, Noailles, Fleury, and Bernis. He could have cited the innumerable lesser prelates who, by virtue of their episcopal seats, were simultaneously feudal potentates and peers of the realm, sovereign rulers of their episcopal cities, princes of the Empire, and princes, dukes, counts, and barons in France.[53] Nor would he have failed to observe that many bishoprics, like Narbonne, Aix, Albi, Bordeaux, Reims, and even Autun, held as portions of their hereditary possessions the presidency of provincial estates and local assemblies in Languedoc, Provence,

Albigeois, Haute-Guyenne, Champagne, and Burgundy.[54] Many like Cardinal Bernis served as ambassadors and advisors of the king. Some, like Loménie de Brienne and Champion de Cicé a few years later, would actually become ministers of the crown. Political eminence was clearly available to bishops of ability who, like Talleyrand, not only had little stomach for diocesan responsibilities, but also, like the future Bishop of Autun between 1788 and 1791, were absentee rulers who preferred to give their time to statecraft, or, like the Archbishop of Reims himself, devoted much time to the establishment of fire companies and organizations of charity, and to the introduction of prize sheep and the reform of education.[55]

Nor could the perceptive youngster remain insensitive to the luxury and princely comforts of the Archbishop of Reims who, by his own admission, in 1786 enjoyed an income of 560,949 *l.* from the see of Reims and its dependencies and 126,005 *l.* from his two abbeys of Cercamp and St. Quentin (compared with the total income of 105,000 *l.* listed in the *Almanach Royal* of the same year).[56] Likewise, hardly had he received Reims from the deceased Cardinal de La Roche Aymon in 1777 when he tore down the ancient Convent of St. Thierry, whose property and furnishings he alienated, to make room for a sumptuous episcopal palace[57] where he resided when he was not living in Paris in his lavish Hôtel de Gramont, rue de Bourbon, acquired in April, 1789 at a cost of 251,542 *l.*[58]

The Archbishop's treatment, judged by Talleyrand's eventual reconciliation to his new profession, was successful, despite the protest of his memoirs, written nearly fifty years afterwards by a contrite sexagenarian who, for the first time in his life, was thinking seriously of his soul. The splendor of 1769 at Reims had been an "intolerable life of empty forms . . . not worth the sacrifice of [his] sincerity."[59]

It is difficult to be indifferent to the sorry lot of a young boy who, in the words of a recent critic, was like an orphan whose parents were still living.[60] Shunted from place to place since the time of birth, passed from a wetnurse in the suburbs to an aged grandmother in Périgord, to stranger tutors in a strict preparatory school in Paris, to an eminent uncle in Reims, and finally to the priests of Saint-Sulpice, he saw his parents only to learn their implacable decision that he was to become a priest. It takes rather little compassion to pardon the *cri de coeur* of an unwanted son who protested that at a time in his life when he needed his parents most he never spent a week under their roof.[61]

However just it may be to acknowledge Talleyrand's opposition as a brooding and resentful adolescent to a clerical career, it is a mistake to accept as veridical the nineteenth-century biographical accounts, the majority of which are either apocryphal or based on imaginary or threadbare evidence, which maintain that his opposition increased in early manhood.[62] On the contrary, a gradually mollified Talleyrand came to realize that advancement in the army was out of the question for someone with his handicap. To add to his misfortune, the other alternative occupations of the nobility were even less promising, because the Talleyrands, who were (or claimed to have been) a clan of stalwart military servants of the monarchy since the days of the first Capetians, had no unusual dynastic representation in the national government, the provincial civil service, or the judiciary. Aside from the army, they had figured prominently in the hierarchy of the Church, and this as early as the fourteenth century when another Talleyrand, Cardinal Hélie, favorite of kings and pontiffs, learned in law, science, poetry, the new humanist literature, and friend of Petrarch, was said to have been a maker of popes.[63] Besides, if Talleyrand had really opposed the ecclesiastical profession as violently as is commonly supposed, the strong-willed and exceedingly intelligent acolyte would have found a way to escape it, as surely as did other "predestined" clerics like Turgot, Chateaubriand, and Fouché.

The reason he did not is that he knew, as history had shown and his contemporaries repeatedly demonstrated, that the episcopate, by offering incomes many of which generously exceeded those of magistrates, governors, and judges, "was the shortest road to influence and opulence." Like Loménie de Brienne, he entered the Church, "studying theology like an Irishman to become a bishop and the memoirs of Retz to become a statesman."[64] Talleyrand would eagerly accept the canonries, benefices, as well as the deputyship and executive offices in the General Assembly of the Clergy which his uncle secured for him. He would accept a bishopric no less eagerly, because it meant vocational success, permanent financial security, and an entry into political life with a minimum of spiritual commitment and social inconvenience. With the majority of French bishops before 1789 he never pretended to be a paragon of virtue in matters of faith and spiritual convictions. Nor was such pretense necessary, for no century either before or after was so tolerant of the misdemeanors and unspiritual behavior among the prelacy as the eighteenth.

In 1770 the Coadjutor of Reims entered his nephew, now called the Abbé de Périgord (the elder man had been known as the Abbé de Talleyrand), in the Seminary of Saint-Sulpice in Paris, where he himself had studied. His own tutor in the seminary, M. Bourlier, was chosen as the preceptor and later became the secretary and best friend of young Talleyrand.[65] It was here at the seminary of the most renowned French bishops since Fénelon, that he was prepared for the priesthood.[66] In the words of one of Talleyrand's colleagues, "an unbelievable futility" reigned among the young seminarians, many of whom, besides the future Bishop of Autun, could not reconcile themselves to their clerical nature.[67] At the same seminary where Turgot crystallized ideas on government and public administration and Loménie de Brienne drew plans for the magnificent chateau and connecting roads at Brienne, Talleyrand was to become seriously interested in politics and diplomacy. M. Leflon has maintained that the fire of 1789 was already burning in the hearts of some of these rebel seminarists—Sieyès, Barrère, Vergniaud, and Talleyrand.[68] To the Cardinal's biographers the entry into Saint-Sulpice was the beginning of a "blind nepotism."[69] To Talleyrand it was here that he was "tempered in the waters of the Styx."[70]

After five years in the seminary an impatient youth of twenty-one, with his early ecclesiastical education behind him, was anxious to achieve economic independence and professional security, which came only through plump benefices and higher Church office. These could not be had, however, at least in principle, until the candidate had entered the subdiaconate, the first major sacerdotal orders.[71] For this reason, and particularly because membership in the General Assembly of the Clergy, for which his uncle had destined him in 1775, also required the subdiaconate,[72] the Abbé took this first major order on April 1, 1775.[73] One of the seminarists at Saint-Sulpice, Philippe Sausin, later Bishop of Blois, recalled that it was rumored at the seminary that the only reason young Talleyrand accepted priestly ties was because he had been promised an abbey "just as soon as he should become a subdeacon."[74]

With the subdiaconate Talleyrand was ready for the fruits of his profession. His uncle did not keep him waiting long. The first link in the chain of clerical patronage had already been forged several months earlier. On January 17, 1775, Talleyrand-Périgord conferred on his nephew the rank of chaplain of the Chapel of the Virgin Mary in the Church of Saint-Peter in Reims.[75] This office was granted an acolyte not yet twenty-one apparently only as a pretext to establish his residence in Reims, one of the requirements he had to fulfill as a deputy of the lower clergy from that ecclesiastical province to the General Assembly of 1775, the springboard to episcopal promotion. This is attested by the fact that Talleyrand never took possession of his canonry, that it was assumed in his name by a canon of Reims on February 3, and that the Abbé resigned it after it had been of service in securing his election.[76] Cardinal de La Roche-Aymon, who was to serve as President of the Assembly, not only secured the election of his vicar's nephew as deputy but also appointed him one of that body's two Promoters. These officers regulated protocol and scheduled debates and received 5,000 *l.* for their pains.[77]

Scarcely two weeks after Talleyrand received the subdiaconate, the prelate of Reims, this time to secure his kinsman a regular income, made him a canon in the cathedral of that city. His letters to the cathedral canons on May 3 requesting this office as a special favor (which could scarcely have been denied the second most important member of the diocese soon to become its titular head) is a mixture of pious exhortation and personal propitiation.[78] The canons, meeting in special session, voted to accept the young Abbé "with greatest honor."[79] Talleyrand, obviously at the signal of his uncle, directed a letter of acceptance to the canons on the very next day, May 4, 1775. The document, written in "a young hand and smacking of the schoolboy," is interesting for no other reason than that it is the earliest known specimen of his justly famous diplomatic skill: "I received with keenest appreciation the favor you accorded me. A great respect for your company, the greatest attachment to its members, the most keen desire to be united with your group, and the friendship, whose tokens you have always given my uncle, are the only claims I can make to deserve it. I hope, Gentlemen, that they can help me retain your kindnesses. I will respond with all my efforts to make myself worthy of them."[80]

The real prize came in September when Talleyrand-Périgord, by royal nomination, secured for his nephew the great Augustinian Abbey of Saint-Denis of Reims. Papal bulls confirming this lucrative office, which by official evaluation furnished eighteen-thousand *livres* a year (but in reality, like all important benefices of France, far exceeded the official published estimate), came on October 3.[81] Still

Genesis of a Clerical Career 19

four years away from the priesthood and having scarcely attained his majority, the young subdeacon now enjoyed an income which equalled if not exceeded that of his parents. A carefree, absentee commendatory abbot, among 850 others in France,[82] with no strings of sacerdotal obligations attached to the enjoyment of the revenues of this richly endowed benefice, Talleyrand on December 4 granted the prior of his monastery full spiritual powers.[83] On January 24, 1776, he deputized a priest of Reims, de Lescure, as *procureur-général et spécial* (an equivalent of a business manager) with full authority in temporal and disciplinary matters.[84]

Sausin's recollection of the seminary rumor is illuminating! It is striking how well the promised emoluments of the Church coincided with the date of the subdiaconate. Talleyrand received a chapel, canonry, abbey, deputyship, and executive position in the General Assembly of the Clergy within five months after having received his first major order! It was not long after that his uncle procured for him the promised succession as Agent-General in the next Assembly (1780), an office of great power and influence, whose occupants were, virtually without exception, named bishops in appreciation of their services to the clergy.[85] Talleyrand on two occasions observed that he was "destined" for this position as early as 1775.[86] It was customary for appointees to be selected well in advance of their tenure. *La France Ecclésiastique* for 1779 formally announced his appointment.[87] There can be no doubt that Talleyrand's uncle had procured this honor, at once from the sense of the memoirs and from the practices of contemporary ranking prelates who controlled all executive positions within the clergy's Assembly into which they introduced their relatives. Moreover, it has been plausibly maintained that in the years before his death in 1777, the senile Cardinal de La Roche-Aymon, who held the key to all ecclesiastical appointments and benefices, was managed by Talleyrand-Périgord, "who would not see his nephew omitted."[88]

Looking ahead to the episcopate, which, after all, was what he was being groomed for, Talleyrand knew he had to have further theological study and full sacerdotal orders. Already in September, 1774, as his last official act at Saint-Sulpice, he had presented a thesis for the baccalaureate in theology entitled, "What Is the Science Which Must Guard the Lips of a Priest."[89] He defended in oral examination before the doctors of the Sorbonne nine orthodox propositions favoring the Scholastics and disputing the errors of Protestants, heretics, and the Leibnizian scheme of world perfection. No votary of daring ideas of protest and reform, Talleyrand inserted nothing in his thesis, dedicated to the Virgin, which could have created a ripple of controversy comparable to the bold views advanced by the Abbés de Prades, Turgot, and Loménie de Brienne before the same faculty. "From official and authentic documents found in the archives of the Seminary of Saint-Sulpice," Bishop Dupanloup claimed, Talleyrand performed with distinction.[90] That he could not have been so ignorant of theology as his detractors would have us believe is clear from the fact that he defended, publicly and apparently with competence during five hours of interrogation by a jury of professional theologians, diverse and complicated propositions.

In April, 1775, he entered the Sorbonne to begin work on the licentiate in theology. According to the records of the faculty he was registered, barely two weeks after having received the subdiaconate, as a "subdeacon of Paris" in the capacity of *hospes* and on June 2 was admitted to the grade of *socius,* the two preliminary steps towards the degree.[91] By November he was already installed in a luxurious two-story house, one of six belonging to the Convent of Bellechasse, rue St. Dominic, in the most fashionable section of the Faubourg Saint-Germain for which, from July, 1777, he paid 2,200 *l.,* and after 1786, 2,454 *l.* per year.[92] It was here that Talleyrand amassed the first of several rich collections of books, fine bindings, and rare editions which he began to gather ten years before the Revolution and sold at auction in London at the time of his emigration to England in 1793.[93] It was here too that he stored his enormous collection of furniture. The list of pieces auctioned in 1795 indicates no fewer than seventy-one chairs, three secretaries, and every manner of sofa, table, and bureau.[94]

With a double salary from the General Assembly, as deputy and Promoter, added to the revenues of his office in Reims,[95] Talleyrand was free from all financial worries during the next three years of study. Through the efforts of his uncle he was accorded two dispensations from Louis XVI exempting him from the prescribed intervals of the licentiate ("on the good and praiseworthy reports made to us on the application to his studies . . . of the Abbé de Périgord") which he received on March 2, 1778, sixth out of a class of eighty-two.[96]

There is no reason to expect his preoccupation with theology to have been either enduring or a matter of conviction. It was merely

Genesis of a Clerical Career 21

part of the job specifications for the executive position for which he was being prepared in the Church. His ideas regarding theology were to be drastically revised at the time of the Revolution when, as part of his famous plan of education, Talleyrand advocated that this discipline, "the most ancient of errors, the source of man's prejudices and unhappiness," should be removed from theological faculties ("dogmatic arenas") and revised under the authority of the nation.[97] This position, however shocking it may appear, did not differ substantially from that of another famous alumnus, the Encyclopedist and translator of Beccaria, the Abbé Morellet. Though a full generation older than Talleyrand, Morellet wrote that the studies for the licentiate "can well be regarded as extremely useless and little worthy of taking the time of. man," and that the students did not take seriously "the theological absurdities" forced on them by their masters.[98]

Talleyrand was perhaps too pleasantly occupied with secular exploits and the brilliant society which assembled at his fashionable apartment in Saint-Germain to think about the indelible bonds of priesthood.[99] He did not turn his attention to ordination until the fall of 1779, and then doubtless only because the office of Agent-General, which he was to occupy the next spring, required it.[100] From this final and irreversible commitment, however, there could be no dispensation.

His faithful uncle was again on hand to direct him into the clergy. While technically still a "subdeacon of Paris," the young Abbé had no connections or promise of advancement in the Paris hierarchy. He might have been ordained by the severe Archbishop of Paris, Christophe de Beaumont, but there were no assurances that he would have been favored. Had he remained in the capital, he might never have realized his clerical ambitions, certainly not so speedily as he wished. However, because he held offices in Reims and hoped to inherit the seat of his uncle[101] (who in 1777 had succeeded as Archbishop), Talleyrand had grounds, as he was surely advised, to excorporate himself from the Archdiocese of Paris and to incorporate himself into the Archdiocese of Reims. It is clear that this change was effected for reasons of professional expediency, since Paris was not only his native ecclesiastical district but, until his episcopal promotion and despite offices held in other dioceses, also his sole place of residence.

Talleyrand made the first move to excorporation with a letter undated but presumably written to his uncle in early September, 1779.[102] The Abbé humbly requested letters of incorporation into his diocese: "The special kindnesses you have always accorded the suppliant, who dares to hope for their continuation, make him desire to be included among the number of those in your diocese." He cited as his main reason for requesting incorporation the desire "to work under the orders" of the Archbishop. His uncle approved this petition on September 14: "in view of his request . . and considering the reasons exposed therein, we consent to receive the suppliant in our diocese."[103] The only condition for incorporation was that the Abbot of Saint-Denis should present letters of excorporation from the Archbishop of Paris. This correspondence between two relatives was no more than a formality. The intentions of Talleyrand and his obliging uncle had certainly been formed in concert before the exchange of these perfunctory missives intended for the record.

Talleyrand's request to the Archbishop of Paris two days later, September 16, was less matter-of-fact.[104] Identifying himself not as a "subdeacon of Paris" but as the "abbé commendataire de l'abbaye de Saint-Denis de Reims," he made known his wish to be incorporated into the Archdiocese of Reims, "in order to work under his [Archbishop Talleyrand-Périgord's] orders." The Abbé de Saint-Denis cleverly noted that the latter prelate had already consented to incorporate him upon receipt of letters of excorporation. On the same day on which he received the petition, September 16, Beaumont granted Talleyrand the desired letters.[105] From his correspondence, it is certain that the Archbishop of Reims was in Paris on September 14. He might well have communicated personally with his elder colleague. The bishops' mutual respect for the ties of family and self-interest together with the prestige of France's first bishopric were enough to secure the Abbé's request. At least this is suggested in the wording of Beaumont's letter granting excorporation. The Archbishop of Paris rephrased Talleyrand's original request "that the special kindnesses accorded by Monseigneur the Archbishop of Reims *his uncle. . .*" (italics added). There was no mention in Talleyrand's letter to Beaumont of any blood relationship, however obvious, between himself and the prelate of Champagne. But this was the first reason cited by the Archbishop of Paris in granting excorporation.

On the very next day, September 17, 1779, the Archbishop of Reims wrote out formal letters of incorporation, "receiving, enrolling,

Genesis of a Clerical Career 23

and incorporating" his relative under the rules of his diocese, and conferred on him "the privilege of remaining indefinitely in [the] diocese."[106] The newcomer, however, was to be advanced to higher orders just like any other member of the diocese, *"cum tamen et protenus nobis placuerit."*

These conditional stipulations, too, were meant only to satisfy the rules, since Archbishop Talleyrand-Périgord almost immediately made his nephew a priest. On the same day that he formally incorporated the young man into his diocese, he provided him with canonical letters authorizing one of his suffragans, François-Joseph de La Rochefoucauld-Bayers, Bishop of Beauvais, to confer the diaconate.[107] Exactly three months later, on December 18, 1779, the Archbishop granted his nephew letters of the priesthood. By special dispensation Talleyrand was exempted from the canonical interval of six months between diaconate and priesthood and was granted permission to be ordained.[108] The next day he was received into the clergy by another officer of the ecclesiastical province of Reims, Louis-André de Grimaldi, Count-Bishop of Noyon.[109]

The same day, December 19, the Archbishop created Charles-Maurice a vicar-general of Reims, granting extensive administrative and spiritual powers in his diocese,[110] just as the Bernis, Montmorency, Loménie de Brienne, Boisgelin, Jarente, Dillon, and Rohan had done for their nephews. This appointment was the last essential condition for episcopal promotion, because it was the avowed intention of the crown to appoint only those ecclesiastics who had already occupied this office, the practical apprenticeship to the episcopate, which placed them close to the government of the diocese.[111] With an easy entrance into the priesthood, with one of the most desirable monasteries in the kingdom, with the Agency-General of the Clergy of France in the next General Assembly—the envied position of every priest who dreamt of becoming a bishop and a statesman—the Abbé's future and an episcopal dynasty of Talleyrands on the ancient throne of St. Remy seemed assured.[112]

II

The General Assembly of the Clergy of France

The body which Talleyrand served in 1775, 1780, 1782, and again in 1785 as deputy, Promoter, Secretary, and Agent-General was the General Assembly of the Clergy of France.[1] This Assembly owed its origin to the fear of royal spoliation during the uneasy quiet before the Wars of Religion. The monarchs of the realm, traditionally on the verge of bankruptcy and eager to find new sources of revenue, devised schemes as far back as Philip-Augustus to put their hands, either by taxation or seizure, on the lucrative holdings of the Church built up through centuries of pious legacies.[2] Chafing under generations of arbitrary royal fiscal impositions and faced with a threat of unprecedented magnitude before the Estates-General of Orleans in 1560, where both the Second and Third Estates boldly advocated the State's seizure of the Church's property under the premise that it belonged to the nation anyway,[3] the Church was anxious to regularize its fiscal obligations and to establish an organ of perpetual surveillance to insure its patrimony against alienations and sequestration. It was to realize both these aims in the creation of the Assembly.

On October 21, 1561, in the Colloquy of Poissy, called originally to compose religious differences between Catholics and Calvinists, the clergy signed its first contract with the king. By its provisions, the First Estate agreed to contribute 1,600,000 *l.* annually for six years, payable from its domains and feudal revenues, to retire the debt on the Hôtel de Ville of Paris. The contract was to continue until December 31, 1567, at which time a total of 7,560,056 *l.* was to be discharged. This agreement which marked the beginning of the Church's contracts with the king and the *don gratuit* which accompanied them ran uninterruptedly until the Revolution.

In return for these revenues the king agreed to guarantee the integrity of the clergy's corporate autonomy. He promised to act on complaints embodied in *cahiers de doléances* (lists of grievances and remonstrances) which the clergy was permitted to submit regularly. Catholicism was declared the official religion of the State. The revenues of all *bénéficiers* (ecclesiastical benefice holders) were to be assured. Despoiled ecclesiastics were to be compensated. The tithes *(dîmes)* were to be paid regularly to the Church by all who owed them. Finally, and crucially, the assessment and division of the clergy's contribution and the supervision of its collection were left to the Church.[4] In a period of civil war, increasing religious and political strife, and grave menaces to ecclesiastical wealth, these assurances constituted a capital victory for the clergy.

The Poissy Contract was renewed after its expiration in 1567 and each ten years during the remainder of the Old Regime. By this agreement the First Estate conceded its fiscal obligation to the crown, a condition which in reality had already existed for some time in France and was, in any case, inevitable with the extension of royal power. But the king's monetary demands on the clergy were now subject to bilateral negotiation and limitation by contract.[5] The necessity to renew the contract and provide for its implementation assured the Church the permanence of its Assemblies and the integrity of its corporate privileges. The clergy agreed to meet periodically and to establish the first links of its permanent administrative machinery in the Syndics-General, prototypes of the later Agents-General, who guarded the Church temporal between sessions of the Assembly and handled the complex finances of the order.[6] From its origins, therefore, the Assembly afforded the clergy not only a means of assuring financial autonomy and of guarding the privileges of its Estate but also machinery to apportion and collect taxes among its membership and a tribunal to judge cases that might arise within it.

Born of economic necessity, these Assemblies were for more than two hundred years a resounding success for the First Estate. In recognizing the permanence and periodicity of the clergy's Assemblies, the kings of France also acknowledged the autonomy of a nationwide administration created outside the pale of royal authority and, in a way, because of its exclusive ends and particularist organization, dedicated against it. The Church was granted rights withheld from the other two Estates of the kingdom: the power to tax itself independently; the right to vote, levy, and collect fiscal contributions itself; the power to retain officials responsible to it alone; and the right to retain permanent authorized representatives to solicit the crown for the maintenance of ecclesiastical prerogatives. The monarchy was under steady pressure at each Assembly to confirm these wide concessions in return for clerical revenues. As late as 1788 the bishops made it clear that they would vote the king revenues only so long as he guaranteed the temporal sovereignty of the First Estate.[7]

From purely financial beginnings the Assembly soon became the sovereign authority and official spokesman of the French Church in matters of administration, discipline, and justice. Although it never obtained the right to legislate independently, which to be sure was impossible after the rise of the omnicompetent State, which subjected all competing authorities to its supreme legislative and executive power, it exercised wide jurisdiction over both spiritual and temporal affairs. It regulated the conduct of its own personnel. It jealously guarded the corporate status and internal integrity of its Estate. With national and provincial councils having fallen into desuetude and without having to resort to an Estates-General, the clergy used the periodic convocations of its General-Assembly, the sole surviving ecclesiastical synod, to treat spiritual questions along with temporal affairs. Not only could it thus combat heresy and incredulity, define its position on a host of questions ranging from Ultramontanism, Jansenism, Protestantism, the fate of the Jesuits, and the reform of the regular clergy, but at the same time it could survey the morals and discipline of the whole body. The kings of France overcame their early distrust of the Assemblies, since, as time went on, they wielded greater influence over their membership and their deliberations.[8] Nor did the monarchy find in the Assembly, whose parliamentarism was the equal and in some areas superior to the Estates-General, the resistance and threats which prompted the crown to convene the latter only rarely and after long intervals.[9] While no other national representative assembly met in France from 1614 to 1789, the clergy's Assembly convened each five years and its national delegates made their voices heard. By the same token the Gallican Church was well aware that the strength of its institutions and the continuation of its autonomy were possible only through the continued success of its close alliance with the monarchy. To the very end, it prided itself on its attachment and devotion to the king and the welfare of the State.

From the Colloquy of Poissy until the Revolution the clergy was convened periodically in both "Ordinary" and "Extraordinary" Assemblies. These Assemblies were made up of representatives of the sixteen ecclesiastical provinces and 116 dioceses already part of France in 1560, at the time of the signing of the first contract with the crown.[10] Excluded both from the Assemblies and the financial agreements with the king was the so-called "foreign clergy" *(clergé étranger)* united to France after 1561, the two archbishoprics of Cambrai and Besançon, and the nineteen bishoprics of Artois, Flanders, Hainaut, Alsace, Lorraine, Franche Comté, Corsica, and Roussillon, including clergy who enjoyed jurisdiction within France but whose metropolitan seats were on foreign soil. The foreign clergy was subject neither to the *don gratuit* nor to the *décime,* the internal income tax each cleric paid to the central clergy, but instead paid the State direct taxes *(taille, capitation, vingtième)* from which the French clergy was exempt. It paid these taxes on a privileged basis accorded by the king to conquered provinces. Indeed, the approximately five per cent of its revenues accorded the State was much lower than that of any other group in the kingdom, and the aggregate was but one-eleventh of what the clergy of France paid.[11]

The Ordinary Assemblies were of two kinds, the "Contract" and the "Accounts." The first met each ten years to renew the clergy's contract with the king and to vote him a *don gratuit.* It was commonly called the "Large" Assembly. Each of the sixteen ecclesiastical provinces sent four delegates to its sessions, making a total membership of sixty-four.[12] Convoked in years in which the last digit was "5," the Large Assembly lasted usually from four to six months and technically was the only Assembly empowered to make decisions binding on the whole Church. It was charged with the verification of the Church's revenues and administration. Talleyrand served as deputy and Promoter in the Assembly of 1775 and as Secretary in the Assembly of 1785.

The second of the Ordinary Assemblies was called the "Accounts" or "Small" Assembly and convened five years after the Contract in the years in which the last digit was "0." Each province sent two deputies to its sessions, making a total membership of thirty-two. Lasting usually three months, the Small Assembly examined the accounts of the dioceses' contributions to the clergy's corporate taxes to the king, and it verified both the income and state of the Church's administration. By the eighteenth century the two Assemblies were roughly equal in authority and scope, save for their respective sizes, which remained the same. Both voted fiscal subsidies, which were of paramount importance to the king; and both had the same authority to deliberate and present their grievances to the crown, which were most important to the clergy. The Assembly of 1780 in which Talleyrand served as Agent-General was an Assembly of Accounts.

Outside the quinquennial series of the Ordinary Assemblies was the "Extraordinary" Assembly. It was called by the monarchy more frequently than the five-year intervals of the Ordinary Assemblies, often during moments of national crisis, for purposes of securing additional financial assistance. The Extraordinary Assembly of 1782, for example, was called to grant a special *don gratuit* to help the king finance the American War.[13] Talleyrand served it as Agent-General and Promoter.

A third type of convocation was the Assembly of Prelates, sometimes called Private Assembly, a small, closed meeting of the bishops, held usually in Paris. Unofficial, the result of no ecclesiastical election, and summoned by the Agents-General for purposes of consultation or advice, the Assembly was not empowered to speak in the name of the entire clergy.[14] As an organ of negotiation with the king and his ministers it proved of inestimable value after the adjournment of the General Assembly, especially during the financial crises of John Law after 1719, in the struggle over the *vingtième* tax with Jean-Baptiste Machault after 1749, in the deleterious judgments of the Paris Parlement against Archbishop Beaumont of Paris after 1752, and in the *foi et hommage* crisis after 1780.[15]

All Assemblies, Ordinary or Extraordinary, were convoked only upon the express authority and licensing of the king, usually in May. Royal letters sent to the Agents-General of the Clergy authorized them to inform the bishops of the date, place, and duration of the Provincial Assemblies which elected the deputies to the General Assembly. The king might, under unusual circumstances, dissolve the sessions of the Assembly. This practice was resorted to during the Assembly of 1785, in session at the time of the tempestuous Necklace Affair, when Cardinal Louis-René-Edouard Rohan, one of the leading powers in the Church, was under indictment by the crown.[16] The Assembly was suspended from September 29, 1785, until July 3, 1786.

Nominally the Church employed democratic methods in electing its General Assembly. It was voted from two representative levels, the diocesan and provincial, and included only the secular clergy. The Diocesan Assembly, made up of the important benefice holders of the diocese, met on March 1 under the presidency of the bishop by license of the metropolitan. From its membership two electoral delegates, the bishop and a clerical benefice holder, were chosen to represent it before the Provincial Assembly which met on March 15 of the year the General Assembly was convened.[17] From this body, which deliberated the affairs and grievances of the province and prepared its *cahier* for the General Assembly, two representatives from both orders for the Large Assembly and one each for the Small were elected.

While these methods of electoral procedure on two levels of suffrage suggested freest parliamentary tradition, and technically claimed a representation of all the secular clergy, they were, by the end of the eighteenth century, quite restrictive. For the first order of deputies consisted of the archbishops and their episcopal suffragans, who had the automatic right to appoint themselves. The second order theoretically was to take in all non-regular elements of the lower clergy regardless of social status but in reality represented the propertied, well-born, non-*curé* priests, who alone could satisfy the clergy's requirements of holy orders, residence, and the payment of clerical income taxes. While the aristocratic bishops, vicars-general, *abbés,* and cathedral canons were represented, the *curés* and vicars "with charge of souls," as they were commonly known, the parish beasts of burden, were excluded both from electing and being elected. After having analyzed the membership of the General Assemblies in the eighteenth century, Professor Gabriel Lepointe concluded that the plebeian *curés* were "totally absent," since they had neither the large benefices which could have permitted them to meet the tax requirement for office in the Assembly nor the social standing to gain admission.[18]

From the credentials of the thirty-two members of the second order presented by the delegations of the sixteen provinces to the Assembly during the years of the last complete quinquennial Assembly (1780-1785), it can be shown that all but one were vicars-general, that is, diocesan officials, hand-picked deputies of episcopal uncles and their colleagues, for whom membership in the Assembly was a jealously sought means of clerical advancement.[19] Where statute called for four or five vicars-general in a diocese, some reported as many as fifteen to twenty of these companions and friends rather than servants of the bishops, who helped make residence in their dioceses more agreeable.[20] It is no coincidence that these well-born hopefuls of the lower order carried the same magical names as the bishops—Loménie de Brienne, Dillon, Barral, Montazet, Cortois de Pressigny, Dulau, Seignelay de Colbert, Chastenet de Puységur, Grimaldi, Osmond, La Fare, Bridelle, Montalet-Alais, Corbeau de Saint-Albin—and that they were easily voted by the Provincial Assembly, which as a body deferred to the electoral wishes of the episcopate. These delegates, like the incumbent Agents between 1780 and 1785, Charles-Maurice de Talleyrand-Périgord and Thomas-Pierre Antoine de Boisgelin de Kerdu, served in Assemblies alongside uncles responsible for their nomination.[21] Many of their group, including Talleyrand, were to become bishops before 1789.

The statements of credentials, or *procurations,* drawn up in the Provincial Assemblies and presented to the Assembly at Paris by each delegate, revealed both the requirements demanded for the office to which he was elected and how he fulfilled them. Initially the deputy must have been *in sacris,* that is, in possession of the subdiaconate for at least six months prior to his election. He was to be in possession of a benefice for at least two years (one year in continual residence) in the province from which he was elected and for which he paid no less than twenty *livres* in *décimes* per year.[22] These rules, in principle, were designed to attract to the Assembly priests residing in the province which elected them and in which they had something at stake. The underlying assumption was that being interested in the welfare of their diocese or province, they would take an informed and creative part in the work of the whole clergy. In practice, however, while residence and tax requirements were of use to exclude the untitled clergy who might aspire to membership in what by 1775 was certainly a patrician General Assembly, they were neither applied nor enforced among the ruling class of the clergy. Frequently deputies were elected who held benefices in other provinces. Often, like Talleyrand and Boisgelin, they were hastily given a benefice in a province in which they did not reside but from which they were nevertheless elected.

It is interesting that Talleyrand as deputy to the Assembly of 1775 fulfilled none of the required conditions. Barely a subdeacon and far from legal tenure, he was given a benefice in the Chapel of Saint Mary in the church of Saint Peter of Reims in order to meet the residence requirements from that province.[23] Nor did he better fulfill the prerequisites for the Agency-General in 1780. He was elected Agent-General from the province of Tours, whose turn it was to elect an Agent. (By a rotating system each of two provinces among the sixteen had the right to elect an Agent for five years. This meant that each province had its turn to elect an Agent every forty years.) Talleyrand had just recently been accorded the Chapel of Saint John the Evangelist in the parish church of Saint Vincent of Tours, obviously for the purpose of his election from that province.[24] Similarly his colleague in the Agency, Boisgelin, though a priest in the Diocese of Saint Brieuc (Province of Tours), was given a chapel by his uncle, the Archbishop of Aix, who assured his election from the Province of Aix, whose turn it was, along with Tours, to elect an Agent.[25]

Deputyship in the General Assembly, like its executive offices, was frequently utilized as a means to obtain preferments. Without the habit of diligent application or requisite knowledge, many young men of great ambition and obscure talents, sons of powerful families, and slated for the Agency or a bishopric, were frequently seated by a *camaraderie aristocratique* and sent to Paris to learn the handling of affairs or simply to attract attention. Were the Assembly not, like the rest of the higher clergy of the latter eighteenth century, discriminatory against all but the highest nobility and blighted by familial patronage, it could have interposed conditions restrictive of age, competence, and experience by virtue of former service in diocesan affairs such as membership in the Diocesan Bureaus, the administrative chambers of the dioceses. These Bureaus would have furnished excellent schools in which the lower clergy could have mastered the ways of clerical business as a preparation for the General Assembly. Allowing the unprivileged clergy to enter the Assembly would have served to bridge the serious class gaps among the clergy of the second order and could have secured it much needed talent and disinterested devotion from a large segment which felt itself excluded. Despite the many flagrant abuses of its statutes, however, the bedrock requirement of enrollment in clerical orders was not relaxed, and the Assembly never admitted laymen in its midst.[26]

Royal influence was another corrupting factor in the election of the Assembly's members. The government used its influence in the provinces through ministers, magistrates, and bishops to secure the election of those delegates who could be depended on to advance the interests of the monarchy. The king, anxious to exclude all radicals and extremists, wished also to forbid the entry of hostile and rebellious parties. Jansenists, Ultramontanists, clerical supremacists, and purists who attacked the luxury of the clergy or the affairs of the king were eminently *personae non gratae*. Conspicuous for their absence from the Assembly during our period among the sixteen archbishops of France were Cardinal Paul d'Albert de Luynes, Archbishop of Sens and dean of the bishops, and Antoine-Malvin de Montazet, Archbishop of Lyon, both excluded because of the intense controversy which had surrounded them and their public positions in the quarrels between the Jesuits and Jansenists and in the reform of the regular clergy.[27] Many elections in the century before had actually been held under royal protection, and in Louis XIV's struggles with Rome, when the Assembly formulated the doctrinal and political bases of Gallicanism and when it received the Bull *Unigenitus* in 1713, both its independence and representative character were notably diminished. Official candidates had been presented at various stages of its history, and coercion was employed. The Sun King excluded some bishops at his will and made others delegates in spite of themselves. Clerical relatives of princes and ministers were invariably assured positions in the Assembly.[28] By the mid-eighteenth century the situation had changed. The General Assembly, which like the Parlements enjoyed a resurgence of independent corporate power, successfully resisted the diminishing interference of the government in the determination of its membership.[29]

The first task of the newly elected General Assembly was to regulate its membership and select the President and officers of the new session. The clergy had its first meeting in Paris at the home of a provisional President, most frequently the highest dignitary of the forthcoming Assembly or the eldest bishop in attendance. In 1780 and 1782 this occurred on the rue des Saints-Pères in Paris, home of Cardinal Dominique de La Rochefoucauld, Archbishop of Rouen, highest dignitary and President-elect of both Assemblies.[30] At this initial meeting the king's letter of welcome was read to the clergy in the new Assembly, expressing the hope that his voluntary gift would be granted.

The provisional President and Agents jointly supervised the credentials and *cahiers* of the deputies.[31] After the members were confirmed in office, their first obligation was to vote a permanent President. By the eighteenth century the earlier practice of multiple Presidents had been abandoned in favor of one chief executive and several "Honorary Presidents" who functioned as executive assistants and took the gavel in the absence of the President.[32] From the reign of Louis XIV the President was designated by the crown several months in advance of the Assembly. He was a prelate who held the confidence

General Assembly of Clergy of France 33

of the king. The king's President was well known both inside the Assembly and out. Accordingly, at the presentation of his candidacy by a member of his province he was elected unanimously. In 1780 and 1782 a member of the second order from the Province of Rouen presented the nomination of its bishop, Cardinal de La Rochefoucauld, together with a panegyric extolling his "experience, discernment, prudence, and moderation" and the distinguished services to his Estate.[33] No one dared to oppose the royal will, which already by the time of Louis XIV had been responsible for several presidential dictatorships in the Assembly, among which the most notorious were the Archbishops of Paris, François de Harlay and Cardinal Louis-Antoine de Noailles, who together ran the Assembly from 1660 to 1715. As Professor Albert Cans observed, "the comedy of election was always played the same way."[34] Cardinal de La Rochefoucauld was replaced by Archbishop Arthur-Richard Dillon of Narbonne as President of the Assemblies of 1785 and 1788 by the pleasure of the king.[35]

The President exercised wide executive latitude in placing before the king and his ministers in private audience important business of the Assembly. He reported the replies of these men back to the Assembly. He explained before the meetings of the clergy the strategy its officers were pursuing in the realization of certain policy objectives and summarized the progress of key issues before the Parlements or the receipt and registration of new edicts on behalf of the clergy.[36] Frequently the President privately enlisted the support of the most powerful and respected leaders of the Assembly, like the pre-Revolutionary Archbishops Etienne-Charles Loménie de Brienne, Boisgelin, Jérôme-Marie Champion de Cicé, and Jean-Marie Dulau, who were invested with the same extensive executive authority before the king, his ministers, and the Assembly.[37]

Besides the President the other two officers whose functions were strictly limited to the life of the Assembly were the Secretary and Promoter. (It is significant that the weightiest responsibilities and obligations of the Agents-General were fulfilled between, rather than during, the sessions of the Assembly.) The President controlled these posts to which he appointed the relatives or protégés of the bishops, the same way as President Charles-Antoine de La Roche-Aymon appointed the nephew of his Coadjutor, Alexandre-Angélique de Talleyrand-Périgord, in 1775. "A bit subaltern to their episcopal dignity,"[38] these junior executive positions were reserved by the bishops for the second order. One Secretary and one Promoter were elected in the Small Assembly and two in the Large. It was customary for the Agents to serve simultaneously as Secretary or Promoter in the Large Assembly, in Extraordinary Assemblies within the term of their service, and finally in the next Assembly, while anxiously awaiting a call to the episcopate and facilitating the initiation of their successors.

"Charged to write and retain faithfully whatever is treated and resolved in the Assembly," the Secretary called the provinces to a vote, read all correspondence received by the Assembly, and countersigned everything sent out. The Secretary, together with the Committee for the Revision of the Minutes was responsible for the preparation of the Assembly's official proceedings according to prescribed rules. He read to the membership each day the minutes which were signed by the President. He also had to scrutinize the inventory of titles of the clergy and other documents of importance.[39]

The Promoter, a kind of floor-leader and manager of protocol, was entrusted "to raise and propose all other affairs that need to be treated in said Assembly," to prepare for debate, and to set the order of deliberations. He might speak on all important affairs and decide on matters pertinent to the smooth functioning of the Assembly and in the general interests of the clergy. It was the Promoter who originally had been empowered to recognize deputies desiring recognition from the floor of the Assembly. Supervising the policing of the Assembly, he also kept a list of committees and their schedules and attended to the daily agenda in order to bring neglected matters before the consideration of the Assembly. The Promoter received clerics of the second order and laymen who presented themselves to the Assembly. It was he who informed the membership of all demands for audiences.[40]

Many of the imposing procedural powers belonging to the Promoter were progressively usurped by the President, who by the middle of the eighteenth century exposed and directed the order of the day, suggested possible solutions in deadlocks, and presented before the Assembly questions whose passage was assured by his high office. It was only the President's imposing authority which could curtail dangerous discussion or threatening scandals.[41]

The functions of the Secretary remained static, and they were less impressive on the whole than those of the Promoter. Both offices, however, like the Agency-General, were coveted stepping stones to the episcopate. Many Secretaries and Promoters not appointed as

Agents were, like their colleagues in the Agency, given bishoprics upon the completion of their terms.[42]

The actual work of the General Assembly was performed by the several committees which comprised it. The deputies of both orders were divided into the various committees which studied all matters of interest to the clergy, drafted reports, made recommendations, and proposed texts of legislation to the Assembly in every field of Church business, spiritual and temporal. The clergy often created new committees when questions of urgency, like the tithes (Committee for the Tithes) and salaries of the indigent lower clergy (Committee for the *Portion Congrue*) required it.[43] Each member served on at least two committees, in which there was an equal representation of both orders. The size of each committee was determined by the relative importance of its task. By the eighteenth century, membership was determined by the President. The President and Agents had access to each group, although they were not expected to contribute to the work of any. The Assembly had the final authority in regulating the operations of each body and frequently instituted rules to this end.[44]

The sessions of the Assembly were called to order and, after the announcement of routine items and deliberation of important matters, were for the most part given over to the meetings of the committees, which submitted reports to a fully convoked parent body on questions assigned them. Out of 130 sessions of the Assembly of 1780 no less than 111 were given over to the meetings of the committees. After winning the endorsement of the committee, these reports embodying decisions, recommendations, or proposed legislation were presented to the full Assembly by the committee chairman. While a two-thirds vote was necessary for acceptance, the proposals of the committee were, in practice, accepted by unanimous vote, particularly in matters of heresy or conflict with civil authorities. Besides providing reports, the committees were also charged with preparing letters to the king and pope on behalf of the Assembly which would be reviewed in plenary session.[45]

The Assembly frequently operated itself as a committee of the whole, withholding from the various delegations certain central problems. Initially, as the supreme tribunal of the French Church the Assembly heard litigations and appeals in matters of ecclesiastical practice or disputed authority, including differences arising from the imposition, division, and collection of ecclesiastical levies. It heard and approved drafts of memoirs or proposed legislation submitted to the king on important subjects such as education, the Philosophers, provincial councils, and the monastic orders. In extreme cases it met to secure judgments of anathema or excommunication against serious violators.[46] The Assembly verified its own accounts and reviewed contracts passed between the king and the Receiver-General of the Clergy. This officer also presented before the Assembly lists of the clergy's expenses and the recovery of its taxes and operation costs from the contributions of the dioceses. The Assembly examined the receipts of its dioceses and ecclesiastical corporations, the salaries of its Agents, officers, deputies, and the personnel of its central agencies, the Secretariat *(bureau du clergé)*, legal staff *(conseil du clergé)*, and Archives. It also reviewed the pensions and bonuses granted in its name. Finally, it verified the fiscal payments of each diocese and the books of the Receiver-General.[47]

The Assembly in the last decade before the Revolution maintained as many as ten committees representing both spiritual and temporal affairs (in Extraordinary Assemblies the number was usually halved). Of this number four are of special importance. These key groups were chaired through successive Assemblies by the same archbishops, the ablest administrative and political leaders of the clergy, prelates who in reality were permanent members of the Assembly, despite the fiction of open-slate voting from the provinces. These same men were to represent the First Estate in the Assembly of Notables of 1787 and to participate in the climactic last General Assembly of 1788— Presidents Cardinal de La Rochefoucauld of Rouen and Archbishop Dillon of Narbonne, and Archbishops Loménie de Brienne of Toulouse, later of Sens, future First Minister; the future Minister Champion de Cicé of Bordeaux; Boisgelin of Aix; Dulau of Arles; Antoine-Eléonore-Léon Le Clerc de Juigné of Paris; Jean-Georges Le Franc de Pompignan of Vienne; and Talleyrand-Périgord of Reims.

In temporal business the dominant committee was the Committee for the Temporal, headed before 1780 by Archbishop Dillon and after that by Archbishop Boisgelin. Displaying prodigious zeal under its able chairman, this committee delivered no fewer than forty-six reports before the Assembly of 1780 and twenty-five in 1782 (out of forty sessions in this Assembly). All questions pertinent to the broad temporal side of the Church's existence—benefices, feudal dues, tithes, clerical taxes, alienations, the administration of the clergy's provincial administrative machinery, contested exemptions, new fiscal levies, salaries of the clergy, acquisition of property, repairs of churches, conflicts with the State over ecclesiastical immunities or illegal tax impositions—came under the aegis of this committee. Composed of eight bishops, an equal number of *abbés,* twelve technical assistants and financial specialists, and the Receiver-General, the Committee for the Temporal reviewed the accounts of the Assembly, classified those of each diocese, and supervised the inventory of all ecclesiastical titles on behalf of the Assembly.[48] Before specialized committees appointed in 1785 were to relieve it, this body also assumed initiative in matters of considerable importance for the Church—the question of salaries of the lower clergy, the protection of ecclesiastical tithes, and the unlawful subjection of the Church to feudal dues.

The Committee of the Ten Year Contract continued the contracts initiated by the Colloquy of Poissy. By the reign of Louis XIV it was obscured by the more important Committee for the *Don Gratuit,* responsible, as its name implies, for the computation and collection of this tax. Voluntary in name only, the gifts were considered an onerous imposition to which the clergy only reluctantly consented. The king sent commissioners to the Assembly to represent him, usually members of high standing like the Intendant or Controller-General of Finances or the Chancellor, who were respectfully received by the Assembly. The Committee collaborated with these officials in establishing an acceptable compromise figure which, presented to the Assembly, was voted immediately and without opposition.[49] Since the sixteenth century the funds specified in the clergy's contract and subsidies were referred to as the *don gratuit.*[50] The gifts demanded by the king were not fixed. They grew larger at each Assembly with the constantly rising deficits and the progressively greater monetary requirements of the State. The clergy, not unnaturally, attempted to give as little as possible. Not without reason the distinguished historian Armand Brette called the negotiations which determined the final settlement "a constant haggling."[51]

The clergy repeatedly used the payment of its gifts together with its charitable and educational work as an excuse for claiming exemption from direct taxes like the *taille, dixième, vingtième, cinquantième,* and other taxation to which the Second and Third Estates were subject each year. Its contracts with the king enumerated at great length the full inventory of its privileges and exemptions together with the amount of the gift and the manner of its collection. Aside from its exemption from all direct taxes it claimed immunity from indirect taxes like the *aides* and from dues like the *droit d'amortissement, marc d'or, franc fief, foi et hommage;* and it was freed from lodging soldiers and major costs of repairing its churches and presbyteries. It also confirmed in each new contract "all the exemptions, privileges, rights, and generally all other things contained in contracts passed between the clergy in preceding Assemblies."[52] It claimed that these immunities carried the sanction of public law; and technically this was correct, for the contract was codified as an edict of the King's Council, letters patent were written out, and it was registered by the Parlements and the other sovereign tribunals, the *Chambre des comptes,* and the *Cour des aides.*

How did the clergy raise the money to meet its fiscal obligations to the king? The eighteenth-century jurist Pierre Guyot conceded that the Church could have alienated benefices in order to pay its taxes, much as it had in the Middle Ages. In time, however, this would have dissipated a considerable portion of its temporal wealth and would have provided an intolerable burden on the ever decreasing number of benefice holders who would have had to pay the ever increasing sums entailed in the gifts demanded by the king.[53] The clergy, therefore, after 1690 preferred floating loans in the name of the First Estate on the collateral of its temporal property. These it could liquidate to its advantage, especially with the amortization assistance received after 1748 from the State, rather than alienations, which meant an inevitable attrition of its sacred patrimony, or the simple division of the burden from the funds of its members, which it had done earlier when the demands of the monarchy were relatively modest.[54] The State favored this policy of borrowing, for it permitted the king to have his money in a lump sum and correspondingly reduced his loans, which were floated at a much higher interest rate than the clergy's. (The State could not borrow for less than eight per cent; the Church paid four to five.)[55]

Each diocese was responsible for discharging a portion of the order's loan. To recover the interest and, in part, the principal of these loans, a clerical income tax was levied, the *décime* (literally one-tenth of revenue) on each benefice, curacy, chapel, abbey, and prebend. From the miserably salaried parish curates to the bishops, every member of the Estate contributed from one twenty-fourth to one quarter of his total revenue according to an eightfold division set by the Assembly of 1760 (previous to which it had been twenty-four). These cumulative loans were difficult to sustain, despite the Church's undeniably extensive wealth and excellent credit. For while Church law provided that the *décimes* of each diocese, set by benefice holders in the Diocesan Bureaus, were to be levied "according to the knowledge they have in conscience of the quality and revenues of benefices and other ecclesiastical property possessed by said benefice holders without any of these taxed being able to exempt themselves,"[56] the bishops, vicars-general, and wealthy tithe-owners, or *gros décimateurs* (monasteries, chapters, canonries) who controlled these bodies were judges and parties at the same time when it came to their incomes, elements which enjoyed most of the tithes without contributing proportionately to the expenses of the cult.[57] It has been frequently demonstrated that among the various means used to undervaluate their own secret incomes and thereby to escape their rightful share of taxes, the bishops and other large tithe-holders falsified the ecclesiastical statements of their wealth with impunity, causing the major burden of taxes to fall on the meager public incomes of the *curés,* who were excluded not only from the General Assembly but also from the Diocesan Bureaus which set the *décimes.*[58] The virtual fiscal sovereignty of each diocese, coupled with the higher clergy's iron control of the diocesan machinery, assured the perpetuation of its unfair economic privileges against an exploited curate class deprived of any way short of rebellion to represent its interests and gain concessions. It also thwarted any sensible reform of a national fiscal regime which brought to the clerical treasury a mere fraction of the Church's annual revenue. The Assembly after 1779 faced determined opposition from *curé* groups openly defiant of episcopal authority and the jurisdiction of the Diocesan Bureaus. Such resistance erupted in Provence and Dauphiné and spread to other parts of the kingdom. The *curés* formed political committees, published papers of protest, named deputies to central headquarters in Paris, received contributions, held regular correspondence, and in several instances attempted to storm the Bureaus by force.[59] With the example of Troyes, where the *curés* had obtained two representatives, the Assembly of 1770 drew up a plan of reform of the Diocesan Bureaus; but fear that change might lead to greater upheaval resulted in its abandonment.[60]

The *décime* was not only a cause of severe hardship for the lower clergy but, as has been convincingly shown, explains the "decisive thrust" of protest they made on behalf of the Revolution.[61] That there were irregularities in the account books of the Diocesan Bureaus was not alone a discovery of modern scholarship. The Assemblies themselves had found the registers "full of frauds and errors.[62] As early as Voltaire and, a century later, Taine, historians suspicious of the absurdly minimized income reports of the higher clergy published in the *Almanach Royal* and *La France Ecclésiastique* insisted that to get at the real figures it was necessary to double the incomes of the bishops and oftentimes triple or quadruple the incomes of the abbeys.[63] Nor was the upper clergy alone in underestimating its revenues. Even the statements of the *curés* made to the Diocesan Bureaus and thence to Paris have been shown to be "manifestly underestimated."[64]

The archives of the clergy reveal no systematic statement of incomes from the dioceses of the clergy of France. This is not strange. Judging from the nearly disastrous experiences with reforming ministers like Machault and Charles-Alexandre de Calonne in forcing the Church to disclose the extent of its wealth, the clergy was reluctant and indeed frequently protested the declaration of its revenues and holdings to an Assembly which never demanded it. Rather the fiscal burden was left up to the Diocesan Bureaus and was divided among the dioceses according to the estimated wealth of each diocese and its ability to pay ("according to the nature, kind, functions, and duties of each benefice").[65] This apportionment of the clergy's corporate tax among the dioceses was called the *département général des décimes*. The Assembly assigned its *dons gratuits* among the benefice holders of the dioceses and left it to each area to raise the sum assigned. According to the last *département* before the Revolution (1755-1765), and in an attempt to recover 31,000,000 *l.*, the Assembly of 1770 assigned dioceses like Paris 2,000,000, Rouen 1,600,000, Le Mans 993,862, Reims 829,773, Amiens 735,976, Sens 715,569, to the poorest bishoprics of the south, Belley 6,586, Vaison 5,843 and Glandève 4,861.[66] The increased *dons gratuits* demanded by the government necessitated a revision of the national division of clerical impositions established in 1755. This was especially true since many declarations were false, unequal increases in the incomes of diocesan benefice holders were not felt in the national taxation,[67] and the control of regional taxation by the higher clergy exempted the really significant incomes from fair taxation. Thus, in the face of undisputed wealth, not unlike the nation as a whole, abuses in the division and collection of its national taxes forced the First Estate, like the State, to borrow. Although the bishops in the last General Assembly of 1788 conceded "the serious and urgent necessity of establishing a more just equilibrium in . . . distribution," the Old Regime passed into history without a new *département*.[68]

In securing additional capital for these loans, the clergy gave preference to ecclesiastical establishments like convents, fabrics, and hospitals which had small sums available for loans. They received four to five per cent interest for their capital besides royal immunity from payment of the *droit d'amortissement* levied on all capital employed for loans. From 1748 the king agreed to remit to the Church 500,000 *l.* each year, and from 1780, one million for thirteen years (to be continued until 1803) in the hope of eventually redeeming the principal on loans contracted on the king's behalf for which a small part of the Church's budget was to be set aside each year after 1806.[69]

Two accounts committees, *Pour les comptes des rentes,* supervised the loans which the clergy of each diocese was obliged to contract to secure the full capital required to meet its gifts to the crown, one at five per cent and the other at four. During the course of the Assemblies the Committees delivered reports on the loans floated, an account of loans outstanding, and the expenses connected with them.[70]

So much for the temporal machinery of the Assembly. The Church spiritual was in the hands of the Committee for Religion and Jurisdiction. Having replaced the earlier Committee on Affairs of Church and Doctrine, by 1750 it was, together with the Commission on the Temporal, the most important delegation of the Assembly. Archbishop Jean-Marie Dulau of Arles succeeded Loménie de Brienne as chairman in 1780. It delivered thirty reports before the Assembly of 1780. To it were assigned all questions of religion and ecclesiastical jurisdiction, spiritual and doctrinal purity, the civil register, vows, education, heresy, the new learning of the Philosophers, clerical discipline, the religious orders, all elements of Church-State relations in matters of cult, and the means to combat secular encroachments on the acknowledged spiritual prerogatives of the Church.

It was this commission which had led the opposition to Protestantism. The earliest levies of the Assembly of Pontoise and subsequent taxes during the Wars of Religion had been voted to facilitate the conversion of Protestants. Strenuously opposed to the Edict of Nantes, the clergy urged its abrogation in favor of legislation disallowing separate religious and civil rights for non-Catholics.[71] Subsequently it applauded the Revocation of the Edict of Nantes in 1685 and the legislation of 1724 and regularly petitioned the kings of France for the execution of these laws on grounds of Protestant political sedition and spiritual disunity. When the spirit of toleration in the eighteenth century, especially after the Calas and Sirven affairs, mollified the literal enforcement of this legislation and when Protestants were no longer subject to the full rigor of the law for preaching, celebrating marriage, and baptizing, the commission pressed for a vigorous adherence to statute and a reaffirmation of Catholicism as the only legal religion in France.[72] Until its last Assembly of 1788 the clergy resolutely pursued its policy through this Committee.[73] One of the factors which explains the decisive anti-royal position of the clergy in its last Assembly was the bitter resentment over the Protestant civil legislation in 1787 and the unwillingness of Louis XVI to rescind it.

On the other hand, the Assembly was generous with funds to attract converts and Protestant ministers, to re-establish Catholicism in areas like Béarn, and to erect schools for new converts. Begun at the end of the sixteenth century under the influence of Henry IV to establish religious unity, the conversion treasury (*caisse de conversion*) reached the sum of 300,000 *l.* per year in 1685, ten times the figure of 1615.[74] Over the protests of the First Estate Louis XIV forced the clergy to continue its huge subsidies, which, once the numerous conversions had ceased and large numbers of Protestant ministers had left France, fell off to 80,000 *l.* in 1691, 57,000 in 1715, and 8,000 in 1785. To secure these sums for the crown during the height of the conversion treasury, the clergy for the first time resorted to borrowing. With considerable justice M. Cans found "it curious . . . that this recourse to loans utilized from 1690, and which was going to create the debt of the clergy, was employed for the first time for expenses made by the clergy for the conversion of the Protestants." Extensive money grants had been given foreign Catholics like James II and his family and Henrietta of England who were attracted to French shores.[75] Besides opposition to Protestantism, the Committee took an active role against heresy within the ranks of the clergy, particularly against Jansenism.[76]

Vying only with the Protestant question in persistence and gravity was the fight waged by the Committee for Religion and Jurisdiction against the Philosophers and evil books. The Church wished to reaffirm its rights in the public approbation and censure of published literature before the kingdom at large as well as in the dioceses.[77] Part of the bitter campaign waged by the clergy for almost forty years against the popular *lumières* of the Age of Reason, whose books, the clergy repeatedly asserted, popularized incredulity, irreligion, and the destruction of morals, consisted in publicly denouncing them and petitioning the king to condemn them. The Sorbonne and the devout made but a weak response to the attacks on the clergy. On the whole it was easier to proscribe the literature than to refute it.[78] To this end the Committee after 1775 drew up and the Assembly approved drafts of royal edicts which aimed at the total suppression and eventual extirpation of the Philosophical party and its menacing productions. These provided an elaborate scheme of punishment (depending on the number of violations) for all authors, booksellers, reading rooms, and public expositions which published, displayed, housed, and distributed the forbidden books, and imprisonment and the seizure of property of all who read them.[79] The clergy found it vexing that already existing legislation did not successfully combat this menace. It complained that the censorship laws of April 16, 1757, "remain unexecuted before the judges of the country," due largely to the liberality of Chrétien-Guillaume de Lamoignon de Malesherbes, head of the censorship after 1750, who opposed them.[80] The Assembly of 1780 conceded that in its battle with godless learning the Church was engaged in an unequal struggle: "The Philosophers are no longer a party, they are popular opinion."

The clergy renewed its campaign against the Philosophers in 1782 by direct appeal to the king, acknowledging that "the dangerous lessons of impiety" had spread "to the farthest corners of the kingdom [against which] the strongest barriers shatter and fall successively," and the ravages of the new intellectuals are "a thousand times more terrible than heresy." It assumed the same initiative against the Kehl edition of the complete works of Voltaire. These books, which by 1780 were flooding the country surreptitiously, despite laws which forbade their entry, and which encountered neither protest by the administration nor precautions by the police, were being "distributed in profusion in Paris and the provinces." The Assembly asked for severer punishment for all those connected with the production and sale of the books—typographers, engravers, artists, editors, publishers, distributors, and booksellers.[81] Three years later the committee, still seeking action from the king, repeated its dissatisfaction with the precautions taken by the State against the works of Voltaire ("the first thirty volumes . . . cross the vast expanse of your states fully and without obstacle") and concluded, "It is time that the voice of the legislator makes itself heard."[82]

At the same time the Assembly awarded subsidies for works of refutation, Christian edification, and religious orthodoxy. It supported by grants translations of the Bible, ecclesiastical dictionaries, histories of the councils, hagiography, and the lives of the Fathers. It also subsidized projects to reprint the works of saints and great churchmen like Bossuet and Fénelon. Under the initiative of Chairman Dulau the Assembly accorded generous pensions and bonuses as high as 4,000 *l*. for refutations of the Philosophers, for works on morals, theology, and oriental languages by the clergy's ablest luminaries, the Abbés Guénée, Pey, Gourcy, Gandin, Gérard, Voisin, Clément, Houbigant, Berthier, and Auger.[83] In 1782 Dulau got the Assembly to approve an increase of 30,000 *l*. in the no longer important Budget for New Converts from which to subsidize works of Christian scholarship in history, eloquence, theology, morals, canon law, liturgy, classical languages, and poetry, and a plan to have the Provincial Assemblies of the clergy provide the General Assembly a statement each five years of the "progress and decadence of ecclesiastical sciences," together with names of authors and titles of books in their part of the kingdom. In 1785 the Assembly cooperated with the king's Keeper of Seals to institute a fund of 10,000 *l*. to encourage worthy projects in civil and ecclesiastical history.[84]

So strongly did the Committee for Religion and Jurisdiction feel about the value of the work of these clerical savants that it urged that their names be sent to the king and his minister in charge of ecclesiastical appointments not only for benefices but also for bishoprics ("the most brilliant rewards and distinguished places").[85] That Dulau's zeal extended far beyond the realities of the situation and that these deserving priests did not stand a chance of getting bishoprics is clear in recalling the frantic jockeying for the few openings in the episcopate among the numerous sons of the nobility for whom by 1789 these places were exclusively reserved.[86]

It is doubtful that the fashionable writers of the Enlightenment stood in fear of these efforts. Nor do they appear to have had widespread appeal to the large reading public of the period or to have seriously influenced the salons and other bastions of current literary

General Assembly of Clergy of France 45

and social opinion. Nor for that matter some of the bishops themselves! According to the Abbé Morellet, longtime friend of a good many, the bishops "knew by heart the greatest part of the fugitive pieces of Voltaire and many pieces of his poems and tragedies." According to Professor Henri Carré, "Its [the Assembly's] declarations and laws remained ineffective."[87]

The Committee prevailed upon the Assembly to press for the re-institution of provincial councils for the good of the Church, the spiritual strength of the clergy, and "national sanctification." Appeal was made to the crown, whose license was required for all such convocations. It was hoped that they might upset the fad of the freethinkers and restore the "former discipline and the golden century of Christianity."[88]

The Committee took an important stand on education. It will be recalled that the State, after considerable popular prodding, invaded the clergy's exclusive domain of education after the dissolution of the Jesuits. Legislation of February, 1763, removed the administration of the one hundred formerly Jesuit schools (out of 562 in France) from the hands of the Church and placed them under the mixed jurisdiction of laymen—municipal officers, local notables, and educators—under the presidency of the local bishop. Faced with the vacuum in education left by the dissolution of the famous teaching order and increasingly alarmed by the influence of the Philosophers and other secular reformers advocating the national supervision of all education, the Committee went on record as opposing any legislation which threatened the Church's instructional monopoly or bypassed the authority of the bishops. At the same time it called for measures to be undertaken by the clergy of each diocese to reform what it conceded was a "deplorable state" of the schools and universities of the kingdom.[89]

Archbishop Dulau's committee secured the renewal of statutes outlawing all public work on Sundays and holidays and worked for a similar order forbidding operation of all coaches and public conveyances. It also vigorously opposed any attempt to diminish the monopoly of the clergy in its control of the civil register, particularly in regard to marriage.[90] The Committee consistently urged the Assembly to demand concessions from the king as the *sine qua non* of continued voluntary gifts. Clerical *cahiers* repeatedly asked for guarantees of Catholic supremacy and confirmation of the Church's control over the civil register, education, and ecclesiastical police.

Of the remaining committees several merit summary consideration. The Committee on the Archives, charged with investigation of the clergy's papers and titles each five years, supervised plans for the easier classification and inventory of the clergy's records, which for 150 years before the Revolution had been lodged in the Convent of the Grands Augustins in Paris. It also supervised the clerical work of the Agents and their staff. The Committee for the Revision of the Minutes was responsible for editing and publishing the Assembly's proceedings together with the reports of the quinquennial Agencies presented to the Assembly by the departing Agents. The Committee for the Servants was set up to prevent the hired men of the prelates from getting into trouble during their sojourn in Paris, which might be as long as a half-year. The clergy instituted a school, supervised by this committee, which taught the servants to read and write and provided the rudiments of mathematics, catechism, and the moral teachings of the Church. The Committee on Coins supervised the design and minting of medals to commemorate the meeting of each new Assembly.[91]

The President also appointed lesser delegations to set up a luncheonette (*buvette*) in two apartments of the convent for the Assembly in session and a committee of the second order to visit prisons, hospitals, and the poor of Paris on behalf of the Assembly and to distribute tokens of its affection in the form of charity.[92]

The Assembly acted as a group in other matters outside the traditional range of spiritual and temporal problems. One was the compilation of its collective *cahier* of grievances and the other the clergy's recommendations for the canonization of French saints. Most important after affairs of religion and finance was the presentation of the clergy's list of grievances, which the Assembly hoped would be redressed by direct appeal to the king, and the drafts of legislation concerning religion and morals, which it expected the crown would accept in exchange for the clergy's loyalty and financial support. It is no accident that the *cahier* invariably accompanied the *don gratuit* at the conclusion of each Assembly.

Each deputy brought to Paris along with his credentials the *cahier* of his province, which, early in the Assembly, was delivered to a special committee appointed by the President which reviewed them for inclusion in the clergy's composite document. The Committee was interested in ascertaining the grievances and problems shared by the greatest number of dioceses, the extent to which they were representative of the Church as a whole, and the priority of their presentation. Particularly stressed were those grievances which threatened the rights and property of the clergy. The complaints were divided into temporal and spiritual articles. In 1780 they incorporated questions of heresy, ecclesiastical personnel, provincial and general councils, unions of benefices, education, illegal taxes, military service, *décimes*, loans, subsidies, charitable institutions, hospitals, and secular justice.[93] The clergy's *cahier* was sent to the king's First Minister or Council which returned it some time later—often not until the next Assembly—with the king's affirmative or negative reply to each question. Archbishop Dulau, annoyed at these delays which had begun in 1755, urged the Assembly to have the Agents press for a quicker response from the throne in order to secure reform of urgent issues, to facilitate the legislative work of the Assembly, and to prevent the delay of publishing its proceedings which reproduced the *cahier* and the king's response.[94] In its dealings with the crown the clergy made it plain that it expected favorable consideration of the pleas presented. But the monarchs of France, including the pious Louis XVI (whose indecisiveness was a source of irritation to the bishops), generally minimized the urgency of the Assembly's demands. Seldom did they concede all the favors requested, and by 1780 virtually never granted the more stringent texts of laws whose application would have an upsetting effect on large groups of the population.

It is significant that in each petition regarding the Protestants, evil books, the Voltaire edition, the conservation of the religious orders, and the provincial councils, which, as have been seen, were objects of serious concern to at least three Assemblies (1780, 1782, 1785), the king provided only vague and dilatory responses. He usually assured the clergy of his love and protection but stated that the present laws were adequate, that he would continue with zeal the policy of his ancestors, that the matters involved "deserve great attention," that he would inform himself on the nature of the clergy's requests, and that the clergy should freely bring similar matters to his attention in the future. Sometimes he simply stated that he would "neglect nothing to carefully maintain good order and to repress abuses," and would see to it that laws were faithfully executed. Occasionally, as in a request for the suppression of monastic unions, he stated that a situation had gone too far for him to consider the clergy's appeal, or, in the matter of provincial councils, refused to grant a request because the bishops had sufficient disciplinary authority already.[95] It is significant that Louis XVI and his ministers did not satisfy the clergy on the major issues submitted. Not without considerable asperity the chairman of the Committee on Jurisdiction pointed out that there was a time after 1560 when the clergy's *cahiers* had resulted in "edicts, declarations, letters patent, and other favorable laws."[96] Well before the advent of the Revolution, this situation had clearly changed.

A second question of especial importance to the clergy, and by this time under the personal direction of the President of the Assembly, was the nomination of French candidates for canonization by the Holy See. It was through the initiative of the Assembly that some of France's most revered saints were canonized: François de Sales, Marie de l'Incarnation, Madeleine de Saint-Joseph, Vincent de Paul, Jeanne de Chantal, Agnès de Jésus, and François Régis. Many of them were under consideration both by the Assembly and Rome for an inordinately long time, as Alain de Solminiac, Bishop of Cahors, whose case was first examined by the Assembly of 1670.[97]

As to the Assembly's deliberations the principle governing all voting was the will of the province. Neither individuals nor dioceses, but only provinces, were represented. It should not be inferred from this that personalities did not dominate the Assembly (and hence the French clergy). The Assembly's operations reflected the same principle of episcopal absolutism which underlay the policy-making of the French Church as a whole, that is, the rigid ordering of affairs by the bishops in accordance with the theocratic and aristocratic tradition of the Gallican Church, in which they were undisputed masters. The carefully selected, well-born lower clergy admitted into the Assembly in the latter eighteenth century presented no challenge to long-established episcopal preponderance. While all important issues were decided by the vote of provinces, lesser matters were decided by head. For a vote to be valid representatives of at least ten provinces had to be present. A two-thirds vote was required to approve all pensions, expenditures, and the records of the Receivers.[98]

While relatively full proceedings of the issues raised before the Assemblies were printed in its proceedings these were not verbatim debates giving full articulation to dissent and disagreement. The bishops, through the medium of the Committee on the Revision of the Minutes, supervised the publication of the lengthy official proceedings (which might be as long as 1,200 printed pages *in folio*) which reproduced what they wished communicated: the text of issues deliberated and resolved, to be accepted and enforced by all elements of the clergy. Except for an occasional reference to unanimity the proceedings never revealed the vote of either provinces or individuals on any matter. By the same token, though the proceedings speak in the name of the whole clergy, it must not be forgotten that the lower elements of the First Estate were excluded from their formulation. Little wonder that the student observing the reception of the Assembly's enactments in the dioceses is struck by the calm indifference paid them by the parish clergy. The proceedings also revealed the central temporal and spiritual issues of concern to all the clergy during the period of the last quinquennial Assembly (though not necessarily resolved by that Assembly), the exact position taken by the clergy, the legal and theological principles connected with each question, and carefully drawn lines of jurisprudence which enabled the clergy all over the realm to be informed in handling its affairs and protecting its rights.

This same principle of enlightening and fortifying the diocesan clergy against lay challenges underlay the preparation of equally extensive and detailed Reports of the Agency-General of the Clergy, published each five years at the termination of the service of the incumbent Agents. The Reports summarized the details and resolution of the leading affairs, spiritual and temporal, which commanded the attention of the clergy and its executive officers during that time. A huge appendix of justificative documents (letters and circulars of the Agents, edicts and laws of the monarchy, court decisions, the *cahiers* of the First Estate and the king's responses, letters to king and pope) provided useful examples on how to face similar questions of adjudicating contested privileges if these should arise, before what tribunals issues were resolved, what bearing pending suits might have for their own cases, and the actual edicts of the monarchy which protected the Church's privileges, whose enforcement the parish clergy was encouraged to demand.

It was no easy matter to keep informed the 130,000 members of the clergy in all parts of a kingdom still largely feudal in its practice of law. It was for this reason that the bishops not only approved huge outlays of money and time for the publication and dissemination among the clergy of its proceedings and Agents' Reports but also sponsored the compilation and printing of an invaluable *Précis des rapports de l'agence générale du clergé de France, par ordre des matières ou extraits raisonnés desdits rapports concernant les princi-*

pales affaires du clergé qui se sont passés depuis l'année 1660 jusqu'en l'année 1780 (Paris, 1786), which summarized the principal problems of the clergy and the classical areas of Church-State dispute during more than one hundred years. It also published between 1767 and 1780 the invaluable collection of the proceedings of the General Assembly from its foundation in 1560 to 1775, *Collection des procès-verbaux des assemblées générales du clergé de France, depuis l'année 1560, jusqu'à présent, rédigés par ordre des matières et réduits à ce qu'ils ont d'essentiel,* competently edited in ten volumes by the Abbé Antoine Duranthon and two successors. Also completed during this time was another extensive collection in thirteen volumes, *Recueil des actes, titres, et mémoires concernant les affaires du clergé de France* (Paris, 1757-1769), which provided in profuse detail a summary of the proceedings of past Assemblies and reports of its officers together with ecclesiastical statutes and historical data governing all offices, organizations, and institutions of the French Church, edicts and decisions of the royal councils and tribunals, and relations with Rome and the monarchy. As part of its policy of sponsoring worthy ecclesiastical projects, the Assembly hoped that not just clergymen but ministers and magistrates of the State and the reading public at large might be interested in reading the monuments of the clergy's deliberations. It conceded, however, that at eighty *livres* per volume (roughly twice the cost of the *Encyclopédie* volumes)[99] and considering the technical nature of the books, they might not sell widely, as indeed they did not, judging from the large inventory of copies still at the printers before the Revolution.[100]

Though difficult to understand for the modern mind accustomed to democratic practice, the clergy of the Old Regime, which was maintained on privilege and tradition, insisted on a literal accordance of precedence and etiquette. During its meetings the Assembly adhered to a set pattern of acts and ceremonies which had been established by long historical usage. The entry and quitting of the Assembly as well as the seating arrangement were determined by the authority and rank of each prelate.[101] There are vivid testimonies in its earlier history of interminable wrangling over the pre-eminence of one prelate's qualifications over those of another, the venerability of his episcopal chair or the strength of his metropolitan primacy, the seniority of his office, the extent of his jurisdiction, the date of his consecration, and the receipt of his pallium. Were this not enough, papal preferences and royal commendations were also brought into play. Frequently a bishop might engage in a feud with a mitred abbot (the superior of a powerful abbey upon whom quasi-episcopal rights were conferred by the papacy) over the wearing of episcopal regalia. The same arguments of the first order were also visited upon the second, which insisted on hierarchical differentiation between deans of cathedral churches and *abbés* or between the eminence of the provinces they represented. Some of these quarrels were taken to the pope or king for settlement. Of the two the latter was invariably the more respected and powerful.[102]

The episcopate sat in a horseshoe around the President according to established rank; and each deputy of the second order sat directly behind the bishop, or bishops, of his province. Certain rules dictated the wearing of choir robes for the deputies of both orders at high Masses, festivals, and celebrations. The oath of office was administered to the entire membership at the outset by the Agent-General. Originally taken by each member on his knees with a hand on a crucifix, Bible, and missal all placed together, by the eighteenth century it was recited aloud by all deputies, who stood bareheaded with their right hands on their breasts.[103] The morning sessions of the Assembly lasted from nine until noon, preceded by a low Mass in a private chapel provided for the deputies in the Grands Augustins. The shorter afternoon session, from three until five-thirty, was preceded by the invocation of the Holy Ghost. With five to six hours of daily labor, exclusive of the special meetings of the committees, the delegates were free on Sundays and most Saturdays, as Saturday was reserved for extraordinary affairs and private requests.[104]

A quorum necessary for the enactment of business was ten of the sixteen provinces with at least one deputy from each province. All voting was by ballot; however, a voice vote was acceptable in matters of bonuses, pensions, and the reception or rejection of the Receiver-General. In theory the Assembly's proceedings were secret. Although the clergy had sworn as part of its oath of fidelity to observe absolute secrecy, this vow in practice was flagrantly violated with the encouragement of the king, who insisted on being informed of its proceedings. It was later unofficially conceded that the tenor of the Assembly's deliberations might be divulged privately, but not personal opinions.[105]

The delegates met the king and the royal family upon the opening and closing of each Assembly as an occasion to manifest their fidelity and obedience to the monarchy. Each member by rank was presented to the king, the queen, and the dauphin. Each of the royal personages was honored with a speech by a clerical designee, which was usually a solemn panegyric to holy religion and an attack on the enemies of the Church. Each member of the royal family then acknowledged the honor of the clergy's appearance. Royal audiences were occasionally requested by the Assembly to present pressing spiritual or temporal matters.[106]

Matters of etiquette were of considerable importance. A manuscript of the Agents in 1752 solemnly complains that, having attended a royal funeral at Versailles, the bishops were not accorded chairs with backs, due them by custom going back to Louis XIII.[107] The Agents in 1785 informed the Assembly that the *Gazette de France* failed to mention that in their royal audience the deputies had been presented to the king by the President of the Assembly, Archbishop Dillon, "conforming with ancient usage." Whereupon the Assembly charged them to have the error corrected and to see "that the same error never again appears in the report prepared by the said *Gazette*."[108]

The Assembly also engaged in a host of lesser ceremonies. It received all visiting dignitaries and representatives of the king and sent delegations to its sick members. It participated in the religious festivals to honor the monks of the Grands Augustins and attended the defense of theses at the Sorbonne, like the famous one Turgot dedicated to it in 1747.[109] The Assembly also suspended session at the death of a great churchman or members of the royal family and ordered a *Te Deum* in their honor. It prayed for the health of the king and his family and attended funeral services on specific invitation of the crown. The Assembly also prayed for the life of its own mortally stricken members, and it commemorated by special prayer the death of its delegates. The Assembly also publicly celebrated the monarchy's military victories.[110]

During the last sessions, besides taking leave of the king, signing the minutes of the Assembly, and presenting the king the signed *cahier* and *don gratuit,* the members distributed alms to the poor, alms which at the discretion of the President ranged from six to ten thousand *livres*. The Assembly officially ended its sessions with a solemn Mass to bless its closing.[111] At the same time the delegates drew their salaries for each day the Assembly was in session: twenty-seven *livres* a day for archbishops, twenty-four for bishops, and fifteen for members of the second order. Each delegate received in addition a daily travel allotment to and from the Assembly, which varied from six days (Paris) to fifty (Albi, Arles, Aix, Embrun, Auch, Narbonne, Toulouse) at the same rate as his salary.[112]

Mention should be made of the meeting place of the Assembly and the costs of its operations. The clergy had purposely avoided the construction of a permanent palace to house its Assembly. The reasons for this are not difficult to find. Not until well into the seventeenth century did the General Assembly meet permanently in Paris. Besides, the clergy wished to avoid exciting public jealousy, certain to arise from the construction of an elaborate structure large enough to accommodate its diversified functions, personnel, and space requirements. Instead therefore of building, the clergy preferred to rent suitable space at reasonable rates. It found adequate quarters in the Convent of the Grands Augustins. A fourteenth-century structure, rebuilt in 1607 and again in 1708, located close by the Pont Neuf near quays of the Seine which still bear its name, it housed the Assembly during the last hundred years of its existence. The clergy paid a rental of 1,200 *l*. after 1760. Besides a large assembly hall it reserved five rooms for its committees and Receiver-General, two for the Agents, two for its Secretariat, two for the President, two for the luncheonette, one for the king's representatives, and one for the preacher of the Assembly.[113]

The Assembly room, reported to be one of the largest rooms in Paris, was the scene of the early sessions of the Estates-General of 1614, the meeting place of the Knights of the Holy Spirit (*cordon bleu*) and occasional sessions of the Paris Parlement. The clergy's Archives were housed in two rooms, one the so-called "Royal Hall," for which the clergy paid another 400 *l*. per year, where Louis XIII was declared king and his mother, Marie de Médicis, Regent in May, 1610, after the assassination of Henry IV.[114] It is easy to understand the clergy's complaints of the room's perpetual dampness, for it was exposed to the weather on the east side by the first court of the convent and on its west side by a second open court.[115]

There were moves under way after 1780 to build a permanent, modern home for the clergy in collaboration with the Curé of Saint-Sulpice, since the Grands Augustins, antiquated, dank, unhealthy, costly to maintain, and direly in need of repair, became inadequate for the growing needs of the Assembly, its Archives, and committees.[116] Archbishop Loménie de Brienne, himself a master builder and creator of the sumptuous palace and estate at Brienne,[117] conceived a plan adopted by the Assembly of 1780. Upon a loan to the Curé of Saint-Sulpice of 150,000 *l.* towards the construction of a parish building, which at the same time would also house the Assembly, the clergy would be virtually released of all rental and maintenance costs on its Archives, library, meeting suites, and chapel, since the normal rental almost equalled the annual interest to be paid the clergy on its loan by the Curate.

Although the motives are nowhere indicated, this plan was never realized. It was reported before the Assembly of 1785 that the agreements with the Curé of Saint-Sulpice were nullified and all monies returned.[118] The archives reveal an interesting correspondence from 1785 to 1788 between Brienne, Pierre-Joseph Antoine, architect of the king, and the Augustinians, complete with designs, plans, estimates, and financial agreements for new quarters.[119] This time the Assembly attempted to interest the monks in a complete renovation and enlargement of its assembly hall and meeting rooms, together with the construction of a spacious new three-story house adjoining the convent houses which would contain the Archives in four rooms, the largest of which was twenty-eight by fifty-two feet, and would provide two rooms for the Agents plus large living quarters for the Guardian of the Archives. The whole—chapel, Assembly, Archives, work rooms, and servants quarters—built and furnished in the fashionable neoclassic style, complete with classical vaulting, Corinthian and Doric pilasters, floor windows, rich parquet floors, marble wall decoration, statuary niches, sculpture, and paintings, to cost between 162,000 and 200,000 *l.*, which the clergy could again advance in lieu of rent and maintenance, and to be ready by January 1, 1789.[120] After two years of negotiations the Augustinians eased out of their initial agreement, noting that "the arrangements made in perpetuity [conditions of occupancy, use of buildings, and especially rental fees] were becoming definitely harmful to one of the parties"; and in letters as early as September, 1786, the king's architect, who had already provided Brienne detailed plans and was engaged to supervise construction, asked for payment of his services, since "the clergy is not at all holding to the execution of projects it made in the buildings of the Grands Augustins."

Preoccupied with pressing temporal problems and immeasurably distressed by the Rohan Affair, which at once cast doubt on the personal immunity of the bishops of France and thrust anew into the light of public controversy the whole problem of the wealth and power of the hierarchical Church, the Assembly did nothing about building itself a new home. It merely ordered its head of the Archives to move the valuable papers out of the humid areas and continued to toy with the idea of one day leaving the superannuated Augustins in favor of the Célestins, rue de l'Observance, where apparently there was plenty of room for its Assembly, chapel, Archives, committees, and private suites.[121] The Convent of the Grands Augustins was suppressed in 1790, occupied by a printer of *assignats,* and in 1797 demolished to make room for the new rue du Pont de Lodi which crossed its grounds to the Seine.[122]

The Assembly, despite frugality and fastidious management of the clergy's finances, continually exceeded the financial limits set for its sessions. The costs of the Assemblies had risen from 69,857 *l.* in 1701 to 657,155 *l.* in 1755 and mounted steadily. The Assembly of 1780 cost 841,958, and the Assembly of 1785, 890,904.[123] The king, who at first assumed a large portion of the operating costs of Extraordinary Assemblies, paid the entire expense after 1745 from the *dons gratuits.* For its ordinary meetings the clergy used funds earmarked for its operating costs, 150,000 *l.* granted by the king, and the remainder borrowed at four per cent.[124] The largest part of these expenses was incurred by the Assembly's lavish gifts, gratuities, and bonuses. It accorded pensions to a mass of schools, seminaries, religious institutions, and persons of all types—famed Catholics, fellow clerics, former servants (or their widows) of the clergy, employees of the Agency, gatekeepers, scrubwomen, latrine cleaners, and messengers of the committees. Bonuses were generously visited on Agents, lawyers, the heads of its Archives and treasury, authors of religious works, ecclesiastical establishments, missionaries, religious, and students dedicating their theological theses to the Assembly. The clergy's pecuniary gifts to converts and converted colleagues were also costly. Finally, the medals and elaborate ceremonies in honor of the Assembly and its guests and the gifts and celebrations honoring royal births, marriages, or deaths entailed important expenditures.[125]

The clergy faced serious problems in the last decade of the Old Regime despite opulence and excellent administration, a parliamentary system lauded by Montesquieu, and the protection of the government. Although the General Assembly must be credited with the effective and responsible management of both clergy and Church in France during the two hundred years of service, its independence and authority were abridged by the monarchy. Its recruitment was faultily one-sided. Its deliberations, in large part a reflection of the Assembly's aristocratic membership, were costly, unedifying, and subject to much wasted time. Its deputies lavished huge sums on ceremonies, bonuses, and pensions. Its distribution of taxes both among dioceses and persons was seriously inequitable and discriminatory. It permitted too many privileged to enter its ranks and granted expensive favors to regions, orders, and persons. It barred from a voice in its government and policy-making an important part of its estate whose loyalty and obedience were nevertheless demanded. Its system of unlimited borrowing, despite undeniable wealth and the probity of its institutions, was fatal; and there was little hope that the clergy could repay the 140 millions of its debt, which grew larger at each *don gratuit*. Indeed, as one informed contemporary remarked, "it was threatened with inevitable bankruptcy."[126] The Revolution saved the Church of France from a fate which threatened economic disaster and social insurrection by depressed groups— phenomena not significantly different from what occurred in the nation at large in 1789.

III

The Agent-General of the Clergy of France: The Office and the Man

If the French clergy on the eve of the Revolution can be conceived as a miniature republic, exercising its authority through the medium of a parliamentary regime, with an electorate on two levels, and national representatives serving under an elected executive, then the Agent-General, responsible to the parliament from which he derived his power and accountable to it for his policies, may in a real sense be considered its prime-minister. While elected by an ecclesiastical province, the Agent was not responsible to it except insofar as his decisions were in conformity with the will and general good of the Church. His task was to represent the whole clergy rather than any province or segment within it, and he owed his final reckoning to the Assembly alone.[1]

Since the General Assembly normally met but once in five years, the Agent-General constituted a permanent executive and spokesman of the clergy after its adjournment and between its quinquennial sessions. As the officer responsible for guarding the interests of the First Estate, and as its chief representative before the government, the Agent-General of the Clergy was acknowledged both by the king and his officials as the Church's first-minister. It was precisely during the years of intercession that the Agent demonstrated his ministerial mettle, for his office was at the center of the vast and intricate machinework of ecclesiastical administration. His duties during the actual Assemblies, when the bishops were at the helm to guide the clergy's ship of state and to formulate ecclesiastical policy, as will be shown, were routinely delineated and of relatively minor significance.

The office of Agent-General was first instituted by the reforming

Assembly of Melun in September, 1579 to replace the several Syndics-General appointed nearly twenty years earlier by the Colloquy of Poissy. The Syndics were invested with broad administrative authority. Two had been assigned to Paris, three to court, and four were employed in various other capacities.[2] Legislation of King Charles IX in 1564 increased their already extensive executive powers by according them "power and jurisdiction" in all disputes and fiscal questions within the First Estate. Becoming more and more the representatives of the king rather than the officers of the clergy in the resolution of economic questions between Church and State, the Syndics gradually became quasi-royal officials. Three years later they asked the clergy to be relieved of their commission so that they could be responsible to the king alone.[3] Within less than twenty years after their inauguration, the Syndics betrayed the interests of their order by approving extensive alienations of Church benefices in the monarch's favor and by using their significant authority in taxes and administration to the advantage of the crown.[4] The Church, understandably, wished to reduce the power of the Syndics, purposely inflated by the sovereigns of the realm and used against its corporate interests. Moreover, large segments of clerical opinion, through the provincial *cahiers* to the Assembly, complained of the Syndics' abuses and petitioned the dissolution of their office. Because the Church required officers to be faithful and responsible to it alone, the nine Syndics were abolished in favor of two Agents-General.

The new appointees were to inherit the broad executive powers of their predecessors, but not the abusive judiciary and fiscal prerogatives which had permitted the Syndics such wide latitude and independence of the clergy. The Agents were, by the express wishes of the clergy after 1621, to reside in Paris. All early distinctions between Syndics at Versailles and Paris were discontinued. All differences in rank among them and the priority they assigned the various affairs of the clergy under their charge were also eliminated.[5] The Agents were to associate themselves more closely with the provincial clergy by formal ties with the Syndic (administrative officer) of each diocese. The latter were obliged to notify the Agents of all legal cases pending against ecclesiastics in their diocese so that the Agents could take the necessary steps on behalf of their protests, remonstrances, and appeals.[6]

The requirements for election to the Agency were originally the same as to deputyship, though later Assemblies demanded a licentiate in theology. An earlier stipulation of the subdiaconate was raised to the priesthood. The possession of a benefice and residence for one year were similarly required but not uniformly imposed.[7] Of these three qualifications Talleyrand, as has been seen, had none in 1775; and in 1780, as Agent, he had only that of clerical orders and a licentiate. He had neither a benefice nor formal residence in the Province of Tours that elected him.

The Agent-General, like the President, seems to have been well known in advance. From Talleyrand we know that he had been intended for the Agency since 1775.[8] *La France Ecclésiastique* of 1779 published his candidacy as Agent-General. The issue for 1781 named the appointees for 1785.[9] The Papal Nuncio in a dispatch to Rome from Paris as early as May 17, 1780 announced the Agents for 1785.[10]

The Agency-General, even more than the deputyship, by the period under consideration had become the property of the higher nobility, which it used for creating reputations or securing wealth for its clerical sons, few of whom had any extensive preparation in theology or administration. *Curés,* theoretically eligible for the Agency as for deputyship, were for nearly a century before 1775 never chosen.[11] The Agents were elected in a plan which divided the sixteen ecclesiastical provinces into eight pairs representing both sides of the Loire: Bourges-Vienne, Lyon-Bordeaux, Rouen-Toulouse, Tours-Aix, Sens-Auch, Paris-Albi, Embrun-Arles, and Reims-Narbonne. By a system of rotation each pair of provinces was given a chance to name the two Agents every forty years.[12] The Provincial Assemblies of the electing provinces voted their Agent early enough so that he could assume his functions which began officially in May. Although ecclesiastical statutes prohibited Agents from being reelected, there were frequent cases before 1735 where Agents were kept for two terms.[13] In the latter half of the eighteenth century, laws forbidding reelection were better enforced. This was due to the Assembly's desire to maintain better control over its appointees, to give each province a chance to name an Agent, and to aid the Agent in securing a bishopric at the termination of his Agency. The king's influence was as strong in selecting the Agents as in appointing the Presidents. Since the Agents were in continual contact with the king, his ministers, magistrates, and government, the interest of the crown in securing agreeable Agents is understandable. No candidate inimical to the House of Bourbon stood a chance of nomination. On the whole, uncle prelates had no difficulty securing from the king the nomination of their nephews. Confirmation by the appropriate Provincial Assemblies was a foregone conclusion.

Relaxation of requirements and abuses in election, however, did not diminish the special qualifications needed for the office if it was to be exercised effectively and with dignity. Indeed, by the middle of the eighteenth century the responsibilities, and hence the power, of the Agency were enlarged significantly, due, on the one hand, to the clergy's ever growing gifts to the king and the dramatic rise of its corporate debt, and, on the other, to the more frequent and regular administrative relations with the regional officers and benefice holders of the kingdom at large. Besides high moral and intellectual standards, a grasp of jurisprudence, theology, finance, and administration was essential to handle the numerous and varied clerical cases and appeals. The Agent needed the agility of mind, the tact and manners of a trained diplomat, and the patience of a priest to resolve the Church's differences with royal government and sovereign courts. The Agency required, too, a profound knowledge of clerical affairs, and for this reason the provinces were called upon to choose as Agents priests who had already participated in an Assembly. Above all it meant a discipline for hard work.

Duly elected, the new Agents usually presented themselves to their outgoing predecessors before the termination of their Agency in order to receive instructions and a recapitulation of unfinished business. The new Agents were also to learn the state of correspondence and communications sent to the dioceses in order to verify the conditions of the clergy's archives and to retrieve papers remaining in possession of former Agents.[14]

At the formal opening of the Assembly the Agents, like the other delegates, presented their credentials which were evaluated and discussed while they remained in an adjoining room. The Assembly had the power to accept the Agents or to reject them, although in practice this never occurred. Once approved by the membership, the Agents took the oath of office. They swore to fulfill their functions faithfully during the five years of their Agency. After taking the oath, they were officially empowered to begin work and were presented to the prelacy, the king, and his ministers.[15] Within the Assembly they were accorded deliberative voice, voted, and signed the official proceedings, as all deputies did.

The powers and duties of the Agent were set forth definitively in the manuscript "Recueil concernant l'agence générale du clergé," promulgated by order of the Assembly in 1767 for the use and consultation of its Agents. With reason the "Recueil" stated that "the Agents carry all the weight of the ecclesiastical hierarchy . . . they are, so to speak, the depositories of the jurisdiction and the temporal of the clergy of France."[16] The Agents served as intermediaries between the clergy and the nation at large in all legal contests and matters of interest to the First Estate. Their first duty was to maintain the unconditional immutability of the Church's temporal together with its traditional spiritual, disciplinary, and pecuniary privileges. The Agents were at once custodians of the vast and intricate institutional network of ecclesiastical administration, attorneys for 130,000 clerics in the 40,000 parishes of the kingdom, and auditors of the First Estate's receipts and expenditures. Their office was responsible for the defense of ecclesiastical jurisdiction and the maintenance of the rights of the clergy against laymen and against its own refractory members.[17] In order to "preciously conserve" the rights, honors, prerogatives, exemptions, immunities, and privileges of the Church, the Agents were expected to assist any ecclesiastic in distress, "even from the most distant provinces."[18] They were commissioned to maintain a strict vigilance over the titles and papers of the First Estate deposited in the Archives of the Clergy.

It was only after the dissolution of the Assembly that the Agents became in reality chief executives. Maintaining uninterrupted liaison with the dioceses, the Agents received their complaints, acted on their behalf, communicated their wishes to proper ecclesiastical or secular authority, sent them information, or advised them. The representatives of the Assembly and the clergy at large quickly learned to profit from the Agents to whom they exposed their complaints. They realized that the Agents, close to the king and his ministers, could impart great weight and prestige to each case. By the eighteenth century each benefice holder was free to appeal directly to the Agent instead of submitting his request through the intermediary of the Diocesan Syndic.[19] The General Assembly, too, frequently forwarded individual cases to the Agent. Since the Assembly was engaged in matters affecting the whole body of the clergy, and since it delegated its power of administrative surveillance to the Agents, it did not, and could not, give individual consideration to even the smallest fraction of pleas received.

Finally, it was the Agents who were the spokesmen of the sovereignty of the Assembly and the whole order before the King's Council, the key organ of royal central government upon which the clergy depended for favorable decrees sustaining its rights and immunities. Between the five-year intervals of the Assemblies the Agents held in their hands the executive, legal, financial, and administrative authority of the First Estate. The unity and permanence of their office, the ease with which they could handle issues and seek solutions (compared to the cumbersomeness and inevitable institutional delays of the Assembly), and the confidence of the clergy all over the kingdom who in their appeals preferred the informality and impartiality of the Agents to the imposing solemnity of the Assembly's prelates made them an indispensable force in the total clerical mechanism. Although technically under the orders of the Assembly which held the mandate and supreme authority over all the clergy, the Agents operated as a semi-independent institution. Indeed, in the view of two scholars the office of the Agents was the most vital administration within the French Church and was more important to the First Estate than the Assembly itself.[20]

The degree of the Agents' intervention was commensurate with the importance of the affair. If it was of a private nature or of little significance to the clergy as a whole, the Agents would not engage themselves or their office to handle it. If it touched the more general order of diocesan affairs, they might intervene or refer the plaintiff to his superior or bishop. However, if a case had bearing for the clergy as an Estate, the Agents lent the full support of the Church to it and frequently took over the affair entirely, including legal costs. In matters affecting two ecclesiastical bodies or two clergy on trial against one another, the Agents were not permitted to intervene on behalf of either.[21] Nor by the regulations of the clergy could they intervene in the name of the order until they had obtained the counsel of the clergy's attorneys.[22] The same regulations forbade them to obtain favors for benefice holders.[23]

In order to retain the weight and prestige of their office and to make their intervention most effective, the Agents sparingly used their appellant powers before the King's Council, his ministers, the Parlements, and the other sovereign tribunals of the realm. When the occasion demanded, they sought permission from an Assembly of Prelates before taking important steps.[24] Talleyrand had his own ideas regarding intercessions, and under what circumstances they were to be pursued. These will be examined shortly.

To plead the cause of the clergy, the Agents were conferred wide appellant powers before the councils and commissions of the government. With the rank of Counsellors of State they had the right to enter the King's Council, his Committee on Ecclesiastical Affairs, and all government agencies to oppose any law contrary to the usages of the clergy.[25] With the right of *committimus,* conferred on the Agents by Louis XIV, they were permitted access to the Great Seal and the king's minister, the Keeper of Seals, for all causes.[26] By royal edict of 1695 they were received in all Parlements and district jurisdictions (*baillages* and *sénéchaussées*) in affairs touching religion, divine service, the honor and dignity of ecclesiastical persons, and matters of general interest to the Church.[27] The Agents also used their extensive powers to see that proposals pending before any secular body should, whenever possible, not prejudice the interests of the clergy, its *cahier,* its royal letters patent, and its accords and conventions passed with the crown.[28] They were also expected to seek the reform or abrogation of prejudicial royal edicts, declarations and letters patent, decrees of sovereign courts curtailing clerical immunities and privileges, and breaches of contract or the *don gratuit* with the king.

The newly elected Agents were taken immediately to the king, his ministers of State, and his Council in order to take charge of the clergy's fiscal accounts with the crown. These contacts with the government permitted the Agents to insure the integrity of clerical privileges and personally to present resolutions and enactments of the Assembly calling for action by secular authorities.[29]

Having established liaison with the government, the new Agents were anxious to resume relations with the dioceses at the earliest moment. For this reason they immediately notified the bishops and Diocesan Syndics of their election in order that they might quickly bring to completion the unterminated affairs of their predecessors. Through the medium of printed letters the Agents informed the provincial churches of the Assembly's enactments or requested information on local conditions necessary for contemplated legislation.[30]

For the welfare of the clergy the Agents informed the dioceses of any lay attempts to curtail ecclesiastical jurisdiction, and they interpreted royal edicts and letters patent explaining innovations or changes. Supervising the cases of the clergy whose holdings had been lost to the State through alienations, the Agents were also required to supervise these transfers.

In matters of finance and temporalities the Agents examined the accounts of the finances, receipts, and expenditures of the First Estate's treasurer, the Receiver-General of the Clergy, and audited the accounts of the Provincial Receivers each three months.[31] They confirmed the proper employment of all funds allocated by the clergy and checked the balance of payments due from the dioceses for their share of the *don gratuit* and other clerical levies. The Agents also proposed to the Assembly sums for the needs of the clergy's various activities and projects.[32]

Duties within the framework of the Assembly, though they cannot compare in importance with those outside it, were nevertheless numerous. Eight to nine months before the first meetings the Agents met with the ministers of the king to secure a date for the new Assembly and royal letters licensing the Assembly. They then sent copies of these letters to the 116 dioceses in the form of circulars ordering the meeting of the Provincial Assemblies and the election of deputies to the next Assembly.[33] Their first duty, three to four months before the opening of the Assembly, was to secure, in concert with the President, a prelate to preach at the opening solemn Mass of the Holy Spirit.[34] Six weeks to two months before convocation the Agents made all arrangements with architects and workers to put in order the Assembly's meeting rooms, the suites of its officers, their servants, and the ministers of the king, and to arrange the buffet in the Grands Augustins. They gave detailed directions for the installation of proper furniture and carpets, down to the number, size, and color for each room.[35] They arranged for a contingent of Swiss Guards to protect the delegates and summoned a company of police to supervise traffic and to assure the tranquillity of the Assembly.[36]

Convoking the deputies at the home of the provisional President, the Agents read the king's letters of convocation, received, reviewed, signed, and later read before the Assembly the credentials of its members and important correspondence. They secured *lettres d'Etat* which immunized the deputies from arrest for debt during the course of the Assembly's sessions.[37] They secured the *licet* from the Archbishop of Paris licensing the Masses of the Assembly in his diocese.[38] Midway between the routine reading of reports, on the one hand, and the assignment of important affairs by the Assembly, on the other, was the middle range of activity, like carrying messages to the king and his ministers and transmitting their replies to the Assembly, reporting on conferences and occasional intercessions before the King's

Council during the life of the Assembly, and announcing dispatches of the government to the clergy.[39]

A large part of the Agents' duties inside the Assembly consisted of directing protocol. They organized and sent the deputies appropriate announcements of all ceremonies, the various Masses of the chamber, and the processions of the clergy.[40] They kept constantly informed of the health and welfare of the king and the members of the Assembly.[41] They arranged royal audiences for the Assembly and were in continual contact with the crown for the negotiation of the clergy's contracts. They printed and distributed to the dioceses the king's reply to the clergy's *cahier,* the provisions of the contracts with the king, and the share of each diocese in the newly approved *don gratuit,* together with instructions on securing loans.[42]

Their functions in protocol were carried beyond the Assembly. The Agents invited the delegates to say Mass at the illness of the king and informed the clergy of the death of a royal prince or prelate.[43] The Agents convoked the bishops in Paris for coronations, royal births and funerals, and high Masses, and handled pontifical Bulls for papal jubilees.[44]

The last of the Agents' prescribed duties was the oral delivery and subsequent publication of a "Report of the Agency," presented to the next Assembly at the termination of their services. This document summarized their activity during the five-year term of office. Until 1700 these reports had been published as part of the proceedings of the Assembly. After that date they were printed separately.[45] The reports represented an accounting of the Agents' ministry as delivered to the sovereign ecclesiastical assembly and exercised in conformity with its rules. The report also furnished a means of showing how the Agents had discharged their office pursuant to the clergy's directives. The principal affairs of the clergy—spiritual, juridical, and temporal—during the past five years were reviewed, including interventions before the king, ministries, and magistracy.[46] The Agents were expected to highlight affairs of particular significance to the Church and to spell out innovations during the course of their ministry that might serve the new Agents, together with main lines of jurisprudence used in their appeals. The report was then deposited with the Committee on the Revision of the Minutes appointed to examine it and its justificative documents. Upon the Committee's recommendation the report and its pertinent appendices were published. Talleyrand read his huge report during twenty meetings of the Assembly of 1785, from the twelfth session, June 8, to the ninety-sixth (out of 150), September 26. It received lavish praise from one of the liberal grandees of the Assembly, Archbishop Champion de Cicé of Bordeaux, chairman of the committee which examined the report. His unstinted tribute to the genius of its authors, the high distinction of their work, and its permanent value to the body of the clergy contrasts strikingly with the kind but prosaic recommendation accorded the report of their predecessors in the Assembly of 1780.[47] "The examination which we made of it can only add once again to the impression which its reading produced in your sessions. To our satisfaction we could not help but admire anew the truth of the principles and the energy of reasoning and the nobility of expression which developed them. It is a monument to the talents and zeal of the gifted hands which shaped it—assured of your perpetual gratitude. The approval which you have given to this important work is beyond all praise we can offer, and your opinion has already assigned it a distinguished rank among those which decorate your annals . . . there is another sign of gratitude more worthy of your former Agents . . . and we especially recommend that you accord it to them. It consists of recommending them to the favors of the king and to empower Monseigneur the Archbishop of Narbonne to transmit your wishes in their favor to Monseigneur the Bishop of Autun [the Minister of the *feuille des bénéfices*]."

In one of the most influential books on eighteenth-century French Church history, *Les Jansénistes du 18e siècle et la constitution civile du clergé* (Paris, 1928), the late Professor Edmond Préclin found Talleyrand's report a mine of economic and juridical detail on the clergy before the Revolution and incorporated into his own work a good deal of its wealth of information on the financial status of the *curés,* the rise of prices, the increase of taxes, and the diminishing value of currency. He concluded that it was his "remarkable report" which brought Talleyrand the episcopate.[48]

The Agents were also responsible for supervising the operations of the central administrative agencies of the clergy, the Secretariat, the Archives, the Council of the Clergy, and the Receivership-General of the Clergy. This important aspect of Talleyrand's functions has been reserved for later treatment.

Having officially terminated the functions of their office, the Agents were given the honorary title *anciens agents généraux* and appointed Secretary and Promoter in the next Assembly, the one in which they delivered their report. They retained a deliberative voice in their province and the right of entry into all committees.

The earnings of the Agent were handsome. The "Recueil" claimed that in the ordinary five-year period the Agent's wages totaled an average of 88,900 *l.* while with an Extraordinary Assembly (as 1782) it rose to 101,800,[49] though the basic salary for this office set in 1715 was only 5,500 *l.* per year.[50] This enormous figure can be broken down into the following rubrics: salary as Agent, 27,500 *l.*; as deputy in three Assemblies, 5,400 *l.*; as Secretary and Promoter in two, 6,000 *l.*; as Counsellor of State, 7,500 *l.*; and expenses (furniture, travel, postage), 8,400 *l.* To this must be added the rich gratuities bestowed both by Church and State: 21,000 *l.* accorded the retiring Agents by the Assembly as an "ordinary" bonus; and 4,000 *l.* as an "extraordinary" bonus; 16,000 *l.* granted by the king on the *dons gratuits*; 3,000 *l.* in special gifts *(bourses)* of the Assembly; and 3,000 *l.* for the purchase of sacred vessels and other accessories required for the celebration of Mass.[51] The size of this sum becomes even clearer when compared with the honoraria of the Assembly's deputies. In a four-month Assembly such as 1780, excluding travel subsidies, archbishops received 3,240 *l.*; bishops 2,880 *l.*; and deputies of the second order 1,800 *l.*[52] Because of their status as attorney-general the Agents could not be deprived of their property for any reason.[53] Finally, they were exempted from the *décime* and the fiscal obligations binding on all other members of the clergy of France.[54]

The salary of the Agents compared well with that of the bishops. Their income of approximately 20,000 *l.* a year often exceeded that of some bishoprics, particularly the poor seats of Provence, Dauphiné, or Corsica. In addition, the Agents were exempted from the heavy fiscal obligations and capital outlays of their superiors and colleagues. It is not surprising, therefore, that some candidates were in no hurry to exchange their Agencies against the purple, especially against the poor and remote sees of the South. One of the reasons Talleyrand waited three years after the termination of his Agency for a bishopric was that most openings after 1785 were either of this impoverished kind, were too far from Paris, or afforded by their nature little opportunity for the exercise of administrative and political talent.[55] With a sizeable income, residence in Paris, continual intercourse with the chiefs of State and Church, and without the administrative responsibilities of a bishopric, the Agency was one of the choicest offices of the First Estate.

The prestige of this office lent it still other attractive advantages. The Agent-General could justly equate his honorific prerogatives before the clergy with those of the hierarchy. In entering the Assembly and the place for the Mass of the Holy Spirit, he preceded all delegates, including the prelates.[56] In the address of the clergy before the king or in the funeral services of the royal family, he led all other delegates and was the first to leave.[57] In signing a contract with the king, he signed first and led the departing procession. In the Assembly and in religious processions the Agent stood at the head of the second order.[58] In the *Almanach Royal* he figured after the bishops and before the *abbés*.[59] These honors, too, were inviting inducements to the Agency.

Finally, each Agent was destined to the episcopate by virtue of his high office. Everyone in the Church knew this. Many Agents were given bishoprics before the termination of their Agencies, providing there was no opposition among the prelacy.[60] An occasional Agent was made an archbishop without having occupied a lower episcopal seat.[61] Often the king took a liking to an Agent and made him a bishop outright. His functions were then assumed by the Promoter and Secretary until the Agent's province could elect a replacement.[62]

The retiring Agents were to initiate their successors in the current business of the clergy. Talleyrand had already in July, 1783 written to his designated successors offering to brief them on important business of the clergy.[63] The President in the name of the Assembly usually acknowledged the services of the former Agents, as a rule early in the new session, and promised to recommend them to the king and his Minister of the *feuille des bénéfices,* which was tantamount to the receipt of a bishopric.

The Agency-General has rightly been termed a steppingstone to the episcopate, considering the large numbers of its occupants who later became bishops. Some of the most influential prelates of the eighteenth century held this coveted place—among them La Rochefoucauld, Boisgelin, Champion de Cicé, Dulau, Broglie, Leclerc de Juigné, Voguë, Luzerne, and Jarente.[64]

What was Talleyrand's role in the Agency?[65] Historians have hitherto been unable to appraise it with accuracy. The reason for this—aside from the complicating effects of a singularly controversial yet oftentimes amusing debate which has been going on for well over

Agent-General of Clergy of France 69

a century between Talleyrand champions and foes about his integrity and morals—is that for each quinquennial term of service not one Agent-General but two were elected and meant to work as a team. Theoretically and constitutionally equal after the Assembly of Melun, "no Agent was to have more rights, privileges, or authority than the other."[66] In practice, however, this provision of ministerial equality proved a chimera. Not only were there traditionally natural inequalities in the ability of the two men presented as Agents, but historically there were dramatic disparities in their achievement in office, their subsequent promotion, and their influence among the clergy as well.[67] What is more, the clergy at large recognized these differences, and there are letters in the archives addressed to the "Premier Agent Général du Clergé de France," usually the abler and better known.[68]

Talleyrand's colleague during the Agency of 1780-1785 was Thomas-Pierre Antoine de Boisgelin de Kerdu, nephew of the powerful Archbishop of Aix, Jean de Dieu-Raymond de Boisgelin de Cucé. Like Talleyrand's uncle, Archbishop Boisgelin helped obtain for his young relative the office of the Agency-General, having previously named his nephew vicar-general of his diocese, Prior of Sainte-Catherine de Suze, and Rector of the Chapel in the Church of Saint John of Jerusalem, the latter two in his Archdiocese of Aix.[69]

If the Abbé de Boisgelin is still recalled today, it is only for his professional association with the distinguished future statesman and diplomat. On October 17, 1787, one year before he became Bishop of Autun, Talleyrand wrote his boyhood friend Choiseul-Gouffier that he "had managed the affairs of his Estate all alone for five years."[70] Thirty years later he acknowledged in his memoirs having discharged the duties of the Agency "almost alone" because a "too public" adventure had cost Boisgelin the confidence of the clergy "from the first months of [the Agents'] functions."[71] Talleyrand was referring to his colleague's liaison with Mme de Cavanac, ex-Mademoiselle de Romans (or Romance), who bore Louis XV a son later known as the Abbé de Bourbon, "the only bastard whom Louis XV recognized."[72] "His indolence, his passion for Madam de Cavanac," he continued, "readily determined [the clergy] to settle on me the whole of the work."[73] That this testimony is indisputably accurate is evidenced at once from the proceedings of the Assembly of 1780, in which the functions of the Agents appear to have been carried out almost single-handed by Talleyrand, also from the testimony of Bachaumont, from another contemporary memorialist, and from the unpublished correspondence of Boisgelin's own uncle. The illustrious publicist of letters and morals reported, under date of February 3, 1781, that late one evening after the Abbé de Boisgelin, "beau brun et superbe cavalier" and his lady had dined together, they retired to her bedroom, where, after a short while, both were surprised by the sudden entry of M. de Cavanac, who caught them, in the words of another account, "in the act" (*en flagrant délit*). The outraged husband seized the fire tongs; the Abbé grabbed the shovel. A struggle ensued. Both men exchanged blows across the face.[74] The frightened beauty shouted for help, a guard entered, "and a frightful scandal resulted." The next day the Agent-General of the Clergy was called before Minister Maurepas, who upbraided him for having chosen "such an hour [for a] tête-à-tête with such a pretty woman." Seeking to excuse his conduct, the Abbé said "he could not do better than follow the example of such and such a prelate whom he named." Whereupon the good-natured Maurepas told him to wait until he became a bishop. Twenty days later the Abbé de Bourbon, taking the side of his mother who was in the habit of receiving prelates and ecclesiastics to advance the fortunes of her son, secured a *lettre de cachet* which exiled M. de Cavanac forty leagues from Paris.[75] "The Abbé de Boisgelin triumphed, and for this reason there is little doubt today that he will remain Grand-Vicar of the Archbishop of Aix and Agent-General of the Clergy."

The Archbishop of Aix, on the contrary, was decidedly less amused. In unmistakable reference to his nephew he wrote his longtime intimate, the Countess de Gramont, on February 9: "And here he is, this imbecile of an Abbé, who upsets—God knows why—the desire I have of helping him. I am told that he will lose his position, that he will be exiled. From what I can see, he will surely lose his abbey, and I don't know yet what this sad affair is all about. Will you tell my brother, to whom I dare not write . . . that I beg him to send me in detail the whole story of our imbecile Abbé. I confess that his name is too unfortunate, and it causes too much scandal in society."[76] Four days later he wrote again, "I finally guessed the adventure of the unfortunate Agent . . . I wrote to him asking for a justification which must come from him."[77] In still another letter the elder Boisgelin confessed that at bottom he was annoyed at the frustration of his generous efforts to secure the advancement of his nephew for whom he had only recently obtained the promise of another abbey, which was being imperiled by this troublesome episode.[78]

"I don't want to lose this abbey," he complained, "and there are a good many others who perpetrated errors of youth and who were not less well treated as a result. If possible we must smooth over everything, excuse everything, justify everything . . . we must not abandon everything for the folly of a moment."

That the higher clergy was disposed to forgive and forget, due obviously to the eminence of the prelate of Aix and the distinction he enjoyed within his order, is plain from references (in his letter) to the all-powerful Minister of the *feuille des bénéfices*, "who took it very well" and who had written the Archbishop pardoning the Abbé, assured that he was not guilty.[79] Another contemporary on February 6, however, observed that as Agent-General, Boisgelin had "claim to one of the first bishoprics, but as a result of this adventure would not wear the miter for a long while." On March 6 he added that the Minister "cannot conceive of rewarding [the] ecclesiastic for this misconduct."[80] Despite exceedingly fortunate connections of birth and influence, Agent Boisgelin was never promoted to the episcopate. He died along with hundreds of other priests during the tragic Paris massacres of September, 1792.[81]

Virtually all of Talleyrand's modern biographers have been disposed to accept his side of the story regarding the question of one-sided ministerial responsibility.[82] This conclusion was drawn, however, merely by accepting Talleyrand's word in his memoirs, not by having studied the actual documents of the Agency. Of two authors who claimed knowledge of these papers (without having made use of any material found therein in their works, however), one, André Leroy, claimed that Talleyrand personally tended the bulk of clerical affairs down to the most minor questions. He arrived at this conclusion after an examination of the major portion of the Agency's documents purportedly revealed Talleyrand's hand.[83] A second authority, Emile Beurlier, repeated this observation, adding that Talleyrand's colleague, "a mediocre man, indolent and little considered, left him the weight and also all the honor of the office."[84]

The other side of the argument was launched in the trenchant and reactionary pamphlets of the Revolution and carried forward by the early hostile and almost exclusively defamatory Talleyrand biographers.[85] Disposed to find nothing good in Talleyrand, the traitor of his class, the villain of the sequestration of the First Estate's temporal property, the architect of the dissolution of the Church's patrimony, governing bodies, privileges, and administration, these mostly anonymous publicists uniformly condemned him as a vicious opportunist and enemy of the faithful.[86] One critic[87] claimed that the future Bishop of Autun "did not fulfill a single function" while in the Agency, his reports and memoranda being prepared for him by one of the clergy's lawyers. Another author[88] went to considerable pains to prove that Talleyrand displayed unprecedented incapacity and that the entire weight of the Agency fell on his colleague, who considered Talleyrand an imbecile, unable to write two serious, "truthfully reasoned" pages. Beyond its acrimony, there is considerable ground to question the veracity of this source, since its key datum, the name of Talleyrand's colleague, is recorded as the Abbé de Montesquiou, Talleyrand's successor as Agent-General after 1785![89] The early Talleyrand mythopoeic biographers, without documentation, insist that several gifted lieutenants were the authors of all his work.[90] It is precisely this school which has contended that of all the projects of greatness and ideas of genius throughout fifty years of public life from the Old Regime to the July Monarchy, not a single one was original with Talleyrand. One modern author, commenting on these biographers who deliberately manufactured injurious legends, aptly observed, "You have to pick your way through hundreds of these to reach the real Talleyrand."[91]

Which of these conflicting versions is correct? The first, however favorable, is based on unproven generalizations. The second rests on irresponsible and unobjective allegations. The only acceptable answer must be based on an examination of the official records of the clergy, the correspondence, memoranda, directives, communications, and final achievements of the Agents.

From May, 1780 until May 1785, the years of the Talleyrand-Boisgelin Agency, there are available the transcripts of 2,001 letters, missives, and decisions sent out by the Secretariat of the Agency. Entitled "Lettres d'Agence, Bureau de l'Agence Générale du Clergé de France," the transcripts of these letters are contained in four large folio volumes, a portion of the vast Archives of the Clergy.[92] This correspondence of 2,001 items was divided as follows: 352 letters in 1780-1781 (May, 1780 to December, 1781); 686 in 1782-1783; 676 in 1784; 251 in 1785 (January to May); and addenda, 1781-1785, thirty-six letters.[93]

Of these 2,001 letters, 1,111[94] carry neither identifying signatures nor the name of either Agent. As the correspondence available in these volumes represents merely the transcripts of letters dispatched, it is highly probable that the originals were signed by or for either or both Agents, or in the collective name of the *agents généraux du clergé de France,* the official signature of the Agents' communications, but were transcribed into the registers without the name of their author. This failure may be explained by the laxness of the Secretariat's scribes, the tending of minor communications by officials of the Secretariat sent out in the name of the Agents, or by the carelessness of the Agents themselves, who did not always take pains to sign their communications.

The only infallible method of determining who actually wrote each letter of the Agents is the almost utopian task of checking the original letters sent to the thousands of parishes all over the kingdom, provided they may have escaped destruction or loss during and after the Revolution and could be located. For it was the original letter which, by the statutes of the Assembly of Melun, was to carry the signature of the Agents.[95]

Of the remaining 890 of the 2,001 letters, thirty-six carry the official signature of the Agents; fifty-six are circulars signed by the Agents; twenty-three are signed by former Agents and officers of the General Assembly of the Clergy; 710 carry the signature of either Agent.[96] Of these 710 items, 602, or slightly less than eighty-five per cent, were penned by Talleyrand and carry his name;[97] 106, or fifteen per cent, carry the name of Boisgelin;[98] and sixty-seven others are directly attributable to Talleyrand's composition. In letters of confirmed authorship Talleyrand mentioned having written letters on the addressee's behalf. But these sixty-seven letters were transscribed without his name.[99] Besides using the official bound transcripts, an attempt was made to locate the originals of these letters in the various unordered cartons of documents. They were located in part and compared with the official transcript versions of the G^{8*} 2617-2620 series. Although dispersed through many series, the numbers on each of the manuscript letters happily corresponds with those in the four folio volumes. Each missive was assigned a number and is, therefore, easily identifiable. Out of the original 352 letters of 1780-1781, a total of 313 of these was found.[100] Of 686 for 1782-1783, 242 could be located.[101] Of 676 letters of 1784, 658 were found.[102] Finally, of the 287 transcript letters for 1785, 267 were traced.[103]

Within the fragment which this manuscript "first-draft" correspondence represents, we are able to identify various unsigned transcripts and reassign authorship of 179 letters. The largest portion of the remainder of the manuscript missives carries no clues of identification. Of the 179 letters, 125 were signed by Talleyrand; and by calligraphic evidence, thirty-one others were determined to be of his composition.[104] None of the letters carried the authorship of Boisgelin. Other curious imprints of Talleyrand's influence are also available in these manuscript letters. Six carry the Abbé de Périgord's "P" in the upper lefthand corner, which indicates his dictation; seven are autograph letters or full manuscripts.[105] Ten bear his signature in reply for the Agents. Two were signed by the Agents jointly. Other letters include those in which the Abbé de Périgord's "P" was crossed out,[106] while letters marked "P" carried other signatures. Several contain his correction of a text or form,[107] and other letters begin with the saluatory "M. l'Abbé de Périgord has the honor," etc.[108]

Other letters were signed for the Agents but were clearly the work of Talleyrand. In some cases manuscript letters were found not recorded in the transcript series.[109] Twenty-one letters carry the closing, "Agents-General of the Clergy," without signature. There are several examples of autograph letters of Talleyrand's composition which he wished sent out under the joint authority of the Agency. Talleyrand frequently wrote "we are" instead of "I am"[110] or "we" instead of "I."[111] These practices are doubtless attributable to his appreciation of the Melun statutes which sought to keep the Agents working together in their correspondence as well as in their directives. Interesting Talleyrand marginalia on letters received were also found,[112] together with corrections of style.[113]

Of the 179 manuscript missives, 156 were certainly written by Talleyrand. Thus, of the letters which can be positively identified as the work of either Agent, 710 plus sixty-seven (probable authorships), plus 156 found in manuscript add to a total 933 out of 2,001 letters. Of these 933, 825 (602 plus 156 plus sixty-seven), or eighty-eight per cent, are directly attributable to Talleyrand. The location of these 179 manuscript letters of verifiable authorship represents 179 errors in faithfully recording the authorship indicated in the official G[8*] 2617-2620 series. It appears certain that the Secretariat, responsible for copying the letters, was interested more in what was written than who had written it.

It is safe to assume that in recording the authors of the letters, numerous other mistakes were made which are not ascertainable from the incomplete records of the Agency. The reasons for this are not alone that many of the unbound originals have been lost or were not scrupulously kept, but, more important, that the Agents neglected to sign their letters or, like Talleyrand, wished them often to pass for the work of both Agents. There are reasons to suspect an even more extensive Talleyrand composition than we can identify with certainty, particularly as he revealed having personally attended to many affairs and letters which, almost two centuries later, could not be located. In matters of his known authorship where an imposing succession of letters bearing Talleyrand's name is suddenly interrupted by an unsigned lacuna and then resumed with letters bearing his name, it is unlikely that the unsigned letters in these series could have been written by anyone but Talleyrand.[114] It is regrettable that there is no means by which the almost 1,100 unsigned letters can be further identified. Besides the 2,001 official letters hundreds of brief informal notes, memoirs, sketches of correspondence, and directions to administrative assistants survive, virtually all of which were written in Talleyrand's hand. Many of these may have been developed into letters by officials of the Secretariat. None of these notes, however, bears numbers corresponding to the official letters series.[115] Similarly, in the shoreless sea of bills, requisitions, checks, statements of payment, pensions, and the other copious documents requiring the approval and signature of the Agents, we find Talleyrand almost unexceptionably the sole representative.[116]

Aside from the consideration of who made and conveyed decisions and retained contact with the clergy as a whole, it is interesting to observe that Talleyrand's influence predominated conspicuously with regard to authorities of both the Church and State. Talleyrand had the undivided confidence of the cardinalate and the episcopate. Not only was he particularly solicited for public and private affairs by Cardinals de La Rochefoucauld (President of the General Assemblies of the Clergy of 1780 and 1782),[117] de Luynes,[118] and Bernis,[119] but he won special praise before two General Assemblies by Cardinal de La Rochefoucauld in 1782,[120] and Dillon, Archbishop of Narbonne, in 1785.[121] His great ability was recognized by archbishops and bishops who wrote or visited him personally to seek his services or praised him for his invaluable assistance on their behalf.[122] Talleyrand even manifested signs of cordial familiarity with prelates like the Archbishop of Bordeaux, Champion de Cicé, the Archbishop of Arles, Jean-Marie Dulau, the Archbishop of Vienne, Lefranc de

Pompignan, and the Archbishop of Embrun, de Leyssin, whom he professed to emulate as a former Agent.[123]

As to the relations of the Agents to the episcopate as a whole, the documents bear out the prominence of Talleyrand's position. Of the 2,001 letters of the Agency, 311 of these were directed to the bishops of France.[124] Of these 311 letters, 137 were found without signature, largely for reasons applicable to the above correspondence, of which these letters were a portion. Of the 174 signed letters one carried the names of the Agents jointly; twelve were of Boisgelin; and 161 were of Talleyrand.[125] Of the 311 letters to the episcopate 276 were found in manuscript.[126] Among these 276, thirty letters, formerly unidentified in the transcripts, are of Talleyrand's composition.[127] Therefore, of the 204 signed letters (one plus twelve plus 161 plus thirty), 191, or ninety-four per cent, were Talleyrand's.

The same high favor was enjoyed with ministers, officers of the crown, and political leaders of considerable prominence with whom Talleyrand, through his office, negotiated the business of the clergy. Vergennes, Turgot, Necker, Calonne, Castries, Ségur, Choiseul, Maurepas, Malesherbes[128] were the most notable. Keepers of Seals, Secretaries of State, presidents of Parlements, ministers of the Council of State, magistrates of royal tribunals, governors, and intendants of provinces were others. His relations with these officers were amicable, and a buoyant sense of understanding and friendliness animated their correspondence. Not only did Talleyrand successfully receive their aid in intercessions on behalf of the Assembly or the clergy, but the ministers again and again volunteered information and aid to Talleyrand in cases which he treated on behalf of the clergy.[129] Many of the king's men dealt directly with Talleyrand, and their response to him was intended oftentimes as their reply to the General Assembly of the Clergy or the Church.[130]

The correspondence of the Agency with the ministers of State (again out of 2,001 letters) numbered 187.[131] Of these, 148 were left in the records of the transcripts without authors. One of these was written by an officer of the clergy; one by Agent Boisgelin; and thirty-five by Talleyrand. Of these 187 letters, 143 were found in manuscript.[132] Thirty-seven among them were found under Talleyrand's name,[133] and one was signed by the Agents jointly. Therefore, of the seventy-five identifiable letters of both Agents, seventy-two of these, or ninety-six per cent, were by Talleyrand.

For the sake of completeness, admittedly at the expense of merely

Agent-General of Clergy of France

summarizing here points to be expanded in the remaining chapters of this book, it is useful to attempt an overview of his ministerial activity by considering briefly the other chief elements which composed it. Talleyrand assumed the leading role in directing the clergy's central administration. It was he who took the decisive initiative in supervising the Secretariat as well as the legal and tax departments. Similarly he assumed the responsibility in the Agency to secure the authority of the clergy and to enhance the strength of the Church. It was he who daringly confronted the king's minister, Vergennes, in July, 1782, with demands for the respect and guarantee of the ecclesiastical temporalities.[134] In like action, to protect the integrity and jurisdiction of the office of the Agency-General, he boldly forbade the Archbishop of Paris to assume independently the authority of convoking episcopal meetings, clearly reserved to the office of the Agents by the statutes of the Church.[135]

When important statements of principle were enunciated by the Agency, the vast majority of the documents indicate Talleyrand as their author. Nowhere will this be clearer than in his interpretation of ecclesiastical jurisdiction and immunities and in his beliefs regarding the immutability of Church property and privileges, the pressing problem which faced the French clergy during this period. In the Herculean task of guiding the parish clergy, insuring their interests, and defending their rights, his letters are represented in overwhelming abundance.

For the most part the clergy readily accepted his advice either in pecuniary matters of importance to the Church or in interpreting legislation regulating its property or personnel. Most of the incoming correspondence and legal cases bearing the name of an Agent was directed to Talleyrand.[136] In the constant struggle to retain ecclesiastical exemptions or to enforce the laws of Church and State among the provincial clergy, the voice of this Agent was heard clearest. In continual contact with the prelacy and the lower clergy. Talleyrand strove to fortify the bonds of orthodox hierarchical authority to the exclusion of secular interferences. As will also be seen, he adroitly resolved serious quarrels between conflicting clerical parties.

The legislation and significant innovations urged by the Agency-General during the years 1780 to 1785 originated with Talleyrand.[137] The crucial augmentation of the salaries of the indigent rural clergy (the *portion congrue*), voted by the Assembly of 1785 and codified by the monarchy in 1786, was made possible only through his work in the provinces and the Assembly. It was he who conceived the "Diocesan Syndic Plan," a highly original and imaginative policy of administrative centralization to strengthen the diocesan clergy and to spare them the disastrous losses of prejudicial legal and judicial suits through a plan of correspondence and periodic contact with the Agents and other central officials of the French Church. So, too, from him came the moves to repulse threats of seizure of ecclesiastical property and to maintain fiscal immunities, to retain the Church's right to the tithes and its maintenance of the civil register, and to secure legislation to determine sacerdotal fitness for the procurement of benefices.

Finally, the *Rapport de l'agence générale* of 1785, the Agents' final report which was to be prepared conjointly, was largely of Talleyrand's composition. This is evidenced from the authorship of individual cases and actions later incorporated into the report and from Talleyrand's correspondence to the provincial clergy, giving assurance of his personal intervention in the majority of them and requesting details for their presentation to the Assembly. This view is also shared by Professor Préclin: "The report of Agents-General Talleyrand and Boisgelin [was] in fact the very complete work of the former."[138] When it came to reporting significant work or initiative from the Agency-General before the Assemblies, it was Talleyrand who addressed them.

In each phase of activity central to the functioning of the two Agents-General of the Clergy during the years 1780 and 1785, the justice of Talleyrand's claims that he had for five years assumed the burdens of his office "almost alone" appears undisputed when judged quantitatively from the authorship of correspondence and administrative detail and qualitatively by the almost exclusive assumption of official responsibility and creative initiative, technically the collective charge of both men. In at least one phase, therefore, of that conspicuously checkered and lengthy career of public service, where relatively full historical documentation exists and can be used to check the veracity of Talleyrand's own version of his official influence, his assertions are resoundingly vindicated by the evidence.

IV

The Agent-General and the Inviolability of the Church Temporal

The severe financial crises of the last decade before the Revolution and the impending national bankruptcy, which the reforms of a half-dozen ministries could not arrest, were fatally to involve the Church of France. The property and privileges of the First Estate were too extensive, its involvement in the political and public life of the kingdom was too far-reaching to remain unaffected. Partly under the sponsorship of the ministers themselves, partly as a natural consequence of the historic envy of ecclesiastical wealth and power by the other two Estates, printed attacks elaborating the familiar sequestration themes of the Philosophers and Economists were launched against the temporal of the First Estate.[1] The clergy during this period, as is clear from the deliberations of its General Assembly and the work of its Agents, stood in mortal fear of losing its wealth.[2] This fear was well founded, because the Church's opulent holdings, considered by many contemporaries to represent one-fourth of the total property value of the realm (a figure disputed by recent studies as excessive),[3] with revenues rivalling or even exceeding those of the national treasury[4] were held to be anachronistic, unnecessary to the functioning of religion, and inadequately administered to serve the public good.

Much to its detriment the First Estate faced these years of hostility and attack with neither the reserves of public sympathy nor the resolute unity of its own membership upon which to fall back. If the Church of France can be said to have enjoyed the allegiance and support of the nation during other periods of its long history, this was no longer the case after 1750, not if we are to credit the testimony of the Marquis d'Argenson and other informed contemporary diarists.[5] By the 1780's the First Estate could no longer claim a popular following among the intellectual and leadership classes of France. The cause of religion had been severely discredited by the long and bitter struggles of the last generation over Jansenism, inside the Church and out. The controversy over the refusal of sacraments and confession certificates intensified the Parlements' dogged stand against the temporal pretensions of the Church, and after 1752 their serious assault on ecclesiastical jurisdiction. The trials and final dissolution of the Jesuits rocked public opinion and drew charges of disloyalty against the clergy. So did the bishops' disagreement first on the need and then the means by which to reform the monastic orders, as demanded by the State, and the bishops' inveterate opposition to declaring ecclesiastical revenues and paying taxes representative of their wealth. Revealed to the world was the partisanship, the selfishness, and the significant cleavages both of fealty and ideology which rent the house of the First Estate.

Nor were these shortcomings tucked away neatly out of sight. In the *Philosophical Dictionary,* the *Homme aux quarante écus,* the *Diatribe à l'auteur des Ephémérides, La voix du sage et du peuple,* and many other popular tracts, Voltaire joined critics like Holbach in *Le christianisme dévoilé* and *Les prêtres démasqués* and Rousseau in *Le vicaire savoyard* to broadcast the economic and social injustices apparent in the organization of a Church which accommodated a handful of patrician bishops and their chosen dependents who led a charmed life at the top and a vast corps of needy, underprivileged, hard-working servants of religion—the mule of the clergy —below. Though loyal to the cult, the curates groaned under the monopoly of power and wealth of an oligarchy which no longer exchanged responsibility for privilege and which offered few examples either of virtue or piety to clergy and nation. Add to this the secularization of religion in the Age of Reason, due in no small measure to the fashionable reign of Deism, begun the century before, which waged battle against things central to the spiritual and disciplinary teachings of the French Church, such as revelation, the divinity of Christ, non-scriptural tradition, the mysteries and sacraments of religion, the apostolic authority of pope and bishops, and the religious origins of morality. And finally, the new political and economic ideas made light of and gradually helped unfasten the bonds of dependence on a Church shackled by tradition and inequality. To add heat to their battle against the traditional usages and established prerogatives

Inviolability of the Church Temporal   81

of the hierarchical Church, the Philosophers found eager cohorts in the Jansenists, Gallicans, *parlementaires,* and *curés.*

The Church of France did not find it easy to refute these charges and to vindicate the sacred cause of religion. Unlike the previous century in which Christian belief was normative and apologists were not only numerous but of puissant stature, the Century of Enlightenment provided relatively few effective defenders with whom the clergy could join forces against the enemies of the faith. The bishops lamented both the sorry defense of clerical apologists against the challenges of the Philosophers and the crisis of recruitment for the priesthood, which appeared as a less desirable vocation in an increasingly antisacerdotal age.[6] That even the Church itself was being sapped by the new literary wave, which had invaded every recess of the kingdom, and that this militated against a show of concerted opposition necessary to refute the attacks or indeed to rise above them is evidenced by the wide diffusion of Philosophic works in religious libraries all over France,[7] by the embarrassing heterodox views among the custodians of religious orthodoxy as revealed in the case of the Abbé de Prades before the Sorbonne,[8] and by the equally incriminating fact that top leaders like Archbishops Loménie de Brienne, Boisgelin, and even Cardinal Bernis were notorious friends and votaries of the forbidden writers. As a body the bishops of France before the Revolution were lustily engaged in every kind of nonspiritual activity.[9]

The First Estate, however forced to the defensive, gave no quarter to public opinion. As Talleyrand admitted, "In its temporal administration, the clergy of the eighteenth century made no concession to the spirit of the times."[10] Determined to hold on to everything it owned, the clergy clung tenaciously to each privilege, which the bishops argued was as sacred as religion itself and indeed a central part of religion. In this policy it faced opposition from the king's magistrates and officers, anxious to see the crown whittle down the extravagant clerical patrimony. This was not new. Increasingly the clergy was to fight its temporal battles with unruly members of its own order who bypassed ecclesiastical authority in favor of the king's justice. Though the monarchy promised to respect the long lists of clerical immunities enumerated point by point in Church-State contracts each five years, or oftener, depending on the frequency of the *dons gratuits,* and while these were given juridical force as official instruments of the crown, registered by the sovereign tribunals of the kingdom, the clergy still found itself obliged to fight for their enforcement before the courts and Parlements of the land. Even though contemporary opinion was no longer sympathetic to the fiscal immunities of the clergy under the fiction of the *don gratuit* and even though the ministers of the king looked favorably on the nationalization of the ecclesiastical domain, it most certainly would have taken a revolutionary reform of the monarchy to separate the Church from the State, which Louis XV decreed "could not be separated,"[11] to deny its powerful voice in public law, to disavow its corporate guarantees universally acknowledged for more than two-hundred years, and to revise the division of social responsibility between the Two Powers. It was in the hope of preventing this and of strengthening feudalism that the bishops of France assumed the calamitous position of disavowing their traditional monarchism in favor of calling for the Estates-General in 1788.

Of the 2001 letters and forty-three official reports that survive Talleyrand's Agency, the vast majority were dedicated to various affairs concerning the temporal, a fact clearly indicative of the growing difficulty experienced by the clergy during the last years before 1789 in holding on to its wealth. These affairs ran the gamut from threats of expropriation of Church property to reform of the parish clergy, the usurpation of clerical prerogatives by lay tribunals, the flouting of episcopal authority, or the refusal, by laymen and clergy alike, to honor ecclesiastical tax obligations.

This chapter proposes to show how Talleyrand during his Agency, the last complete quinquennial term in the Old Regime, defended the Church by maintaining the inviolability of its temporal, the gravest single issue which faced the body of the clergy in the decade before 1789. Talleyrand's work during these years can be focussed about five main considerations. The first concerned what he thought to be wholesale governmental seizure. The second, pertaining to the Church's feudal obligations, involved the clergy's attempt to keep secret and out of the government's hands the exact extent of its wealth. The third had to do with the safeguarding of the most valuable portion of the temporal, the tithes, and the attempt to combat insurrectionary tendencies among the indigent lower clergy, who depended on them for their livelihood. The fourth concerned an attempt to stop the alienations of Church property which seriously attenuated the clerical patrimony. The fifth, a bold and ingenious plan to secure the Church against future lay attacks by strengthening the bonds between provincial clergy and the central administrative machinery, will be considered separately in a later section.

Clearly the greatest danger to the ecclesiastical domain was nationalization or outright seizure. Despite threats of sequestration the Church temporal survived the Old Regime intact. The last three monarchs before the Revolution were stout defenders of orthodoxy, who professed paternalistic responsibility for the welfare of the Church, a policy openly encouraged by the medieval theories of sacerdotal kingship revived by Bossuet.[12] They adhered to the religious programs defined by Louis XIV by which the king was protector of the Church with the "open and free disposition of all property, secular as well as ecclesiastic, to use . . . according to the needs of the State."[13] The Very Christian Monarchy only halfheartedly, sometimes even grudgingly, countenanced the fiscal proposals of its ministers against the clergy, such as the *capitation* of 1695, the *dixième* of 1710, and the *cinquantième* of 1725, which sought a more generous portion of clerical wealth in taxes.[14] The same was true of bold schemes like Machault's permanent *vingtième* of 1749, the corollary edicts prohibiting all further acquisition of clerical property by mortmain and demanding the compulsory declaration of revenues of all clerical benefices, and Calonne's land tax (*impôt territorial*) and plan to reimburse the debt of the clergy of 1787. Both attempted to abrogate the Church's fiscal immunity by making taxes permanent, equal, and universal, thereby subjecting the clergy's holdings without exception to the same fiscal obligations as the other two estates.[15]

Crucial issues were at stake in the proposals of Machault and Calonne. For deprived of its fiscal autonomy and subject to taxes as everyone else in the kingdom, the clergy no longer had any excuse for separate corporate existence, symbolized by its General Assemblies, Agents-General, permanent central agencies, Diocesan Bureaus and Provincial Assemblies. Though founded originally for economic reasons, that is, as organizations which facilitated the payment of periodic subsidies to the crown, these elements of centralizing authority worked to enhance the administrative and legal power of the First Estate and by the eighteenth century came to constitute a formidable and articulate vehicle of institutionalized protest to royal policy. The existence of the clergy's huge cumulative corporate debt, which grew larger at each Assembly, contracted through loans, the results of its *dons gratuits* to the crown, guaranteed the continuation and integrity of machinery which voted, raised, and repaid them. But with its debts reimbursed by the State, there would be no need or justification either for its contracts or the continuation of its vast and potent institutions of corporative privilege and pressure. The Church was acutely aware of the grave perils to its traditional hegemony inherent in these measures of Machault and Calonne, and it fought fiercely—and successfully—not only for their defeat but for the removal of the ministers responsible for them. In December, 1750 the clergy threatened to call for the Estates-General against royal despotism in levying taxes,[16] essentially similar motives which impelled it to do the same thing in 1788. The pious but indecisive Louis XVI did not relish a reputation as a latter-day Diocletian, and like his grandfather in 1749, he disavowed his Minister in 1787, abandoned the proposed land tax, and capitulated to the fiscal autonomy of the clergy, thereby rejecting one of the soundest antidotes to France's chronic insolvency. As Talleyrand cogently observed about the body of bishops of 1789, of whom he was one, "When the pecuniary interests of the clergy were attacked, the defense was general."[17]

In the summer of 1782 in the thick of the American war, Talleyrand thought the king was preparing to seize the temporal. On June 28 the semi-official *Gazette de France* published the Emperor's announced intention of appropriating for the crown the property of the Austrian clergy, which would bring to the public treasury "more than 100 millions in revenue" after providing an annual wage for all clerical persons, lay and regular.[18] The Agent was mindful of the ever-mounting government deficit in France, the huge expenditures for the war, the perennial want of French kings, and the Church's enemies who coveted her wealth. The failure of Pope Pius VI's journey to Vienna, several months earlier, to dissuade Joseph II from his course[19] and the fear that similar plans might be on foot by other Catholic powers caused Talleyrand grave apprehension. On July 2 the Agent-General wrote a long letter to Vergennes, Foreign Minister, chief advisor of the king, and a well-known admirer of Joseph's ecclesiastical policies,[20] insinuating that the government was behind the publication of the article to foment popular feeling for a policy similar to the one then proclaimed in the Empire.[21] Stating that the *Gazette de France* together with its directors and editors enjoyed an extraordinary reputation for informed and responsible reporting, Talleyrand apprised the Minister that the article "gave rise to a host of reflections scarcely favorable to the clergy of France" from many who see it as an official journal. The article might whip up public opinion already disposed to conclude, after the pope's recent failure to deter the Emperor from his announced course of sequestration, that his project would be "adopted by all the Catholic powers" of Europe. Coming as it did so close upon an election of another General Assembly of the Clergy, the article was being used by some "to force the clergy to great sacrifices by the threat of a great revolution." In a classical exhortation worthy of the diplomat he was to become, Talleyrand concluded:

> Your sincere love for religion is too well known, Monsieur; I am too convinced of your respect for law, of your justice, of the breadth of your lights, of the prudence and wisdom of your views, to permit these reckless and indiscreet reflections to cause me the slightest fears. But the more you consider them ill-founded the more I would like to hope, Monsieur, that you will order that articles in which the *Gazette* reports the affairs of the Austrian clergy be presented in a manner which permits no room for interpretations capable of rekindling the envy and blind hatred of some persons against the ministers of the Church.

Talleyrand's letter urging the Minister to use his authority to alter the text of the *Gazette* and censor future articles, thereby allowing no quarter to the enemies of the Church, was tantamount to a request for suppression. Three days later Vergennes wrote Talleyrand what he really wanted to know, that Louis XVI—unlike his Imperial brother-in-law—had no designs on the Church's domain.[22] The crown takes no hand in the writing of articles which appear in the *Gazette* and, therefore, "can in no wise vouch for the truth of the facts contained in it." Further, the government has no "secret view" of possible sequestration of ecclesiastical properties. Even "if the king had the intention of seizing the administration of ecclesiastical property," Vergennes continued, "he would consider it below his dignity as well as his authority to sound out in advance, by devious ways, the feeling of his subjects in this regard." After informing Talleyrand that the article may have "produced a disagreeable sensation for the clergy of France," Vergennes invited Talleyrand to request the editor of the *Gazette* to print "whatever retraction or modification" he judged appropriate, which, he assured the Agent, would be inserted in the next copy and "passed under the eyes of the king and his ministers."

Talleyrand's action was taken, as he honestly stated, "to justify the confidence with which the clergy honored [him]" as their monitor, responsible for the wealth and welfare of the Church and sensitive to any innovation which threatened either. Unsure how the omens of expropriation in Austria were to be interpreted or what their bearing might be for France and the other Catholic Houses of Europe, Talleyrand, it appears quite certain, was not so much interested in muffling the article as sounding out the government on the possibility of sequestration. That these were, in fact, his motives are attested by the fact that neither the Agent's correspondence nor the records of the *Gazette* reveal any trace of a letter written to its editor, and no retraction was printed in subsequent issues of that journal.

It is only in understanding the importance of this exchange that Talleyrand's peculiar position before the Extraordinary Assembly of the Clergy, three months later, can be explained. The king convoked the Assembly on October 10, 1782, only a few months before the humiliating destruction of the French fleet in the bloody battle between Admiral Rodney and the Count de Grasse in the Dominican Islands, in order to ask for an extra *don gratuit* of fifteen millions to help sustain the burdens of the American war. The clergy was indignant at this request, because the king had promised (through the offices of Talleyrand himself) that additional money would not be solicited between 1780 and 1785.[23] Talleyrand surprised the Assembly on October 18 by an impassioned and unprecedented appeal for the speedy ratification of the king's demands. This was a daring stand, not only because affairs such as determining the voluntary gifts were usually outside the Agents' authority once the bishops were convened in their Assembly but also because these officers were charged to oppose all schemes of the State not in the best pecuniary interests of the Church.

His argument was brief and skillfully constructed.[24] The king's promise of 1780 had been made in good faith, but "unforeseen losses and urgent needs" of the war, impossible to calculate in advance, left the king no other choice but to summon the Assembly. The money would be an inexpensive investment for the Church's security, the strength of its petitions, and the safety of its temporal. The gift would also buy popular prestige and the king's continued support, so necessary to guarantee both the ecclesiastical domain against its many foes and the success of its litigations before the king's tribunals, and, for purposes of discipline, the enforcement of the Assembly's enactments among the lower clergy. Moreover, the clergy owed the nation an example as the spiritual leaders of the people; and because peace was the basis of the Church's mission, it was obliged to aid the king in the emergency of the war. "The sacred principles which contribute to constitute in you the First Body of the State . . . the confidence of the sovereign . . . the veneration of the people [and] the sacred duties of the ministry" demand this of the clergy.

Clearly the most compelling reason which motivated the Agent's stand—though this did not figure in his dramatic elocution—was the fear of the clergy's wealth expressed in the Vergennes letter. Because of his closeness both to the business of the clergy and the royal government, Talleyrand realized more clearly than other members of his order that a sure way to prevent the king, desperately in need of money in the crisis of the war, from resorting to the precedents of Joseph II, as important segments of official and non-official opinion would have him do, was to incur a monetary sacrifice through a higher voluntary gift. In advocating this policy, he was only reminding the clergy what it had been forced to do in 1695, 1710, 1726, and 1750, and what it was again to do in 1789.[25] The vote of the Assembly to grant the appropriations came immediately after the plea of the Agent-General.[26]

If the State could not nationalize the Church's property, it could at least tax it. But to tax, the government had to ascertain the exact state of ecclesiastical income and holdings. The clergy, understandably, was determined to keep its wealth a closely guarded secret—a secret so well guarded, in fact, that even modern historians are still left guessing at its real extent.[27] The clergy made no secret of the taxation of its dioceses and benefices. As a matter of fact it printed in voluminous detail the fiscal contributions of all its dioceses in the proceedings of the Assemblies for all to see. On the contrary, its financial situation and the real revenues of its dioceses were tightly guarded secrets. Ignorance on the part of the government appeared the only assurance of the clergy's financial immunities and the sole barrier to new taxes. Clerical estimates of Church wealth were intentionally minimized to make its fiscal obligations as modest as possible. But, logically, the same motives which led the clergy to conceal its wealth impelled the king to ascertain it. The monarchy, convinced that the clergy was paying a disproportionately modest portion of its revenues, lent its support to attempts to make the First Estate contribute more.

The king had two ways to determine the extent of clerical property. First, by legislative authority the clergy could be forced to disclose the value of its benefices. This was attempted (unsuccessfully) in laws of August 17, 1750, which required all holders of benefices to furnish the government within six months a statement of annual benefice income, and of August 5, 1787, by which the crown argued that the *don gratuit* was unfair to the State and placed undue burdens upon the lower clergy.[28] Only a revised fiscal contribution under the newly proposed *vingtième* would at once equalize the burden nationally and yield revenue more representative of the Church's holdings. Second, as suzerain and conformable to feudal practice the king could demand of all ecclesiastical benefice holders the *foi et hommage*, which was merely the traditional feudal oath of fidelity and submission, but which carried with it the vexatious *aveu et dénombrement*, the vassal's obligation to provide his lord within forty days of the oath a detailed description of the full property of a fief, together with its appurtenances, revenues, rights, and prerogatives—justly characterized by an informed contemporary in 1775 as "a branch of the barbarism of feudal law which still governs the kingdom."[29] This was done by an edict of December 29, 1674, renewed on November 10, 1725.[30] But from 1726 the clergy procured stays of execution (*arrêt de surséance*) of this decree each five years until the end of the Old Regime.[31] In 1775 the king appointed a mixed commission of Church and State to investigate this matter;[32] but right up to 1789 it resulted in no change. Until the Revolution, therefore, neither feudal procedures nor legislative authority forced the clergy to reveal the extent of its holdings.

There is no doubt that before 1785 the clergy considered the *foi et hommage* as one of the cardinal threats to its temporal autonomy. It was repeatedly referred to in the Assembly as a "revolution."[33] The spokesmen for the clergy made no secret of the fact that the king's ministers, notably his Inspector of the Domain, considered the clergy's exemption illegal and that everything would be done to quash it.[34] The First Estate was prepared, if necessary, to wage the same war of attrition fought thirty years before against Machault's *vingtième*, where the fear of an official state inventory of its possessions was even more dreaded than the tax itself.[35] The stay of execution until December, 1785, it was announced in 1780, "appears to be the last," and the clergy could no longer hope for a prolongation.[36] Accordingly Cardinal de La Rochefoucauld announced before the Assembly of 1782 the formation of what might be called a committee of clerical safety, a permanent committee of surveillance, study, and political action to mobilize the clergy for victory. It was made up of the bishops, the members of the Assembly's Committee on the *Foi et Hommage,* the Agents-General, the clergy's attorneys, and outside specialists in feudal and canon law, who met at regular intervals at the Cardinal's Paris mansion.[37] The Assembly voted to hire other specialists, as required for the case, urgent to both the First and Second Estates, and to empower the Agents to convoke special meetings of the bishops if necessary.

The Archives of the Clergy contain huge and learned treatises, written by distinguished canonists (the Abbés Bouquet and Parent), which proved the immunity of the Church's titles from the beginnings of the monarchy.[38] Two powerful memoirs of book size in 1783 and 1784 were directed against the arguments of the Inspector of the Domain.[39] In a letter of March 8, 1781, Talleyrand indicated that the Abbé Bouquet had presented 2,000 charters proving the Church's exemption, and that he had gathered another 3,000 relative to ecclesiastical foundations.[40] Such importance was attached to these researches that the bishops accorded not only lucrative gratuities to Bouquet and Parent but went as far in 1781 as recommending Parent (Bouquet died in July, 1781) to the Minister of the *feuille des bénéfices* for the highest rewards the Church was capable of bestowing. The Assembly of 1785 accorded him a life pension of 3,000 *livres* annually in acknowledgement of his ten years of "unyielding work, indefatigable zeal, and rare wisdom . . . in the important cause of the *foi et hommage.*"[41]

Cardinal de La Rochefoucauld pleaded for the suggestions and the assistance of every clergyman of the realm in collecting titles of exemption. He proposed a correspondence to rouse the dioceses, giving "the state, cause, and plan of our defense."[42]

Thanks to the skill and determination of the clergy, the unwillingness of the monarchy to precipitate another crisis with the Church, and the timeliness of the Rohan Affair, which galvanized the zeal of the bishops for the cause of their order, the First Estate won the battle. Fearless, even bold, in pursuing the king for a definitive showdown on this issue and confident of victory ("the law is on our side"),[43] the bishops secured a meeting with the king's ministers of

State during which the opposition collapsed. A docile Keeper of Seals reported that he had prepared the text of a law which "condemns the pretensions of the clergy in the exemption [but] takes all measures to render the enforcement less onerous for the present and more advantageous for the future."[44] This admission of weakness and indecision on the part of the monarchy was even more advantageous to the clergy than the five-year exemptions of the past; for, as the jubilant Assembly was informed, no decision would be forthcoming "for a considerable time," probably not before the Assembly of 1790, and then there was the expectancy of a favorable ruling. Nor was there any longer the fear of a "fatal deadline" or legal action before the courts, the *Chambre des comptes,* the *Bureaux des finances,* and the *Commission du domaine.* Proud of its victory, the clergy published a book of 186 pages in 1786 in which it reproduced the choicest arguments on its behalf, taken from the numerous papers written by its specialists, and a *précis* of the successful defense of its immunities before the king's ministers.[45] Secure that "the clergy can rest peacefully," the Church weathered the rest of the Old Regime without fear of the *foi et hommage.*

It was Talleyrand's job as Agent-General to keep the secret of his order and to help the provincial clergy do the same.[46] As a subdeacon of twenty-one and a member of the key Committee for Religion and Jurisdiction in the Assembly of 1775, Talleyrand had encountered this thorny question for the first time. The king's political primordiality was in reality threefold: he was at once political sovereign, supreme protector and guardian, and feudal suzerain. On the basis of the last, Louis XVI could have insisted on the *foi et hommage* at his accession in 1775 if he had chosen. Instead his two brothers and their cousin the Duke of Orleans lost no time to press their feudal claims against the Church. The clergy recognized that there was legally no way to escape the demands of the *foi et hommage* exacted by individual nobles such as the king's brother the Count of Provence.[47] The hierarchy conceded that it lived "in a precarious and uncertain state under the sole power of the stays of execution accorded [it]."[48] It sought immunity by virtue of the supernatural character of the priesthood, the edicts of the king, and the usages of common law which traditionally immunized the clergy. It maintained furthermore that its fiscal contributions freed it of all feudal and patrimonial charges.

After 1780 the contest was taken up anew by the Duke of Orleans.

Inviolability of the Church Temporal 91

Although he enjoyed revenues from his ducal *apanage* of nearly four million *livres* (3,945,782), three times more than the Count of Provence and seven times that of the Count of Artois,[49] the Duke was reportedly close to bankruptcy due to extravagant living and lavish expenditure and avoided financial ruin only by continued borrowing.[50] His financial administrators used every device to augment existing sources of revenue and to tap new ones.[51] The *foi et hommage* held out hope for just such a windfall. Talleyrand coordinated the administrative procedures of his order between 1780 and 1785 to thwart these threats and to secure renewed stays of execution. From the first moments of his Agency Talleyrand was in the thick of the struggle over the *foi et hommage*. In November, 1780 he was appointed secretary of a committee of bishops and lawyers under the presidency of the Archbishop of Paris, which met regularly during 1780, 1781, and 1782, and again in 1784 and 1785, to prepare the clergy's defense and to meet the commissioners of the king. The Committee charged him with the preparation of its proceedings, the correspondence with the dioceses, and the redaction of the official papers.[52]

Until 1782 his official argument had been that the *foi et hommage*, like Machault's proposed inventory of 1749, attacked the very manner in which the clergy held its property.[53] To impose it on the Church, therefore, would destroy the principle of private property. Since the king and his family no longer enforced these feudal rights against the clergy, the Duke as a royal prince could not either. The clergy held its feudal property immediately from the king, therefore it did not recognize intermediary seigneurs. By royal decree the churches in the Duchy of Orleans enjoyed the same privileges as those in the king's domains. Thus, by threatening the churches of Orleans and Chartres with the enforcement of the *foi et hommage*, the Duke by "absolutely arbitrary exceptions" undermined royal will and authority.

Reflecting the clergy's confidence of victory in this affair by 1785, Talleyrand went further.[54] The question was whether the Church owed feudal responsibilities for its property even to the king. He attempted to prove that from the time of the Romans through the Capetians to 1785, Church lands were allodial, that is, held without recognition of feudal superior. Royal charters and monuments of all races of French kings repeatedly confirmed this right in the interests of religion. Therefore the clergy as citizens recognized the king as sovereign and monarch but rejected his quality as suzerain, that technically did not exist for the Church.

The Agent admitted privately that the clergy was on unsafe ground. The law of 1674 had formally rejected the Church's immunity from the *foi et hommage*. Royal stays of execution only postponed a final decision. "Without touching the heart of the question," Talleyrand wrote in his memoirs forty years later,[55] "[they] suspended the execution of the laws." The State rejected the Church's arguments of immemorial allodiality as "null and abusive." Because the clergy could claim no "authentic titles" to prove its exemption, it could not legally oppose lay demands for that obligation.

The king, who was not eager to precipitate all-out war with his clergy, particularly as he gave it so little satisfaction in its other grievances, harmlessly reassured it that he would discuss this matter with the Presidents and attorneys of his sovereign courts before undertaking any statute of importance to Church or State.[56] As for the royal brothers and the Duke of Orleans the clergy secured oral agreements, from the former in 1780 and from the latter in 1782, to postpone action on the *foi et hommage* in their appanages until 1785.[57]

Through the office of the Agency Talleyrand secured two royal stays of execution in 1780 and 1785 which enabled the clergy to guard its immunities and to keep secret the extent of its wealth for well over one hundred years in clear defiance of royal legislation. In this, as in so many other facets of the ecclesiastical temporal, it was only the good will of the king or, as was stated in the August 23, 1780 decree of his Council which granted postponement, "his benevolence for the clergy of his kingdom" that saved the First Estate from the enmity of its foes.[58]

The clergy's patrimony consisted of lands, buildings, rents, leases, and profits from various investments, and of feudal-patrimonial dues and services. The single most significant portion of its property was the tithe (*dîme*), the revenue used to defray the costs of the cult, due the Church by all who owned land and enjoyed its fruits. Despite its name the tithe was not a constant one-tenth of agricultural produce, but varied markedly all over France from one-seventh in Lorraine to one-sixtieth in Dauphiné or Provence. One-thirteenth has been offered as a figure representative of the country as a whole.[59] The tithe yielded more to the clergy than any other single direct tax received by the State; as a matter of fact, it totaled slightly less than two-thirds of the combined revenues of the *vingtièmes, capitation,* and *taille*.[60]

The tithe was under constant bombardment in the eighteenth century. The Philosophers, Physiocrats, large groups of farmers and lower clergy, and the king's Committee on the Administration of Agriculture under Minister Vergennes, Lavoisier, and Dupont de Nemours (1785-1787) attacked it as fiscally arbitrary, a barrier to the perfection of agriculture, and as a deterrent to economic growth.[61] The Parlements repeatedly disputed its divine authority.[62] It is no surprise that the Church fought innumerable attempts by laymen and clergy alike to escape payment. Archbishop Boisgelin announced before the Assembly of 1788 "that there was not a diocese [in France], scarcely a parish whose inhabitants did not contest before their pastors a part of his subsistence which he held by law."[63] This money was supposed to provide a decent living to thousands of parish *curés* who assured the maintenance of religion all over France. Most of the rural clergy, deprived of these incomes intended for their support, did not themselves possess the tithes.[64] Instead they worked for a woefully insufficient stipend, ironically called the *portion congrue* (adequate emolument), paid them by the tithe owners (*décimateurs*), the titulars of benefices in whose churches these *curés à portion congrue* discharged sacerdotal functions. As a result of centuries of infringement the vast majority of the tithes (five-sixths according to Henri Marion) had fallen into the hands of *gros décimateurs,* that is, bishops, canons, religious, schools, seminaries, hospitals, Knights of Malta, commendatory abbots, and occasionally laics who were often non-residents of the parish where religious services were discharged. They took their name from the *grosses dîmes* which they collected, the most common and extensive (hence the most valuable) fruits of the parish.[65] The *curés* of these parishes, who technically had the right to the tithes levied in them, held but one-sixth of the total. Thus only a fraction of the tithes actually benefitted the *curés* directly, or for that matter even the faithful of the parish, upon whom rested the support of both pastors and churches, and who viewed with hostility the subversion of indigenous tithes by outsiders who extracted unearned revenues without commensurately supporting the cult of the region. The *curé* as sole tithe owner was a rarity.[66]

The clergy in the Assemblies of 1780 and 1782 was greatly disturbed by unfavorable decisions rendered by the Parlements of Provence, Brittany, Flanders, and especially Languedoc (Toulouse), which submitted jurisprudence inimical to the traditional tithe rights of the Church by redefining conditions for their payment and by according liberal exemptions.[67] By the second half of the eighteenth century the clergy encountered increasing difficulty in securing payment of the tithes because of numerous legal disputes and conflicting interests of ecclesiastical and lay parties and because of the marked increase in decrees, edicts, and regulations which granted exemptions.[68] The right of the clergy to collect the major tithes (*grosses dîmes*) on the common cereal grains called the *gros fruits* or *solites* was not disputed. But the courts granted exemptions from certain tithes called *novales,* exacted on land newly cleared of forest, and from such lesser tithes (*menues dîmes*) as green tithes or *insolites* (millet-grass, vegetables, hemp, wood, saffron, peas, beans). The Church was involved in widespread court actions to secure payment of these tithes.[69] The clergy protested that the jurisprudence of the Parlements was inadmissible because the tithe had historically been more extensive than these bodies conceded, that the former law specifically mentioned the tithes on *insolite* crops, and finally that the Parlement of Toulouse had itself conceded the legitimacy of the lesser tithes and by its decisions made payment obligatory.

Talleyrand's weightiest problem in this domain, by his own admission, came as a result of the decision of the Parlement of Normandy (Rouen) on May 3, 1784, which renewed an earlier decision of July 16, 1749. It acknowledged the clergy's legitimate title to the *solites* but reduced them to four (wheat, rye, barley, oats) and obliged the tithe owner to prove that he had collected the tithes on *insolites* (which it defined as all crops not *solite*) for forty consecutive years as a condition of future payment.[70] While recognizing that landowners could not legally escape the tithes by transferring arable land into meadow land, the decision decreed that owners were not obliged to keep under cultivation more than one-third of their lands subject to the payment of the tithes.

The decision of the Parlement threatened the churches of Normandy with the loss of no less than one-half of the tithes paid in a province in which agricultural crises had already occasioned serious famines, hunger, riots, and pillaging.[71] It increased the already bewildering numbers of court cases involving the *insolites*. It reversed traditional practice by making all proof in contested tithes incumbent on the *décimateur,* who received, rather than on the *décimable,* who paid, regardless of the length of time crops had been under cultivation. It suppressed the fundamental rule that all new crops were subject to payment of the tithes and made the tithe owner prove that the tithe in litigation was *solite* and collected regularly for forty years to secure payment, where formerly the tithe payer had to prove it *insolite* to secure exemption.

Talleyrand wrote soon after that this "most extensive and most dangerous legislation" threatened to cripple the tithe owners not only of Normandy but also of the whole realm,[72] for if once the precedent were established of allowing the payer to free himself from what the Church considered his legitimate tithe obligations, regardless of the clergy's ability to prove forty years' possession, then nothing could prevent all payers from doing the same. The current decision is in violation "not [of] a divine institution which is perpetually thrown at us" but of common law, universal jurisprudence, and established usages as old as the monarchy itself, acknowledged in France "long before Charlemagne" and in Normandy for the past six hundred years. The tithe is not a voluntary payment, but a duty levied on all fruits of the earth without distinction, and Talleyrand cited Montesquieu as a partisan of the Church's rigorous retention of the tithes. The Parlement's decision, the Agent asserted, "assailed the holiness of property, spread alarm, consternation, discord, and anarchy," and increased the suffering of the *congruiste* priests who lived from these receipts. He appealed to the General Assembly for authority to seek its suppression and, with the aid of the clergy's legal department, received rulings from the King's Council on June 8, 1785 and July 27, 1786 which suspended it. Despite this victory, however, the king refused to accede to the repeated demands of the Assemblies for a new law defining the payment of the tithe which could have reversed the unfavorable jurisprudence delivered by the Parlements.

There were many cases of abusive tithe exemptions sought by clerical parties. The Lazarists and the Order of Malta tried to prove exemption by invalid papal Bulls going back to Innocent III or Bulls never ratified in France.[73] *Curés* in Clermont refused to pay their bishop for certain crops under the pretense that these did not fall under the category of taxable crops and because the local seneschal twice sustained them in their decision.[74] Some sought exemption of arable lands under the pretext that these were forested or not under cultivation.[75] On the whole the Agent had little difficulty recovering alienated tithes. Those which had fallen into the hands of laymen were, generally speaking, not difficult to regain, since both canon and common law forbade such possession.[76]

Inextricably bound to the payment of the tithes was the fate of the salaried *curés à portion congrue*. Their salary was fixed by joint action of Church and State. Between 1686 and 1768 it had been set at 300 *l*.[77] In 1768 it was raised to 500. The *cahiers* and other contemporary documents testify to the great economic need of this group whom generations of historians have lauded as "the most intelligent and educated portion of the country population"—clergymen, schoolmasters, counsellors, and auxiliaries of secular government, respected by Turgot (whom he called his "local subdelegates") and other statesmen, who announced edicts, laws, and treaties, aided justice, and maintained the civil register.[78] From their small grants the *curés* had to pay the costs of their household, the maintenance of their house, and minor repairs on their church. Their homes often served as a center for the sick and indigent of the parish and a refuge for some member of their family. They were invariably expected to contribute to communal causes. Beyond this, the *curés* were obliged to pay the clerical income tax, the *décime* which constituted their heaviest single expenditure. Many complained that their receipts after expenses did not permit adequate food or clothing. There is no longer any doubt that this group, forced after 1690 to pay a disproportionate share of its income in *décimes*, sustained the heaviest burden of taxation within the First Estate.[79]

Talleyrand reported cases where many *congruistes* were not even given the full 500 *l*. guaranteed them by law.[80] There were innumerable instances of suffering caused by the selfishness of unscrupulous tithe owners who welcomed legal technicalities and subterfuge to avoid paying the *curés*. Between 1768 and 1789, when legislation raised the *portion* to 700 *livres*, many *curés* obtained no more than 100, 140, 180, and 300.[81] "Almost everywhere where they were reduced to the *portion congrue*, *curés* and vicars lived miserably."[82] The tithe owners, whose tithes were to be used for the relief of the poor and the maintenance of the parish churches, were equally delinquent and parsimonious.[83] Innumerable cases are recorded of tithe owners who extracted as much as 24,000 *l*. but did not contribute a sou to the poor of the parish. Moreover, the question of who was to repair the churches was so complicated and controversial and the decisions of the courts so contradictory that the tithe owners whose responsibility was clearly defined in legislation of 1695, also

Inviolability of the Church Temporal 97

managed to evade their duties in this area. The tithe was no longer fulfilling the purpose of its institution. Save for the valiant efforts of the *curés* who nourished the flame of religion in the parishes—and who, if they received the tithes at all, received a disproportionately small amount—services were no longer exchanged for the tithes which the faithful of France had been legally obliged by the Church to pay since the Council of Macon in 585 and by the State since Charlemagne's Capitulary of 801. Letters to Calonne, the Controller-General of Finances, between December, 1783 and March, 1784, demanding payment from even the king as tithe owner to priests in Antibes who had not been paid for seven years, are typical of the Agent's attempts to end the negligence of tithe owners, large and small, and to secure just payment for the *congruistes*.[84]

Many *congruistes* appealed directly to Talleyrand for aid. The Archives of the Clergy reveal many tracts addressed to him representing the protests of large segments of poor priests all over France. Some were privately printed. Most of them bore the same title, "On the Inadequacy of the *Portion Congrue*."[85] All of them insisted on what subsequently has become abundantly clear, that their stationary incomes could not keep pace with the erratic rise in prices and soaring costs of living in the thirty years preceding the Revolution.[86] With this in mind it is not difficult to explain the assaults on the Church by groups of rebellious *curés,* particularly in the poorest provinces of Provence and Dauphiné, who tried by force to subvert the legitimate authority of the bishop and Diocesan Bureaus. These *curés* constituted themselves into permanent committees to deliberate, present grievances, name deputies to Paris, receive contributions, and maintain correspondence with their membership.[87]

What began in Dauphiné spread to Brittany, Berry, Anjou, Orléanais, Bordelais, Languedoc, and Flanders. Manifest in their agitation was the resentment against the opulent and indifferent ecclesiastical hierarchy, who, according to the testimony of one of the most informed and reliable sources of the period, enjoyed 95 millions out of a total clerical revenue of 140 millions, leaving 45 millions to sustain the scores of thousands of parish priests who guaranteed the function of the cult in the nation.[88] With average episcopal income of 37,500 *l.* about 1750, compared to the *portion congrue* of 300 *l.,* the *curés* enjoyed an annual income of less than one per cent of that of the bishops.[89] The more miserable vicars received less than one-half of the *curés'* salary! Coupled with poverty was their exclusion from a deliberative voice in the government either of the diocesan or the national Church, clearly portending their later espousal of the social protests and egalitarian reforms of the Revolution.[90] The correspondence of the Agency between 1780 and 1785, both by its abundance and seriousness, leaves no doubt that the *portion congrue* was the foremost internal question facing the clergy before 1789.

It was not alone genuine humanitarian compassion for the suffering of the lower clergy which impelled Talleyrand to act on behalf of his indigent colleagues. He was too astute not to see the dangers behind the collective action which the *curés* had already assumed to force concessions from the bishops. After the crisis of the refusal of sacraments the *curés*, who previously had been little preoccupied with the Five Propositions of Jansenism and its rigorous moral strictures, began to advance in earnest the presbyterian ideas which inspired their *cahiers* of 1789 and which were to play a significant part in the organization of the Civil Constitutional Church.[91] Against Rome many became Gallicans, and against their bishops, Richerists. Not only did large numbers demand a representative role in the General Assembly of the Clergy alongside the bishops and *abbés*, but others wished to suppress its pontifical despotism and one-sided preoccupation with finances by banishing it altogether in favor of national and provincial councils.[92] Under the pervasive influences of Richerism, presbyterianism, and laicism, priests of the second order, tired of subjection to their episcopal masters, insisted that the Church belonged to all the faithful and proclaimed themselves equal to the bishops as judges of the faith, that the power of the keys came to them by ordination, and that they could not be removed from office for any reason whatever. The *curés* found certain ideas of St. Cyran, Arnaud, and Quesnel sympathetic, particularly their view of the Church as an autocracy of priests, representatives of the faithful who play a central role in the government of the Christian community. These bold doctrines, which added fuel to their economic grievances, were to prove disastrous to Church discipline and unity.[93] As M. Préclin observed, "Behind the theological doctrine in reality was couched a powerful revolutionary ferment, a movement of independence and revolt against established authority."[94]

Advancing the argument that this rebellious contagion was a threat at once to the authority of the State as well as the Church, Talleyrand appealed to the king in 1781 to promulgate laws outlawing all unauthorized meetings and organizations of *curés*.[95] He received a preliminary act of the Council of State on April 28, 1781 which forbade all *curés* to assemble and formulate programs.[96] Government support in suppressing the insurrections of the lower clergy came in the order of March 9, 1782, which declared it illegal for *curés* not constituted as legitimate corporations or communities to assemble without permission.[97] This is another dramatic example of how the Church, which guarded its economic privileges tenaciously from the State, still depended on it for the maintenance of its internal discipline.

Talleyrand realized that repressive legislation alone would neither mollify the poverty of the *curés* nor check their devastating attacks on the Church. The only sound solution was to increase their salaries. His first encounter with this particular problem came as a member of Loménie de Brienne's Committee on Religion and Jurisdiction in the Assembly of 1775. The Committee proposed to relieve indigence by securing capital necessary for a higher wage through the union of benefices and the suppression of useless ones. This plan was similarly under serious consideration by the Assembly of 1780.[98]

Reporting before the Assembly of 1785,[99] he summarized the opinions of the entire clergy which he had studied since the Assembly of 1780 requested him to circularize the clergy on this subject.[100] He conceded the free play of selfish interests on all levels. Vast segments opposed an increase for personal reasons and merely urged a more effective execution of the already existing legislation of 1768 on the *congruistes*. Others favored local laws dependent on local needs and special monetary concessions to less fortunate areas. The bulk of these suggestions favored the tithe owners rather than the victims whose futures were at stake. Some tithe owners refused to support any increases which would help pay *curés* of other dioceses. Many even refused to pay their own. Others insisted (quite correctly) that the expedient of uniting benefices was too arbitrary and slow to meet the needs of the lower clergy. The jurisprudence of the former statute, moreover, had become subject to innumerable and often contradictory interpretations in the courts which required redefinition by a new law. Only a rigidly uniform law of Church and State could overcome the selfishness and irregularities of the tithe owners and the massive disparity in wealth between dioceses.[101]

Talleyrand's argument for the increase went straight to the point. The prime concern of the clergy in the former legislation of 1686 and 1768 which had set the level of the *portion congrue* had been to insure each *curé* an "honest subsistence" as compensation for his services. In order to determine a just income, the clergy voted to guarantee a salary equal to the price of twenty-five *setiers* (300 bushels) of wheat. Not only did the constant rise of prices, the weakening value and reduced buying power of money take a serious toll on the static income of the *curés*, but the 500 *l.* assigned in 1768 fell far short of the mark in buying the bread needed for survival seventeen years later.[102] An honest subsistence of 300 *l.* in 1686 and 500 in 1768 could in 1785 "be represented by a sum not less than 700 *l.*," an absolute minimum if the intentions of the clergy, in the spirit of its earlier legislation, were to be fulfilled. Talleyrand confessed that the inspiration for his argument that the original intentions of the clergy were not being honored by permitting the high cost of living to deprive the lower clergy of the modest wages assured by law came from the logic of Malesherbes and Rulhière, who pleaded toleration for the Protestants as the true meaning of Louis XIV's religious policy imperfectly realized by his successors.[103]

The Assembly approved this figure. The wording of the royal edict of September 2, 1786 which legislated it ("the progressive rise in prices of all objects necessary for an honest subsistence having weakened the value fixed in money")[104] was strikingly reminiscent of the Agent's phraseology.[105] The edict, however, proved a Phyrric victory; for by 1789 only a few Parlements had registered it (key Parlements like Brittany and Guyenne withheld approval), and the Revolution came without its having really been applied.[106]

Talleyrand never forgot the deplorable financial situation of the lower clergy. His famous motion of 1789 provided them a substantial pay increase.[107] The Civil Constitutional Church officially adopted his proposal for employing the *curés* at 1200 *l.* plus additional benefits.

As has been seen, the attempts of the monarchy to secure a greater proportion of clerical wealth by taxation were repeatedly frustrated. It was, therefore, logical that the crown was not anxious to permit the clergy an unlimited aggrandizement of its non-taxable mortmain lands as it had for centuries since the Middle Ages. Royal decrees of December, 1666, and particularly of August, 1749,[108] forbade the clergy to receive any type of property—lands, buildings or income— either by donation or purchase except by express authorization of the king through letters patent, registered by the sovereign courts, "after a public inquiry into the usefulness of the proposed acquisition." The crown intended that the law should make it impossible for the Church to acquire new property, and the First Estate acknowledged that "the edict of 1749 deprived the Church of the freedom to acquire."[109]

Since the clergy was virtually deprived of the capacity to increase its temporal, it was imperative that wise administration and investment should prevent its diminution. But the French clergy of the eighteenth century were on the whole inept administrators who did not use their wealth prudently but instead lost much revenue through improvident commercial and agricultural leases, contracted debts on the collateral of churches, and often alienated holdings under their charge.[110] It is well to recall that it was through the bankruptcy of the Jesuits' commercial enterprises in the Antilles that the Parlement of Paris commenced proceedings which resulted in their suppression and expulsion from France. The temporal history of the Church of France is redolent with cases of hardship occasioned by abuses, blunders, and eventual loss of real property.

It made little difference to many ambitious clerics that by canon law they were mere usufructuaries of property belonging to the faithful.[111] They might enjoy the revenues of property under their supervision, but they were bound to respect its integrity. Many clergy contracted obligations of enormous proportions without the consent of their bishops. Once furnished with letters patent, they could with impunity alienate holdings consigned to them on the flimsy grounds that such alienations benefitted the Church.

Alienation represented a malady practiced on all levels of the French Church. The episcopate owed an example to the lower clergy, but some of its less spiritual members, such as Rohan, Loménie de Brienne, Champion de Cicé, and Boisgelin, alienated considerable holdings of their churches or abbeys for private gains.[112] While the debts of secular ecclesiastics were essentially personal affairs, the same did not hold true for monasteries and religious communities, whose debts fell upon successive generations. The debts of these houses were adjudged, even by contemporaries, as scandalous.[113] Some clerics alienated ecclesiastical property to acquit former indebtedness; others did so to procure luxuries. One alienation usually meant another, for new titularies of benefices, parts of which had already been sold by predecessors, were obliged to sell more to honor previous obligations. Many religious houses were completely ruined.

Poverty and poor management of the monasteries were contributing factors for their reform by the Commission of Regulars in 1768.[114] From 1775 until the Revolution uncanonical sales and leases had become so widespread that the Assembly sought the assistance of the king to prevent further disasters caused by the clergy's negligence and audacity.[115]

Talleyrand met many of these cases in his five years as Agent. Sometimes he frustrated minor alienations either by clever diplomacy and the skillful cajolery of clerical parties or by fortunate appeals to royal justice.[116] But when it was a question either of large-scale alienations, loans taken on clerical property, or the seizure of conventual property due to the inability to meet the arrears on loans, intercessions proved fruitless.

Talleyrand reported to the Assembly of 1785 a typical case involving the Cistercian Abbey of Chaalis in Picardy.[117] In 1767 it had contracted 900,000 *l*. in loans to liquidate pressing debts. The religious were unable to maintain their annual payments of 50,000 *l*. and fell further into debt. Since they could not pay the long overdue arrears on the principal as demanded by their creditors, the courts proclaimed the seizure of the abbey's property. This seizure was confirmed by the crown on March 31, 1784 against Talleyrand's plea. The courts did not accept the Agent's arguments that alienations were illegal, that priests were only custodians of property entrusted to their safekeeping by the faithful in order to honor God, to insure the functions of religion, and to care for the poor. Ecclesiastical property, Talleyrand insisted,[118] could never legally find its way into lay hands.

After all he had to say about the sacred principles of property, Talleyrand could not deny the rights of a creditor to recover his capital. But it could only be regained, he maintained, from the revenues, not from the immovable property of the abbey, since the religious did not own what was only committed to their charge by the faithful. Any other interpretation "would destroy the principles of the inalienability of ecclesiastical property." Chaalis was paying dearly for the "vices of administration," and so was the whole clergy "in seeing immense possessions consecrated to the Church pass into foreign hands."[119] Ecclesiastical property was not only sanctified by the will of God and the divine canons of councils, popes, and Church law, but it was also enshrined in royal capitularies, Imperial codes, letters patent, feudal titles, judicial decisions, Church-State contracts,

Inviolability of the Church Temporal 103

and public and common law. Property was an unassailable whole. The clergy's property could not be destroyed without destroying all property. If ecclesiastical titles were not assured the same guarantees reserved for all others, then the principle of property would be a mockery. All property and rights once granted the Church were irreversible.[120] They were not subject to judicial review by lay courts. Revocation of ecclesiastical privileges therefore belied the right of property assured by government and law.

These were interesting arguments which during the Middle Ages had been acknowledged by the monarchy and its judiciary. By the eighteenth century, however, they were lifeless anachronisms which neither side, clerical nor lay, really believed or honored. No one realized better than Talleyrand that the faulty administration of temporalities occasioned disastrous losses to the whole order of the clergy. With the lesson of this case and others of a similar nature, he appealed to the Assembly of 1785 to approve a measure prohibiting all alienations of ecclesiastical property, either sales, exchanges, leases, or loans on the part of benefice holders, religious corporations, and communities, except upon the express approval of the local bishop, thereby correcting the "excessive facility to form loans and the neglect exercised by many houses in the use of funds."[121] Under the strict aegis of the bishop the recourse to loans or sales would be immeasurably reduced, he believed, and the intentions of the king to conserve the Church's patrimony would always be fulfilled. "Ecclesiastical establishments need no longer be exposed to the danger of succumbing under the weight of their obligations." The Assembly accepted this proposal, and until 1789 sought its promulgation by the government.[122]

From the foregoing cases it is clear that Talleyrand was an implacable foe of alienations. In other cases he tried to prove that each title and foundation of the ecclesiastical domain was not only inalienable but also irrevocable in perpetuity.

The Abbé de Rastignac, Abbot of St. Mesmin (Diocese of Orleans), attempted after 1780 to recover several privileges of his abbey which had been alienated by a predecessor in 1611.[123] The most important of these was the collection of the tithes. Rastignac offered to compensate the present owners the sum paid for the alienated privileges. This was rejected. He then went to court. Talleyrand intervened on Rastignac's behalf before the King's Council, arguing that the abbot of the seventeenth century had ignored ecclesiastical law which prohibited laymen from receiving the tithes. An ecclesiastic might alienate the revenues of his benefice with the permission of his superiors, but never the property which "religion divides between the service of the churches and the needs of the people . . . forming a universal patrimony, a perpetual domain." This domain is irrevocable because that was the wish of its founders who desired to preserve for all time the patrimony of the faithful. Nor could long possession legitimize a title when its nullity was known to its possessors who illegally retained it. Finally, the sale was invalid, since confirmatory letters patent were never secured. Talleyrand called on the king to sustain the plea of Abbot de Rastignac in conformity with the statutes of the realm. The King's Council in May, 1784 ordered the return of his abbey's alienated rights.[124]

In 1784 Agent Talleyrand represented the clergy in a litigation with the King of Sardinia, Victor Amadeus III. This cause represented the high point of his dedication to the clergy's temporal. It was well enough known for the Bishop of Autun to refer to it in his motion of October, 1789 to prove that he had always had the interests of the Church at heart, and that his plan for nationalizing the ecclesiastical temporal was in harmonious conformity with the policies he had advocated as Agent-General of the Clergy.[125]

The case involved the reversibility of donations. In 1407 Amadeus VIII, Count of Savoy, deeded his mansion in Lyons to the Celestines of that city for use as a monastery. A clause was inserted providing that the donation would revert to the family if it were dissipated, transferred, or alienated in whole or part without the consent of the Counts of Savoy. In 1778 Pope Pius VI suppressed the order, whereupon the Archbishop of Lyons took title to its property for "pious and useful works." The King of Sardinia, as legitimate head of the House of Savoy, refused to recognize such a seizure and demanded the return of his ancestor's property on grounds of alienation. The case was settled on January 12, 1784 by a decision of the Council of Dispatches in favor of the king, who sold this property the next year to meet the wedding expenses of his son and the sister of Louis XVI.[126]

The Agent reported the case to the Assembly of 1785.[127] The attempt of the King of Sardinia to regain the donation of his ancestors threatened to make all ecclesiastical foundations revocable. If every donor could reclaim his gifts, there would be no end to claims for reversion of donations. Foundations to the Church were unalterable. The donor after giving his gift becomes completely separated from his property. Since the donor sacrificed his property in order to render homage to God, it became the patrimony of the "universal Church which presides over His religion." Hence the true owner was not the person at all but the Church. The claim that the Celestines ceased to exist is neither valid nor just, because all properties given to "religious establishments belong to them irrevocably and will always constitute a part of their domain, regardless of the revolution which a particular establishment, for which they were destined, may suffer."

By a careful exegesis of the clause of reversibility, Talleyrand claimed that suppression and alienation were by no means the same thing. True alienation would have occurred only if the religious expressly consented to the relinquishment of their property. But the Celestines did not alienate their holdings as the crown claimed in ordering reversion to the House of Sardinia. They were suppressed by authority of the papacy. Therefore the clause rescinding their donation through alienation was not binding. "All gifts made to the Church are perpetual and indefectible."

Five years later, in October, 1789, at the time of his famous sequestration motion, Talleyrand claimed that his current arguments for the State's nationalization of the clergy's temporal, so long as it assured the clergy an adequate subsistence and maintained the cult, were in keeping with those advanced in 1784.[128] The State, he maintained, established a long-time precedent of seizing the Church's property during times of emergency, particularly since this property did not enjoy the same guarantees as others, being given not in the interest of persons but for the performance of services. There was no violation of property, since the State fulfilled the intentions of all donors and guaranteed the services of the cult.

The Abbé Maury, chief orator of the Right in the National Assembly and well known for his insatiable ambition to succeed both in society and among the clergy,[129] led the First Estate against the motion. He proclaimed to the Assembly in October 13, 1789 "that the doctrine loftily professed by M. l'Abbé de Périgord in 1784 forms a strange contrast to the principles of M. l'Evêque d'Autun presented before this tribune in 1789."[130] Maury correctly observed that the Agent tried to prove then (as he did all through his Agency) that the Church owned its property "in the most rigorous sense," that this property was more incontestable and more sacred than the property of other citizens, that the house of the Celestines was the property of the Church, regardless of the clause of reversion stipulated by the Count of Savoy in the act of donation. Talleyrand, his antagonist observed, "solicited by the ascendancy of his own principles," had taken this stand in 1784 from his own initiative to impress the clergy with his zeal.

Maury, using the same absolute arguments on the sanctity and immutability of clerical property Talleyrand had used all through his Agency, was ready to publish the former Agent's long memorandum of 1784 if the Bishop of Autun disavowed the assertions or the principles which he had formerly defended "with force." Here is one of the first of so many turnabouts in the public career of the future statesman, for a disavowal was never forthcoming.

V

The Agent-General and the Maintenance of Ecclesiastical Jurisdiction

The First Estate could not be assured of respect either for its spiritual primacy or temporal wealth unless each link in the chain of ecclesiastical authority was firmly secured. Internal discipline presented a severe problem for the French Church in the latter Old Regime beset with disobedience and disrespect for the traditional lines of command within its house. Provincial clergy in all parts of the kingdom ignored the legislative enactments of the General Assembly, particularly in fiscal matters; many disavowed the traditional ties of obeisance to bishop as well as to Diocesan Bureau. Episcopal hegemony was disputed in matters as central as ecclesiastical appointments, discipline, unions and dissolutions of clerical corporations, alienations, and even pastoral affairs. A significant part of the Agent's time was given to reconciling bishops and their priests, entreating both to resolve differences amicably for the good of the Church and the peace of the diocese, and attempting to discourage the entry into their disputes of laics who only corrupted spiritual purity and disrupted the unity of the clergy.

As Agent, Talleyrand conceived and adhered faithfully to a clear and sensible scheme of hierarchical authority which served to guide his policies before the State and with dissident parties inside his order. Indisputably the top priority was the welfare of the clergy and the integrity of the whole First Estate. Below this was the Assembly, whose sovereignty within the order he repeatedly proclaimed, and without whose legislative and judicial supremacy the First Estate could never hope to achieve a uniform body of laws and usages governing the practice of religion, the administration of its benefices, and the conduct of its personnel. Within the Assembly and responsible for the uninterrupted enforcement of its resolutions, was the Agent-General himself. Guardian, dispassionate judge, the Agent had to determine the priority of each petition for intervention directed to him and the Assembly. At the same time his ministry was responsible for legal measures either remedial or innovative to secure the well being of every clergyman. Below the Assembly stood the bishops, the executives of the provincial churches. Already as a journeyman in the Assembly of 1775 Talleyrand realized that episcopal supremacy was the indispensable guarantee of ecclesiastical discipline and the structural health of the dioceses. Without this there was no guaranteeing the application of the Assembly's enactments, the uniform administration of each parish, and the means to combat centrifugal influences of factious clerical individuals and groups.

The titles of the clergy, from the Assembly of Melun onwards, gave the Agents clearest authority in all matters touching ecclesiastical jurisdiction on all levels of Church and State. Within the First Estate their constitutional competence could not be contested by any member. They were conferred extensive powers in presenting remonstrances before the king, his Council, his Parlements, and other tribunals of the kingdom, and in "seeking cassation of decrees . . . rendered by encroachment on ecclesiastical jurisdiction."[1] Similarly it was the Agents who were expected "to stop the too frequent encroachments of . . . magistrates who by their own authority establish themselves as judges of the most spiritual cases"[2] and "to seek the retraction of their decrees" which frequently upset the uneasy peace of the dioceses. Since clerical litigation almost always involved the episcopate in one way or another, and ". . . when ecclesiastical jurisdiction was being attacked in the person of these prelates . . . it [was] the ministry of the Agents-General to defend it."[3]

A word must be said here about the clash of spiritual and lay authorities. By Talleyrand's time these encounters were but the last installment in the battle of rival jurisdictions which had been going on in France since the time of Philip-Augustus. The Church could not easily forget that it had once been the State for millions of Frenchmen—that its laws, justice, institutions, culture, administration, its definition of social relations and moral values were binding on the nation. The Reformation and the simultaneous rise of the modern monarchy took a heavy toll on the Church's claims to supremacy and effectively weakened its dominant legal position. The royal mastery over aristocratic feudalism was to render the Church subservient to the State and transform ecclesiastical power to its service. Instead of permitting it to remain outside the State, however, the monarchy conferred on the Church public functions and accorded it important privileges, but subjected it to lay law determining its rights and duties to the State. As the Church became less central in the lives of the French, the State absorbed and extended the vast authority its rival had formerly wielded, a victory enhanced by the strength of its governmental institutions, the efficacy of its administration, the latitude of its competence, and the superior allegiance of the nation. Long before Montesquieu there was no question that Frenchmen were governed best by the State. But until the ultimate triumph of the State in the Revolution, the Church never conceded this and in defiance still attempted to wield independent legal and judicial power. These were disputed at once by the King's Council, ministers, magistrates, and sovereign courts—good Catholics all—but for the most part dead set against the political pretensions of the Church. Though they may have been willing to accommodate the First Estate in those individual appeals which lay at the heart of Talleyrand's office, they would not tamper with the elemental principles which sustained the State's primordiality.

The history of ecclesiastical jurisdiction in the years before 1789 is a baleful tale of numerous legal contests and diminishing spiritual influence. The tides were quietly but inexorably flowing against clerical privilege. For nearly three centuries before the last Estates-General it was the State that appointed the bishops and thousands of commendatory abbots, canons, and priors. The Concordat of Bologna of 1516 had already made the king the master of the French Church, and the principle of temporal over spiritual was sustained two-hundred-and-fifty years later in the dissolution of the Jesuits. The government soon after invaded the exclusively spiritual domain in reforming education, and it legislated with impunity on behalf of the Protestants. If it failed to tax the clergy in 1750 and 1787, this was only out of its own lack of resoluteness. The plans of its ministers, reinforced by the popular sentiment of Philosophers, *parlementaires,* financiers, and bourgeoisie to abrogate the Church's status as a separate and autonomous force within the State, awaited only the Revolution for realization.

Increasingly in the eighteenth century ecclesiastical tribunals lost jurisdiction over clergy to secular justice. A national network of Church courts, under the direction of the bishops, still survived in each diocese with appellate jurisdiction vested in archiepiscopal chambers and national councils. While the competence of these courts had once extended to all cases of the clergy, spiritual, criminal, and civil, and even to spiritual trials of laymen (as in marriage), by the end of the seventeenth century it was limited in practice to personal and disciplinary actions of ecclesiastical personnel.[4] The clergy could try minor misdemeanors of its members, but serious cases came under shared jurisdiction with secular tribunals, always anxious to enlarge the scope of their authority at the expense of their clerical counterparts.[5] With the extension of royal power and justice, the clergy became subject to lay courts for all secular questions, property, debts, and civil crimes. Although it was generally acknowledged that ecclesiastical jurisdiction included such things as heresy, simony, marriage, and the tithes, these were disputed by secular tribunals whenever they impinged on political and civil rights, social interest, and property—as unavoidably they did.[6] For this reason contests involving tithes and contracts were considered secular matters and invariably came before the king's judges. Similarly, because the assignment of benefices and difficulties involved in their possession could trouble public order, of which the king was the ultimate guarantor,[7] royal magistrates invented arguments to seize exclusive jurisdiction, to circumscribe ecclesiastical courts, and to divest them of portions of their natural competence. While it is true that royal legislation of 1695 reaffirmed the jurisdiction of Church tribunals in the matter of sacraments, religious vows, holy office, ecclesiastical discipline, and other purely spiritual matters,[8] the First Estate fought an unremitting battle for the recognition of these prerogatives and continually appealed to the king against the illegitimate jurisdiction of lay courts. To make matters worse, clerics in litigation frequently appealed to civil courts, not only because their decisions were more swift but also because they carried the greater weight of the State and, with the laws of the land solidly behind them, were more easily enforceable.

Besides superior strength and prestige, lay justice claimed still another powerful advantage in its competition with the Church. Anyone in the realm, including clergy, could file an *appel comme d'abus* (appeal against abuse) before a Parlement, by which the judgments of an ecclesiastical tribunal could be challenged by lay courts.[9] While in most cases the Parlement in the course of appeal could not suspend the ecclesiastical decision, yet it achieved virtually the same effect by having the decision "devolve" on the Parlement. While the *appel* had been intended as an "extraordinary remedy . . . not to be employed except on important occasions where the public is concerned," so commonly was it used for "slight matters" by refractory priests, and so serious was the appeal to secular justice over the heads of diocesan superiors, that the bishops obtained from Louis XIV an edict of April, 1695, defining the respective jurisdictions of the two courts.[10] The monarchy never favored the clergy's pleas to reform the noxious *appel comme d'abus* but agreed only to reassert at periodic intervals the full force of the legislation of 1695.

The determination of the clergy to maintain an independent judiciary as part of its corporate legal autonomy resulted in headlong collision with the masters of secular justice, the Parlements. A decisive cause of the First Estate's weakened internal authority must be laid to a half-century of conflict between Robe and Mitre. Its acute stage was reached between 1750 and 1766 in more than fifteen years of hostile acts and declarations by the Parlements (particularly the Parlement of Paris) against the bishops, the Archbishop of Paris, and the General Assembly of the Clergy occasioned by quarrels over Jansenism, Gallicanism, the confession certificates, the refusal of sacraments, and the ratification of the Bull *Unigenitus*.[11] In the ensuing battles of jurisdiction between magistracy and episcopate, the Church's temporal and disciplinary primacy was breached, and aggrieved clergy found welcome refuge in the Parlements of the realm, at once to evade and defy the courts of their order. At mid-century *parlementaires* and bishops were locked in grim combat, a combat renewed both in the poisoned atmosphere of the Church's ugly three-year war against Machault and the *vingtième* and at a time when the tide of bitter animosity set in against the clergy for their attempts to silence the popular Philosophers and to champion the equally unpopular Jesuits. Episcopal Gallicanism vied with Parliamentary Gallicanism. Each side insisted on its own superior patriotism. Each extolled its virtues as champion of legality and monarchical orthodoxy. Each, finally, hurled accusations of disloyalty, subversion, and usurpation against the other.

The Parlements considered themselves less a servant of the king in whose name they rendered justice than "the defender and restorer of public liberties."[12] Though they paraded as the savior of France and the champions of national sovereignty against the despotism of Louis XV, they were in reality a clique of "outward liberals" who disguised their social conservatism and political egoism behind a banner of patriotism and sought power and privilege in the narrow interests of their class.[13] From their vaunted authority as custodians of the fundamental laws of the kingdom, they fancied themselves in a contractual, reciprocal relationship to the crown. Their remonstrances against its laws were in reality not just a desire to share sovereignty but rather the design to confer on the nation and themselves, to the exclusion of the king, the decisive role in law. Referring to the history of the Parlements during the last fifty years of the Old Regime as "a half-century of culpable errors and blindness," Roger Bickart concluded that the *parlementaires*' "insurgence against the spirit of their very function [was directed] against the monarchy which placed it in their hands."[14]

Throughout the course of its struggle with the judges, the Church stoutly asserted its right of spiritual independence and paramount authority in administering the sacraments, enforcing clerical discipline, and expounding the faith. It came under savage indictment of the Parlement for this and for having "broken" the laws of the kingdom by disloyal allegiance to the pope, to whom it had appealed against the persistent Jansenist heresy. Its boastful claims of legal autonomy in regulating these issues on its own authority allegedly subordinated the power both of the king as supreme protector of the Church, his subjects and domestic tranquillity, and his Parlements, in which resided the protective vigilance of the nation's rights. The Parlement of Paris complained that *Unigenitus* was not only illegal as a rule of faith, because it had not obtained the sanction of the Universal Church in Council, but also that it compromised the fundamental law of the kingdom in levelling threats of excommunication and relieving subjects of their oath to the king.[15] The bishops correctly interpreted this opposition as part of the Parlements' campaign to undermine the Church's jurisdiction and retorted that religion was endangered, ecclesiastical justice jeopardized, and episcopal prerogatives shattered by the Parlements' usurping decisions in spiritual questions on grounds that they invaded public peace. This weakening of religion was not only an affront to God but also assailed the authority of the king. In its "Acts of the Clergy" of August, 1765, aptly called "the most important ecclesiastical act of the end of the Old Regime,"[16] itself a statement of spiritual absolutism not unlike the bold political pretensions of the Parlements, the bishops enjoined the acceptance of *Unigenitus* and proclaimed the infallibility of the Church in doctrine, in rules of faith, in determining fitness to receive the sacraments, and in the conduct of its personnel. It also pronounced the doctrine of the "Two Powers" by which Church and State "in reciprocal union" are "sovereign, independent, and absolute." Because spiritual authority transcends the civil power, the prince is obliged to obey the ministers of Jesus Christ.[17]

The Parlement of Paris replied by ordering the burning of the "fanatical and seditious" Acts. The General Assemblies of the Clergy, it was pointed out, the symbol of defiant exclusivity and not the national council of the clergy's dreams, were nothing but "purely economic assemblies" which existed at the pleasure of the king in order to vote him taxes. The Church is neither superior to nor independent of the secular power. Church statute and discipline have no force as laws of the kingdom except by the consent and confirmation of the king. The *appel comme d'abus* becomes more than ever necessary to thwart the clergy's illegal enterprises. The clergy must be forced to acknowledge the supremacy of the State over the Church and the law of the land over spiritual independence.[18]

While Louis XIV nearly a century before had made himself the supreme tutelary magistrate of his realm and made the direction of the Church one of his primary cares, Louis XV shunned this responsibility and was incapable of forceful responsive action. The irresolute king, fearful both of the clergy's claims of immunity from his own power and the belligerent assaults of his Parlements, did come to the rescue of his Church. Short, however, of forcing "general and absolute silence" on both sides in May, 1766, as he had in the past,[19] Louis XV could not compose the conflict of rival jurisdictions, thereby encouraging the Parlements to resume hostilities that continued unabated during the remainder of the Old Regime. As for the Church, without a decisive monarch, with implacable foes in the courts of the land, and beset with divisions within its own fold, it turned to the papacy for aid and comfort.

In the hope of strengthening its disciplinary hold over the diocesan clergy, an authority effectively undercut by the Parlements, the Church petitioned the crown for the reinstatement of the provincial councils. Only two councils, Toulon in 1704 and Embrun in 1727, were convoked in the course of the eighteenth century and, like the General Assemblies, required royal authorization. Such a violent storm of controversy had been unleashed by the Council of Embrun, which suspended the exiled Nestor of Jansenism, Bishop Jean Soanen of Senez, that the kings of France permitted no further councils.

Though the General Assembly repeatedly insisted on the spiritual necessity of the provincial councils, the monarchy was unwilling to augment the authority of the bishops and stood firm in opposing them.[20]

To whom could the clergy appeal against the hostile Parlements (whom Marcel Marion called the clergy's "redoubtable enemies")[21] which rendered negative decisions in every manner of clerical jurisdiction, spiritual as well as temporal, and which, anxious to whittle down the authority of the bishops, had invented the *appel comme d'abus*[22] to exempt priests from the supervision of their episcopal superiors? To whom could it turn to reverse equally inimical enactments of the *Cour des aides* (manned by the same families and animated by the same ideas) and the king's provincial magistrates and tax officers? From the end of the sixteenth century to the end of the Old Regime the clergy sought strength in the King's Council, the monarchy's supreme court and Council of State.[23] In the transition from feudal to administrative monarchy at the end of the Wars of Religion, the kings of France created modern departments, among which the Council was most important, to fight sectionalism and the political pretensions of feudal classes, to achieve administrative uniformity, and to subject the kingdom to the supreme authority of the crown. The definitive organization of the Council was the work of Richelieu and Colbert. It was endowed with the widest competence— judicial and legislative—in economic, financial, and religious affairs and was granted authority to render decrees, prepare ordinances, and issue edicts and letters patent.

The King's Council enjoyed extensive spiritual and temporal authority in matters of religion. It could interpret the rights and judge the litigations of bishops, chapters, and collators. It could pass on the interior regime, the secularization and suppression of monastic orders, convents, abbeys, priories, and collegiates. Its authority also extended to unions of institutions and benefices to episcopal manses and to other religious establishments. The Council also judged contests between ecclesiastical chambers and clergy under their jurisdiction. It could interfere in the temporal administration of the clergy by orders governing all constructions and repairs of ecclesiastical edifices. Its approval was required for all acquisitions, alienations, and exchanges of property, regardless of importance. Finally, it was before sessions of the King's Council and through the intermediary of the Chancellor (the king's executive officer in his councils and head of justice in the kingdom) that the General Assembly delivered its *cahier*, settled the *don gratuit* and the contributions of the foreign clergy, and received authorization for the dioceses to contract debts in their payment.[24]

As Counsellors of State the Agents enjoyed the right to speak and present affairs of importance to the clergy before the King's Council. Personal appearance was of greatest advantage when clerical questions were deliberated. The Agents could provide explanations and respond to objections more effectively than anyone else in the clergy. In contrast to letters directed to ministers which may have been filed away or forgotten, presence in Council was an excellent device for gaining attention and refreshing memories. After 1777 the Agents' appellant power was completed by the right to enter the Council's subsidiary Bureau of Ecclesiastical Affairs before which questions of concern to the First Estate oftentimes appeared before being reported to the Council. "It even frequently occurred that some important cases were definitively judged by this Bureau and consequently did not even pass before the Council."[25] To insure the Agents' intervention the greatest weight, all appeals before the Council (as well as before the King's Great and Private Councils and the Paris Parlement) required the authorization of the General Assembly or Assembly of Prelates.[26] The Report of the Agency, which provided a résumé of the principal affairs during the quinquennial ministry of the Agents, gave extensive attention to those cases which required intervention before the Councils.

In addition, the Agents were in continual contact with the Secretary of State for Ecclesiastical Affairs, one of the king's four Secretaries of State, "those bureaucrats transformed into high and powerful functionaries . . . [who] exercised a preponderant influence in high spheres of government,"[27] and upon whom many favorable decisions before the Council, the king's officers, and other tribunals of the realm were dependent. The authority of the Secretary was such that he could secure from the king and his Chancellor decisions in form of decrees (*arrêts du conseil*), which need not even have been deliberated in the sessions of the Council.[28]

The Secretary was the official intermediary between crown and First Estate and worked intimately with the Agents-General. From him the Agents solicited and received the king's order for the time and place of convocation of the General Assemblies and permission for their opening and closing. The Secretary, as head of the king's ecclesiastical commissioners, informed the clergy of the royal demands of the *don gratuit* and other extraordinary levies and prepared the contract with the clergy. It was through the Secretary that the bishops received briefs and acts of the Court of Rome.[29] A grateful clergy, unconcerned with what today we might consider peculation, accorded the Secretary a gratuity of 15,000 *l.* and a lesser bonus for his assistant at each Assembly.[30]

The clergy, on the strength of its acknowledged corporate status, its landed riches, its *dons gratuits* contractually granted the crown, and its unique position as permanent legal representative of the Church and its interests, could appeal to the Council in its own name. The First Estate had access to its justice for decrees overruling and annulling prejudicial decisions of the Parlements and other tribunals, for the enforcement of legislation against insubordinate lower clergy and for the maintenance of its fiscal and temporal exemptions. The Assembly, usually through the less formal and more flexible and swift offices of the Agents, could appeal to the Council either by private conferences with its officers, by solicitations before the body or the Chancellor, by remonstrances or direct appeal to the king, or by the ultra-official "request"—a written resolution of the whole order to the sovereign, requesting favorable action on an urgent matter of collective concern. The appeals of the clergy, used sparingly, were for the most part crowned with success, and most decisions of the Council left the clergy in possession of its temporal and disciplinary jurisdiction. This was due to the fact that the clergy made it its business to know the judges handling its appeals; indeed, the bishops on the basis of their historical participation in the old Curia Regis controlled a certain number of places on the Council to which ecclesiastics committed to the interests of the order were appointed. In addition to the Agents other designated members of the Assembly could speak at its sessions and, if necessary, could appeal above the heads of the Counsellors and even the ministers to a king generous and committed to the welfare of his clergy. As a recent historian of the Council observed, "All this came about as if the State had not yet been conceded a life independent of its subjects, as if nothing were yet strictly administrative, as if the king were in effect the father of the [clerical] litigants."[31] Though the Council righted many of the clergy's grievances, no one questioned whose authority was superior. And it was equally clear to whom the clergy had to appeal in composing difficulties before the courts of the land and with its own members. While the Church won many litigations, victory derived not alone from the merits of its cases but from the king's desire to preserve ecclesiastical jurisdiction from the stalemate of crippling decisions imposed by his own Parlements and magistrates. One may rightly ask whether these were victories at all if, in the last analysis, the clergy's authority was vindicated by unpopular royal intervention in the procedures of justice.

The principle at the heart of the Agent-General's office was the obligation to retain the Assembly's status as the sovereign body in all affairs of concern to the First Estate. Talleyrand understood this precept from the first moment of his Agency. He delivered before the Assembly of 1780, having been in office but three months, an extreme, authoritarian definition of the Assembly's jurisdiction which revealed a frankly conservative dislike and distrust of innovation challenging it.[32] The Assembly's jurisdictional and regulatory supremacy manifested itself above all in having its edicts and statutes, together with those of its institutional representatives in the diocese, the Diocesan Bureau, honored by every segment of the clergy.

The most frequent affront to the central authority came in the refusal of individual clergy to honor tax obligations defined by it. On September 25 Talleyrand revealed the details of a refusal of payment of *décimes,* ordered by the Diocesan Bureau of Pamiers, by canons of the Abbey of St. Valusien. The canons refused to pay the amount established by the Assembly of 1775 because, so they pleaded, it exceeded the rate paid by other diocesan tithe owners of equivalent revenues. To defend their stand, the religious threatened recourse to secular justice. The chamber appealed to the General Assembly in support of its decision. At stake, Talleyrand insisted, was the very sovereignty and dignity of the Assembly. It had already decided this and similar issues by "solemn judgments of 1775." If it were to authorize the Diocesan Bureau to determine the *décime* by principles of class other than those already laid down by it, the resulting classification would no longer retain the fixed and invariable proportion of each taxpayer, which lies at the heart of "all the wisdom of your administration." This in turn would automatically create a precedent impossible to control, and "we would see the reappearance of that arbitrariness which you wished to dispel forever." The decisions of the Assembly, as the Church's "sovereign chamber," were binding on all the clergy. From it there could be no appeal—especially not to the illegitimate offices of secular courts. In conclusion he asked the Assembly to refuse the renewal of a case already decided by one of its predecessors and, lest its authority be undermined and its statutes subjected to arbitrary interpretation, to judge the Abbey's claims as "without foundation." The Assembly unanimously approved this proposal.[33]

During the five years of his ministry the Agent had intervened against many other clergy defiant of the Assembly's authority. Two typical cases will suffice. The first involved the religious of the Cistercian Abbey of Relecq (Diocese of Saint-Pol-de-Léon) who refused to pay the *décime* on grounds that it was excessive. The religious appealed to the Rennes Parlement which sustained their plea against the Diocesan Bureau.[34] A second involved a priest, Ribeaucourt, *Curé* of Coutres (Diocese of Amiens), who refused to pay his *décime* and appealed to the Paris Parlement against the diocese. In both cases the Agent appeared before the King's Council and pressed for the recognition that only the Diocesan Bureau, with a full inventory of the tithe owner's property, was in a position to impose an equitable tax.[35] Secular tribunals were without competence in matters bearing completely on ecclesiastical administration. These rights were solemnly recognized by the king in his contracts with the clergy, which repeatedly specified the superior jurisdiction of the Diocesan Bureau and, upon appeal, the provincial chambers in all matters concerning taxes. For both cases Talleyrand secured a decree of Council on August 10, 1784 returning jurisdiction to the Diocesan Bureau and, upon appeal, to the provincial chamber.[36]

A second issue presented to the Assembly of 1780 involved the Assembly's supremacy in matters of ecclesiastical discipline. The Cathedral Chapter of Lombez refused to elect one of its members, absent without permission, to the Diocesan Bureau. Irregularities in the chapter's statutes, the unsuccessful canon protested, prevented his election. Rebuffed by the diocesan body which refused to seat him, he appealed to the Seneschal of Toulouse, who not only ordered his reinstatement but fined the Diocesan Bureau 1,000 *l.* in damages.[37]

Talleyrand approved the action of the Bureau, for secular courts, he contended, could not legitimately judge jurisdictional disputes involving clerical offices and personnel. Were the question merely one of procedure between a canon and his chapter, he told the Assembly, it would constitute only a "private quarrel incapable of commanding your attention or distracting you from the major and general affairs

Maintenance of Ecclesiastical Jurisdiction 119

with which you are occupied." Rather it "attacks your rights, your most acknowledged privileges." Contests involving clerical discipline may be tried only in ecclesiastical courts, to the exclusion of secular tribunals. "This is a principle which you have always sought to maintain and upon which your temporal administration rests." Should the clergy surrender its spiritual authority to a secular party incompetent to treat ecclesiastical affairs, it would lose its power by default to lay courts and would have sanctioned a situation which could only diminish its respect and authority among the clergy and undermine the unity and uniformity of its administration and spiritual supremacy. Soon broader questions would be brought to the secular tribunals, "and you will see established . . . a jurisprudence which you will not be able to revise. Gradually your administration will escape you, or at least your ecclesiastical chambers will lose the exclusive jurisdiction which your vigilance has conserved for them until now."[38]

Furnishing abundant examples of past usages to illustrate the argument that the Church never admitted the authority of lay tribunals in its internal affairs, he urged it not to do so now. The Diocese of Lombez had requested the Agents to appeal this case before the King's Council. Talleyrand asked the Assembly to support this request so that he might secure an edict to confirm the Bureau's decision. This permission was immediately granted.[39]

On the whole, the King's Council was quite willing to accept the General Assembly as the clergy's supreme court in contests over the *décime,* by excluding the challenges of lay courts and by ordering the settlement of disputes by the Assembly. Without this exclusive competence it would have been impossible for the clergy to pursue to far flung tribunals contentious benefice holders and high dignitaries who may have held rights of *committimus* and other privileged jurisdiction.

As to the Agent's views regarding the deliberations of the Assembly and its authority to enact the laws of the clergy, these were perhaps best described in a letter to a *curé* in the Diocese of Nîmes on June 7, 1782: "It is not without having carefully considered and without having weighed with the greatest exactitude all kinds of considerations that the Assemblies of the Clergy pass resolutions . . . The views of administration which precede these resolutions are pure, disinterested, and tend only to the general and individual good of the clergy . . . The resolutions of the Assemblies of the Clergy require no justification and . . . owe explanations to no one."[40]

The sanctity and awe with which Talleyrand regarded the Assembly he served as first-minister was matched only by the dignity and importance he attached to his own office and the enormous respect he secured for it, as a result, from both Church and State. It was before the Extraordinary Assembly of 1782 that he left the clearest definition both of the range and complexity of the Agency. The twenty-eight year old Agent was not willing to wait the usual five years before giving the clergy a reckoning of his ministry.[41] Welcoming each opportunity "to enter the stage of public affairs," anxious to win the eye of prelacy[42] and to convince them of his zeal for their affairs, the Agent used this report to show the Assembly what he had learned during his first two years in office. In this departure he cited the authority of two distinguished archbishops, Dulau of Arles and Champion de Cicé of Bordeaux, both sitting in the audience of the Assembly, who, as former Agents, delivered similar reports to the clergy ("the great models that we always have under our eyes").[43]

He opened with an unveiled bid for favor. He thanked the Assembly for the opportunity to serve, "to turn to your talents and your lights, to draw your principles from your wisdom, and to direct our views towards your prudence and your designs." "The career of the Agency becomes from day to day more difficult to execute. Far from being discouraged . . .," however, he was bringing to the Assembly for its review and counsel the chief cases of his incipient Agency, all of which were to figure in definitive form in the Report of the Agency of 1785. The apprentice diplomat, who was trying out on the bishops the language of his future profession, qualified his remarks. Though he would speak of matters touching the entire order, he should not be accused of neglecting the interests of its individual members: "God forbid that anything that concerns a single member of the clergy should become alien or indifferent to us."

Talleyrand then proceeded to review the indispensable conditions which the Assembly should require of all cases before authorizing the Agents to intervene on its behalf and in its name. It was dangerous for the First Estate of the nation to commit itself to risky and costly litigations except in affairs touching the vital interests of the whole clergy. The greatest mistake is to pursue private or personal issues "unless it can be compensated by the promise of success." The number of interventions before the secular power must be cut to the bone to insure victory in cases that count. Neither should the Church risk its honor, its prestige, and its authority on unimportant trials or repeated unsuccessful intercessions. One defeat inevitably brings others: "Thus your authority would lose its weight and would find itself less strong at an important occasion when it was necessary to win an important case." In only one type of private case should the Church intervene, that is, when repeated judgments of the same kind destroyed principles or compromised interests of common concern to the whole clergy, and then "with all your strength . . . all your measures are justified."

Talleyrand practiced what he preached. He did not hesitate to inform clergy singly what he told them collectively, that the continued bad faith and unfavorable decisions delivered the First Estate by secular courts should make every prelate and cleric determined to use ecclesiastical tribunals whenever possible. To the Diocesan Syndic of Cahors he wrote that secular authorities were hostile to the Church, and even the King's Council "views with jaundiced eye all that tends to multiply the number of privileged."[44] Opposing the State was difficult—"one does not always fight with advantage against the domain."[45] As for receiving cassations from the Council overruling unfavorable decrees of Parlements, Talleyrand noted in a letter of November, 1781 to the Bishop of Clermont that they were increasingly more difficult to obtain, particularly against the Paris Parlement whose judgment the Council respected.[46] To the *Curé* of Morainville (Diocese of Evreux) he wrote the next year that "The Council becomes from day to day more difficult in the matter of cassation."[47]

The increasing difficulty in obtaining favorable decisions before the courts, together with the Agent's determination to maintain the strength of his office, led him to accept personally only a fraction of the hundreds of demands with which the clergy bombarded him and to reject all those which might jeopardize the credit and prestige of the order. He maintained this stand to bishop and priest alike. To the Bishop of Limoges in May, 1782, he refused a personal plea to enter a case concerning the tithes which the clergy could not hope to win: "As Agents-General we believe we would be compromising our ministry and the interests of the clergy by risking before the [King's] Council a plea which certainly would be rejected."[48]

To the *Curé* of Nogent-le-Rotrou (Diocese of Séez) he wrote two years later that his intercession in an affair of a union of a chapel to a parish church could be effective only where some degree of success was evident. "I would fear to compromise the functions of my ministry by fruitless measures."[49] To a cleric in Châlons-sur-Marne who requested information on the conditions of the Agent's intervention, he wrote in February, 1784 that the Agents concerned themselves only with affairs of common interest to the clergy.[50] Again in September, 1783 he specified that his intervention was "reserved for those affairs which by themselves or by their consequences interest the clergy [and] cannot apply to private discussions."[51]

Not only private discussions but all personal affairs were ruled out. Were these to be assumed by the Church, Talleyrand asserted in a letter of October 5, 1782, "We would not be received before any tribunal to protest a judgment rendered against us."[52] To a canon of Sarlat he wrote succinctly in September, 1784, "I will by no means risk my opinion on an affair which is personal to you, and having no interest whatever to the clergy at large, I cannot involve our counsel."[53]

Occasionally his intercession rather than helping might impair the clergy's cause. He noted to the *Curé* of Nogent-le-Rotrou, "It would be premature for me to appear in [your] affair . . . it would, in case of necessity, deprive the clergy . . . of a resource that it could still count on."[54] In many instances the Agent took a real interest in the personal problems of clerics but confessed his hands were tied: "I would like very much to be of some help to you, but the functions of my ministry do not extend to affairs of this nature."[55] Against the charge of favoritism in a case where several clerical parties appealed to him, he insisted that the interest of each ecclesiastic was of equal concern to him. To the *Curé* of Pommeraye (Diocese of Caen) he wrote in March, 1785: "Between the members of the clergy . . . all interests are equally dear to me. The duties of my place in these circumstances impose on me the most exact neutrality . . . all I can do is to interest myself for neither one nor the other."[56] There were very few exceptions to Talleyrand's iron rule governing intercessions. Occasionally he intervened on behalf of those, like the Ursulines of Toulon, who were subjected to a tyrannical fiscal imposition without either the means to secure counsel or the ability to protect themselves against the government.[57]

On behalf of those for whom he offered direct intercession, there were varied means at his disposal. As has been seen, his office permitted direct access to the king's ministers, national and provincial administration, and the courts. Beyond this he used his influence and personal appeal to officials handling cases he judged particularly important. Talleyrand wrote to the President of the Parlement of Paris requesting an opportunity to speak with him personally about a case concerning a *curé* in an obscure parish, "to place under the eyes of M. le Président d'Ormesson a precise account of this affair . . . which will be judged next Tuesday. The Agents take a real interest in this *curé* who is personally not at all at fault, and they are confident that the age and irreproachable conduct of this *curé* will be taken into consideration."[58]

Cognizant that the power of his office was not far removed from the respect it commanded, Talleyrand demanded and secured respect for the prerogatives of the Agency-General from officers of State and clergy alike. Neither the king's bishop, minister, nor the Cardinal-President of the General Assembly were exempted from his insistence on legal propriety. On June 6, 1782 the Archbishop of Paris, Leclerc de Juigné, a prelate of considerable ability and universally admired for his piety, invited to his palace by circular letter the bishops present in Paris for a Private Assembly of Prelates.[59] As soon as Talleyrand got wind of the intended meeting, which was the very same day, he wrote the Archbishop that the Assembly was illegal because it abused a statute of the General Assembly of 1715 which empowered the Agent-General to convoke all meetings of prelates in Paris by his own circulars upon the orders of the oldest bishop or archbishop then in Paris.[60]

Talleyrand politely informed the Prelate of Paris that in arrogating the powers of the Agent's office he had overturned the ordinances of the Assembly which ordered the Agents to regulate such convocations. Without recourse to their ministry, therefore, such "an arbitrary meeting could lead to unfavorable interpretations by administration and public . . . could endanger the rights of the Church and its prelates, and could compromise the interests of the clergy." Recalling that the Archbishop was himself a former Agent (between 1760 and 1765), "whose ministry was exercised in a manner to excite equally the gratefulness of the clergy and our emulation," he observed, "the Agents are charged with affairs too important not to be informed of extraordinary meetings so that they can instruct the bishops on the subject upon which their counsel might be needed." Talleyrand hoped Leclerc de Juigné recognized the dangers involved in violating the clergy's rules and that the prelates would gather in conformity with statute. Otherwise, he warned, he would press for the rights guaranteed his office: "I am so convinced of the dangers which could result from the infraction of our practices that I believe myself obliged to prevent them and to summon them to the spirit of the statutes of 1715. I dare believe that your kindnesses for me will spare me this measure and that the reply you will be good enough to give will authorize me to confer with you tomorrow before nine o'clock on this subject."

The style and language of this letter are strikingly similar to the one he addressed three weeks later to Vergennes on the possibility of the seizure of the Church's temporal, in which Talleyrand likewise used the language of a skilled diplomat to conserve each privilege of his office. That the officers of the clergy agreed with Talleyrand's position in this matter is evidenced by the fact that the outline of his arguments was recorded in the "Recueil concernant l'agence générale" to advise future Agents on the duties and prerogatives of their office.[61]

To the king's Secretary of State for Religious Affairs, Antoine-Jean Amelot, Talleyrand insisted on September 9, 1780 that it was customary for all edicts, declarations, and laws solicited by the Assembly of the Clergy before the King's Council to come to the Agents for approval before being made public.[62] The Minister replied five days later apologizing for this inadvertence and promised that henceforth this usage would be respected and all papers would be sent him as soon as possible.[63]

In a letter of December 21, 1782 to Cardinal de La Rochefoucauld, President of the Assemblies of 1780 and 1782, the Agent expressed "astonishment at the form of a letter" sent by his secretary which at once lacked the respect due his office and was unworthy of the Cardinal's dignity.[64] La Rochefoucauld, who was fond of Talleyrand, wrote him an autograph letter addressed to his home in Bellechasse, apologized for the incident, and asked him to send back the letter in question.[65]

Talleyrand frequently reminded the clergy of other prerogatives vested in his office. On June 20, 1782 he wrote that all titles kept in the clergy's Archives were confined to his "vigilance" and that copies of papers could not be legalized "by anyone but ourselves."[66] The Abbé de Rastignac, for whom Talleyrand had recently won a case regarding the alienation of tithe privileges belonging to his abbey, wished to publish that Agent's correspondence during the litigation. Pointing out that "this was absolutely contrary to the usages established in the Agency" and modestly disclaiming the worth of his own letters, he noted that no laws forbade the Abbé from making extracts of this correspondence if he chose.[67]

Having examined in what terms Talleyrand interpreted the powers of the General Assembly and his own Agency, we have yet to consider the last but fundamental link in the chain of clerical jurisdiction, the episcopate. From the Agent's numerous legal actions and letters applicable to the contested authority of the bishops over the clergy and churches of their dioceses, it is possible to reconstruct a clear picture of the significance he attributed to episcopal supremacy. Anxious to sustain the inviolate authority of the Church through its laws, Talleyrand realized this was possible only if the bishop of each diocese remained the undisputed head of that part of the Church consigned to his care.

The rule of the bishops was most frequently contested by unfavorable decisions or, as Talleyrand put it, by the interference and incursions in spiritual affairs of secular tribunals, particularly the Parlements, in which clerical offenders found sanctuary against their masters. Frequently overruling and even nullifying the authority of the bishop, the courts rendered decisions usurping traditionally exclusive episcopal jurisdiction, that is, supervising the administration of regular clergy, conferring ecclesiastical titles or exemptions, controlling schools and selecting teachers, and assigning ecclesiastical benefices. Further the Parlements preempted the episcopal right of appointments, determined competence for sacerdotal candidates, conferred spiritual offices, granted canonic institution, and even administered ecclesiastical penalties and censure. They frequently overruled bishops who revoked sacerdotal rights from unworthy priests, regulated ecclesiastical property, and granted or withheld permission to unite benefices. In short, for some time before the advent of the Revolution the Parlements felt themselves adequately empowered to pronounce on all clerical affairs, temporal as well as spiritual.[68]

The chief preventive of lay interference, and even Talleyrand conceded its inadequacy, was the moral obligation of the clergy to have recourse only to ecclesiastical tribunals as the sole legitimate judge of spiritual matters. Where pleas were too late or inapplicable, the Agents and lawyers of the clergy fought suits brought against the bishops in lay courts and, when possible, used influence with the king's ministers and magistrates. Talleyrand not infrequently wrote ministers asking for a transfer of jurisdiction from courts (like Parlements) to individual ministries (like the Controller-General of Finances), aware that litigations pending before the courts frequently were decided against the Church and hoping by transfer to receive favorable decisions.[69] As the late Professor Glasson observed, the clergy was far more successful in its appeals before the king's *gens de finance* than before his *gens de justice*.[70]

Talleyrand solemnly warned priest and bishop alike to stay clear of secular offices. He reminded the Bishop of Montpellier, who considered removing a case pending before a provincial ecclesiastical tribunal to a secular court, that it "would trouble the order of jurisdiction and interrupt the ordinary course of justice" and that beyond these tribunals and the General Assembly there was no further appeal.[71]

In the large number of cases which Talleyrand personally managed on behalf of the bishops, we have singled out the most important which demonstrate, first, what episcopal powers were subjected to contestation during this period; second, what authority Talleyrand believed indispensable to secure the structure of traditional spiritual jurisdiction; and third, the means he used to realize these objectives.

A dispute initiated by the Abbeys of St. Vaast and St. Bertin (Dioceses of Arras and St. Omer) against their bishops seeking exemption from episcopal jurisdiction led Talleyrand to argue the imprescriptible superiority of the bishop over the regular clergy of his diocese.[72] The second half of the eighteenth century witnessed a dramatic rise in the number of monastic houses seeking exemption from episcopal jurisdiction through the offices of the crown.[73] The Assembly from 1775 appealed to the king for the appointment of a committee to examine spurious titles used by the regulars to evade episcopal control and to arrest this abuse. Rejecting the abbeys' plea that Maria Theresa had granted them exemption under Austrian occupation, Talleyrand contended that the statutes of the Church "from the Council of Chalcedon to the Holy and Learned Council of Trent" empowered the bishop to exercise full control over the regulars of each diocese. This authority was founded, too, on common law which empowered the bishop to assure public order and tranquillity in his diocese and on legislation of 1695 which placed both regular and lay clergy under episcopal jurisdiction regardless of their claims of immunity. The Church, "always an enemy of exemptions" (that is, within its own ranks, surely not as an Estate against the laws or levies of the crown), could only regard such pretensions as fatal to episcopal jurisdiction. Therefore no exemptions possessed by these or any other abbeys could free them from their diocesan ordinary, "since episcopal jurisdiction is imprescriptible." Talleyrand asked the Assembly of 1785 to pass this affair on to his successors to seek an annulment of the decrees which the abbeys had secured from the Paris Parlement confirming their immunity.

The power of the bishop over the regular clergy of his diocese could also be extended to the dissolution of ineffectual unions of regulars.[74] In 1774 the Archbishop of Auch dissolved a collegiate benefice belonging to the Praemonstratensians of his diocese, formed in 1466 by the prelate's predecessor and the Count d'Armagnac. The bishop was empowered to dissolve a union if and when the religious, by reason of paucity, ceased to render the prescribed services responsible for their foundation. The Archbishop did just this on grounds of the order's greatly reduced numbers, declared the benefice vacant, and assigned it to other collators. The religious contested the prelate's authority before the king's Great Council, claiming that episcopal power was not sufficient to suppress a monastic order and that only the pope could dissolve their organization.

The Agent strongly defended the bishops' power of dissolution and nomination, accorded by the early Church and confirmed by subsequent councils and concordats. In February, 1781 he secured a favorable decree from the Great Council, a decree not difficult to obtain, since the government was anxious to wrest jurisdiction over monastic communities from Roman and foreign hands in favor of French bishops.[75] With this victory Talleyrand vigorously exhorted each bishop to exploit this "right which belongs to all of you in your dioceses and which you hold by ordination and your episcopal character."[76] The same episcopal privileges, he maintained, extended to the property of suppressed orders, like the Jesuits, together with jurisdiction over clerical personnel dependent on these benefices.[77]

By the same token the bishop enjoyed supreme authority in the union of benefices in the diocese. In 1782 the citizens of Parthenay (Diocese of Poitiers) sought money to build a hospital and to appoint new teachers for their schools. They petitioned their bishop to declare a union of four defunct monasteries, the revenue of which would revert to the township for its announced enterprises.[78] When that prelate requested time to consider their proposals, the townspeople took the case to the Paris Parlement demanding the union of these benefices and the impoundage of their revenues. Talleyrand intervened and denounced the citizenry for assuming the role of judge in a matter "where they have no rights." The burden of his defense was not a new one for him. It was that these monasteries were consecrated to God and given to the Church for specific spiritual purposes by pious founders. Only the bishop, as representative of the Church in his diocese, was empowered to interpret the intentions of the donors and the fate of their gifts. Talleyrand secured a decree of August 31, 1784 from the Paris Parlement which approved a union of two of the benefices and directed the townspeople to pay a fine and court expenses.[79]

Closely related to the seizure of ecclesiastical property by secular authority, but far more dangerous, was lay control of spiritual offices. Talleyrand reported to the Assembly of 1785 a case of lay collation by the Municipality of Limoges of a benefice formerly the property of the proscribed Jesuits. To the Archbishop of Vienne he referred to this as "one of the most important cases the Assembly assigned [to him]."[80] He argued that the conferral by laymen of spiritual office constituted the gravest interference in the spiritual office of the Church. Since a benefice with charge of souls is a strictly spiritual office in which laymen have no authority, they cannot confer them. While kings and other lay persons legitimately could name priests to exercise sacerdotal functions in their private chapels, just as soon as these institutions served souls other than the family of a prince or lord they became a church of the faithful and an office of public ministry subject to strictest regulation by ecclesiastical authority. This principle was sustained in a decision of the Paris Parlement in May, 1781.

Other decisions of Parlement forced clerics to discharge involuntarily the functions of their ministry. The Grenoble Parlement forced a priest in the Diocese of Valence to perform, against his opposition, a marriage ceremony involving a Protestant.[81] Talleyrand contested the decision. "The Parlement exceeded the limits of its jurisdiction by forcing ecclesiastical administration of the sacrament." Not only is a lay court without authority in spiritual affairs, but it endangers the sacramental function of the Church, and, to the detriment of society, endangers marriage as a legal contract.

The judgment of the bishop was the authoritative criterion in determining sacerdotal competence, in eliminating unworthy candidates for the priesthood, and in conferring the *visa* of occupancy. The edict of April, 1695, a lengthy ordinance of fifty articles governing ecclesi-

Maintenance of Ecclesiastical Jurisdiction

astical jurisdiction, gave the bishops widespread power they long had sought over the lower clergy of their dioceses.[82] The bishops were not only solely empowered to grant canonic institution of benefices for the legal occupancy of sacerdotal office, from which lay tribunals were forbidden to interfere, but they were confirmed as judges of the morals, doctrine, science, age, and other qualities of the lower clergy, with the right to remove those judged unfit. Their extensive inspection power, which developed parallel to that of the Intendants, gave them the right to visit all churches of the diocese, including monastic communities, to verify the conduct and residence of priests and to evaluate their efficiency in education, assistance, and the civil register.[83] Bishops could grant and revoke the right to preach, to administer sacraments, to supervise discipline of the regular clergy, including those who claimed episcopal immunity, and to confine religious to their convents.[84]

What the law granted with one hand, however, it took back, to a certain extent, with the other. For the bishops or their vicars-general could be challenged as judges, and their sentences, ordinances, and jurisdiction could be disputed in matters ranging from the assignment of benefices to the conferral of sacraments, the taking of vows, and ecclesiastical discipline before any Parlement of the land by recourse to the *appel comme d'abus*. In the words of the eighteenth-century canonist Jousse, "the *appel comme d'abus* is a way open not only to the subjects of the king but also to foreigners in the kingdom to aid those who find themselves oppressed by ecclesiastical enterprises and to destroy or reform those [abuses] that archbishops and bishops and their officials or other ecclesiastics may judge contrary to the liberties of the Gallican Church, to the holy canons, to the liberties of the kingdom, and to the authority of the king."[85]

The appeal of the lower clergy to secular justice in defiance of the bishops, whose disciplinary authority the law manifestly tried to strengthen, caused the higher clergy considerable alarm. The law also embittered the *curés*, who found their activities, indeed their credentials and conduct, subject to the permanent judgment of the bishops, and who found the protective jurisdiction enjoyed in the Church against their masters destroyed by the edict. The law of 1695 played no small role in fanning the Richerist ardor of the lower clergy, in influencing the *curés* to accost the bishops and vicars-general with Presbyterian Gallicanism, in accentuating the lower clergy's resentment at being further excluded from divine government, and in encouraging democratic ideas within the Church. The papers of the clergy's lawyers during the period under study indicate that the refusal of the *visa* was widespread among the bishops of France.[86]

The juridical situation of the *curés* itself was quite complicated. While subject to nomination by the local bishop, they were more often nominated by *abbés*, priors, canons, abbesses, and lay seigneurs. It has been estimated that one-fourth of the nominations escaped the clergy altogether, including the bishops, by resignations *in favorem*, whereby a *curé* could designate his successor and secure his title by a patent from the Court of Rome.[87] Regardless of the source of his nomination, however, the Edict of 1695 assured the diocesan bishop or his vicar-general a monopoly on the conferral of canonic title and thus ultimate spiritual and disciplinary jurisdiction. The bishop attempted whenever possible to regain lost rights of nomination; and when new parishes were created, he secured those rights if he could.

Buisonnier, a priest in the Diocese of St. Dié, received a benefice resigned in his favor. He attempted to get from Rome canonic provision granting title.[88] The pope, presumably on the recommendation of the bishop, refused. Whereupon the Bishop of St. Dié retracted the priest's power of preaching and confession and refused to confer on him a benefice with charge of souls. Appealing this action to the metropolitan (Vienne) and thence to the eldest bishop of the province, both of whom denied confirmation, he appealed to the Grenoble Parlement which on August 31, 1782 ordered that he be given title to his benefice.

The question, the Agent wrote, reduced itself to the attempt of a secular authority to usurp the sacred right of canonic confirmation always held by the Church. "Secular authority may not in any case give the power to dispense holy things, to exercise functions purely spiritual. Secular authority cannot force ecclesiastical superiors to confer these powers on subjects they believe unworthy." Canonic institution involves the conferral of sacred functions and therefore can originate only from the spiritual power "by virtue of the power of the keys." The secular power cannot "repudiate, dissemble, change, or modify this rule, because it is founded on the essence of religion [and] is at the base of the administration established by Jesus Christ Himself."

Writing to the king's Minister of the Royal Household, the Baron Louis-Auguste Le Tonnelier de Breteuil, in February, 1785,[89] Talleyrand challenged the decision of any secular power which endangered the hierarchical principles involved here. Only the diocesan bishop had the authority to determine spiritual qualifications and sacerdotal capacity. There could be no further legitimate appeal. Since purely supernatural forces were at stake, and because they could not render judgments, secular courts have no spiritual powers. He called on royal authority to return to the king's statute of 1695 which assured the right of conferring the *visa* exclusively on the bishops. Without it, a candidate remained an intruder, regardless of the decisions of lay authorities. He secured an order of June 25, 1784 which recognized that Buissonier held his benefice illegally.[90]

Talleyrand exhorted all the bishops to exploit their powers of canonic confirmation and revocation guaranteed them by the same Edict of 1695 for the greater good of their dioceses. In January, 1783, the Agent advised the Archbishop of Tours to sustain the judgment of one of his suffragan bishops who refused the *visa* "without being bound to explain the reasons" to a priest who had violated holy orders. He added that in order to discourage clerics from seeking canonic institution from secular authorities, it was incumbent on the prelacy to judge fairly, to use skillful negotiation, and to assure their clergy the same justice "among their natural judges" that they could secure in secular tribunals. The Bishop of Lisieux revoked the powers of conferring the sacrament of penance on a priest in his diocese, a priest of unsuitable character named Maury. Talleyrand suggested that the priest be dropped "like a tree which bears no fruit." The Agent claimed that a priest could not confer the sacrament to absolve sin if he was himself guilty of moral turpitude. Maury is as much an intruder as if he had never been granted canonic confirmation, for he does not have the sanction of his bishop nor has he shown the "submission, obedience, and dependence of secondary ministers towards their first pastors." The Rouen Parlement, to which Maury appealed, acknowledged the bishop's authority by a decree of March, 1783, and ordered the priest to pay a fine and damages.

Episcopal supremacy in the determination of spiritual qualifications of priests extended also to the religious. The Bishop of Meaux ordered a regular, de Villiers, canon of the Congregation of France, to retire to his abbey because of disobedience to his superiors. Upon appeal de Villiers was exonerated of this sentence by the Paris Parlement.[91] In letters to d'Ormesson, President of the Paris Parlement, and Joly de Fleury, attorney-general,[92] Talleyrand argued that by law the bishop was empowered to dismiss a *curé* without previous warning for crimes and misdemeanors, or if the *curé* was adjudged unworthy of leading the faithful both by the statutes of the Congregation and the laws of the kingdom. The Parlement's decision ran contrary to the "intentions of the sovereign," who was anxious to assure the calm of the dioceses. Moreover, the Edict of 1695 "becomes more necessary every day . . . to the conduct of the large dioceses." He asked the Parlement for a favorable decision which would encourage all other tribunals to honor the statutes of the realm guaranteeing the bishops this fundamental premise of their authority.[93] The favorable decision sought against de Villiers was granted on February 20, 1783.[94]

Encouraged by this ruling, Talleyrand advised bishops to exploit the power recognized by the courts of removing undesirable clergy. He approved the actions of the Archbishop of Rouen who revoked the vicariate of an unfit priest and of the Bishop of Clermont who unseated a hospital chaplain of depraved character.[95] He backed the Bishop of Saintes who deprived the *Curé* David of Saint-Brunet, "already known in the courts for his temper and violence," of all sacerdotal functions for having publicly insulted a government official and his family during the course of holy service in December, 1780. On April 28, 1781 David received an order from the Bordeaux Parlement reinstating him in his office and functions. Talleyrand, appealing this decision on grounds of secular incompetence in matters of clerical discipline, secured a cassation from the king in his Council of Dispatches on March 14, 1783, and with this the Bishop of Saintes appealed anew to the Bordeaux Parlement which reversed its earlier order and condemned David to fines and expenses.[96]

Akin to the bishop's authority to determine clerical fitness was the right to oversee the conduct of priests. This right was jeopardized by groups of dissident *curés* who, openly defiant of the monopoly of political and economic power in the hands of the bishop and the Diocesan Bureau, organized to elect their own candidates to that body. In the Agent's view these movements constituted an attempt to destroy the foundations of ecclesiastical discipline. He had reported to the Assembly of 1782 the case of a priest in the Diocese of Vienne, Henri Reymond. Six years before Reymond had published an influential Richerist tract (*Les droits des curés et des paroisses considérés sous leur double rapport spirituel et temporel* [Paris, 1776]) which fulminated against the overtaxation of the *curés,* their exclusion from a voice in the temporal and spiritual affairs of the diocese, and their social ostracism by the aristocratic hierarchy. The author argued that the *curés* were equal to the bishops by divine ordination and as successors to the apostles and were the only legitimate owners of the tithes. Reymond, who by 1780 had become a spokesman of the lower order of the clergy, convoked an organization of *curés* to elect a candidate to the Diocesan Bureau of Vienne, from which they had been effectively barred. Once assembled, this organization pressed its grievances and made a bid for representation. The Agent described them as "a reprehensible ferment of turbulent spirits setting a fire which was ready to burst forth in that diocese."[97]

Similar movements had been launched in Provence and Dauphiné by *curés* who pressed in concert for an increased *portion congrue* and who, much to the ire of the bishops, had been accorded permission to assemble by the Parlements of Grenoble and Aix in 1779.[98] But this assembly, Talleyrand asserted, was only a "pretext" for the establishment of permanent committees of protest which deliberated, published papers of protest, named deputies to a central headquarters in Paris, received contributions, and held regular correspondence "overtly contrary to episcopal jurisdiction." The rebellion threatened the Church with armed force to secure its demands. It could not permit priests under any pretext to question the formation of the Diocesan Bureau or forcibly to alter its constitution by the intrusion of illegal candidates. To do otherwise would "accredit their unjust and dishonoring accusations and encourage the spirit of trouble and disorder which would be as contrary to the tranquillity of the dioceses as to the service of His Majesty."[99]

As ministers of religion priests could not constitute themselves legally into separate bodies. "No law ever accorded them this privilege." Their unions were merely brazen attempts to assail the authority of the bishop: "The bishop is the head of the diocese. He is its first pastor. Priests cannot therefore separate their interests from his or search out any other representative except him or the Syndic General who aids him in his functions. It is to the bishop that belongs the government of the churches of his diocese, the inspection of all that might interest the ecclesiastical order, the right to convoke assemblies which the welfare of the diocese demands ... all assemblies of pastors to which the bishop is not connected are by these reasons alone illegitimate assemblies."[100]

For their part, the bishops in the Assembly were alarmed at the ominous political organizations of the *curés congruistes* which had erupted in various parts of the kingdom.[101] Archbishop Boisgelin assured his colleagues that the king would put down such seditious movements as he had in the past.[102] The *curés*, on the other hand, complained bitterly of episcopal absolutism, apparent not only in the renewed application of the law of 1695 which fixed the rights of the bishops over them but also in their exclusion from a representative voice in the clergy's affairs in the diocese, province, and nation. Their attempt to storm the Diocesan Bureaus was only part of the struggle to regain a share in ecclesiastical government, in which they were members and in which their interests were at stake, and to achieve a voice in the division of taxes. The all-powerful bishops, *abbés*, and canons, who controlled assessments, saw to it that the *curés* carried by far the most onerous burden.[103] Their rebuff, the call for their suppression by members of their own order who used the Edict of 1695 against them, and the unjustifiable delays in augmenting the *portion congrue* only intensified the antagonism and real crisis of division between the two clergies which, as one recent historian put it, reached a point of virtual civil war.[104] The economic, social and moral position of the privileged members of the hierarchy was in large part determined by the aristocratic mores of their class. In intimate contact with the king and his ministers, the bishops monopolized the power of the First Estate and isolated themselves from the mass of their clergy whose economic and social position became increasingly desperate in an age of rampant inflation and feudal reaction.

The bishops, even the most evangelical, did not resist the temptation of showing the *curés* that "they were of a different race."[105] The bishops' scorn for the lower clergy was manifested not alone in barring them from the government of the cult, from political activity within their own estate, as well as from the assemblies and estates of the dioceses and provinces, but also in actually removing *curés* disagreeable to them.[106] Having evaded any effective control, either by the king, who divested himself of the direction of the Church in favor of his episcopate, or by the pope, whose authority was in "prolonged eclipse" in the second-half of the eighteenth-century, the bishops showed themselves "vigorous and rigorous" to the lower clergy.[107]

Little wonder that *frondeur* priests defied the orders of the Assembly and the admonitions of bishops more concerned with administration than religion. Little wonder that they felt scant kinship for a handful of spiritual seigneurs whose distinguishing mark was *"esprit de cour, esprit aristocratique, esprit de corps,"*[108] and whose wealth, luxury, immorality, pride, and skepticism they hated, masters who seldom consulted their priests, who were oblivious of their problems and, even more, of the conditions of their dioceses where many were absentee rulers. Little wonder, finally, that the political position of a class profoundly aware of its inferiority was allied to the *tiers*, and that when the time came, the *curés* scornfully repudiated privilege and took revenge at once on their arrogant bishops, their avaricious *gros décimateurs*, and their insolent noble lords by abandoning them in favor of the Revolution.[109] By maintaining rigidly their reactionary stance, by clinging stubbornly to practices no longer acceptable to the lower clergy, the bishops unwittingly abetted the revolutionary furor. For at the head of the clergy in the Estates-General of 1789 were to figure the "long despised and oppressed" *curés*—Grégoire, *Curé* of Embermenil in Lorraine; Gouttes, *Curé* of Souppes near Nemours; Le Cesve, *Curé* of Sainte-Triaize; Jallet, *Curé* of Chérigné; and Ballard, *Curé* of Poiré in Poitou.[110]

It is significant that Talleyrand should have become the outspoken foe of sacerdotal democracy and the freedom of association among the lower clergy, and that he played such a highly personal role in combatting all popular organizations of priests. He viewed them simply as grave perils to the existence of the ecclesiastical hierarchy and episcopal authority he was charged to defend, an authority which had no intention of accommodating the demands of the lower clergy for a representative voice. Moreover, as he wrote to the king's ministers, he feared that the contagion, nourished by "intrigue . . . weakness . . . seducing promises . . . advantageous change" might engulf the whole Church. However hard the Agent worked to meliorate the clergy's economic situation by a more sensible salary, to have compromised with the *curés*, he believed, would have fed the fires of revolution.[111] Though Talleyrand was an astute and resourceful politician, it should not be forgotten that at the same time he was an aristocrat, of the same class and loyalties as the bishops whose morals he shared and whose company he was anxious to join. He promised the Assembly he would secure legislation "to stop the disease at its source."

It is unmistakably evident that here, more than in any other facet of its temporal operations, the Church required the authority of the

State to restore order. It is both significant and ironic that in order to make good his promise, Talleyrand had to appeal to that same secular justice he denied the clergy. It is not surprising that many members of the First Estate looked critically and even hostilely on the principle Talleyrand never ceased to proclaim—that the General Assembly had the supreme right to review the conduct of ecclesiastical persons and to establish ordinances regulating their conduct—"the most natural tribunal to terminate with justice and equity all dissensions that might arise among us."[112] But while the Agent ardently longed for the day when the Assembly might regain sovereignty in all cases involving the spiritual, it was apparent that victory, even in questions involving its own personnel, carried the liability of State authority which secured it. In the last analysis the Church remained powerless in affairs which threatened force within its own ranks. It could save itself only through the intercession of the crown.

Talleyrand's strategy in securing the help of the secular arm was that rebellious priests not only destroyed spiritual peace but also endangered the lives of French citizens and posed a threat to the authority of the monarchy. These seditious groups, "difficult, ambitious, jealous of power, enemies of subordination,"[113] which organized into separate bodies for political action, could be fatal to the peoples of the State." The Agent wrote to the Keeper of Seals that since these rebellions had always centered about the organization of the Diocesan Bureaus, the General Assemblies had attempted to prevent trouble by enacting ordinances governing the uniform composition and organization of each chamber.[114] The government, he continued, had as much at stake in guaranteeing the constitution of the Diocesan Bureaus against the *curés* as did the Church, for it was this body which was responsible for collecting the *décimes* used to amortize the king's *dons gratuits*. Irregularities in their composition and operations would necessarily prevent the payment of the clergy's taxes to the State.

Though he asked the king's assistance, Talleyrand was not anxious to submit the Church's diocesan machinery to secular review, and he was careful to point out that the judicial surveillance of spiritual institutions rested exclusively with the clergy's Assembly. He was only requesting legislation to quash illegal organizations of *curés* which menaced Church and State alike.

As has already been observed Talleyrand secured decrees of the King's Council on April 28, 1781 and March 9, 1782 prohibiting all *curés* not instituted as legitimate corporations or communities to assemble without permission.[115] In a letter of March 20 Armand-Thomas Hue de Miromesnil, Keeper of Seals, acknowledged Talleyrand's broad initiative and interest in this edict and brought news of its registration by the Paris Parlement.[116] On the same day the Agent replied, expressing the hope that the law "would suffer no difficulties" before the other Parlements and courts of the kingdom.[117] In succeeding communications the Agent was informed of the progress of the edict before the remaining Parlements.[118]

Talleyrand used his authority to dissuade *curés* from initiating steps to form associations. He warned a cleric of Bordeaux that "each time the *curés* have wanted to combine, the clergy was opposed to their enterprise."[119] To the *Curé* of Marolles (Diocese of Blois) he wrote in September, 1784[120] that all unions of *curés* into separate bodies "to form their demands by secret associations" were strictly forbidden by law. Only by charging an attorney ("however without preliminary assembly, association, and agenda") to present their claims before the Diocesan Syndic could the *curés* legally present their grievances.

The disciplinary jurisdiction of the bishops was undermined not alone by disobedience and organized protests but also by unauthorized alienation of temporalities by lower clergy. Alienations had been a serious problem since the seventeenth century.[121] The Assemblies after 1780 were profoundly disturbed at the magnitude of alienations, illicit loans, and improper use of the clergy's immovable property (especially by the regular orders) all over the kingdom ("Blind cupidity . . . negligence, and avidity pose a threat to the clergy's own house [and] destroy episcopal jurisdiction").[122] Talleyrand regarded alienations as a foremost enemy of the Church temporal and undertook every means to assert the authority of the bishop over the propertied patrimony as well as the spiritual personnel of the First Estate.

One case involving the Abbé de Chatre and his superior, the Bishop of Le Mans, illustrates the Agent's personal initiative in preventing this costly abuse.[123] The Bishop sought the aid of Talleyrand against de Chatre, who without obtaining his permission proceeded to alienate an important portion of his benefice by public sale. In a letter of February 9, 1785 the Agent assured the Bishop that he would do all in his power to stop this sale, and "should all other methods fail," he would invoke the aid of the approaching General Assembly. The next day the Agent wrote to the violator. His letter, a combination of forcefulness, tact, and loosely veiled intimidation, worked the trick in prompting de Chatre to call off his proposed plans to alienate property in his charge.[124]

The first part of the missive presented a humorless recital of "canon law and the ordinances of the kingdom" which condemned the illegality of his acts. Then followed arguments quite familiar to the readers of the Agent's letters: the sanctity of ecclesiastical property; its inalienability except by "evident necessity or great utility"; the illegality of usufructuaries to "denature" the perpetual patrimony of the faithful; the obligatory recourse to the only legitimate authority, the bishop; and the irregularity of securing royal letters patent authorizing the sale without episcopal consent.

The next section passed from legality to the threat of punishment. His bishop could successfully take action against him, and "in my quality of Agent I would be forced to aid and abet his opposition with everything in me." He professed deep shock that the clergy had learned of the present project through the newspapers. Should his case come before the General Assembly, the clergy would certainly place de Chatre on its list of the infamous. Talleyrand then reminded the Abbé of his success in similar cases during the course of the Agency where violators "disposed to heed my warnings" called off similar enterprises. De Chatre was advised to do the same "to avoid costing you . . . an unpleasant scandal." Talleyrand terminated the problem within a week. On February 18 he wrote the Bishop of Le Mans that "ancient maxims [and] personal considerations appear to me to have banished forever the decision he had taken."

Talleyrand was too perceptive not to see that the Church was powerless to retain certain essential tenets of its internal discipline except by outside help. Adroit diplomacy and skillful blandishments might work to stay the hand of some refractory clerics bent on alienation; but, obviously, they were not effective in each case, certainly not in the many which never even came to the attention of the Agents. Only the government (which did not share the Church's apprehension in the matter of alienations and, on the contrary, welcomed the surrender of its mortmain privileges) could by legislative action prevent the erosion of its patrimony. The draft of a law making all alienations, loans, and personal use of Church real estate illegal except upon the approval of the bishop, proposed by Talleyrand and resoundingly favored by the Assembly of 1785, lay on the desk of the king during the remainder of the Old Monarchy.[125]

Maintenance of Ecclesiastical Jurisdiction 139

It should not be inferred from this that alienations were a monopoly of the second order of the clergy. Archbishop Boisgelin, the same chairman of the Committee on the Temporal who decried the pernicious consequences of alienation and the excesses of the lower clergy before the Assemblies of 1780 and 1785, was himself guilty of selling half the land and *seigneurie* of Jouques belonging to his episcopal see for 200,000 *l*. And he was joined by fellow *politiques* bishops who resorted to this illegal device to augment their revenues.[126] There was of course no way to curtail the enterprises of the bishops whose laws were binding on all members of the First Estate except themselves.

Talleyrand lent his assistance in another case which threatened the authority of the bishop over his clergy, this time within the Diocesan Bureau itself. The Bishop of Tarbes wished to replace the Roman breviary used in his diocese by the Parisian, despite the displeasure of five of the fourteen members of his diocesan chamber.[127] The Agent informed the prelate that Church law fully authorized him to make such a change and "there was more than one example where the changing of breviaries was authorized against the pleasure of the chamber." But he advised the bishop to yield to the wishes of his vicars in the interests of peace and harmony.

Another element of challenged episcopal authority involved the bishop's right to control seminaries and schools within his diocese. Education before 1789 was the obligation of the Church, not the State, which accorded no budget for public instruction or for the maintenance of schools. The bishops recruited, supervised, and paid the teachers, and judged the ability, doctrine, and morals of masters called on to teach in the public schools, the majority of whom were clergy of various teaching orders.[128] One important case during the 1780-1785 Agency involved the Bishop of Oleron and the Barnabites of his diocese who had assumed, against his wishes, the supervision of the local seminary and the property united to it. The religious obtained a ruling of the Pau Parlement confirming their control. In a letter to a member of the King's Council, Talleyrand objected to the illegality of this decision which struck "at the precious part of the bishop's authority which confides to him alone the task of forming and instructing young ecclesiastics and, as a consequence, the choice of ministers charged to supervise them in the seminaries."[129]

Talleyrand secured a favorable edict from the Council in November, 1781 which decreed that the bishop was free to appoint all persons worthy of his confidence for the education of young clergy in the seminaries. The Agent appealed to the Assembly of 1782 to consider exploiting this favorable decision by drafting a law embodying these proposals consolidating the bishop's authority over education, thereby discouraging the recurrence of similar cases.[130]

Episcopal authority in education and the right of episcopal surveillance in matters of doctrine and morals extended also to lay teachers. In 1781 the Bishop of Boulogne relieved a teacher, Gollio, of his duties on charges of unbecoming conduct.[131] Gollio appealed to the local Parlement and obtained a stay permitting him to retain his position. Upon appeal of the bishop, backed by the Agent, an order of June, 1782, received from the Seneschal of Boulogne, declared Gollio's post vacant and permitted the parish to appoint a replacement.

Talleyrand was by no means anxious to arrogate to the Agency-General the powers which he painstakingly sought for the bishops. He redirected to the bishops pleas of clergy directed to him concerning powers vested in the episcopate. A priest in the Diocese of Bourges asked the Agents for permission to say Mass in a neighboring chapel for a certain number of days. Talleyrand replied that only the Archbishop of Bourges could grant such a request.[132] Solicited by a *curé* in the Diocese of Autun for aid in a criminal trial in which he was involved, Talleyrand answered he must first inform his bishop.[133] The Agent approved the zeal of a *curé* of Fontenay (Diocese of Lisieux) who wished to expose the "reprehensible conduct" of a man and woman of his parish, but he confessed this was a problem whose jurisdiction lay outside his Agency, and that the priest must appeal directly to his bishop.[134]

The Agent received innumerable petitions from *congruiste* priests who wished the Assembly, and frequently the Agents themselves, to supplement their miserable incomes. In most instances Talleyrand replied that it was unfortunately not in his power to come to their aid with funds from the clergy's treasury, whose "fixed destination cannot possibly be reversed without disturbing the order established by the Assembly."[135] Hoping that the Assembly of 1785 would see fit to raise the *portion congrue,* he asked the *curés* to seek the assistance of their bishop, and above all, to avoid secular courts. Likewise to diocesan clergy requesting higher pensions to meet rising costs of living, Talleyrand replied that this fell within the responsibility of the local bishops.[136]

Occasionally the Agent referred one bishop to another, particularly when matters of benefices and jurisdiction involved more than one diocese. In June, 1782 he redirected to the Bishop of Autun a letter from the Bishop of Quimper regarding the union of chapters outside his jurisdiction.[137]

Talleyrand also meant to preserve the demarcation lines between metropolitan and bishop. The Bishop of Alais asked the Agents if he might decree a union of chapters without the permission of his metropolitan. Talleyrand judged that such action could be challenged as an *appel comme d'abus* before secular justice. Since Church law placed the highest authority in the metropolitan and since this was the surest means to avoid expenses and delay, he directed the bishop to the Archbishop of Narbonne, who, he assured him, would gladly receive his petition.[138]

The Agent sought not only to maintain but, whenever possible, to widen the jurisdiction of the bishops. He warmly received a petition of several houses of nuns who, wishing to renounce the right of exemption from their bishop, inquired about the steps to be taken to submit themselves fully to episcopal authority. In a large autograph memorandum Talleyrand outlined the legal procedures involved and applauded such a policy, always favorably received by Church and episcopate.[139]

Talleyrand who had worked so hard to keep secret and out of secular hands the exact extent of the clergy's temporal wealth exercised similar caution with regard to its treasury of spiritual jurisdiction so that it, too, would not escape the clergy. He warned the personnel of the First Estate, prelacy as well as lower clergy, to avoid all scandals and public discussions which could offer the secular authorities a pretext for abridging it. In March, 1785 Talleyrand wrote: "Ecclesiastical jurisdiction is in our day attacked so openly from all sides that all discussions which might compromise it should be avoided with greatest care." He warned bishops to refrain, to the point of granting embarrassing concessions to their priests, from all issues which would bring the Church either unfavorable publicity or which might arouse the enmity of *curés* against their superiors. Concerted protests of the lower clergy, he warned, would result in costly contagions among the dioceses and encourage their colleagues to take cases against their bishops to secular courts to the abasement of ecclesiastical discipline. Failure to recognize these facts could undo the Agent's labors and even undermine his office, dedicated to obtaining laws for the needs of the clergy.

Unfavorable publicity, too, might prevent the passage of needed laws or the revocation of abusive statutes. He warned the bishop of Le Mans in the case of the Abbé de Chatre in February, 1785 to avoid scandal and especially not to expose himself to an adverse judgment of the courts which might not only result in defeat for him but would also render more difficult the clergy's securing a law against alienations. In a similar action he warned the Bishop of Séez to proceed cautiously and moderately against priests of his diocese who had met secretly and defied his authority in diocesan matters.[140] He granted that the bishop could denounce these deliberations before the government, but that this "rigorous method" should be used only as "the last extremity and after all other means to lead [his clergy] to better dispositions had been exhausted."

Talleyrand's excellent administrative ability—to strike immediately at the heart of a problem, to discard the unimportant, and to devise simple and effective solutions—is further demonstrated in a communication to the Bishop of Luçon in September, 1784.[141] The Church was involved in judicial unpleasantness due to the appeal of parishioners who protested the actions of a zealous clergyman who forced them against their will to recite the ritual act of faith in presenting a child for baptism. Remarked Talleyrand: "It is sometimes dangerous to expose [to laymen] the coolness and indifference which greets ecclesiastical ceremonies, and on a good many occasions a prudent silence is preferable to publicity in a scandal whose example could become contagious. This is what is practiced in Paris where, as you know, there are, more than elsewhere, Catholics who show little zeal for the ceremonies of the Church." The *curé's* task is to do his job and avoid all difficulties for the Church. His parishioners ought to observe the ritual "by persuasive exhortations rather than measures that might irritate and embitter." In any case, the difficulty of obtaining favorable decisions from the government in these cases and others like them "make us feel more and more the necessity of avoiding all kinds of scandal."

It becomes apparent in studying Talleyrand's record as defender of ecclesiastical jurisdiction that we are dealing with a man whose formal outlook, limited objectives, insistence on order and legality before all else, and unswerving sense of duty are essentially those of a higher public servant charged with the responsibility of group direction and institutional management. We do not encounter in his writings a formulator of lofty precepts, an author of uplifting messages or exciting interpretations, or an oracle of a novel philosophy. The task of the Agent-General did not call for these. It would be grossly unfair to have expected them of him. As Agent, Talleyrand was called on to deal with questions in the less exalted realm of law enforcement and to champion, before the clergy and government alike, contested privileges and unpopular causes. By a vigorously orthodox and authoritarian approach the young Athanasius sought traditional solutions to traditional problems on behalf of traditional institutions. What made his task difficult is that by the time of the 1780-1785 Agency appeal to tradition was no longer respected as it once had been, and the Church was on the defensive for a considerable part of what it owned and decreed. Indeed, as we have seen, ecclesiastical authority was subject to serious opposition from among the clergy as well as from unsympathetic magistrates which required periodic reassertion through the intervention of the king. Impatient and distrustful of change that might disrupt the status quo he was appointed to defend, Talleyrand upheld the Church's interests resolutely, never once questioning the presuppositions of its power, the righteousness of its task, or the justice of its policies.

The difference, however, between young Talleyrand and any hack was the fertile mind, the resourceful administration, and the flexible policy of accommodation he brought to his office. He won the confidence and esteem of the Assembly after only two years in power. Though his reports to the bishops hardly eschew exuberance and pedantry and, admittedly, are redolent with conservative views to command attention and win approval, he displayed rare skill in handling clerical business. Critical, cautious, imaginative, prudent, Talleyrand early understood the strengths and weaknesses of ecclesiastical administration, as well as the dangers presented by a divided house and hostile neighbors. He was fully alive to the challenges to ecclesiastical jurisdiction presented by organized groups of *curés,* taxdodging clerics, extortionate benefice holders who squandered their patrimony, absentee cathedral canons, and immoral priests abetted by the Parlements and secular tribunals. Adding to this a genuine fear of the uprooting consequences of innovation and pervasive effects of deviation in an institution whose strength resided in its ability to resist change, he was prompted to uphold the absolute sovereignty of the General Assembly among the dioceses and the bishops within them. Any other course, however enlightened, would have reflected a policy of compromise and change or a relaxation of customary discipline which in no wise characterized the temporal policy of the Church in the latter Old Regime, which, by Talleyrand's admission, and by its own, was an enemy of innovation.[142]

Having seen how he used his office to defend the authority of his order at the higher levels, there remain the considerable obligations of the Agent for the welfare of the massive body of lower clergy, the interests of individual ecclesiastics, and the privileges of their churches.

VI

The Agent-General as Servant of the Clergy

Below the Assembly and the episcopate lay the vast numbers of parish clergy. To their body the Agent-General had five chief responsibilities. The first was to secure the codification of acts and resolutions passed by the Assembly. The second was to act as spokesman and herald, empowered to keep colleagues throughout the nation informed of all issues of concern by communicating and, in certain cases, securing information. The third was to act as attorney to the remotest parishes of the land, clarifying rights and immunities and counselling clerics in need of assistance. The fourth was to assume the role of peacemaker and, on occasion, judge, to assure harmony between factions of priests. And finally, the Agent was an intercessor, and, at times, an actual party to the litigations of the clergy.

After the Assembly adjourned the Agents were expected to cooperate with the government to obtain for the First Estate the registration or enforcement of laws already passed and to seek the promulgation of statutes demanded by former Assemblies. Frequently the Agent might not only suggest the text of laws, as Talleyrand did in the *portion congrue* or alienations, but might lend the weight and prestige of his office to press for the passage of statutes conformant or useful to the clergy's interests, as with the *foi et hommage* and tithes. These laws, as has been shown in preceding chapters, touched all matters vital to the Church spiritual and temporal, disciplinary as well as financial. The job of the Agent was to procure legislative and legal force for the Assembly's resolutions in order to ensure the inviolability of ecclesiastical jurisdiction and to protect the privileges and property of each parish.

First as executors of the Assembly's decision, the Agents were responsible for securing the king's letters patent and Acts of Council which confirmed the clergy's *don gratuits* and the annual assistance newly augmented after 1780, accorded by the crown to reimburse its loans.[1] Upon procurement of these letters from the king, they were to be registered by a decree of Parlement.[2] Archbishop Loménie de Brienne reported to the Assembly of 1780 that on July 7 he and Talleyrand had seen the king's ministers to procure the desired letters patent confirming the voluntary gift, in conformity with the Assembly's deliberations.[3] One month later they were empowered to seek the registration of these letters from the President of the Parlement of Paris,[4] which were granted on January 30, 1781, and registered on March 13.[5] Similar letters and registration were to be procured authorizing four per cent loans to amortize these gifts.[6]

On behalf of the Assembly and to seek the registration of laws already promulgated, Talleyrand had other contacts with the Parlements. The Agents were asked by the Assembly of 1780 to appeal to the Paris Parlement for the registration of a law of 1769 which provided that unions of benefices contracted for the profit of bishoprics, cathedral chapters, seminaries, hospitals, and colleges were immune from legal suits.[7] They were also charged to secure before the several Parlements the registration of letters patent fixing the number of benefices classed as *gradués,* that is, for which the possession of university study and an academic degree were prerequisite.[8] They were charged to secure the prompt registration of a decree protecting the Church's lesser tithes.[9] The Assembly of 1782 asked the Agents to solicit the king for a new text of a law to end abuses originating in unfavorable decisions of the Toulouse Parlement depriving the Church of traditional tithe revenues on its domain, rights confirmed by earlier legislation.[10]

Similarly, the Agents were charged to renew the guarantees of laws which had not been observed strictly since their promulgation. Against the forced purchase of salt imposed on the clergy despite its confirmed *(gabelle)* exemptions, Talleyrand was charged to seek a new edict to confirm the legal guarantees of former legislation against both forced salt purchases and the searching of ecclesiastical premises for any reason by *gabelle* collectors.[11] Finally, the Assemblies of 1780 and 1782 commissioned Talleyrand to seek the codification of proposed legislation against evil books, particularly the works of Voltaire and against the composition, printing, sale, and distribution of prohibited books; and for the policing of all bookstores, reading rooms, and public fairs displaying literature coming into France.[12]

A second segment of Talleyrand's legislative responsibility concerned the promulgation of texts of laws drawn up from the clergy's *cahier* or requests for the revival or enforcement of statutes already on the books. To obtain these, the Agents were expected to petition the king.[13] As has already been seen, Louis XVI was evasive, dilatory, and unwilling to give satisfaction to the appeals of the First Estate. Often he did not reply from one five-year Assembly to the next. It occasionally occurred that the king possessed the *cahiers* of two Assemblies at the same time.[14] Talleyrand secured Louis' response to the *cahier* of 1775 for the Assembly of 1780. The *cahier* of 1780 he received in record time, on November 23, 1782, only two years after the Assembly of 1780 submitted it.[15] This *cahier* was obviously made ready in time to conciliate the clergy convened in extraordinary session for purposes of voting the king an extra gift of 15,000,000 *l*. In the report of his Agency in 1785, Talleyrand outlined the ten points of the 1780 *cahier* which he had solicited on behalf of the clergy. Examination of these points is illuminating, for they embodied the important litigations in which Talleyrand intervened in defense of the spiritual and temporal jurisdiction of the First Estate and reflect the difficulties encountered by the clergy in realizing the guarantees of the king's laws in the parishes. The remarks of the king or his Keeper of Seals were appended to each point.[16]

The first case concerned the possession of benefices by clerics denied the *visa*. The king ordered the enforcement of the Edict of April, 1695, which stipulated that only bishops could confer canonic institution. The second forbade any ecclesiastic to be provided a benefice with charge of souls secured either through patents from Rome or by resignation in favor without first having exercised sacerdotal functions for two years and without having been approved for confession or preaching for at least four years. In presenting this before the Assembly of 1785, Talleyrand asked that, for the "spiritual good of the people and the honor of the clergy," a system of competitive selection should be introduced among all candidates seeking benefices with charge of souls in order to assure the recruitment of the worthiest clerics. The Assembly greeted this proposal with enthusiasm, and the Committee of Religion and Jurisdiction drew up a selection plan for the dioceses together with a memorandum recommending it to the Keeper of Seals.[17] Other provisions in the *cahiers* attempted to prevent bigamy, to facilitate the unions of collegiate churches, and to clarify what benefices might be placed in the possession of *gradué* priests. Article eight specified that all curates dependent on benefices united to colleges formerly held by the Jesuits should be placed under the authority of the local bishop. To this the king's minister replied that he did not have the required details to judge the situation properly. Article nine was aimed at abolishing all alienations. The clergy stipuated that, no longer able to extend its patrimony, it must do all in its power to stop the "dissipation of Church property" and the multiple abuses of clerics who wantonly alienated temporalities in their charge. The law which Talleyrand sought would make it impossible for the clergy, individuals as well as corporations, to initiate any steps leading to alienation or loans engaging the property or revenues of churches as collateral without the full knowledge and approval of the local bishop.[18] The king left this point unanswered. Nor did Louis XVI reply to the tenth plea, a renewal of the laws of 1686 and 1768 which provided for the payment of vicars by local tithe owners.

Talleyrand exercised independent initiative in proposing promulgation of new statutes on behalf of the clergy. Nowhere is this better evident than in his attempt to quash a law of May 12, 1782, regulating the entry of vital statistics in the baptismal registry and to secure more favorable legislation in its place. Baptismal records were but one portion of the civil register (marriage and burial being the others) whose custody the Church jealously guarded until the Revolution. By Article Four of the hitherto prevailing law of April, 1736, the parish priest, upon authority of the higher clergy, regarded himself free to enter in the registers whatever facts regarding parents and children he believed pertinent.[19] This power had been subject to frequent abuse and resulted in the registry of humiliating and discriminatory data, especially against Protestants.

The plight of the Huguenots is well known. After 1685 they were subject to four hundred discriminatory laws, ordinances, decrees, and declarations; barred from the professions; limited in their employment; subject to proselytizing harassments of local clergy and judges; and forced to deliver their children to the Church to be baptized and educated. Indeed, as has been recently maintained, they were "second class citizens . . . deserted by their pastors, suspected by their neighbors, bullied by the authorities, separated from their children, living under a cloud of fear and apprehension."[20] Although some Protestants in the course of the century successfully evaded the obligation of delivering their children for baptism, no valid birth or, for that matter, marriage and sepulchral records could be entered except by the parish priest.

Commonly inserted references in the baptismal registry regarding illegitimate marriages and bastardy ("of an alleged marriage unknown to us" or "of a father and mother of the So-Called Reformed Religion") were injurious to children and calumnious to parents.[21] In the text of the law of 1782 the king acknowledged that priests had abused their authority over the registry by erecting themselves as judges of the "facts and merits of the depositions of parents and godparents whose personal feelings . . . by different clauses or enunciations" resulted in the recording of prejudicial data.[22] The 1782 law reinterpreted Article Four of the 1736 law and forbade clergy to insert on their own authority anything contrary to the facts communicated by those bringing children for baptism. The Assembly of 1782 strenuously opposed this assault on its privileges, attempted to get an immediate stay of execution, and charged the Agents to seek the revocation of this legislation on grounds that it imperiled the Church's immemorial custodianship of the civil register.[23]

We may hastily summarize Talleyrand's lengthy and detailed arguments before the Assembly of 1785 on behalf of the clergy's custody of the civil register.[24] The priest is a public minister holding the confidence both of Church and State. Acting in the public interest, he fulfilled with scrupulous exactitude and truth the sacred charge of recording the birth of citizens. Priests never knowingly inserted falsehoods. Charges of discriminatory emendations and illegitimacy were calumnies raised by enemies of the faith. It was equally false and scandalous that priests in charge of the records were illiterate, intolerant, and animated by hatred and distrust, and that the registers were full of strikeouts, erasures, and marginations,[25] even though the new law credited these beliefs by reducing rather than enlarging the influence of the parish priest. By the new law the priest could no longer be responsible for the veracity of facts entered in his registers or the probity of persons delivering children for baptism. "The remedy prescribed by the declaration is more pernicious than the malady itself," and in attempting to reform "a very rare abuse," the law provides abuses more numerous and grave. Moreover, the 1782 law was but one part of a movement to wrench the civil register from the hands of the clergy whose historic rights were attested by centuries of royal edicts.

While working to suppress the law of 1782, Talleyrand encountered suits before the Parlements lodged by legitimately married Protestants who protested the prejudicial insertions of the clergy and refused to bring their children to the Catholic Church for baptism.[26] The Agent advised the Bishop of La Rochelle, who faced such a case in defense of his diocesan clergy, and who in 1787 was to take the lead among the bishops in defying the Protestant civil legislation, to tread cautiously before the anti-episcopal Parlements and to instruct his priests to ask Protestants nothing other than what they asked Catholics.[27] Judicial decisions rendered in their favor, he maintained, were fatal precedents threatening the "disruption . . . of the sacred depots of society." Fearing the usurpation of the Church's civil authority, on the one hand, and the reversal of public law and opinion in favor of a minority excluded from both religious and civil liberty, on the other, Talleyrand urged the suppression of the 1782 law and the readoption of the 1736 law which assured full authority over the baptismal registry. A royal edict of July 20, 1787 provided for the execution of Article Four of the 1736 law as it stood prior to 1782.[28]

For two reasons the recapture of control over the baptismal registry by this edict was of relatively minor consequence for the Church. First, it was virtually nullified by the famous Protestant laws of November, 1787, four months later. This legislation acknowledged the injustices inflicted on the Protestants who by 1750 were gradually realizing progress in the public practice of religion, the increase of synods and recruitment of pastors, an increasingly favorable position before law and justice, and widespread sympathy through the writings of the Philosophers.[29] These factors in large measure explain the promulgation of the 1782 statute in the first place. The law of November, 1787, made possible by the writings and agitation of Malesherbes (who wrote two powerful papers on the marriage of Protestants in 1785 and 1786), Rulhière, Lafayette, Breteuil, and Rabaut de Saint-Etienne, removed the Protestants' "civil death" by permitting legalized marriage outside the Catholic Church and the recording of marriage, baptism, and death bans in the appropriate registers before either *curé* or local judge without reference to religion.[30] The second reason is that the clergy's Assembly of 1788, deeply disturbed by the 1787 legislation and actively engaged in its repeal, feared the eventual loss of the coveted privilege of the civil registry, already breached by these laws, and petitioned Louis XVI for a new law stronger than the 1736 statute.[31]

Agent-General as Servant of Clergy 151

The second duty of the Agent-General on behalf of the whole clergy was to act as its courier to keep the provinces informed of issues and enactments both of the Assembly and the civil government and to solicit views and information.[32] The earliest regulations of the Agents' office required them to keep the clergy abreast of developments of interest to the dioceses of France and to their priests by "pastoral letters, memoranda, and instructions" sent to the bishops and the Diocesan and Metropolitan Syndics.[33] The easiest way of communicating information efficiently and uniformly was through printed circular letters. Most letters were sent in two versions: one to the bishop, containing forms of address and information meant exclusively for the episcopate; and another to the Syndics, who were to communicate its contents, chiefly temporal, to the clergy of the diocese. All letters were signed by both Agents and sent out by the Secretariat.[34]

The circular letters were of two kinds, reflecting the two sides of the Agent's role—as messenger and poll-taker. One, sent from Paris, gave information about Church and State. It may be divided into the three sub-units of edicts and laws passed in favor of the clergy, of financial matters, and of ceremonial functions. The second circular requested information, opinions, and local usages from the dioceses to secure data needed by the Assembly for effective policy and legislation.

One hundred and forty signed circular letters survive the Talleyrand-Boisgelin Agency.[35] In brief analysis an attempt will be made to determine how they fulfilled the Agents' responsibility to keep provincial churches informed, to provide for their welfare, and to enforce the Assembly's statutes within each reserve.

The Assembly required the Agents to publicize "edicts, declarations, and decrees rendered in favor of the clergy."[36] By a circular dated November 8, 1780 the clergy was informed of the current state of the *foi et hommage* dispute with the Duke of Orleans together with news of the recently-granted five year postponement.[37] Another circular announced the king's replies to the clergy's *cahiers*.[38] Others reproduced decisions of the Assemblies, recapitulated important problems resolved and pending, and summarized enactments and contracts between Church and State and edicts and laws binding on the dioceses.

In economic affairs the letters fulfilled an important service. They informed each diocese of the financial engagements taken in the name of the whole Estate and the means of their reimbursement, together with permission and instructions enabling the diocese to negotiate loans to acquit its assigned share of taxes. Circulars of October 25 and November 8, 1780 authorized four per cent loans as in 1775.[39] The *don gratuit* affected the clergy of each diocese, since each benefice holder contributed through his assigned *décime*. A circular of December 11, 1780 outlined the procedures involved in engaging loans on behalf of the Church and the role of the Diocesan Syndics, who received all revenues of the diocese before turning them over to the Provincial Receiver and Receiver-General.[40] A circular of June 21, 1781 authorized the Diocesan Syndics, in conformity with the Assembly's enactments, to borrow at four per cent all necessary additional sums to acquit the *don gratuit*. It also printed the clauses governing the payment of the clergy's gift to the king as provided by contract.[41] A circular of November 4, 1782 announced that loans for the Assembly's gift of 1782 would be taken at five per cent.[42] On April 3, 1783 Talleyrand sent the Syndics a copy of the contract signed with the king in 1782 and his letters patent confirming the clergy's gift.[43] Others revealed the extent of the clergy's economic commitments and the state of its fiscal finances.

Letters were also used to announce the distribution to bishops and diocesan centers of newly published official documents—proceedings of the Assemblies, final reports of the Agents-General, and the fourteen-volume *Recueil des actes, titres, et mémoires du clergé*[44] —of paramount importance in keeping the dioceses informed of their rights. Letters of September 7, 1783 announced the availability of the printed proceedings of the Assemblies of 1780 and 1782, and one of December 10, 1781 announced the reports of the Agents of 1775-1780.[45] Each bishop and diocesan officer could receive a copy by signing and returning a receipt enclosed with his circular.[46]

A fourth purpose of the communicative circular letter announced forthcoming Assemblies and ceremonies. As already observed the Agents had the obligation to prepare the convocation of the General Assembly, eight to nine months in advance of its inauguration, by calling for the meeting of the Provincial Assemblies which voted its membership. The Agents sent out letters reprinting the king's order of convocation and inviting the metropolitans to call into session the Provincial Assembly of their province. Archbishops also received copies of another letter, directed to their episcopal suffragans, indicating the convocation of the Provincial Assembly.[47] Talleyrand's

Agent-General as Servant of Clergy 153

circular for the Extraordinary Assembly of October, 1782 was sent out June 26,[48] two days before his important letter to Vergennes. That for the Ordinary Assembly of May 23, 1785, was sent on August 21, 1784.[49] In others he requested the metropolitan to send him, as soon as possible, the names of the deputies elected to the General Assembly, indicating that each was to be provided with credentials in good form as stipulated by the General Assembly.[50]

As regards ceremonies the Agents invited by circular the prelates of the kingdom to a *Te Deum* commemorating various public occasions.[51] They transmitted invitations of the king together with supplementary information on ceremonials, the extent of the clergy's participation, and the invitation of the Archbishop of Paris to receive all bishops in his palace during their sojourn in the capital. One letter dated October 24, 1781 announced a ceremony to commemorate the birth of the Dauphin; one of November 24, 1781 a victory over the English in America; one of December 4, 1783 the proclamation of peace; and another of March 30, 1785 the birth of the Duke of Normandy.[52]

The circular served also to notify the episcopate of the death of a fellow or former prelate, that is, a cardinal, archbishop, bishop, or non-consecrated bishop.[53] The Agents requested prayers in the dioceses for the soul of the departed churchman by the traditional phrase "we beg you to order, in the manner you judge most fitting, prayers for the rest of his soul."[54] The circular letter was also used for announcements of funeral services of members of the royal family and for the king's wish that all prelates assist in Paris.[55] The only such event during Talleyrand's Agency commemorated the death of Empress Maria-Theresa of Austria. A letter of May 26, 1781 invited the prelates to participate.[56] Similar announcements were to be made of the coronation or illness of the king. News of papal Bulls governing jubilees were also sent out by letter.[57]

The second kind of circular letter served as a medium for obtaining rather than diffusing information—for securing opinions, suggestions, and conditions in the dioceses with a view to future legislation or to guiding the Church on certain questions. During Talleyrand's Agency such letters were devoted to temporal matters and education.

The Assembly of 1780 charged the Agents to write a letter on the *foi et hommage* informing the clergy of the stay of execution granted it.[58] The First Estate was given three years to collect titles and declarations proving its immunity from this feudal duty. The dioceses were requested not only to locate all titles in their possession proving immunity but also to give an account of their properties, titles, and founding charters to the commissions of the Assembly charged with the surveillance of the *foi et hommage*. In a letter of March 5, 1781 Talleyrand requested that they submit their titles promptly to the Assembly.[59]

Another circular involved the *portion congrue*. The Assembly of 1780 charged Archbishop Boisgelin's Committee for the Temporal to investigate the means of augmenting the established 500 *l*. It wished to ascertain the local prices of twenty-five *setiers* of wheat, used as a measure of the cost of living, whether the figure of some of the provinces was less or more than the 500 *l*. currently assigned (used to determine "honest subsistence") and the actual salary of the *curés congruistes* of their diocese. It charged the Agents on October 6 to solicit the views of the bishops on the means to resolve this problem. The Agents' circular dated November 8, 1780 asked that all data relative to local changes and variations of prices, including the views of the Diocesan Bureaus, be sent before January 1, 1785.[60]

Before the Assembly of 1782, two years later, Talleyrand reviewed the disappointing response to this circular.[61] On behalf of the Assembly the Archbishop of Bordeaux, Champion de Cicé, commissioned the Agent to submit another letter renewing the instructions of the Assembly of 1780 and stipulating that the bishops were to present their views on the *portion congrue* to their Provincial Assemblies, whose resolutions would then be brought to the Assembly of 1785 by their selected representatives.[62] In conformity with this order Talleyrand sent out a circular on May 10, 1783 reminding the bishops of the deliberations of the Assemblies of 1780 and 1782.[63]

Two letters were sent out to secure data on the state of education in France. On September 20, 1780, Archbishop Dulau, Chairman of the Committee for Religion and Jurisdiction, reported to the Assembly that the rights of the Church in regulating public instruction were being impeded by an edict of February, 1763 which, upon the fall of the Jesuits, conferred important administrative powers in education to judges and magistrates.[64] This challenge, added to what, by the prelate's admission, was the "deplorable state" of educational institutions in France, impelled the Assembly to secure legislation fortifying the clergy's traditional right of supervising public instruction. He wished to obtain information on local conditions governing the organization of schools and universities, the choice of teachers, the discipline and supervision of studies, and the status of temporal and spiritual administration. The Agents were to write on behalf of the Assembly to the bishops of France and to report their findings to the next Assembly.

Six days later Talleyrand read to the Assembly the draft of a letter he proposed to send. It was immediately approved and was mailed on November 8, 1780.[65] This document was remarkable at once for its precision and breadth of inquiry. The Agent hoped that the data secured by it could lay the foundations for the reform of national education in France. In nine questions he requested a wide range of opinion on the "plan of education most proper to make religion loved and respected, to conserve the purity of morals, to encourage competition, to give a taste for sciences, and to render pupils capable of fulfilling in society the functions to which they may be destined." He asked for the number, quality, and classes of schools and universities in each diocese; the selection and merit of their programs of study, teachers, and administration; abuses in their governing statutes; the character of their temporal endowment; the results of the legislation abolishing Jesuit schools; abusive or useless practices in education; the conferral of degrees; the prudence of increasing clerical control over education; and suggestions for a system of recruitment of teachers and principals. It is likely that the information assembled from the dioceses of the realm, together with personal interest in one of the most challenging tasks consigned to his care by the clergy, contributed significantly to the ideas behind Talleyrand's own plan of national education presented to the National Assembly in September, 1791.[66]

Because of the inadequate initial response to this circular during the first two years of its distribution, the Agent recommended before the Assembly of 1782 that another letter be sent to the dioceses to secure their views, because of the "extreme importance of the matter . . . closely allied to the cause of religion, morals, and patriotism [and] whose happy success would console us for the evils which afflict us."[67] The Assembly ordered the Agents to resubmit their circular of 1780 and to exhort the bishops to return their responses by July 1, 1784, thus enabling the Agents to evaluate the returns and prepare an instructive report for the Assembly of 1785 embodying their own views and research.[68] Though this letter was sent to the bishops on May 7, 1783,[69] no report was made in 1785, and educational reform was lost behind the other more pressing temporal issues which faced the clergy on the eve of the Revolution.

The circular also enabled the clergy to combat incredulity. As has been seen, Archbishop Dulau convinced the Assembly of 1780 to encourage by subsidy the composition of works of religious devotion and refutation to combat heresy and the subversive doctrines of the Philosophers. To this end, a circular letter was sent to the prelacy inviting their Provincial Assemblies each five years to communicate to the General Assembly a résumé of the progress of "ecclesiastical sciences," together with the names of living authors and a précis of their works. The most worthy were to be rewarded from the Budget of New Converts, enriched for this purpose in 1782 by 30,000 *l*.[70] In their circular the Agents stipulated that this information should be returned by October, 1784.[71]

In principle the circular letters were intended to enlighten every clerical element of the dioceses. If in practice this happened, it was done only through the intermediary of the bishops and Syndics, the only parties who received them. Talleyrand took a strong hand in keeping secret the circulars addressed to the bishops. In several instances these letters had fallen into the hands of disgruntled *curés* and contributed to serious disciplinary disorders. The confidential matters contained in the bishops' circulars were not meant for the eyes of the lower clergy, who were to receive them as interpreted by the bishop. In a letter to the Bishop of Châlons-sur-Marne Talleyrand expressed indignation at negligence which permitted episcopal letters to circulate among his priests: "Our circular letters are not written to be known to the *curés* with the same arguments we believe necessary to use in addressing the bishops . . . you will recall what we had the honor of pointing out already, that our letters must not be communicated except to those persons whose ministry appears necessary to you for the execution of [a] project, and these persons alone are the Diocesan Syndics and chamber."[72]

That each response from the diocese was essential both to retain the bridge of communication between Paris and the provinces and to permit the Assembly to legislate in the interests of the entire clergy is clear in Talleyrand's letter to the Bishop of Tréguier in August, 1783: ". . . it would be very difficult for the Agents to draw up divers systems . . . proposed to us for the next Assembly to judge unless our lords the bishops instruct us of the facility or obstacles these plans might encounter in their areas, and unless they reflect on the resources, needs, and subjects of their dioceses. For our particular work in such matters we place our confidence principally in your zeal and lights."[73]

It is apparent, even from this brief consideration of the circular letter, that its importance cannot be overlooked. Quite aside from the advantages of surveillance and law enforcement within the First Estate, it afforded a means of direct personal communication between Paris and each parish in the realm. Each diocese had its direct relationship to the central clergy. Each had a chance to voice its views and to make sure the Assembly continued to legislate in the interests of the entire body. To Talleyrand the circulars were indispensable if the clergy was to remain informed and united for the sake of its spiritual responsibilities and the defense of its domain. His Diocesan Syndic Plan, to be considered in the last section of this book, envisaged an extension of this vital representative principle.

The Agent-General was also the legal adviser of the clergy in the 40,000 parishes of the kingdom. By prelates and *curés* alike he was asked to clarify immunities, to define authority provided in ecclesiastical and lay statutes, to approve positions vis-à-vis parishioners, and to consider requests for aid. He imparted to clergymen his official and personal opinions, and he explained their responsibilities. When necessary, he denied the validity of a cleric's case or his attempts to secure a favor or exemption. He insisted always that ecclesiastics must inform themselves of their rights in the interest of retaining contested privileges. He encouraged the solution of less pressing and local problems by the clergy without interference from either Agents or Assembly.

In only a small proportion of cases reported to him did Talleyrand actually intervene before ministers and secular tribunals. He frequently refused to risk the capital and good name of the clergy, the efficacy of his office, and his precious time on ill-founded or personal claims. These views he stated openly and repeatedly before the Assembly of 1782 and practiced consistently. In important quarrels between clerical parties Talleyrand occasionally acted as impartial referee and pacificator.

It required prodigious energy and a huge personal correspondence to act on the numerous memoirs and protests which came to his desk from clergy all over the kingdom—from thick discourses and petitions to increase the *portion congrue* to private demands for personal monetary compensation, from requests to receive the complete *Gallia*

Christiana to anti-papal diatribes, from tracts disputing episcopal supremacy to those proposing agricultural reform and "The Perfection of Linens in France."[74] It required, too, voluminous correspondence to guide clerical contestants, to direct their suits, and to provide them needed legal and technical information. It was clear that the burden of important affairs of temporal administration and the supervision of the Assembly's central agencies made it impossible to act on each problem brought to him. Yet, it will be recalled, Talleyrand's record in correspondence dispatched is all the more remarkable for the attention given to the large number of individual cases.

The obligation of the Agents to receive all requests, petitions, and protests of the clergy was a central reason for the establishment of their office in 1579.[75] By far the most significant portion of pleas received by Talleyrand requested either the clarification of jurisdiction, spiritual and lay, according to statutes of both Church and State or advice on steps to be taken in pending court actions. In answering these requests, the Agents might send five memoirs in a single missive. There are numerous examples in the Agency's archives of three to seven memoirs sent at the same time and to the same recipient.[76]

It was Talleyrand's task to decide for uninformed and disputant clerical parties which ecclesiastical body or persons and which secular tribunals or officers enjoyed proper competence. To the Dean of the Chapter of Belley he answered that the authority of the bishop alone was sufficient to oblige all clerics to participate in a divine service or public procession, though they were not subject to his authority in private processions of the Chapter or collegiate churches.[77] To the Bishop of La Rochelle Talleyrand confirmed that it was the bishop who was the head of all hospitals in his episcopal city.[78] The Archbishop of Tours wished to confirm his authority before proposing a change in ritual for his diocese and asked whether the consent of the chapter was necessary. Talleyrand replied that because of the ritual's twofold character, as dogma and as ceremonial rite, the chapter need not be consulted about the first but should be about the second, since it was jointly responsible for the public cult.[79]

The Bishop of Le Mans asked whether tax commissioners might enter a convent at will. The Agent replied that this practice was incompatible with conventional usage which required the bishop or public judge to give permission to any public officers before entering ecclesiastical establishments. Without this permission the occupants had the right to refuse entry.[80] To a *curé* in Berry who had written to ask who should decide the rules governing the preliminary possession of a prebend given a new collator, the Agent replied that these powers rested with the chapter.[81] The Chapter of Avranches asked if it could elect a member to the Assembly of Municipal Notables. Talleyrand replied that for the sake of peace and conciliation the electors should defer to the legitimate ecclesiastical authority, "the first ecclesiastical body of the diocese," the Diocesan Bureau.[82] In matters involving secular authority, Talleyrand wrote the Diocesan Syndic of Evreux that, though his chapter must have recourse to the Rouen Parlement for legal authorization to procure a loan of 75,000 *l.* for the reconstruction of the local seminary, the Parlement had no right to influence the chapter's deliberations and administration.[83]

Lower clergy raised questions about the plenitude of their powers. The *Curé* of Bargemond (Diocese of Fréjus) asked whether a priest was obliged by law to give a noble advance notice of a coming *Te Deum*. The Agent replied that this was not required beyond public announcement of the forthcoming service.[84] A canon of Corbeille (Archdiocese of Paris) asked to what degree the chapter was responsible for payment of a fellow canon studying theology in the seminary of Chartres, how much should be paid by it, and from what revenues. Talleyrand replied that the amount was dependent on the usages of the chapter and that the tithes and the *lods-et-ventes* (revenues due a seigneur at the transfer of a vassal's property) were particularly desirable for such purposes.[85]

A *curé* Charlin complained that the inhabitants of his village convoked a town assembly by sounding the bells of his church without permission. The Agent observed that in principle the bells belonged to the community. Therefore in public emergencies and other extraordinary causes it might use them without his authorization.[86] However, in cases touching divine service, processions, or public prayers, the community must ask permission. The Agent added a note of caution, as he frequently did, not to antagonize the secular authority by an unpopular stand: "I can only invite you to conciliate minds by mildness and good conduct."[87]

To an obviously overworked *curé* of Sillards (Diocese of Poitiers) who asked how many communicants were needed before his bishop would consent to establish a vicariate, difficult to obtain from bishop and tithe owner alike (and "for which [the *curé*] had to display great energy and give proof of persevering tenacity,"[88]), Talleyrand replied five-hundred generally, depending on the conditions of the roads and other geographical factors.[89] The Agent received an inquiry regarding special favors conferred on the clerical servants of royal princes. He notified a priest of Montigny (Diocese of Rouen) that whereas the prince was granted special honors in the blessed bread, holy water, a seat in the choir, and incense, his clerical servants had rights only to the blessed bread and a distinguished place in the choir.[90]

Several clerics wished to know who was legally bound to contribute to the payment of the *portion congrue* of a new parish. Talleyrand replied that every tithe owner owed a share in this obligation according to his income.[91] In answering a query as to whether the estate of a deceased regular priest should devolve on his parents or his order, the Agent replied that by law it must revert to the order in which the priest had been a member.[92]

Talleyrand devoted much energy to clarifying fiscal and feudal immunities guaranteed the Church. Questions were always asked about direct taxes, especially the *capitation* and *taille*. In one letter Talleyrand quoted the royal edicts of 1701 and 1710 which freed the clergy of France from the payment of personal taxes for whatever motive.[93] To another he reiterated this right "constantly enjoyed by the clergy of France" for all ecclesiastics "engaged in holy orders or living clerically."[94] He gave a similar reply in the matter of the *taille:* "It is usual that the ecclesiastical order and its benefice holders are exempt from all personal imposition on their property."[95] The same was true of the *vingtième*. The Agent assured all inquirers of the clergy's exemption of this tax on all clerical property.[96]

Clergymen wrote Paris asking whether feudal services could be extorted from titulars of ecclesiastical lands. Talleyrand replied, "property belonging to churches is exempt from all feudal servitude to the domain."[97] An order of Benedictine nuns in Orleans inquired whether they were subject to the *foi et hommage* because of the controversy in that province. Talleyrand informed them of the recent stay of execution granted the clergy.[98] There were also questions of the clergy's exemptions from the *franc fief,* a tax paid on inherited real estate.[99] The Agent informed the clergy of its exemption of the *franc fief* on property inherited by the Church after 1777. He advised a prior to present a receipt of his inheritance bearing a post-1777 date in order to insure himself against paying this tax.[100]

Innumerable inquiries concerned the question of who was to pay the costs of maintaining and repairing edifices of the cult. The Edict of April, 1695 obliged the tithe owners to maintain parish churches and presbytery houses, though it freed them from major repair costs.[101] The negligence of tithe owners was notorious, and, especially in Flanders, Brittany, and Champagne, resulted in deplorable consequences for their churches. *Cahiers* "almost everywhere" (130 out of 150 published by Sagnac and St. Leger)[102] deplored the dilapidation of ecclesiastical edifices and voiced the indignation of impecunious *curés* and inhabitants (whose tithes paid their upkeep) who had been forced to sacrifice in order to pay for major repairs, needed because of faulty maintenance. The higher clergy was alarmed at once by the *curés'* demands that the tithe owners be forced to pay these costs, which had been ordered by decrees of the Parlements of Provence in 1772, and by letters patent issued in Flanders in 1773 and 1784 assigning repairs to the tithe owners. The Assembly of 1785 tried without success to have these decrees withdrawn.[103]

The Agent's stand here naturally reflected the policy of the hierarchy. To the Bishop of Châlons-sur-Marne Talleyrand wrote that repairs of a church must be paid by parishioners as receivers of the sacrament and divine service. These rights were confirmed by the king's contracts with the clergy.[104] To a *curé* in St. Quentin (Diocese of Laon) Talleyrand replied that the maintenance costs of churches, however, must be paid by the clergy regardless of its income category, since the faithful were responsible only for "major repairs."[105]

The Agents reminded clerics of still other lesser corporate immunities. The clergy was exempted from the excise on wine when this product constituted its sole or main income.[106] It was also free from the burial tax levied on the populace for place in the cemetery, since ecclesiastics were interred within the church.[107] The Assembly of 1780 charged Talleyrand with the case of a priest of Châlons-sur-Marne who had been denied his right to receive gratis his share of community wood. Instead, the local seigneur subjected the priest to the payment of the *droit de feu,* the tax paid by each citizen for wood taken from the seigneurial forest. The Agent informed the priest to press for the recognition of his rights. By his residence and the nature of his functions he was the first citizen of the community, entitled to all the communal privileges claimed by others without payment of feudal excises.[108]

Personal immunities were also subject to question. One of these included the *patrouille,* or patrol, and the lodging of soldiers in ecclesiastical property. Both canon and temporal laws insured full freedom from this "personal servitude to which persons consecrated to the service of the altar have never been subjected."[109] The Agent informed the Bishop of Sarlat that an edict of 1774 extended the clerical immunity from military service, patrol, and billeting of army personnel to the body of servants of the episcopate and the lower clergy.[110]

Besides reminding clerics of their personal immunities, Talleyrand frequently instructed them on how legally to escape demands for payment of taxes by exploiting the Church's corporate exemption. He also outlined the conditions they had to fulfill to enjoy certain economic benefits. To one priest he suggested the means to inherit the money of a deceased cleric without being subject to the *droit d'amortissement,* the tax paid the seigneur upon acquisition of landed property.[111] To the *Curé* of Saints (Diocese of Auxerre) the Agent explained the local customs to be observed before he could receive property left him by a clerical colleague.[112] Talleyrand instructed another inquirer that the Church was often compelled to pay the *droit d'amortissement* along with other domain duties even in constructing edifices for the instruction of children or for the care of the sick, "which have often placed obstacles in the way of works of charity."[113] The Abbey of Hautvilliers (Diocese of Reims) complained of having been assessed by the township for local repairs. The Agent wrote that the forced payments of these repairs constituted "an attack on the privileges and immunities of the clergy." The Abbey might be relieved of this charge by immediately informing the local Intendant.[114]

Talleyrand sent clerics minute instructions on how they might avoid payment of certain duties. One case involved the demand of the *foi et hommage* which came up before the renewal of the clergy's stay of execution. Before signing any declaration recognizing the claims of his seigneur, the priest was to search all papers "as exactly as possible" to ascertain whether he or his predecessors had at any time signed a similar declaration demanded by the seigneur which would make the cleric subject to the feudal demands of his lord. Should he find nothing, the *curé* was instructed "to entreat [the seigneur] amicably" to produce the declaration which he must possess to verify that his demand was not an "innovation." Should

Agent-General as Servant of Clergy 163

he refuse this "way of reconciliation," the cleric was not to yield to his demands. Should the seigneur take proceedings against him, it would then be easier to advise him on "the course . . . to take."[115] To another canon of Chartres, Talleyrand explained the legislation regarding the *foi et hommage,* instructing him to inspect carefully his church's titles of fiefs, incomes, and acquisitions in order to establish their non-feudal character.[116] In a similar case, declining to intervene personally, Talleyrand spelled out the procedures to be followed in presenting an appeal before a secular court.[117]

As still another aspect of his advisory capacity to the clergy, the Agent reviewed the merits of cases for adjudication submitted by individual priests and communicated his opinions regarding chances of success. The *Curé* of Trannes (Diocese of Troyes) wished to take to court a plea to gain more revenue from his tithe owner, the monastery which paid him, partly in cash and partly in food. Talleyrand replied that by the salary and provisions accorded the *Curé,* the monastery was justified in refusing additional payment. His case would stand little chance of success in court: "There is ground to believe you would succumb."[118] A clerical workman wished to appeal to the local Parlement to recover back salary owed him by the Church. Talleyrand stated that on the strength of his case he had no chance for victory in any appeal.[119] In other instances, where it was not a case of winning or losing but supplying information regarding court actions, the Agent cautioned priests and parishes that lengthy litigations and appeals involved heavy costs which could ruin them, or in his own words, "it would cost you dear to raise suits, prepare and pursue a judgment, expenses which are beyond your resources."[120]

Drawing from large experience in appeals, Talleyrand passed out helpful hints which the clergy might adopt for the success of pleas. He warned the Bishop of Châlons-sur-Marne that the subordinate whom he charged to submit a plea on his behalf should watch his language and excise from his brief such terms as "extravagant pretension," "outrageous vexations," "frightful paradox," "criminal concussion," and "an infinity of similar expressions which could only prejudice his case." He continued, "It is by solid means that you must construct a legitimate defense. Heat and passion have ruined the best cases . . . I therefore beg you, Monseigneur, to ask him to change the style of his memorandum, to limit himself to a simple exposition of the facts, and to place more measure and moderation in the development of his case . . . basically nothing seems to me worse founded than pretension."[121]

To the *Curé* of Blaize (Diocese of Langres) the Agent again strongly recommended the use of restrained language in appeals: "I cannot insist too much that you order your lawyer to use more measured terms in your defense."[122] The *Cure's* case was pending before the *Cour des aides,* where, according to Talleyrand, nothing was more perilous than false pretensions and novelties.[123]

Talleyrand also gave his opinion to clerics who asked for it. He replied to the Bishop of Le Mans regarding the prudence of electing to the Diocesan Bureau the brother of a deputy already there. The lawyers of the clergy with whom he discussed this proposal opposed it because similar cases in the past had always occasioned trouble.[124] The Bishop of Rieux asked the Agent about punishing non-residing and absentee clerics. The Agent answered that many ecclesiastics were absent not only on Sundays but on other solemn occasions from the churches in which they held benefices. For such residence abuses he suggested they should be punished by the deprivation of their prebendal incomes.[125]

The Agent also passed on advice helpful to the dioceses. He informed a priest of Gaunot that in order to avoid any trouble with government officials, it was important to exercise great care in keeping public records and to pay the stamp-tax *(droit de contrôle)* on them, since these were subject to periodic inspection by State authorities.[126] He counseled the Diocesan Syndic of Agde to retain communications in important affairs which past Agents had sent together with those still to be sent "so that they can serve to inform your successors."[127]

Much as Talleyrand was anxious to conserve the privileges of his order in legitimate cases, he was stern in reproving clergy for illegal exemptions. He did this in order that the Church might not squander its strength and prestige on unimportant cases. Talleyrand wrote a *curé* in the Diocese of St. Claude that he had no legitimate grounds for seeking an exemption of his choir from the charges of the tithes: "there is no title which exempts you from this charge."[128] To an Abbé Raforin he wrote that he could not escape the *droit d'amortissement* on a legacy received in return for saying Mass for a departed parishioner. Since he received the grant as a private person, rather than in the name of the Church, he no longer enjoyed the immunity of mortmain and accordingly no longer enjoyed the clergy's corporate exemption.[129]

With the same forcefulness the Agent opposed cases of illegal ecclesiastical property exemptions. To a priest who wished to free his farm and garden from the *taille,* granted normally only on the Church domain, he wrote, "This is not ecclesiastical property by its nature . . . the privilege of exemption applies only to property belonging to the Church."[130] Nor could the *taille* exemption be claimed, he wrote a *curé* of Evreux, where private property was accepted by donation, succession, or purchase.[131]

Talleyrand also rejected innumerable petitions of clerics seeking exemptions for ecclesiastical or non-ecclesiastical personnel. The *Curé* of Champmotteux (Archdiocese of Sens) wished to free his gardener from military service. Talleyrand replied that the law exempted only servants rendering personal service to ecclesiastics.[132] To the administrators of the Collège de St. Brieuc he wrote that the office of clerk of ecclesiastical records, by Church law and practice, could be maintained only by a cleric. Hence the Collège was denied permission to retain a layman in this post.[133] To the *Curé* of St. Pierre de Mailloc (Diocese of Lisieux) Talleyrand wrote that the clergy was exempted from the *corvée* (road labor), but this could not be applied to sextons or servants.[134]

Some ecclesiastics thought they were immune from costs of legal suits in which they were litigants, costs which they hoped would be sustained by the General Assembly. This misconception the Agent quickly dismissed: "This is by no means the usage [of the Church] . . . besides, the clergy does not have enough funds to sustain in its name all private suits which might interest each benefice holder of the kingdom."[135]

The extensive advisory powers of the Agent-General over the clergy also included censure when this was necessary. He did not hesitate to rebuke clergy for ill-advised acts. Even to the door of the episcopate he occasionally delivered reprimands. He told the Bishop of Montpellier that his decision to remove a case from an ecclesiastical to a secular tribunal was contrary to every law and tradition of the Church.[136] To the Bishop of Châlons-sur-Marne he insisted that certain powers enjoyed by the episcopate, like regulations against working on Sundays, could be held only conjointly with the State.[137] A more serious matter involved the Bishop of Bayeux, who in March, 1781, through the offices of a subordinate, distorted to his advantage a statement of income demanded by Necker for purposes of the land tax *(impôt territorial)* and the newly constituted Provincial Assembly.[138] Talleyrand upbraided the prelate for this dishonest practice: "When one charges someone else with his affairs, one has to be scrupulously truthful . . . [anything] contrary to the truth of the facts must find us free from deception."[139] The Agent wrote to Minister Necker apologizing for this incident.

Occasionally Talleyrand reproved the timorousness of ecclesiastics in cases where their exemptions were incontestable and needed only to be announced to be honored. He wrote to a canon of the Chapter of Sarlat emphasizing that the law against billeting soldiers in episcopal and chapter houses was so well known and honored that he did not have to tolerate the orders of the municipal authorities who ordered the billeting. "A simple protestation against this enterprise . . . would suffice to prevent all further steps which could come as a consequence."[140]

As a last aspect of his advisory responsibilities to the clergy, Talleyrand took the trouble to remind certain clerics that they were presenting cases to him in which neither the Assembly nor its Agency-General could be implicated but which, rather, might easily be satisfied if those in question merely informed themselves and assumed proper initiative. These reminders ranged in consequence from a letter to a canon of Bourganeuf (Diocese of Limoges) on the eve of the Assembly of 1785, in which Talleyrand informed him that he, and not the Abbé de La Rochefoucauld (his predecessor), had occupied the Agency during the past five years,[141] to the frequent exchanges with ecclesiastics in the district of Orleans and Chartres whose feudal titles, incomes, and duties Talleyrand repeatedly urged be studied to combat the claims of the Duke of Orleans for payment of the *foi et hommage*. To the Bishop of Bayeux Talleyrand acknowledged complaints of irregularities in one of his priest's baptismal registry and the manner in which he baptized a Protestant child, which had excited the vigilance of the magistracy. The Agent advised the prelate to inform himself better of the complaints involved against the *curé*. The bishop should not only observe the behavior of his priests but should also ascertain whether they discharged their duties in conformity with diocesan usages.[142]

The lack of proper information too often deprived the clergy of judicial victories. To the Archbishop of Paris Talleyrand wrote that one of his subordinates had never taken the time to read properly the appropriate titles of the law before seeking an exemption from the *droit d'amortissement* on new acquisitions: "Here is the real matter upon which you must insist. I invite M. l'Abbé de Launday to reread with attention the decree . . . he will find in the preambule the real principles of the matter and the means to oppose victoriously the demand of the officials in charge."[143] Talleyrand wrote another cleric that he had no chance for victory in an appeal, because he had not taken the pains to acquaint himself with the law by a careful reading of the appropriate statutes.[144] To the Vicar-General of Verdun (part of the foreign clergy), who sought an exemption from the *droit d'amortissement* on property attached to his house, Talleyrand answered that his chances for success could easily be determined by reading the law: "Take the time to read it with care, and you will convince yourself easily that it is virtually impossible for establishments not of the clergy of France to derive favorable action."[145]

Besides adviser, Talleyrand served frequently as pacificator and arbitrator between dissident groups of clergy or members of the same body. The Agents were interested in their quarrels, because they endangered the tranquillity of the diocese and threatened to spread to other dioceses or wind up before secular tribunals. A good example of Talleyrand's personal involvement was a case of May, 1784 between the Congregation of the Oratory of Orleans and one of its members.[146]

The Congregation opposed the acquisition of a canonicate by one of its regulars, a member of the cathedral chapter. The Oratory believed that the functions of the priest's new office were incompatible at once with the common life, the observance of its rule, and submission to a regular superior. The Congregation therefore wished, upon threat of expulsion, to exact another oath of obedience from the priest in question. The regular refused this, and both parties appealed to the Agent.

Talleyrand attacked the statute of the Congregation responsible for such an unjust demand. By the laws of Church and State any ecclesiastic, regular or secular, with the requisite qualities and capacity was able to accept any type of clerical office despite the wishes of his Congregation "[which] is not a separate religion." If a priest were suited to possess Church office before his entry into the Congregation, he was able to retain it after—"reason alone destroys this statute."

Further, there was no precedent in either Church or State for the present decision. Members of the Oratory "are not held captive by indissoluble chains." Nothing is more conformant with the state of the Oratorian and for the "perfection of the sacerdotal spirit" than the acceptance of an ecclesiastical charge, wholly compatible with the duties to his order. The Church is free at all times to call upon any member whose services are of advantage to it. The Congregation could legally discharge the regular only if he declared that he no longer wished to be associated with it. It could not demand a new oath except as the ecclesiastic's refusal implied an incapacity to possess the benefice in which he had been canonically instituted. It cannot inflict a punishment before the existence of a crime.

The Congregation's statute, Talleyrand concluded, was contrary both to reason and justice and destroyed the rules of equity, the rights of the candidate, the authority of the collator, and public law in matters of benefices. He advised a solution by compromise—that the cleric renounce his canonicate and the Congregation annul its statute. The affair was decided in conformance with this principle. Informed of the Congregation's decision, the Agent wrote that he was "charmed" by the successful compromise, "desiring especially peace and union among the different bodies of the clergy" and the tranquillity of the dioceses.[147]

The Agent's last duty on behalf of the clergy was to intervene before the State in cases of necessity. Where information and counsel were not enough to protect clerical rights, there remained the extensive power of the Agents either as administrators of suits or as actual parties in litigation before ministries and tribunals. The Agents intervened most often before the King's Council, less often before the Grand Council and Paris Parlement, but never before the provincial Parlements.[148] Of interest here are the Agents' appeals, not the presentation before the tribunals of the land of formal cases which were entrusted to the attorneys of the First Estate. Their intercessory efforts were for the most part concerned with fiscal matters and directed against attempts of magistrates and tax collectors to subject the clergy to direct and indirect taxes or to services contrary to the immunity of the First Estate. Where the loss of individual cases threatened the legal principles behind the clergy's universal exemption or in a case where victory would serve to clarify or strengthen it, the Agents intervened. As Talleyrand put it, "We take a real interest . . . in affairs whose consequences could be prejudicial to

Agent-General as Servant of Clergy 169

the clergy if the real principles . . . are not reestablished in all their vigor."[149]

Subjection to the *taille*, from which the First Estate was exempted and about which Talleyrand supplied guidance to many clergy, necessitated frequent intervention from Paris. As requested by the Assembly of 1780, Talleyrand secured exemption for religious in the Diocese of Condom whose farmers were arrested for non-payment on Church lands.[150] A *curé* of Germigny in the *généralité* of Paris was placed on the *taille* rolls for a house attached to his parish. The Agent intervened before the Intendant of Paris pointing out that "secular and regular ecclesiastics are immune and exempt from all *tailles*, dues, charges, and impositions from which seigneurs and noble persons are exempt."[151] Moreover, the clergy's *taille* privilege embraced the totality of its ecclesiastical property. The Intendant honored this appeal and revoked all taxes imposed on the *curé*.[152]

The Agent also went to the rescue of ecclesiastics of Alençon who were subjected to the *taille* on land which produced food destined for their use.[153] In appeal to the local Intendant the Agent pointed out that to recognize this tax would render meaningless and illusory the Church's exemption. The Intendant in a letter to Talleyrand accorded the exemption.[154] Whenever possible, Talleyrand tried to extend the *taille* privilege. From the Intendant of Orleans he secured an exemption for a tonsured teacher, even though he still did not have full sacerdotal orders.[155]

The Agent used essentially the same intercessory methods against two other direct taxes, the *capitation* and the *vingtième*. Against the first, pressed illegally against one clerical party, he appealed to the Intendant of Amiens in July, 1780, referring to the laws of 1701 and 1710 which specifically exempted the clergy, "an immunity which all ecclesiastics engaged in sacred orders or living clerically have always enjoyed."[156] The Assembly assigned the Agent the case of Ursuline nuns in Toulon forced to pay the *vingtième* on a loan of 13,000 *livres* taken to pay their taxes. Talleyrand secured letters patent in May, 1781, basing the nuns' exemption on the Edict of 1749 and a decision of the King's Council of 1751.[157] In March, 1783 Talleyrand appealed to Vergennes requesting the reversal of an order of the Intendant of Metz which had placed the Collège de Sedan, formerly Jesuit, on the rolls of the *vingtième*.[158]

The Assembly referred to the Agents complaints of numerous ecclesiastics in Auxerre and Nevers who had been subjected to a municipal *don gratuit* and whose letters patent of exemption were declared inapplicable by municipal officers.[159] Similar municipal taxes were levied against a newly appointed receiver of *décimes* in Cahors. Exemptions from local taxes as an employee of the clergy were denied by the Intendant of Montauban. Talleyrand secured them upon appeal.[160]

The Agent took a firm stand in cases of taxation to which the clergy had never before been subject. To Minister Calonne in July, 1784, Talleyrand protested as unprecedented and "a surprise levied against religion" a tax of eight sous per *livre* levied on Church revenue from the performance of religious services *(casuel)*—baptisms, marriages, burials, vows, novitiates, and taking of orders—pointing out that these "vexations would obviously fall on the most indigent of the clergy," for whom these revenues constituted an important part of income.[161]

A second large area of intervention had to do with the preservation of corporate exemptions from indirect taxes. Subjection to the salt tax *(gabelle)* was a common abuse. No tax was more hated by the French people than the *gabelle,* which "had for the entire duration of the Old Regime a capital and ever increasing importance in [France's] fiscal history."[162] It surpassed by far in yield the product of the *capitation,* exceeded the *vingtième,* and almost equalled the *taille.* By the king's Edict of December, 1680, and its contracts with the crown, the clergy was exempted from this duty.[163] Yet this guarantee was commonly flouted by the king's judges and was in periodic need of reassertion. The Assembly of 1782 charged the Agents to intercede on behalf of the *curés* of Saunay (Diocese of Bourges), forced to take salt despite their protests and fined 150 *l.* in defiance of the clergy's rights. They were also to secure from the government a reiteration of the edict of immunity to protect the clergy in the future.[164] Talleyrand, who conferred with the Controller-General of Finances, was convinced that the law of 1680 was still clear and binding but that the trouble lay rather in the rapacity of local tax collectors who, defiant both of statute and Church-State contracts, tyrannized helpless ecclesiastics. In reporting back to the same Assembly, the Agent referred to this case as a test of the integrity of the clergy's contracts with the king which, instead of a safeguard, had become a "fatal weapon" used against it. Were the contracts with the crown a simple formality to be openly abused?

On this issue rested the sanctity of the Church's "too visibly attacked" privileges.

The question of the *gabelle,* he continued, also suggested a second enormous problem, namely, the means by which a defenseless rural clergy could protect itself, its property, and its privileges against the tyranny of powerful agents of the crown or private tax officials. It was this case and the sympathy for poor rural priests, without influence, far from counsel, and reticent to engage in costly and unequal contests with more powerful contestants, which provided the first inspiration for Talleyrand's Diocesan Syndic Plan, which would place the resources of the diocese and the clergy's central agencies at the disposal of clergy in distress.

The Assembly of 1782 charged the Agents to intervene on behalf of ecclesiastics in Provence forced to pay the *droit de l'huile* on their oils in violation of clerical privilege.[165] Equally clear titles against taxes on the sale of wine *(droit de gros)* were disregarded by other local authorities who insisted that the clergy's exemption extended only to certain types of wine. The Agent brushed this allegation aside pointing out that the exemption covered all wines. From the *Cour des aides* he secured a decree of July 31, 1782 to prove it.[166] Talleyrand also obtained upon appeal to Minister Necker in September, 1780 a suspension of payment of a ledger stamp tax *(droit de contrôle)* in the election of a church warden *(marguillier)* ordered by the tax farm.[167] The Agent pointed out that an edict of 1740 exempted the clergy from this tax. He secured the same exemptions against a similar order of the Intendant of Brittany in June, 1782, this time on the stamp tax levied on baptismal registries in the Diocese of Nantes.[168]

The good will of the king's ministers and their fondness for Talleyrand are apparent in like action concerning the *marc d'or,* a tax payable on the cutting of fresh forest reserves, from which the clergy was not exempted. Talleyrand took the complaint of clerics subjected to the *marc d'or* before an Assembly of Prelates in Paris before intervening (as the Assembly's law of 1715 required in important appeals).[169] Before the Controller-General of Finances, Jean-François Joly de Fleury, in March, 1782, he pointed out that many ecclesiastics depended on forest revenues for their livelihood and that payment of this excise threatened poor communities with ruin, since it took a large share of their revenues. The minister accorded this exemption to Talleyrand, who secured similar privileges for several charitable institutions.[170]

A third broad category which prompted direct action involved the performance of services not applicable to the clergy. For a *curé* of Dauphiné who was ordered to render *corvée* service along with his servant and two horses, Talleyrand secured a repeal from the Intendant of Lyon.[171] While it was easy to obtain exemption for the priest whose holy office automatically freed him, the Agent had to plead that the servant and horses were absolutely necessary to the ministry of his parish, composed of several widely-separated hamlets. He made a similar appeal to the Intendant of Bordeaux in February, 1781 seeking exemption from a pecuniary commutation of the *corvée* paid for a servant of a priest.[172] Since the Church's *corvée* exemption applied not only to roads but to bridges and public works, Talleyrand received an exemption from Minister Necker on behalf of the Bishop of Bayeux, who had been charged this tax on the rebuilding of a bridge.[173]

Like the *corvée,* military service and the housing of military personnel were other clear clerical exemptions. In attempting to secure the exemption of a servant from army service, Talleyrand appealed to the Minister of War, the Marshal Philippe-Henri Ségur, pointing out that the requested exemption was conformant both with law and spiritual necessity, since the servant aided the *curé* in divine service and in collecting the tithes "which constituted the support of the curate."[174] Before Joly de Fleury, Controller-General of Finances, in September, 1781, he demanded respect for laws exempting priests from the obligation of housing and supporting soldiers and constabulary.[175] Before the Intendant of Paris in July, 1783 he demanded the immediate withdrawal of troops lodged in property of a Parisian church.[176] Occasionally a cleric was forced to render patrol service, which Talleyrand condemned as "a personal servitude to which persons consecrated to the service of the altar have never before been subjected . . . it would be strange that ecclesiastics exempt from lodging soldiers should be constrained to pay for patrol service."[177] It is clear from the correspondence of the Agents that Talleyrand attached considerable importance to the question of housing military personnel. In a letter of September, 1784 he signified his intention to include this matter in his final report to the clergy "in order that |the monarchy] can be apprised of means to accord *curés* the justice |the clergy] seeks and to maintain them in their privileges."[178]

Although the king's Edict of April, 1695 was clear in exempting the clergy from major constructions and repairs of churches, the

Intendant of Champagne ordered the Chapter of Joinville to pay for repairs on its church. Talleyrand advised the clergy not to expend tithe revenues on these repairs and appealed to the Intendant, pointing out that laws of Church and State obliged parishioners, not the clergy, to repair churches, enclose cemeteries, and provide suitable lodging for their *curés*.[179] Since the law charged the parishioners to pay the costs of constructing the church, they must also be responsible for its repair. "This conclusion is not a simple deduction, it is the law itself." The Intendant acknowledged the chapter's exemption and by an order of October 12, 1781 provided the restitution of all funds used in repairs.[180]

Talleyrand was commissioned by the Assembly of 1780 to aid clerics of Agen who were similarly forced to expend their tithe revenues on church repairs. He secured a suspension of the sentence against the clerics from Joly de Fleury, citing the Edict of 1695 which freed the clergy from presbytery repairs and reminding him that ecclesiastical tithes were under no circumstances liable for such payment.[181] On the authority of the same legislation he intervened on behalf of a *curé* of Brignolles (Diocese of Aix) who was forced by the townspeople to pay repair costs of the belfry.[182]

Hoping to prevent the recurrence of such cases as the Chapter of Joinville or the *curés* of Agen and to secure a clear affirmation of the clergy's privileges, Talleyrand communicated a detailed memorandum to Joly de Fleury and the Toulouse Parlement in July, 1781 outlining the Church's position that royal statutes fully exempted the tithe owners from all presbytery repairs.[183]

VII

The Agent-General and the Administrative Machinery of the Clergy

It was natural that the two young and usually inexperienced Agents-General invested by the clergy each five years with positions of enormous range and complexity could not discharge their obligations unaided. Nor, indeed, were they expected to do so. Like the executives of any extensive organization, public or private, the Agents depended on the assistance of an experienced, professionally trained staff for the technical data and counsel from which intelligent and responsible decisions could be made. They also relied on regional representatives, who, removed from the central arteries of administration and policy-making, enforced the clergy's directives uniformly and efficiently. This chapter will investigate the administrative machinery of the clergy—Secretariat, Council of the Clergy, and Receivership-General—which provided the Agents secretarial, legal, and financial assistance in handling the overwhelming mass of correspondence, judicial contests, and the audit of the clergy's finances for which the Agents were held responsible. The strength and permanence of these established organs, whose members served far longer than the five years of the Agents, compensated at once for the lack of expertise or the unpredictable capacity and zeal of the incoming Agents and insured continuity from one Agency and Assembly to another. Indeed, the nature of the clergy's temporal regime, its rigorous centralization, and the needs of the periodic General Assemblies required such a permanent organization. These offices, in effect, constituted the Agents' general staff. As an integral institution of the clergy, separate and semi-independent of the Assembly, the Agency-General was provided with personnel and subordinate offices whose bureaucratic administrative organization was strikingly modern

Administrative Machinery of Clergy 175

and fulfilled much the same function for it that the Agents and the committees of the Assembly fulfilled for the parent body.

The first of the three permanent agencies was the *Bureau de l'agence* or Secretariat. Although the Agents had secured some kind of administrative assistance as early as the seventeenth century, no formal or permanent machinery was established until 1748.[1] The task of the Bureau was twofold: to discharge the secretarial tasks of the Agents and to maintain the Archives of the Clergy. The vast increases in correspondence which occasioned the establishment of the Secretariat in the mid-eighteenth century were due to the Agents' extended exchanges with the king's ministries, magistracy, and judiciary, and to the intensification of clerical business with the dioceses. In the first instance, preferring to spare their coveted power of direct intervention in favor of working behind the scenes by personal negotiations and appeals, the Agents directed to the government innumerable requests, petitions, or complaints touching all affairs of clerical interest and dispute. More often, as has been seen, they resorted to writing rather than utilizing their rights to appear personally before the King's Council or Parlement.

The second increase was due to the steadily rising volume of correspondence received from diocesan clergy anxious to enjoy the protection, favors, counsel, and intercession of the Agents. By extensive letters the Agents communicated the results of their consultations with the clergy's legal staff together with technical advice or reports on the progress of a given litigation. Detailed files of all cases were kept. Some were made available to each diocese concerning events of particular interest to it. The Agents also communicated to the Diocesan Syndics matters of economic and legislative concern to their diocese.

The Secretariat also filed, in order of importance, letters and requests of diocesan correspondents to serve the Agents on behalf of litigants and also for the preparation of their final report to the Assembly.[2] Separate filings were made available to the Agents in affairs in the process of appeal or adjudication. Those of lesser significance were filed away in cartons entitled *"lettres isolées."*[3]

Both the Secretariat and the Archives were combined under the single direction of the "Chef du bureau de l'agence générale du clergé" and "Garde des archives." In charge of this double department since 1775 was Henri-Gabriel Duchesne (1729-1822). Duchesne secured the reversion of this position (from the Assemblies of 1765 and 1772), as was customary since the seventeenth century among the lay offices of the First Estate, lawyers, receivers, and guardians, from a close relative, M. de Beauvais. Beauvais had served as Guardian since 1742 and as first Director of the Secretariat upon its creation in 1748 until his death in 1775.[4]

It was in the Secretariat that all the correspondence of the Agency was prepared and that all written work, the maintenance of records, and related clerical functions connected with that office were discharged. The Agents were aided in their correspondence by the Guardian of the Archives. The statutes of the Assembly stipulated that for purposes of the Agents' correspondence, the Guardian would come to the home of the Agents at least twice a week, at which time they would sign all letters prepared in their name and return them for mailing.[5] At these meetings the Agents also communicated their decisions on letters received. If the affair were of routine character, the composition of letters was left to the Guardian, which the Agents might approve and sign at the next conference. Letters of important affairs were either closely supervised or personally dictated or written by the Agents. All significant cases involving matters of law or judicial procedure, as will be indicated presently, were sent to the clergy's legal staff for advice and assistance.

The relations of Talleyrand and Duchesne were productive and cordial in sharing the responsibilities of what was a huge correspondence of complicated and intricate legal-administrative matters. From directives in the archives, it is clear that Duchesne functioned not only as Director of the Secretariat but also as Talleyrand's administrative secretary, who arranged his schedule of appointments and correspondence.[6] With the ceaseless flow of incoming diocesan communications, Talleyrand took full advantage of the powers granted him to use his staff to alleviate the burdens of the correspondence.

Duchesne classified all incoming mail according to a specially arranged order for distribution to the Agents. Given the quantity of letters for which he took personal responsibility and the large number of persons, from cardinals to curates, who accepted Talleyrand's generous invitation to direct their problems personally to him,[7] he displayed remarkable capacity in having studied and assimilated the vast majority. This is verified by his marginalia in letters received,[8] by the instructions he gave Duchesne in the treatment of appeals,[9] and by his personal interest in important litigations which he subsequently directed to the clergy's lawyers for advice.[10] This capacity is further evidenced by his personal replies to hundreds of memoirs sent to him from the dioceses. In them he demanded information on the state of a case, the lawyers responsible, and the means by which he might accord his offices.[11] It is not surprising that most of the incoming letters bearing the name of either Agent were directed to Talleyrand, variously referred to as "Monsieur l'Abbé de Talleyrand de Périgord," "l'Abbé de Tailleyrand de Périgord," and "l'Abbé de Talleyrand."[12] Expressions of gratitude for his services are a common occurrence in the papers of the Agency, like a letter of July 16, 1784 from a representative of the clergy of Bourg-en-Bresse (Diocese of Lyon) whom the Agent had aided in a case of unjust subjection to the *vingtième:* "The clergy of these provinces will never forget what it owes you; your name will be preciously preserved in its annals."[13]

Nor is it surprising that Talleyrand availed himself to the fullest of the Secretariat's assistance, not only to keep himself informed of all issues brought to the Assembly and the Agency from the 116 older dioceses as well as the dioceses of the foreign clergy, but also to keep the machinery of the central ecclesiastical government in efficient running order. Given the Agents' many demanding responsibilities before clergy and government on behalf of the Assembly, the provincial churches, and other agencies, the clergy did not intend them to become ensnared in a maze of paper work. The Assembly of 1748 unanimously voted to institute the Secretariat to reduce the Agents' labors.[14] That he required more assistance than the overworked Duchesne could supply is clear from letters which indicate that M. Mannay, future Bishop of Trèves, mentor at Saint-Sulpice of both the Agent and his uncle, the Archbishop of Reims (who named him Vicar-General of Reims), was being used as part-time personal secretary as early as 1781.[15] M. Mannay, whom, in the words of one cleric, Talleyrand "honored by his confidence,"[16] not only communicated with Duchesne and other officers of the clergy upon Talleyrand's orders but occasionally informed clerical parties, who appealed to Talleyrand, of the Agent's decisions and solicitations on their behalf. This is perhaps the earliest proof of what all through Talleyrand's life was his well known practice of *savoir faire faire,* the spreading of the burdensome tasks on broad backs capable of sustaining them so that the resulting liberation from routine matters permitted the time and energy to concentrate on affairs requiring a higher talent. That the use of a private secretary was a thoroughly normal procedure is indicated at once by letters in which Talleyrand refers openly to Mannay in addressing himself to clerical parties with whom he was in communication and by the practice of the Assembly of according gratuities to the private secretaries of outgoing Agents.[17] Judging from the immense number of cases he handled personally and the energy in pursuing issues to successful conclusion for scores of clerical parties, there is no justification, as his detractors have claimed, for charges either of laziness, insincerity, or of a reliance on assistants who were the authors of all his work.

It was customary for the Secretariat to turn out an average of thirty communications a day in the form of letters, memoirs, and messages. The number was frequently as high as fifty. In a letter to the Diocesan Syndic of Agen, Talleyrand outlined a plan "which [he] believed [he] had to establish" to permit the Secretariat to handle more effectively the questions, problems, and requests for information from the dioceses. The Agent incorporated his reply to each request in a separate statement, attached to which was a master letter which explained and correlated the chief observations and conclusions contained in individual memoirs.[18]

He seems also to have practiced frugality in the operations of the Secretariat. To conserve paper, the Agent used the obverse side of manuscript drafts of his letters to write instructions to Duchesne regarding the operations of the *Bureau de l'agence*. Happily these precious and illuminating directives have survived, only because Duchesne was interested in retaining the original drafts of the Agents' letters on the other side. Most of these cryptic notes carry no date whatever, but they can be roughly identified chronologically by observing the dates appearing in the Agent's drafts on the opposite side, which, upon cross checking in the G^{8*} 2617-2620 series, prove to be practically identical.[19] Almost all of them during the 1780-1785 Agency were in Talleyrand's small, vertical, almost undecipherable handwriting, and most of them were written in the formal eighteenth-century style of the third person singular.

Talleyrand wrote Duchesne frequently in order that together they might work out matters at Bellechasse. In a typical invitation, characteristically dated "this Monday afternoon," the Agent notified Duchesne that he was sending him for the Archives the registered documents of the *Chambre des comptes* and the king's letters patent confirming the clergy's voluntary gift.[20] All secretarial drudgery, particularly tasks involving the preparation of several copies of a letter, were handled independently by the Guardian.

Duchesne was also used to ascertain the explicit instructions of the Assembly or the current state of matters charged to the Agents. In order to seek the recovery of the papers held by a former Bishop of Séez, as requested by the Assembly of 1780, Talleyrand wished to learn of all previous steps initiated in this matter by his predecessors. In February, 1781 he asked the Guardian to send him "right away" a copy of the deliberations of the Assembly regarding these papers and its exact instructions.[21] In a second note he asked for the records of his predecessor, who had similarly been active in the recovery of these papers.[22]

Talleyrand also utilized the Secretariat's Director to check on the progress of all individual cases requiring the intercession and correspondence of the Agents or to refresh his memory on particulars.[23] He also solicited the Guardian to send him the files of certain cases housed in the Archives in order that he might prepare replies in actions which required his personal attention or which were pertinent to his final report. In a note of March, 1784 Duchesne communicated these to Talleyrand with an added word as to the merits of one case which might be included in the final report of his Agency.[24]

In replying to conventional matters which required neither the personal attention nor the decision of the Agent, Duchesne wrote out drafts which Talleyrand had corrected and either had signed immediately or had requested to be rewritten with additions or emendations.[25] There are many examples both of Talleyrand's orders to the Guardian to attend to the composition of certain letters and of other letters dictated by him. In order to acknowledge to the recipient that Talleyrand was responsible for the authorship of these dictated missives, Duchesne used a particular form in which Talleyrand, by name, addressed the recipient in the third-person singular: "M. l'Abbé de Périgord has the honor to present his respectful compliments to M. the Archbishop of Tours . . . as these decrees are cited in the memoir, M. l'Abbé de Périgord begs Mgr. the Archbishop of Tours. . . ."[26] or again, "M. l'Abbé de Périgord who read the memoir concerning the tax levied for the repairs of a bridge . . . believes that this demand is an attack on the privileges and immunities of the clergy. M. l'Abbé de Périgord thinks, therefore, that M. l'Abbé . . . could make formal request to M. the Intendant to request his release."[27] That Talleyrand was responsible for these letters and many others of the same form is unmistakable. Letters by his own hand, however, were neither as wan nor as formal as those sent out for him.

It is clear from the operations of the *Bureau de l'agence* and the statements of its chief that Talleyrand possessed the last authority in running this agency. Even during his absences from Paris he insisted on being notified of the operations of the Secretariat and the business of the clergy. He received wherever he was the clergy's transactions, correspondence, and requests to which he invariably replied.[28] Duchesne on various occasions wrote for his directives.

What was the role of the Abbé de Boisgelin? It is not inconceivable that the Director of the Secretariat held the functions of the second Agent as well during Talleyrand's absence. We have found no records of his either in directing the operations of the Secretariat or in manuscript orders to the heads of agencies similar to the numerous dispatches of his colleague. In a letter of October 23, 1784 Duchesne wrote Talleyrand, who was in Reims at that moment, for authority to make arrangements for the renovation of the meeting quarters of the Assembly. From his remarks it is clear that the second Agent was in Paris at the time.[29] Almost a month later the Guardian laid before Talleyrand more pressing cases, requesting authority to act in his absence.[30] Duchesne, instead of charging the Abbé de Boisgelin with significant affairs within the province of the Agents (Boisgelin failing to take the initiative himself as required), discharged them himself. Duchesne also wrote the Receiver-General of the Clergy in matters which touched the supervisory functions of the Agent-General's office.[31]

Certainly without the aid of the Director and the staff of the Secretariat, Talleyrand would have been crushed by the burdens of his office. Nor was his task facilitated by the apparent indifference of his colleague who, as has been shown elsewhere, was responsible for a modest fraction of the correspondence and acts of the Agents. Despite rigorous assignments there are only a few indications in the two-thousand letters that Talleyrand was late in replying to affairs submitted to him. These were occasioned either by illness which had kept him from his functions or when, by his own confession, he was in no hurry to communicate bad news concerning the fate of cases decided against the addressee.[32]

The documents of the Secretariat indicate that Talleyrand here, as in other matters, exceeded the limits of his office in treating the business of the clergy. The correspondence reveals that he encouraged the clergy to appeal to him at his home for the success of their affairs and that, in fact, *curés,* abbots, bishops, and archbishops came to Bellechasse to discuss their cases with him.[33]

He seems also to have won the loyalty and affection of his lieutenant in the Secretariat together with its staff. His good-humored leniency is exemplified in a note dated November 30, 1784: "The Abbé de Périgord begs M. Duchesne not to be disturbed at the sight of the big packet he is sending him . . . There are perhaps only two or three affairs worth presenting to the Council of the Clergy. If it should take M. Duchesne more than five minutes to glance through the others, he is requested to put off the examination to another day."[34]

The Secretariat was at the same time the depot of the Archives of the Clergy. From the earliest moments of the establishment of its temporal administration after the Colloquy of Poissy, the clergy realized the importance of housing and, whenever possible, extending the registers of its official enactments, the manuscript official proceedings of its Provincial and General Assemblies, together with all instruments, edicts, acts, decrees, and letters patent confirming its privileges, immunities, and royal correspondence.[35] Nowhere is the clergy's reliance on its records and ordinances, the sources of the legal distinction which made it the first order of the realm, more clearly stated than in the preface to the "Recueil": "There is no body of the kingdom which does not reserve to itself uniform rules applicable to different events. Each member is bound to conform to them. It is always the spirit of order which is introduced to prevent arbitrary innovations."[36] "As every other good administration rests on examples,"[37] it is imperative to protect all the clergy's "writings and memoirs, even the most secret," by which its traditional practices are confirmed and its rights and exemptions established from generation to generation.

Though servants were charged to protect the Archives since the time of its formal establishment in September, 1579, the office of "Garde des archives" seems to have been founded as recently as 1705.[38] When M. de Beauvais was made "Chef du bureau de l'agence générale" in 1748 he had already held the title of "Garde des archives."[39] A directive as early as 1726 addressed to the Assembly by its Committee on the Archives recommended that the Archives "should be conferred on a man of letters versed in law who can study them and inform himself fully on what they contain."[40]

It was here that the several series of documents and source collections of interest to the clergy (in addition to the correspondence to and from its officers) were classified and housed. The most important of these consisted of all edicts and decisions rendered in ecclesiastical affairs since the eleventh century, the letters and circulars of the Agents, the Agents' memoirs and requests, the consultations of the legal staff and canon lawyers, the minutes of the Council of the Clergy, the letters of ministers and public officers, and the published edicts, declarations, and judgments of the government. The Agents were also obliged to deposit all titles of temporal or spiritual jurisdiction, the manuscript proceedings of the General Assembly, the reports of their Agencies, the accounts of the Receiver-General, the listings of all liquidated and outstanding loans and revenues of the clergy, and letters patent rendered in the Church's favor.[41] Although the vast records of the clergy filled two large rooms of the Grands Augustins, the major portion was occupied by its financial records. The various series of its papers related to the Agency between 1727 and 1788, placed in chronological order, indexed by subject, and bound, as ordered by the Assemblies after 1748,[42] totalled 374 folio volumes. Eighty-nine of these were composed of the clergy's memoirs and requests pertaining to its jurisdiction, property rights, immunities, and temporal administration and privileges.[43] Fifty-four volumes recorded the consultations of the Council of the Clergy and other distinguished jurists on questions of canon law and jurisprudence;[44] 17 volumes, the minutes of the Council of the Clergy between 1766 and 1788;[45] 148 volumes, the opinions of the distinguished jurist of the clergy, Jean-Jacques Piales (1720-1789), between 1754 and 1787;[46] and 66 volumes, the letters of the Agents.[47]

M. Duchesne considered the sixty-six volume collection a "bible" in the profession of the Agents, "a real code of the science of ecclesiastical affairs," a storehouse of information and procedure which could guide their operations and considerably shorten their work and researches. From the letters of their predecessors, the Agents were expected to learn how to treat similar affairs during their ministry.[48] Duchesne, a hard worker, lover of detail and systematic organization, wrote that before the new collection of letters was begun in 1748, the Agents searched in vain through the labyrinthine collection of unindexed papers. "Indexes were necessary," the Director succinctly remarked, "so I made them."[49] He was justly proud of this "particular effort" which placed the 24,000 letters of the Agency over the previous sixty years in systematic order and permitted the location of cases and persons "at a glance." Quite correctly he referred to them as "a precious monument . . . where one can find the origins, the conclusions, and the chain of affairs whose resolution was either fortunate or unfortunate."

Duchesne was also at work on several other voluminous collections ordered by the Assembly of 1775.[50] One was a chronological collection of edicts, decisions, regulations, and laws delivered in favor of the clergy.[51] This was meant to bring up to date the magistral collection *Recueil des actes, titres, et mémoires concernant les affaires du clergé de France,* which stopped at 1715. Another was a systematic inventory and cataloguing of the papers of the Receiver-General from the sixteenth century. Before, Duchesne admitted, these had been "scattered pell-mell, without order, without distinction, and with precious titles intermingled with useless drafts." Third, he was in the midst of a reorganization and inventory of the whole of the clergy's papers, ordered by the Assemblies of 1775 and 1780.[52] Finally, he planned eventually to prepare subject indexes for all the series of the clergy's papers (including the ninety-six volumes of registers of the edicts of Parlements) and files of all titles entering the Archives. For the completion of these projects, "working without respite twelve to fourteen hours per day" for twenty years and with but one assistant, Duchesne successfully appealed to the Assembly of 1785 for a rise in salary from 6,500 to 8,500 $l.$,[53] a very respectable figure when one considers that the salary of the Guardian in 1748 had been but 1,500 $l.$,[54] and that the basic salary of the Agents before supplements was 5,500 $l.$[55] The Assembly of 1780 granted him a gratuity of 6,000 $l.$, 3,000 more than was accorded by the Assembly of 1775.[56] The Guardian's duties reflected the same dramatic increase in the clergy's temporal activity that affected all branches of its central administration after 1775, for by 1785 he was obliged to double his staff by the addition of two more clerks.[57]

The Guardian maintained a pragmatic system of organizing current documents entering the Archives. Each was filed by subject. Separate headings were available for Agents' letters to ministers, requests pending, and judgments and decisions received. All other papers, letters, and information on affairs were arranged in alphabetical portfolios by the title of the case to which they referred so they were easy to find. Papers relating to concluded questions were transferred to the rubric "settled cases," which could serve the Agents in preparing their final report. "Memoirs and Requests" and "Acts and Decisions" were kept in their own files until they were numerous enough to be bound.[58]

Though the Guardian was named by the clergy, he "worked under the eyes and on the orders of the Agents."[59] Officially charged to register all papers entering the Archives, the Guardian was responsible for keeping all records in proper order and form. Already by 1723 the Assembly ordered that "not a single paper" could leave the Archives with any borrower, however distinguished, without the authorization of the Agents and without appropriate receipts.[60] The Agents and the Guardian alone kept the keys to the double-locked Archives.[61] In the absence of the Guardian someone was always on duty. A perpetual agenda listed items borrowed and the names of borrowers.[62]

Since the time of the Assembly of Melun the Agents had been charged to make cumulative inventories of the clergy's papers and to communicate to their successors the condition of the Secretariat at the end of their Agency, "to serve them better and to assure the clergy that nothing had been lost."[63] They also delivered up the keys of the Archives at this time. A written verification of the Archives was submitted to the Assembly each five years and reviewed by its Committee on the Archives.[64] The Agents were also bound to return any papers which may have remained in their possession, since these were the property of the clergy.[65]

The Agents were also the printers of the First Estate, responsible for publishing all matters of relevance to the order. The Assembly of 1715 required them to print and distribute to the clergy all edicts, declarations, and decrees rendered in favor of the clergy.[66] Nothing could be printed for the clergy without their specific order.[67] Under their direction the Secretariat sent out the circular letters and proclamations to the bishops and other authorized personnel announcing clerical measures and enactments of the Assembly. And under similar supervision it was charged to oversee repairs of the Grands Augustins, to prepare the convocation of the General Assembly, and to notify the Provincial Assemblies of their first meeting.[68]

What was the situation of the Archives during the Talleyrand-Boisgelin Agency? The Archives in 1780 were still located at the Convent of the Grands Augustins, to which they had been moved in 1625.[69] Conformant to instructions of the Assembly of Melun that the clergy's papers be kept in Paris, they had been housed between 1579 and 1625 in the cloister of Notre-Dame.[70]

Duchesne wrote Talleyrand that the Grands Augustins, like many medieval conventual structures by the time of the eighteenth century, was in a condition of near ruin. The Assembly's quarters were especially bad. Though it had been rebuilt by the clergy in 1715 at its own expense, the building, according to the Augustinians in 1760, "was so defective that it was constantly in need of repairs . . . hardly livable . . . humidity ruins everything . . . all the chimneys smoke . . . and fires cannot be built without danger of conflagration."[71] Crowded, inadequate for the growing needs of the clergy, excessively damp and humid, its structural timbers rotten and in need of replacement almost everywhere, it was feared that the eventual deterioration of the clergy's documents would result unless they were moved elsewhere.[72] Duchesne constantly pressed Talleyrand to urge the Assembly to seek a new home "cleaner, more comfortable, and less expensive" and provisionally to gain approval for major expenditures to renovate the Convent.[73]

We have had occasion to examine Archbishop Loménie de Brienne's arguments before the Assembly of 1780 in favor of abandoning the Grands Augustins' "humid and unhealthy suites, its narrow Archives exposed to all accidents, a chapel where the slightest absence of sun results in darkness" in favor of "a place more healthy, more suitable, more worthy of the dignity of the First Order of the State."[74] With the failure of the Saint-Sulpice plan and others similar to it, the French clergy of the Old Regime was never destined to see a new home. For eighty-five years before the Revolution it had convened in the Convent of the Grands Augustins.

The same Assembly of 1780 took a vigorous lead in placing the Archives in order. Its Committee on the Archives, under the chairmanship of François de Bonac, Bishop of Clermont, presented a lengthy report acknowledging the "greatest vigilance and assiduous pains on the part of Monsieur Duchesne" but admitted that "confusion and disorder [still] reign there today." It urged a total reorganization and inventory of the clergy's papers, which had last been accomplished in 1695.[75] Duchesne provided the Assembly a comprehensive, detailed plan of classification under five groupings, which he hoped would be ready by 1785: religion and jurisdiction; benefices; temporal property of the Church; privileges, franchises, and immunities; and temporal administration.

The Assembly ordered the Guardian to continue the work of providing inventories for the three large series of the clergy's papers (Agents' letters, memoirs and consultations, deliberations of lawyers), which from 1775 to 1780 had grown from 111 volumes to 173, indicating once again the accentuated rise in temporal business during that period. The Assembly further ordered the Guardian to continue the collection of edicts, ordinances, regulations, declarations, and decisions of the king's courts and councils and to catalog the papers of the Receiver-General which, before Duchesne, had been stored in sacks, "condemned to dust and obscurity." In order to arrest the needless proliferation of the clergy's minor papers and to help solve the crucial space problem in the crowded Archives, the Assembly approved the Guardian's suggestion of destroying the huge stores of duplicate receipts of loans floated at least thirty years before, which alone took up almost a single room. Finally, it ordered all benefice holders to inform the Agents by letter of court decisions favorable to the jurisdiction and temporal of the Church.

It is interesting that the spirit of administrative unity within the clergy was in the air during the last years of the Old Regime, prompted, as we have seen, by the attacks of the courts on the Church's temporal privileges and by questions like the *foi et hommage* which brought the higher clergy after 1780 to a state of emboldened tension. Not only did the central clergy try to draw the lines of communications with the provincial churches closer to Paris, but it attempted to strengthen the legal bonds and juridical immunities of the rural communities to protect the privileges of the whole company. Not only were benefice holders to report judicial decisions to Paris, but by orders of 1785 each diocese was to send an inventory of its Archives to constitute a general depot in Paris, "a center of unity . . . for the choice of means of defense . . . [since] the different dioceses are but one and the same family charged to defend and preserve together the same laws and a common patrimony."

The Diocesan Bureaus in the cities of Parlements were to send the Agents copies of the registration of edicts, declarations, letters patent, and decrees on the jurisdiction and temporal of the clergy to permit Agents and lawyers to be informed of local usages and local acts or decrees employed in its defense and of interest to other dioceses. The clergy's lawyers were also to be informed of laws, regulations, and decisions of the various courts regarding the rights, property, and ecclesiastical privileges of the Church. For dioceses negligent in the maintenance of their archives the present order was intended "to excite a useful vigilance." The Assembly of 1785 acknowledged that work continued in the rationalization of the clergy's records.[76] The Guardian had not been able to complete the new inventory or the new collection of edicts and decisions, largely because of the enormous clerical problems connected with the Extraordinary Assembly of 1782 and the heavy burdens of keeping ahead of the daily problems and papers entering the Archives.

Actually completed by Duchesne before 1789 were valuable introductory summaries together with chronological and alphabetical indices for the three large series of papers. These were significant contributions to the work of the Assembly and the Agents. Remaining unfulfilled was the intention of the Guardian to provide an index for all titles of the clergy and the collection of all official edicts and enactments of interest to the First Estate. Similarly, the new general inventory of the Archives to replace the one made a hundred years before also lay incomplete at the time of the Revolution.

The Assembly of 1780 also charged the Agents to undertake all measures to recover for the Archives missing Church titles and papers.[77] This was not new. As early as the Assembly of 1715 Agents had been ordered to recover the manuscript proceedings of the Assemblies of 1635 and 1682, held by several bishops and lawyers of the clergy.[78] They were to recover ecclesiastical documents retained after his Agency by Bishop d'Aquin (1665-1710) of Séez.[79] An interesting correspondence after 1780[80] reveals that the documents in question were extensive, reaching back to 1438 and numbering nearly a hundred registers, account books, notebooks, reports, and statements. The Assembly of 1780 accorded 1200 *l.* for the recovery of these papers which were in the hands of a priest of the diocese, the Abbé Bailly, who had bought them from the former servants of d'Aquin and offered them to the Assembly. The Bishop of Séez, who described Bailly as "honest, disinterested, and industrious," also lent his good offices for the delivery of these papers to the clergy in Paris.[81]

That Talleyrand appreciated his responsibility for assuring that all official instruments reached permanent deposit in the Archives is illustrated by a letter of October, 1780 to M. Amelot, Secretary of State for Ecclesiastical Affairs, requesting confirmatory letters *(let-*

tres d'encadrement) securing the crown's financial aid in the reimbursement of the clergy's loans taken on its behalf: "It is the duty of our ministry to see that all important dispatches are deposited in the Archives of the Clergy."[82] As to the role Talleyrand may have played in modernizing the Archives, the Assembly of 1785, in praising what had been done during the past five years, specifically recognized the zeal of the Agents and the work executed under their direction.[83]

The second permanent agency under the direction of the Agents-General was the Council of the Clergy. "Attorneys of the Clergy" had been appointed as early as 1595. By 1640 they were constituted into a body.[84] By 1727 they met periodically to deliberate in common affairs submitted to them by the Agents.[85] During the period 1780-1785 the Council consisted of four attorneys, three of whom were assigned to cases of the First Estate which came before the Parlements and the fourth to the King's Council.[86] The attorneys were experienced jurists, men who in 1780 had already been in the service of the clergy for some time. The Abbé Rat de Mondon received his office by reversion in 1760; Messrs. Laget Bardelin and Vulpian in 1765, and Rigault in 1775.[87] Earlier in the century the lawyers had been the appointees of the Agents. By the time of the Talleyrand-Boisgelin Agency they were no longer named by the Agents except in the intervals of the Assembly, although they had considerable influence in presenting candidates to the Assembly (as Talleyrand did in 1785)[88] which made all appointments.[89] So dramatic was the increase of clerical adjudications and the need for legal assistance after 1780 that the Assembly of 1785 increased the Council by the services of four lawyers with rights of permanent tenure upon vacancies which occurred there; three, Messrs. Camus, Gaignant, and Hervé, "Attorneys in Parlement" and a fourth, Sanson du Peronnet, "Attorney in Council."[90]

It is certain that the Agents could not have fulfilled the consultative, intercessory, and appellant obligations of their office without the advice and aid of the Council. Their frequent recourse to the lawyers, therefore, was both natural and necessary when it is recalled how many of the affairs charged to the Agents involved legal suits, litigations, and court appeals before the Parlements and other sovereign tribunals.

Under the presidency of one of the Agents the Council met once every two weeks (except during their vacation between September 7 and November 12) and oftener as a weighty schedule of cases

Administrative Machinery of Clergy 189

warranted.[91] Convened at the home of the eldest of the clergy's lawyers before 1771, the Council met at the residence of one of the Agents after that date.[92] The Agents enjoyed fullest freedom to place before the attorneys matters of consequence to the Estate.[93] In cases of urgency the Agents could convoke the lawyers in extraordinary session. Even during their vacation they could send pressing matters to whichever lawyer was in Paris, and he in turn was to consult his other colleagues before rendering an opinion. During the Assemblies, to permit delegates direct access to counsel, the attorneys met in the Agents' suite in the Grands Augustins. As their services were required, they were invited to join the deliberations of the committees. Talleyrand was assisted in his collaboration with the lawyers by the Guardian of the Archives. With an assistant the Guardian attended each meeting, presented affairs communicated by the Agents, and took notes. He also prepared the journal of deliberations in which the Council's decisions were entered at each conference, and which all present signed, and passed on decisions to interested clerical parties. The lawyers received copies of all documents printed in the name of the clergy. All documents communicated to the lawyers were collected. The Receiver-General might participate in the deliberation of cases which fell within the sphere of his interest and activity.

The demands for information and assistance which entered the Agency each day were carefully read by the Agents or Duchesne, and those in need of attention were distributed to the lawyers in advance, particularly those involving interpretations of statutes, jurisprudence, or questions of property and jurisdiction. Every conceivable subject of temporal business was discussed in their conferences: contested tithes, *tailles, vingtièmes,* legacies, dues and services, presbytery repairs, scandals and trials of clergy, marriage and baptism of Protestants, the refusal of the *visa,* the housing of soldiers, the supervision of schools, alienations, the care of cemeteries, burial in church, rights of hunting, seigneurial privileges, the discipline of regulars, the interpretation of contracts and wills, episcopal rights, and many others.

The Agents' letters of response to the dioceses incorporated the findings of the attorneys. The Council's analysis and decisions usually sufficed to guide the legal counsel of embarrassed or harassed clergy. Many clerics faced legal action through chicanery, laziness, or ignorance. Others required not only assistance but too frequently rescue by the Agents.

The attorneys judged the relative importance of each case submitted to them and stated their opinions or advice. Each attorney delivered his report on cases assigned to him by the Agents to a full meeting of the Council, which then discussed it. Revealing the lines of his reasoning, authorities and precedents, and the nature of his conclusions, the attorney then exchanged views with his colleagues. Having fully explored in concert each question, a vote was then taken to determine the official position of the Council. No vote, however, was taken until the proposals had been given at least two readings before the Council and then usually formulated in the following ways: "The undersigned who have examined the above memoir judge that the best course to take in the present state of the affair would be . . . ." or again, "The undersigned Council which read the above consultation as well as the memoir, judge. . . ."[94] This method of outlining objectives, exchanging opinions, and studying alternatives, assured each important affair the interest and participation of all the lawyers and reduced the margin of doubt and error in preparing a case before the courts. The Council's meetings were concluded after each member had signed the minutes.

If the Agents were absent from the meetings of the Council, the lawyers communicated opinions or wrote out the essentials of law connected with a given case and communicated them to Talleyrand.[95] According to the records of the Council, compiled by Duchesne, the Agent within two days sent the results of these conferences to benefice holders together with his own letter.[96] The lawyers not only advised the Agents on the merits of each case but also pointed out instances where appeal to the government (often the specific minister involved)[97] might be a distinct asset to its success, calling attention to the particular state of a dispute which, injurious to the clergy, required the intervention of the Agents.[98] The Guardian acknowledged in the records that Talleyrand wrote to the king's ministers as recommended by the Council.[99]

The consultations and deliberations of the Council from 1727 to 1788 constitute a huge and valuable library of eighteenth-century jurisprudence. Duchesne, who put his name down as the editor of the series, went to considerable pains to point out that the "precious collection" was no doctrinaire compilation, no "elementary treatise . . . on ideal applications . . . of possible events."[100] Rather it was an "isolated and exhaustive" gathering of specific treatises and dissertations "in common law, in decrees and ordinances, in regulations and jurisprudence applied to known facts [and] to real and existing contestations." The consultations of the clergy from 1727 to 1775, a period of nearly fifty years, had been collected in twenty-three volumes.[101] During the next thirteen years alone, from 1775 to 1788, the collection nearly doubled. The entry of each meeting gives a full listing of the cases presented, prefaced by the uniform phrase "affairs treated before the Council of the Clergy" and followed by the date.

Talleyrand took as strong a hand in managing the Council as he had the Secretariat. The reasons for this are not far to seek. Initially it is clear from his correspondence, both to the lawyers and to the dioceses, how dependent he was on the knowledge and judgment of the clergy's legal staff in highly technical questions. Second, unlike the *Bureau de l'agence* the lawyers had no permanent administrative chief within their own ranks. This office was to be occupied by the Agents. Talleyrand assumed the responsibility for the operations of the Council, for dividing the cases among the lawyers, and for preparing the schedule of its sessions.[102]

The Agent's fundamental task in coordinating the work of the Agency-General with that of the Council was to communicate cases which came to him in order to receive guidance and recommendations on the appropriate legal defense. It was typical for the Agent to assign cases to the four permanent members of the Council. He successively named the attorneys, informed each of the case for which he would be responsible, and assigned to each letters and supporting documents received from the dioceses: "M. Vulpian, letter of the *Curé* of Germini and the observations on the memorandum of M. the Archbishop of Tours; M. l'Abbé Rat, memorandum of the Visitandines of Crest and religious of St. Morassey; M. Rigault, letters of a *curé* of Ahun and the *Curé* of Saunay; M. Laget, letter of a *curé* of Tours."[103]

In the unhurried atmosphere of the eighteenth century, the Council was normally allowed as long as three weeks to a month to decide strategy on cases submitted. Frequently the Agent requested a report in shorter interval, occasionally at the next meeting.[104] This short notice was reserved either for an important case which had to come before the clergy at the first opportunity or, conversely, routine cases which the Agent wished to dismiss promptly.[105] Also without extensive formal preparation, the attorneys were expected to brief the Agents on the implications of new decisions of Parlements and the King's Council and their applicability to cases under examination or to the clergy at large.[106] At other times they were to interpret memoirs, official titles, or letters of an appellee in litigations.[107] It was not rare for Talleyrand to request such a report or consultation in one day, "since the affair is several months late and might degenerate into a serious contestation if this consultation is delayed any longer."[108] He asked similar service on grounds of the relative simplicity of a given affair or the need of a very brief outline: "M. l'Abbé de Périgord requests M. Rigault to examine the enclosed letter and memoir . . . as it is a question of only a word in this affair, M. Rigault is requested to discuss it tomorrow before the Council."[109] In large and important issues subject to long consideration by the Council, Talleyrand asked the lawyers to report at the next meeting on new papers being added to their dossiers for additional study.[110]

It also appears certain that Talleyrand placed as much reliance on Duchesne in the operations of the Council as he did in the Secretariat. The Guardian was entrusted both to place affairs before the Council and to report to it.[111] A letter of Duchesne on June 23, 1784 suggests in fact a threefold division of authority in the running of the Council, with Talleyrand at the top, the Guardian of the Archives in the center, and the lawyers below.[112]

That Talleyrand owed a substantial debt to the lawyers for imparting the necessary legal knowledge and technical formulations to important cases in his charge cannot be disputed. He did more, however, than simply prepare the sessions of the Council and divide the cases among the lawyers. He frequently consulted them on less broad affairs which he wished to handle himself, affairs which did not require the attention of the entire Council or were of a confidential character whose details he was reluctant to reveal. In a letter of May, 1782 Talleyrand asked one of the attorneys "what the response ought to be" in a case involving detailed procedures before the *Cour des aides*.[113] In March, 1785 he asked another to return documents and letters with his comments in order to guide him in drafting suitable replies. He set a deadline of five days for this.[114]

The lawyers' judgment was usually respected. Besides their first duty of protecting clerical titles and immunities, the lawyers were expected to submit judgment on the merits of individual cases and the advisability of the Agents getting involved. In a typical instance M. Laget advised against Talleyrand's entering a case in which a cleric was indicted for having maligned important people. He believed this case could jeopardize the Agents' influence and therefore should not be risked.[115] The Council deliberated another typical case involving a Mlle Danguet, who claimed a reimbursement of income from the clergy due her from capital left in trust. Complications were involved because the clergy refused to recognize the claims of a minor without legal guardians. The lawyers advised Talleyrand to have the girl paid "while there was still time," because the clergy could not convincingly refute the girl's strong case and because the provisions of the law favored her.[116]

From the records of the Council it is apparent that the attorneys' recommendations were incorporated not only into the daily handling of routine cases but also in the cases Talleyrand presented to the Assembly, like the baptismal registers and the bishops' refusal of the *visa*.[117] Besides interpretation and counsel Talleyrand had recourse to the lawyers in every manner of legal and juridical technicality.

Though he was at perfect liberty to do so, Agent Talleyrand never gave the impression that he was the author of the Council's advice. He often quoted verbatim the opinions of the attorneys or simply summarized their decisions. He would often prelude his remarks by "the lawyers think that" or "the lawyers do not doubt that."[118] The genius of young Talleyrand lay not merely in rubber-stamping his lawyers' opinions. Not himself a professional legist, though schooled in civil and canon law, he exercised much good sense and understood clearly what was at stake in each case. Without getting bogged down in technical details, he used his judgment on how best to utilize the suggestions of his lawyers within the needs of the clergy and the wishes of the Assembly.

Of course, the actual responsibility for all counsel and decisions emanating from the Council rested with the Agents. To be sure, the lawyers were seasoned specialists whose opinions were invaluable in determining the main lines of the law, the most appropriate and effective means of procedure and argument, the chances for success or the risk of failure in this case and that. But in the last analysis the attorneys were nameless technicians who provided information on legal actions whose application in the courts or in affairs of state lay squarely with the Agents. The task of piecing together legal advice within the framework of general policy and of weighing the implications of legal battle within the broader context of Church-State relations was theirs. The official proceedings and documents of the clergy never mention the lawyers, but rather attach to the Agents exclusive responsibility—and credit—for handling affairs.

That Talleyrand realized the inestimable importance of the Council as a permanent adviser to the Agents is clear from his eagerness to introduce his successors to the functions of this important agency at the first opportunity. As early as July 9, 1783, fully two years before the official commencement of his Agency, the Abbé de Montesquiou was invited by Talleyrand to the Council where important questions, of interest to his successors, were to be treated.[119]

Of Talleyrand's supervisory authority within the three permanent agencies of the clergy, that portion associated with the Receiver-General of the Clergy was most routinely and uniformly delineated. The Agents were furnished neither the incentive nor the necessity to innovate in this department. Their responsibility was primarily one of surveillance and confirmation, to insure the conservation of the clergy's revenues, to prohibit unauthorized expenditures, and to certify by periodic audit that Church funds both in the dioceses and in the capital were being employed for purposes for which they had been appropriated.[120]

The Receiver-General, like the Agents, was a minister of considerable stature. In one sense he occupied the most crucial administrative post in all the First Estate, for, responsible for the payment and recovery of all clerical taxes and subsidies to the king, he provided the *raison d'être* for the continued existence at once of the Assembly and the extensive temporal machinery of the clergy. Combination minister, treasurer, banker, chief tax-collector, and auditor of the Church, he was, like the Agents, accorded the privilege of entering the King's Council. He was inscribed in the fourth class of the *capitation* reserved for the high nobility of the Robe.[121] He received not only honorific privileges but also a princely salary of 135,000 *l*. in addition to gratuities (the Assembly of 1770 accorded him a bonus of 162,000 *l*.)[122] which were intended to help defray his office expenses, the wages of his clerks in the provinces, and collection and account costs. He was permitted to pass on his office by reversion to relatives. Little wonder that the Receivership was respected and sought after by wealthy bourgeoisie. The son of a

Receiver-General of the early eighteenth-century, M. Ogier, became a *président de chambre* of Parlement; and the son of his successor, M. Senozan, a former lace merchant of Lyon, married the daughter of the *président à mortier* of the Parlement of Paris and future Chancellor, Guillaume de Blancmesnil-Lamoignon, and became one of the richest men in Paris.[123]

M. Bollioud de Saint-Jullien, Receiver-General during the Agency under study, acknowledged with pride before the Assembly of 1785 the fifty years of his life he had given to the clergy.[124] He had inherited his office from his uncle, M. de Senozan, in 1735 "as a reward for his services." He secured the reversion of his office, in turn, first for his son, by the Assemblies of 1765 and 1775, then for his nephew, M. de Quinson, by the Assembly of 1785. With reason the clergy considered this office a pivotal appointment. The Assembly ordered an extensive private investigation before confirming the candidate. Unlike the Diocesan Receivers, who bought their offices and were appointed for life, the Receiver-General was named by a two-thirds vote of the Assembly for a tenure of ten years, subject to renewal or dismissal at the signing of each new contract with the king.[125] Resisting the temptation of venality, common on all levels of magistracy and tax collection in the seventeenth and eighteenth centuries, the clergy kept the office of Receiver-General, of considerable importance both to Church and State, a revocable, dependent, salaried position securely under its vigilance and control.[126]

The Receivership-General, alongside most of the clergy's other national and diocesan machinery, was originally instituted by the Colloquy of Poissy in 1560 to oversee the sums collected from the benefice holders of the First Estate in payment of its contract with the king.[127] The Receiver's duties included the periodic auditing of all the accounts of diocesan and provincial chambers and the transmission of all *décimes* to Paris twice a year.[128] With the sums collected he was to guarantee the execution of all monetary obligations binding on the clergy under the provisions of its contract with the king and the settling of all sums demanded by the clergy's creditors.

As Agent, Talleyrand was commissioned to check the receipt and expenditure accounts of the Receiver-General each three months along with those of his counterparts in the provinces, the Diocesan-Receivers.[129] At each five year Assembly, and in the presence of the Agents, the Receiver-General presented a formal reading of his accounts. At the renewal of the contract the Assembly appointed several committees to audit the accounts of the Receiver and the statements of loans outstanding and reimbursed which were printed in the Assembly's official proceedings.[130] By the rules of the clergy "no act relative to the administration of the clergy's economic affairs could be commenced without first being approved by the Agents."[131] Talleyrand approved with the marking "vu par les agents" the *décime* receipts of the Receiver, the expenses of the Assembly, and the salaries of its deputies and employees. He also reviewed the Church's revenues and pensions.[132] Besides this he approved a multitude of miscellaneous expenditures of the Assembly from letter wax to leather bindings.[133] He audited the money grants to the new converts as well as all other recipients of Church bonuses.[134] He was similarly held accountable to the Assembly for a contingency fund of 3,000 *l.,* established by the Assembly "for necessary expenses."[135]

The Assembly of Melun also intended the Agents to supervise all accounts involving spoliations of dioceses, the result of war or destruction by natural forces. The Agents might grant special privileges in the payment or the exemption of the *décime* as the proven merits of individual cases warranted.[136] As part of their responsibility for guaranteeing the funds of the clergy and to insure their proper use by the Receiver in conformity with the directives of the Assembly, the Agents together with the President were commissioned by the Assembly of 1780 to supervise the procurement of loans at four per cent to cover the clergy's latest *don gratuit* of thirty millions. These sums were to be delivered to the Receiver-General.[137] The Assembly of 1782 gave the Agents similar permission to supervise all means to borrow sums up to sixteen millions at five per cent, in the name of the clergy and by the same means as outlined by the Assembly of 1780.[138] With the consent of the eldest prelate in Paris they fixed the schedule by which the Receiver set the rate of amortization of the clergy's debts and principal on its bonds. From the correspondence of the Agency it is clear that Talleyrand utilized M. Duchesne as liaison in his work with the Receiver-General in the same way he had with the Council and the Secretariat.[139]

Before leaving the subject of the Agents' general staff, one or two observations are in order. Henri-Gabriel Duchesne, its most prominent member, was more than a mere scribe or amanuensis. Commonly referred to by the bishops as the "secretary of the clergy," he was the administrative link between Agents, lawyers, receivers, and secretaries. He was also a learned specialist in administrative usages and Church history, *avocat en parlement*,[140] and the Agents' *aide-mémoire* for the Assembly's decisions, for the state of all current problems before the order, and for outstanding obligations of the clergy to government and benefice holders. An executive assistant who prepared a vast quantity of first-draft letters and memoirs for the Agents and the committees of the Assembly and upon whom Talleyrand on occasion depended for the preparation of substantial preliminary briefs of cases, Duchesne was a cultivated man of considerable legal and literary talents who once had been considered for the editorship of the Assembly's collection of proceedings, begun by the Abbé Duranthon.[141] Before 1789 he was hard at work on an imaginative and huge inventory summarizing the technical and diversified operations, offices, and titles of the First Estate. It was Duchesne who was the author of *La France Ecclésiastique* for sixteen years, between 1774 and 1789. Under the sponsorship of no less a personage than Buffon, he published a *Manuel de naturaliste* in 1770. Six years later he completed a three-volume *Dictionnaire de l'industrie . . . les sciences . . . et les arts*. After the Revolution severed his connection with the clergy, he continued his literary and scientific labors in biography, poetry, and a French translation of the comedies of Terence and wrote articles for dictionaries of agriculture and natural science. His superb organizing skills were challenged as Referendary Counsellor of the Napoleonic *Cour des comptes*, between 1807 and his death fifteen years later, where he was charged with putting its archives in order and preparing repertories to facilitate the use and research of formerly unordered documents.[142]

The clergy was indeed blessed with officers who gave their lives to its service. When one considers the vast paper work and the numerous monuments of detail, patience, effort, and personal concern for the Church's business left behind by men like Beauvais, Senozan, Bollioud de St. Jullien, and Duchesne, who served uninterruptedly in proud family tradition through several generations in the course of the eighteenth century, one is impressed by their zeal and fidelity for the welfare and safety of the First Estate. Solicitude and efforts like these had few, if any, equals in the civil service of the State.

To accomplish their twofold task of surveying the operations of the Church in the provinces and administering the decisions of the Assembly to the remotest parish, the Agents had to rely on the Diocesan Bureaus and provincial *Chambres supérieures des décimes*.

The first body was established in 1567 and confirmed by the Assembly of Melun.[143] The Diocesan Bureau like the General Assembly had been instituted for almost purely financial considerations, since its job was to set and collect the *décimes* from all benefice holders to acquit the diocese's share of the clergy's corporate debt.[144] Under the presidency of the local bishop, and located at the seat of the bishopric, it assumed administrative direction of all clerical affairs of the diocese.

Regulations governing the constitution of the Bureaus were vague or nonexistent. Some chambers met irregularly, twice a year or upon notice of the bishop; others met regularly, as often as each several weeks. With no consistent rules for membership either, the Bureau was composed of usually eight to ten deputies (though the number might be as low as four or as high as twenty-seven), usually the chief benefice holders of the diocese. The methods of electing deputies varied greatly, from direct election and cooption to designation by bishop or groups of benefice holders. Similar confusion reigned in determining constituency representation among the clergy in the election of deputies and the duration of their terms of office. Altercations were frequent over the presence of the bishop in the Bureaus, growing out of charges that he impeded liberty of discussion and election.

In these "closed and unchecked circles . . . abuses were possible and in fact quite frequent." Some deputies of the Bureaus were not even members of the diocese. Some never appeared. Others enjoyed immovable tenure. Improprieties crept into the operation of the chambers, the most serious being the unjust and even arbitrary assessment of the *décime* among benefice holders. In some Bureaus deputies paid themselves lavish salaries and diverted funds for personal use. In others administrative expenses multiplied and official monies were used for gifts and charity.[145]

To correct difficulties in the composition of the Bureau and to achieve better administration and internal harmony, the Assembly of 1770 promulgated a reform plan for the Diocesan Bureau of Troyes which included a fivefold division of benefice holders by class (cathedral chapters; collegiate chapters; *curés;* simple benefice holders; regular communities of both sexes) who voted deputies to the chamber for regular five-year terms. *Curés* "under any pretext" were not to exceed two members, regardless of their numbers in the diocese.[146] Except for the Diocese of Troyes the plan of 1770 was not adopted. Some bishops rejected it outright as inapplicable to their dioceses.

Besides supervision of the financial operations of the diocese and the collection of all ecclesiastical taxes, the chamber audited the accounts of the Diocesan Receiver. It was empowered to take measures against delinquent tithe owners and judged all tax complaints and controversies, up to twenty *livres* for the *décime* and thirty for the *don gratuit*. Sums which exceeded these figures could be brought by appeal before the provincial chamber. It also considered petitions of exemption from the *décimes*. These exemptions, long subject to serious abuses, were accorded those who through alienations, local disasters, or military invasions lost a part or all of their income.[147] Exemptions were also accorded persons who claimed favors by reason of services rendered to Church or State and to privileged segments of the clergy: the cardinals, the Order of Malta, the Jesuits (before 1763), the Visitandines, and certain provinces like Béarn.[148]

Attempts had repeatedly been made to curb abusive exemptions in the *décimes,* to end the discrimination of the richer North against the poorer dioceses south of the Loire that carried a heavier proportion of the corporate debt, and to simplify the complicated twenty-four fold division of benefice holders established in the sixteenth century. In 1760 and 1770 the division was reduced to eight, with benefice holders paying from one twenty-fourth to one quarter of their incomes in *décimes*.[149] This reform, however, did not bring with it the end of exemptions or discrimination against the *curés* who before 1768 paid 60 *livres* out of their *portion congrue* of 300 *l.*[150] Nor did it force the opulent prelates and their aristocratic cohorts who controlled the chamber to surrender a fairer share of their incomes to ecclesiastical taxation. The virtually sovereign dioceses themselves were largely responsible for this, for they were hostile to all declarations of revenue and, even before the central clergy, repeatedly refused to reveal the extent of their property and incomes.[151] The clergy in its last Assembly acknowledged the universal complaints of benefice holders and "the serious and urgent necessity of establishing a more just balance in [the] distribution" of clerical taxes without, however, upsetting the privileged position of the hierarchy.[152] Finally, the chamber voted the assessment of purely diocesan debts, expenses, arrears, pensions, seminary costs, and wages among benefice holders.[153]

The executive legal officer of the Bureau was the Diocesan Syndic, who shared with the episcopate the responsibility of insuring the retention of the temporal and spiritual rights of the diocese, the proper observance of its regulations, and the privileges of its members.[154] He served as the representative of the diocese before local magistrates and judges and received legal actions against local clergy whose redress he was to seek in court. He functioned as intermediary between the benefice holders of his district and Paris. Along with the bishop he received from the Agents-General all communications meant for the diocese. Chief among these was the diocese's allotment for the payment of the *don gratuit*. While the quota for each diocese was computed by the General Assembly, each diocese was accorded the right of dividing it among its benefice holders in proportion to income.[155] After 1745 the Syndics were obliged to render an account to the diocesan chambers of all acts pending in the General Assembly.[156] The Syndic also received the opinions and orders of the Agents in all matters regarding ecclesiastical administration and the laws passed by the Assembly. By the directives of the Assembly of Melun the Syndic was to retain a periodic correspondence with Paris in order to inform the central authorities of diocesan conditions and the current state of legal suits and litigations.[157] There is no evidence in the papers of the clergy that this important provision was respected until Talleyrand resuscitated it in his Diocesan Syndic Plan, to be examined directly.

The second essential servant of the diocese was the receiver. A layman, Catholic by faith, resident in the seat of the diocese, and owner of his office by purchase, he was responsible for supervising the collection of the *décimes* set by the chamber.[158] Personally responsible for his administration, he was required to present regular accounts to the Diocesan Bureau. He could be present at its sessions to express his views on the recovery of taxes. Depositing the *décimes* collected, he verified the receipts and supervised the accounts of the Church collectors under his direction.[159] The Diocesan Receiver transferred his diocese's contributions to the Provincial Receiver, who centralized all the sums of the dioceses in the province for the Receiver-General in Paris. Scrutinizing the sources of revenue in his diocese for monthly reports to the chamber and biannual reports to the Receiver-General before May 15 and January 15, he was obliged to report *décimes* collected, those yet outstanding, and the total contributions of his diocese to the provincial treasury.[160] The

Receiver-General, in turn, reviewed the contributions of all benefice holders within the 116 dioceses and seventeen tax areas called *généralités*.[161] Each diocese was a partially autonomous financial unit, at least insofar as it was expected to recover by *décimes* and loans the full share of the corporate debt assigned to it. Its tax accounts which reached the Agents in Paris for final confirmation had been subject beforehand to the scrupulous examination at once of Diocesan Syndic, Diocesan Bureau, Provincial Receiver, and Receiver-General.[162]

Less important and functioning largely as an intermediary between the diocesan chamber and the General Assembly were the eight *Chambres supérieures des décimes:* Paris, Lyon, Toulouse, Bordeaux, Rouen, Tours, Aix, and Bourges.[163] Established in 1580 (Bourges in 1585), these Chambers were composed of eight to twenty-two members, generally appointed by the bishops for terms of five years, whose duties were similar to those of their diocesan counterparts.[164] The bishop, who controlled the Diocesan Bureaus, also sat by right in the Chamber. The archbishop presided. The Chamber served as an appeals tribunal in cases involving more than twenty *livres* in the *décime* and thirty in the *don gratuit*. It employed the services of judges of local Parlements, prelates, and district magistrates (preferably clerical members, since "the clergy was loathe in the extreme to mix laymen in its own affairs, especially financial, even if they were the best Catholics in the world") in these appeals, beyond which there was only the General Assembly.[165] It offered its justice, like the Diocesan Bureaus, without cost. Each Chamber also had its Metropolitan Syndic, whose duties were largely the same as his diocesan counterpart, only considerably reduced, since his authority extended solely to the metropolitan city. It frequently occurred that both offices were held by the same individual.

The office of Provincial Receiver, referred to above, was abolished in 1719 and never reestablished. In its place auxiliary offices of the Receiver-General were established in the cities of the seventeen *généralités* and manned by clerks who took an oath to the Receiver-General who paid them and subjected them to close surveillance. These clerks were of marginal importance compared to the Diocesan Receivers. As noted above, the *décimes* of the diocese passed through the hands of the provincial functionaries before being sent to Paris. They were also expected to pursue cases of delinquent payment and other operations ordered by the Receiver-General.

The Provincial Chambers did not expand or achieve the importance of the Diocesan Bureaus. Though they proudly claimed to be sovereign tribunals, and though the king often regarded them as quasi-royal courts and protected their jurisdiction from the incursions of his own magistrates,[166] their functions were largely supervisory, and they lacked the means to enforce their decisions.[167] The crown repeatedly made it clear that the Chambers held power only upon its permission. Their one-sided membership, too, was resented by the lower clergy. As Professor Lepointe pointed out, "The bishops occupied an excessive place in them; they can be reproached also for an insufficient knowledge of law and perhaps a certain partiality, in any case a too frequent inobservance of the rules."[168]

VIII

Talleyrand's Legacy to the Church

Charles-Maurice de Talleyrand-Périgord proved a model Agent-General who spared no resource to protect the wealth and personnel of the First Estate. Every avenue of the clergy's major temporal business between 1780 and 1785 reveals the imprint of his activity. To Talleyrand, under the central authority of the French Church during this period, can be traced the most important enunciation of administrative practice governing the lower clergy, ecclesiastical revenues, the modernization of the clergy's corporate organization, and the maintenance of its privileges, jurisdiction, and fortune against attacks from inside the Church and out.

Talleyrand left behind, too, an impressive residue of legislation enacted both by Church and State. Most notable were statutes governing the *portion congrue,* the tithes, and the outlawry of illegally organized *curés.* His opposition to sequestration and alienations resulted in enactments requiring episcopal approval for all loans or sales of ecclesiastical property. Intimately connected with this work was legislation which assured the Church's continued control of the baptismal registry and laws determining sacerdotal fitness for the procurement of benefices by competitive means.

Talleyrand's legacy to the Assembly at the termination of a brilliant term of service was a correspondence plan which he termed a "Diocesan Syndic Plan," named, as has been seen, after the administrative officer who executed the decisions of the Diocesan Bureau and acted as the representative of his diocese to the Agents and before the government.[1] Unlike much of the Agent's former work which had been directed to specific aspects of ecclesiastical business, this plan was designed to include the temporal problems of the entire clergy. As an attempt to realize administrative centralization, the plan provided for a permanent and periodic collaboration between diocesan officials (bishop, Syndic, and Diocesan Bureau) and the clergy's central agencies (Agents, legal department, and Secretariat). It was a means to transform the Church into a compact, integrated superstructure capable of deriving maximum benefit from its administrative officers and agencies by resolving all contestations within the clergy's ranks without the costly interference of lay justice. The plan would thus prevent future attacks on its authority, privileges, and wealth. It had "no other design than the interest, the advantage, the legitimate defense of the rights and property of the clergy."[2]

Talleyrand believed that the former use of circulars and the Syndics' correspondence, intended to cement the clergy, while useful, was undependable and spasmodic. Nor was it successful either in awakening popular interest or widespread response.[3] As Agent he had always been hampered by the lack of proper information at the right time. Rarely did clerical parties involved in lawsuits send him the right documents, titles, or warrants involved in their cases. Many applied for aid without sending any of these. Others appealed to the Agents too late, many not at all. Few clerics were sufficiently informed in law or legal procedure to defend their threatened interests. Few were even aware of their rights or the means of protecting them. In hundreds of cases, recourse to the Agents for advice, legal knowledge, and intercessions in litigations testified to this. Through fear, ignorance, and indifference, the parish clergy lost case after case in the courts. Misdirected piety and generosity, the fear of a stronger antagonist, the impossibility of incurring the expenses of court and adjudication, or the risk of losing cases and with them the revenues that constituted their livelihood were all considerations.[4] The clergy's hesitancy, Talleyrand wrote, "prepared the weakening and the decadence of the principles which protect[ed] the entire body."[5] The state of clerical jurisdiction in the dioceses was so precarious that legal assurances of Church privileges were obtained on an *ad hoc,* individual basis. Timid clergy were frequently challenged or overridden in the exercise of their corporate rights. Where loss of individual cases threatened the legal principles behind the First Estate's universal exemption, or where victory could clarify or strengthen them, the Agents were forced to secure enforcement through favorable court rulings or appeal to the king's officers. Each victory of precedent and renewal of the full vigor or privilege obtained led Talleyrand to exhòrt the bishops to press for these rights in their dioceses. With diocesan officials taking a more interested part in the administration of their churches, the Agent hoped he could arrest the popular recourse to secular tribunals, which usurped episcopal authority in all branches of spiritual and temporal jurisdiction, and get local clergy to enjoy without fear or constraint the full measure of its rights.[6]

The operation of the plan was simple. A questionnaire was to be sent to each benefice holder by his Diocesan Syndic to inquire if he were engaged in a lawsuit of any kind. If so he was to reveal its subject, tell against whom it was directed, at which tribunal it was pending, at which stage the proceedings then were, and whether he was plaintiff or defendant. The Diocesan Bureau was to meet fifteen days after the circulars were sent out to review all ecclesiastical contests in the diocese. The Syndics, fully conversant with conditions and litigations within their jurisdiction, would cooperate with bishop and diocesan chamber and conjointly separate affairs of concern to the entire clergy from those of local interest. All affairs judged worthy of review by the general clergy together with all supporting titles and documents were to be sent to the Agents each three months. Thus a permanent correspondence between Syndics and Agents was to continue uninterruptedly.

Many substantial advantages would accrue to the Church through such a plan. First, it was a means of strengthening the office of the Agency-General and the central machinery of the clergy. Since these agencies did not terminate their operations between Assemblies, they had to be informed constantly of all diocesan problems in order to fulfill their obligations as permanent guardians of the clergy. The correspondence would bring all branches of clerical administration under the eyes of the Agents. It would permit a more effective assistance to benefice holders by revealing the existing differences in diocesan usages, the diversity in applying Church law, and the decisions of various courts interpreting them.[7] It would simplify and eventually reduce clerical contests and render "the corps of the clergy more imposing still and more respectable."[8]

Second, as Talleyrand believed his experience in the Assemblies of 1775, 1780 and 1782 proved, the plan would be of great advantage to the Assembly itself. For the same lack of knowledge which retarded his activity as Agent had dogged the operations of the Assembly's committees which constantly complained of the "insufficiency of instructions or details" so necessary for intelligent legislation. Finally, he hoped the plan would secure an advantage to the clergy as a whole. It would tie the rural clergy closer to the center. It would provide agreement in the conduct of ecclesiastical affairs among members of the clergy, benefice holders, Syndics, bishops, Agents, and the Assembly. To a better informed clergy it promised increased victories in litigations, which, in turn, would enhance its prestige and power in lay courts and before the State. This added strength would generate greater confidence among the clergy in appealing its cases. The plan, at least in principle, would introduce harmony between Church and State in that it "would stop the source of contestations."[9] Finally, the Diocesan Syndics could assume their proper share of the burden of questions and detail which overwhelmed the Agents.

Talleyrand outlined the essentials of his plan for the first time to the Extraordinary Assembly of 1782.[10] The inspiration for the plan grew out of extortions of tyrannical tax farmers who forced poor priests to pay the salt tax despite the clergy's exemption, for whom "one or two examples sufficed to establish a usage, and a usage became an imperious law."[11] It was a product of reflection and wide experience over ten years, during the "meeting of three consecutive Assemblies":[12]

> "Permit us, Messeigneurs and Messieurs, to dare to propose here a project which our zeal for the conservation of your privileges makes us believe possible or, at least, desirable. Your immunities are most often attacked in the persons of poor ecclesiastics without influence and far from counsel which they need to be guided in their defense. Frightened by an unequal struggle against gold and power and the inextinguishable subtleties of their adversaries, they give in or succumb after useless complaints and obscure protests. The tax farmers, proud of a first success, soon multiply their enterprises . . .[13] [and the lower clergy] are misled by the detours of chicanery, dazzled by sophisms, intimidated by influence, tired by delays, put off by appeals, overpowered by expense. Thus anxiety and disgust take hold of them, and they lose no time to appeal to your Agents."[14]

Almost a year later, on October 26, 1783, he completed the plan and in the form of two circulars announced it to the episcopate and Syndics, outlined its provisions, and solicited cooperation.[15]

The unilateral proclamation of a measure of such widespread significance for the entire Church was a bold step susceptible of criticism from conservative elements of the hierarchy. Comment was almost immediately forthcoming from Cardinal Bernis, Archbishop of Albi and French Ambassador to Rome, who complained that Talleyrand had exercised extraordinary authority in a plan of daring innovations to ecclesiastical administration. Talleyrand replied[16] that his correspondence plan was provided in principle by the Assembly of Melun of 1580, the clerical Assembly which definitively reorganized the Assembly of the Clergy in its current form; that the Assembly of 1785 alone could approve the plan and give it "final perfection and stability"; and that the statutes of the clergy empowered him to renew provisions of Church law as he judged necessary. To Jean-Marie Dulau, Archbishop of Arles and leader of the Ultras in the Assembly, the Agent justified his acts by the encouragement received from certain members of the prelacy (like Cardinal de La Rochefoucauld, President of the Assemblies of 1780 and 1782 and a cordial friend).[17] Having "long meditated this project before publishing it," he released it in advance so that even after only two years of operation he might report its usefulness to the Assembly of 1785. It could start at once to mend the abuses of the secular power and conserve the property of the Church.[18]

There can be no question from Talleyrand's correspondence that his haste was prompted by the conviction that costly attacks on the temporal made immediate action mandatory: "Your rights openly attacked from all sides demand prompt execution to stop the progress of an evil whose consequences appear to threaten the whole ecclesiastical order."[19] "Inviolable from our standpoint, as well as from the standpoint of each citizen, is that sacred right of property, which is so much the base and purpose of all societies . . . the infraction of the former carries necessarily the ruin of the latter. . . . Our defeats stem from our own weaknesses . . . the evil is easier to cure . . . when the cause of the evil is in ourselves."[20] To the Syndic of Dijon he added: "Here there is only one property-holder, property is in common. We need a head to watch it."[21]

Archbishop Loménie de Brienne wanted to add to the plan by replacing the static Metropolitan Syndics by "Syndics-General" who would be located in the town seats of the Parlements and would act as liaison between Diocesan Syndics and Agents. They could communicate the most important affairs of interest to the clergy and, with knowledge of jurisprudence, could act as on-the-spot Agents in cases requiring immediate clerical intercession. Talleyrand hailed this amendment which he asserted could easily be accommodated to his plan. The Assembly of 1785, however, sent it to committee for further study and immediately promulgated the Talleyrand program.[22] Loménie's initiative here reveals that seasoned administrators of the Church, as well as the representatives of both orders of the clergy, acknowledged the need for preventive temporal legislation.

As early as 1782 Talleyrand knew he would have trouble persuading the clergy as a whole to adopt his plan. Though he tried to keep it conservative by welding it to the iron base of the Assembly of Melun, it was not at once unanimously received.[23] If he could not present the Assembly of 1785 a report of the plan in operation, it was because for more than two years after 1783 he spent his energies on a vast correspondence personally soliciting every bishop and Syndic of the kingdom to offer suggestions and criticisms and to accept the plan.[24] After two years of hard campaigning and voluminous correspondence, Talleyrand got his plan accepted by virtually every bishop.[25]

The situation was quite different with the Syndics. While the bishops were concerned mainly with dangerous precedents or departures from established usages, the Syndics resented the additional burdens of responsibility required in a plan in which they were at once guarantors and prime functionaires, or as Talleyrand put it, "the Agents of each diocese . . . our necessary cooperators."[26] There are scores of letters and lengthy memoirs in Talleyrand's hand in which he refuted their objections that the plan's provisions would occasion resentment at once from benefice holders and courts; that the average Syndic lacked the talents and ability to counsel his benefice holders; and that it would increase his already considerable duties and responsibilities in the diocese.[27] The Agent's replies were consistently diplomatic and idealistic, always in the order of pious exhortation, flattery, or discreet reminders of sacerdotal responsibilities, pointing out that benefice holders and courts alike could find no fault, since the plan intended to end rather than encourage all contestations: "In official business" talents and ability were less important than zeal and industry, which, with experience, "render even mediocrity useful." True the plan would increase the Syndics' load, but it would also increase their prestige and their usefulness as well as the strength of the entire clergy.[28]

To the occasional Syndic who refused to relinquish his authority to the Bureau, the Agent replied that all agencies of the diocese were working towards the same end and their only effective work could be in concert. He also used a common device of assuring them that their bishop had already approved the plan and that it was his wish that the Syndic should, too. Talleyrand granted that his plan could not be perfected overnight. Only a gradual, evolutionary movement could get the clergy to use it and the Syndics to administer it: "It must not be announced with too much *éclat*: its entire execution must be the work of time and confidence."[29]

On September 26 the Assembly of 1785 applauded the Diocesan Syndic Plan and enacted its essentials in four articles.[30] The Assembly went only so far as "to invite and exhort" each benefice holder, Syndic, and bishop to accept it. Because the plan was formally sanctioned and enacted by the bishops in their Assembly, it can be assumed that all dioceses attempted to use it. From the discussion of cases contained in the Diocesan Syndic reports forwarded by the Agent to the Council of the Clergy, there is evidence that at least eighty-three dioceses actively used the plan.[31] In a letter of 1785, towards the end of his Agency, Talleyrand wrote that the "greatest number of dioceses" had adopted the plan.[32] That the volume of this correspondence entailed in the plan added considerably to the work of the legal department is indicated by the appointment of four more attorneys to its staff.[33] The President of the Assembly of 1785 informed the deputies that the affairs of the clergy had considerably multiplied "and would continue to multiply even more by the effect of the proposed correspondence."[34]

It would be difficult if not impossible to speculate quantitatively on the extent to which the Diocesan-Syndic Plan conserved the ecclesiastical temporal in the three years it was officially in operation before 1789. Yet, there is no doubt that this plan which struck at the heart of the Church's administrative weakness, and which proposed to remedy the cause of its reverses, was the most imaginative attempt in the years before the Revolution to revive the lethargic, age-ridden diocesan administration. It was also the one realistic way to protect the property, privileges, and jurisdiction of the First Estate against the challenges of laymen, and to make its entire personnel "united and unanimous in all that concerned the defense of the Church"[35]—a condition which never obtained in the ranks of the clergy in the latter eighteenth century.

* * * * *

It is time to take stock of Talleyrand's achievement as Agent-General. Viewed as a whole, his work betrays an almost obsessive sense of institutional unity. To him each possession and privilege constituted a sacred and immutable charge if the clerical patrimony was to remain a cumulative inheritance and an autonomous spiritual and temporal force. Not a shred of authority or property could be relinquished either to the alien, usurping jurisdiction of lay courts or to the refractory voices within the clergy without weakening the principles of immunity, ownership, and discipline which made the First Estate a corporate phenomenon unique in France. All the acts of the Agency, the inspiration for his reforms and proposed legislation derived from this premise. His work against illegal unions of priests who threatened the discipline as well as the property of the Church, his attempted outlawry of clerical alienations, his stand on the *foi et hommage* and the alodial nature of ecclesiastical property, the immunity from fiscal-feudal-patrimonial impositions, the irrevocability of foundations and the famous case of the Celestines of Lyon, his authoritarian statements on episcopal supremacy—all of these must revert to the Church domain. Even the ingenious Diocesan Syndic Plan, although it intended to fortify the Church on every level by insuring the rights of each benefice holder in litigations, and although designed to tighten the grip of the legitimately constituted authorities over the diocesan clergy, had at its root the concern for the conservation of the temporalities of each parish.

Indeed, more than personal conviction or professional orientation, this stand was obligatory for an official made captain of the ecclesiastical temporal and charged to defend its integrity and wealth. The Church spiritual was not his main concern. It was left to the bishops and the Assembly.

With undaunted constancy Talleyrand confronted the ablest ministers of his time, Vergennes, Necker, and Calonne, with old fashioned arguments about the inalienability of the clergy's temporal and its tax immunities—more typical of the spirit of the Age of St. Louis than Voltaire. To how many Parlements and magistrates did he address the age-old canonic doctrines of the unassailable sanctity of ecclesiastical property, to which he added the fashionable Lockean corollary that once the right of possessing property were trespassed, the principles of ownership were voided and the traditional institutional bases of society itself were thereby endangered. And what—

ironically—better proved the truth of these assertions than Talleyrand's own motion of October, 1789?

No one in the order of the clergy in the waning Old Regime better divined the source of the clergy's reverses vis-a-vis the State, and no one worked harder for appropriate reforms to overcome them. Talleyrand sensed the ever increasing menace posed by lay power in the form of tax collectors, local magistrates, or the Parlements themselves which undermined the foundations of spiritual discipline and jurisdiction and attenuated the Church's exclusive regulation of religion and its personnel. To combat this, Talleyrand-jurisconsult mobilized the legal-juridical guarantees confirmed by statute and sanctified by tradition, and Talleyrand-attorney secured before the king or his officers favorable decisions and cassations of abusive court decrees. To counteract insubordinate ecclesiastics who sought the offices of secular tribunals, Talleyrand reverted to a well-defined and consistent scheme of hierarchical authority. At the summit there was the Assembly, the supreme authority. It shared power with the bishops upon whom the Agent depended as the backbone of order in the dioceses, as the enforcers of the statutes of the Church, and as the foundation for reform. This was particularly true in the preservation of ecclesiastical property, the prevention of alienations and the illicit confederation of *curés,* the determination of sacerdotal fitness for priests seeking benefices, the control of the baptismal registry, and, once again, his own Diocesan Syndic Plan. He continually searched methods which would strengthen ecclesiastical jurisdiction at the top level of the Assembly and episcopate and would exclude injurious and divisive influences of lay tribunals. At the bottom there was the lower clergy who not only discharged sacramental-sacerdotal functions and submitted to the authority of the first pastors but also protected the patrimony consigned to its trust. Each cleric was to enjoy the aggregate of rights and immunities granted the Church and with the aid of the Agents was to repulse lay attempts to withhold or abridge them. Talleyrand jealously guarded the prerogatives of the clergy which were most frequently assailed in the person of local priests. His efforts culminated in a correspondence plan which the clergy enacted in 1785.

Politically, Talleyrand feared the seditious organization of disaffected clergy of the Fourth Estate, the *curés congruistes.* He realized clearer than most of the bishops that only by guaranteeing them adequate subsistence could the Church preserve its discipline and wealth, insure the efficacy of its spiritual mission, reduce the incidence of lay interference, and avoid clerical insurrection. This concern led him to advance legislation, officially adopted in 1786, which raised the priests' salaries.

Economically, he vigorously resisted any attempt to cut off the Church's fiscal receipts, especially the tithes. Against clergy and laymen alike he fought all attempts to evade payment to legitimate tithe owners. He was severe with laymen (including the king) and priests alike who refused to honor their obligations to the *portion congrue*. Nor was there either patience or kindness for clerics who refused to meet their *décime* obligations or contested the figure assigned by the Diocesan Bureau.

Administratively, the links of command from Paris to the provinces had faltered in the course of the eighteenth century, resulting in local catastrophes, the demoralization of poor clergy, and costly losses for the order. The Agent attempted to put the household of the parish clergy in the same good order as he had the central agencies in Paris. In these administrative tasks, in his legislative work, and in making himself accessible to the clergy at all times, he enjoyed the full confidence of prelacy and priests, officers of the State, and lieutenants of the Agency.

Talleyrand's fear of royal government, commonly shared by all elements of the First Estate, did not blind him to the need for compromise and enlightened self-interest. He displayed the judgment and acumen for which he was later to become justly famous in advocating a generous *don gratuit* as the cheapest method all round to secure the Church's property and to assure the king's continuing good will. He advocated relinquishing the excesses and abuses of the ecclesiastical temporal, according reasonable concessions, and rejecting unpopular or illegitimate demands of clerical parties which only increased the incidence of litigations and costly conflict which, in turn, taxed the clergy's wealth, energy, and influence.

For Talleyrand the Agency proved an apprenticeship of statesmanship in the most rigorous sense. From his functions in the Assembly he acquired invaluable parliamentary and ministerial experience, an acute sense of tact and reserve, and a feeling for official language and the *mot juste*. In dealing with the bewildering multitude and diversity of officers, groups and persons, lay and spiritual, and in appeal before magistrates and Parlements of the State with whom he was in ceaseless contact, he learned the vocabulary of politics, the give-and-take of diplomacy, and the securing of concessions and agreements from the other side by negotiations and counter-proposals. His contacts with the king's ministers and Versailles provided an inside view of court life and plentiful lessons in the gentle art of intrigue, personal influence, and the game of men and politics.

In the Secretariat he developed administrative proficiency. He learned how to separate out the important, and he received practical instruction in the division of labor and responsibility. Indeed, Talleyrand's later idea of civil service as "the link between government and governed, the locus of particular and of general interests, of public authority and individual freedom," which a recent scholar called "the forerunner of its present-day sociological definition,"[36] was first conceived and practiced as the titular head of the clergy's administrative organization.

In the Council of the Clergy he gained wide legal knowledge and pitted his legal wits against sophisticated legal minds steeped in an impressive juristic tradition which went back to the Middle Ages. It was here, too, that he defined and practiced those first notions of legitimacy of ownership and authority, destined to reappear in 1814 under a not so different form. His superintendence of the finances of his order and his collaboration with the Receivers added to his already considerable knowledge of economics and national finance. If we are to believe Bachaumont, Talleyrand saved the day for the Receiver-General of the Clergy, M. Bollioud de Saint-Jullien, who, with two millions of the clergy's funds tied up in the bonds of the Discount Bank, sent the Agent on October 30, 1783 to a meeting of the stockholders to advise him on "the situation of the Discount Bank and to learn the fate [of the clergy's bonds]."[37] Talleyrand, we are informed, though in the company of well known financiers like Panchaud, Dunolé, and Beaumarchais, proved himself "the most distinguished" and as a result of his eloquence was named one of the five commissioners of the bank, a position he declined "as too contrary to his estate."

And finally, from the hundreds of clerical parties, whose affairs he made his own, he learned how to gather opinion, to make decisions, to practice moderation, and to compose by adroit politics seemingly irreconcilable points of view. These skills Talleyrand employed all through his career as minister, diplomat, financier, and politician.

Revealed in the clerical ministry of 1780 to 1785 were the main lines of Talleyrand's future development. His intellectual powers and creative originality were already clearly evident. The qualities of statesmanship—imagination, keen judgment of men and issues, a peculiar endowment for hard work and detail (though this has rarely been appreciated in Talleyrand), a splendid memory for facts, synthetic ability, administrative and diplomatic skill, and the power of swift and inspired decision—all sources of his later reputation—were clearly visible to his hierarchical superiors. They were equally apparent to the ministers of government with whom he negotiated the affairs of the clergy and to his own successors who admitted being "jealous to follow in the steps of our predecessors [and] to follow the same zeal."[38]

In a memoir submitted to Napoleon and published in 1800[39] on the qualities essential for appointees to the Foreign Office, Talleyrand defined under the categories of "soul" and "mind" the elements of a consummate politician. In the first category he put circumspection, discretion, detachment, and the elevation of sentiment that makes a man feel "all that is great in the function of representing his nation abroad and of guarding within the conservation of its political interests." Under mind, he included a penchant for the study of political relations, a faculty for seizing problems promptly and well, and a certain "breadth of ideas" which reveals detail as part of the whole. While he was speaking of secular politics, to be sure, it is apparent that these same skills were practiced by the author, twenty years before, in the temporal service of the Church of France.

On the other hand, how explain the ultra-conservatism and dramatic zeal of the figure whom the history books have traditionally put down as the indolent idea-peddler of talented feudatories? There are two explanations; the first is personal, and the second is implicit in the political position of the clergy on the eve of the Revolution. During the years of his Agency Talleyrand's steadfast ambition, and the reason for his appointment to that office in the first place, was to become a bishop. The Agency was commonly accepted as the vestibule of a bishopric. Everyone in the Church knew that. But in the jungle of competition between numerous ecclesiastical noblemen vying for the few bishoprics available, Talleyrand realized that he could be no ordinary Agent, especially if the reports of his easy morals during the period have any truth. He was out to impress his superiors by surpassing the requirements of his office[40] and by adopting a conservative posture congenial to the tradition-bound hierarchy so that there could be no just grounds for depriving him of his well-earned prize. Desire for promotion and the will to advance provide the first explanation.

The second is to be seen in Talleyrand's gifted adaptation of ecclesiastical policy. From the crescendo of clerical court contests, the increase of forced sales of clerical property, the rising influence of the Parlements in ecclesiastical jurisdiction, the serious social cleavages within the French Church, and the growing advocacy of sequestration it is clear that the First Estate was frightened and apprehensive about its patrimony. The official stand of the French bishops before 1789 was to give no quarter to popular opinion and to hold on to their corporate privileges in whatever way possible. The Church's answer to Calonne's plans for a clerical income tax of 1787 and the king's request for more clerical funds in the agony of 1788 was, on the one hand, to scuttle the Notables and discredit the minister[41] and, on the other, to grant the king a pittance, to join hands with the proscribed Parlements, traditionally the clergy's arch foes, and to lend its enormous prestige and authority to the radical elements which clamored for the Estates-General.[42] Resolved to fly from its age-old monarchism and only true friend, the king, into the arms of magisterial aristocrats whose only answer to national crisis was the resurgence of selfish caste power, the episcopate revised its policy of conciliatory coexistence based on the theory of immemorial privilege in favor of bold nobiliary pretensions and denunciations of royal despotism inspired by Montesquieu. It is a sobering historical reality that the bishops greeted the Revolution as the only way left to hold on to their temporal, never dreaming that its arrival would have the disastrous effect they were trying to avoid—an upheaval that would rob the Church and its leaders of the wealth, power, independence, and unique corporate status enjoyed in France for centuries. This explains the conservatism and orthodoxy of Talleyrand's Agency. As Agent-General he was the spokesman, the executor, but scarcely the architect of clerical policy; and however adroit and imaginative his diplomacy and innovating techniques which facilitated the clergy's objectives, their main course was predetermined by others.

Within less than a decade the priest who had been the pride of his order and the uncompromising champion of its privileges became in the popular image the Judas who provided its disestablishment. The young acolyte who had entered the Church without love was prepared to leave as a liberated prelate without hate. Once 1789 came and

Talleyrand, now a bishop, had nothing more to desire from an unpopular Church, whose service he never wanted to join anyway (and from which he was already planning an opportune exit), he could afford to abandon his former policy of intransigence, now thoroughly anachronistic and unpopular. His future professional ambitions were national statesmanship, political economy, and diplomacy; and his new patron, to replace the one he helped dispatch, was the State. But this is another story and still another of the "Lives of Talleyrand."

Notes

NOTES TO INTRODUCTION

[1] *Annales politiques, civiles et littéraires du dix-huitième siècle, ouvrage périodique par M. Linguet,* Vol. IX (Londres, 1780), p. 116.

NOTES TO CHAPTER I

[1] This practice was quite common among the social peers of the Talleyrands. "The nobles who led a courtly life in Paris and Versailles, even the nobles of the provinces, seriously neglected the education of their children. No sooner born, they were placed in the hands of a wetnurse to stay as long as possible." (H. Carré, *La noblesse de France et l'opinion publique au XVIIIe siècle* [Paris, 1920], p. 194).

[2] An older brother died when Charles-Maurice was three. (A. Pichot, *Souvenirs intimes de Monsieur de Talleyrand* [Paris, 1870], p. 15.) His lameness, like virtually every other incident of importance in his life, is enveloped by a dense growth of exaggerated polemic and ill-tempered controversy. Historians are still arguing the origins of this affliction. L. Bastide, (*La vie religieuse et politique de Talleyrand-Périgord* [Paris, 1838], p. 14), representing the old school, and J. Vivent (*La vie priveé de Talleyrand* [Paris, 1940], pp. 17-18), the new, present a case for its congenital origin. A. Marcade (*Talleyrand, prêtre et évêque* [Paris, 1883], p. 12) and C. K. McHarg (*Life of Prince de Talleyrand* [New York, 1857], p. 9) argue that its genesis lay in an injury inflicted by pasture animals while an unsuspecting urchin ran wild on the plains of Périgord. His niece, Mme de Dino, and confessor, Mgr. Dupanloup, adopted Talleyrand's own account (*Mémoires du Prince de Talleyrand, publiés avec une préface et des notes par le Duc de Broglie* [Paris, 1891], I, 7 [hereafter cited as Talleyrand, *Mémoires*]) that he fell from a highboy. This version is current among most biographers. A writer of science fiction of the last century, Dr. Cabanes, who called himself a "medical psychologist," sought to prove that Talleyrand's "evil" resulted from the relationship between lameness and an unhealthy brain, called "atrophic cerebral lesions." This, according to Cabanes, also explains his immorality and peculiar *état d'âme.* ("Conversations avec M. le docteur Luys, les lésions cérébrales chez les pieds bots, le cerveau de Talleyrand," *La Chronique Médicale* [Paris, 1894], I, 35.) Two writers who assisted and transcribed the autopsy of Talleyrand's brain, on the other hand, alleged that it had the health and vitality of a man of forty. (G. Place and J. Florens, *Mémoire sur M. de Talleyrand, sa vie politique, et sa vie intime* [Paris, 1838], p. 141).

[3] By letters patent secured from Louis XIII in 1613, the unbroken succession of the Talleyrands as sovereign Counts of Périgord was confirmed. (P. de Guilbourne Anselme de Sainte-Marie, *Histoire généalogique et chronologique de la maison royale de France, des pairs, grand officiers de la couronne, et de la maison du roi,* Pol Potier de Courcy, ed. [Paris, 1881], IX, Part 2, 80).

218   *Talleyrand: Statesman Priest*

[4] The famed warrior tradition of the family extended back to the days of Hélie VI of Périgord and the first Capetians. Monluc and Admiral Jean de Vienne were relatives. Ministers Mortemart, Chamillart, and Colbert were also in the family. His godfather, Gabriel-Marie de Talleyrand, step-brother of his father, was Governor of Berry. (Sainte-Marie, *Histoire généalogique*, IX, Part 2, 79-80; Archives du Séminaire de Saint-Sulpice de Paris, "Registre des Naissances et Baptêmes," vol. 1754; C. de Saint-Aulaire, *Talleyrand* [Paris, 1936], pp. 16-17). Similarly his maternal d'Antigny forbears were brigadiers of armies. (G. Lacour-Gayet, "L'enfance de Talleyrand et le collège d'Harcourt," *Revue de Paris* [1926], p. 800).

[5] H. M. Brougham, *Historical Sketches of Statesmen who Flourished in the Time of George III* (London, 1843), I, 162.

[6] F. Lagrange, *Vie de Monseigneur Dupanloup* (Paris, 1883), I, 223.

[7] *Notice historique sur la vie et les travaux de M. le prince de Talleyrand* (Paris, 1839), p. 4.

[8] H. Carré, P. Sagnac, E. Lavisse, *Louis XVI, 1774-1789* (*Histoire de France*, IX, Part 1, E. Lavisse, ed., [Paris, 1911]), p. 149. Cited hereafter as Lavisse, *Histoire de France*.

[9] Talleyrand, *Mémoires*, I, 7.

[10] H. Sée, *La France économique et sociale au XVIIIe siècle* (5th ed.; Paris, 1952), pp. 83-88; Carré, *La noblesse de France*, pp. 56-92.

[11] *Souvenirs de Jacob-Nicholas Moreau*, G. Hermelin, ed. (Paris, 1898), I, 95.

[12] M. Dumolin, "La maison natale de Talleyrand," *Revue Historique du VIe Arrondissement*, XI (1929), 44-46.

[13] *Souvenirs de la Marquise de Créquy, 1710-1800* (Paris, 1834), I, 234.

[14] Papers of G. Lacour-Gayet, "Lettre #1 de la Comtesse Arthur de Voguë."

[15] Talleyrand, *Mémoires*, I, 34.

[16] Archives Nationales de France [henceforth cited as "A.N."] T 89.

[17] 54,370 *l.* (A.N. T 88).

[18] In 1778 he married Madeleine-Henriette Sabine Ollivier de Senozan de Virinville, who combined ancient titles of nobility with vast landed wealth. Her inheritance included the lands and Marquisat of Rosny, the lands and County of Senozan, the lands and Marquisat of Sennecey, the lands and Marquisat of Falavier together with "other lands, fiefs, and seigneuries." (A.N., T 89).

[19] Talleyrand, *Mémoires*, I, 7.

[20] The Freudians have made much sound about Talleyrand's handicap and forced profession, which they agree was the turning point of his whole life. To Edmund Bergler, "Talleyrand's hatred of the Church was not alone his defense against an unpleasant organization, it was parental authority personified, which he battled in the Church, and which he battled with greatest hatred." (*Psychoanalytische-biographische Essays* [Vienna, 1935], p. 27). R. Laforgue (*Talleyrand, l'homme de la France: essai psychoanalytique* [Lausanne, n. d.], p. 48) found a second cause of Talleyrand's abnormality in the absence of maternal affection, having been reared in a society which prevented mothers from fulfilling their natural roles. G. Ferrero believed Talleyrand's accident accounted for his inexplicable predestination to revolt against all powers and regimes. (*Reconstruction of Europe: Talleyrand and the Congress of Vienna, 1814-1815* [New York, 1941], p. 30). A half-century before the Freudians, but a harbinger of their views, Talleyrand's friend, the Baron de Barante ("Discours prononcé à la chambre des pairs, le 8 juin, 1838 à l'occasion du

décès de M. de Talleyrand," *Etudes historiques et biographiques* [Paris, 1857], p. 373) saw in this infirmity his compulsive need to seek "a lavish standard of living" through dissipation and luxury.

[21] It is particularly in this context that Talleyrand's words of contrition to Pope Gregory XVI on the eve of his death (May 17, 1838) have meaning: "The respect for those to whom I owe my life by no means forbids me to state that my entire youth was directed towards a profession for which I was not born" (reproduced in B. Nervo, *La conversion et la mort de M. de Talleyrand: Récit de cinq témoins* [Paris, 1911], pp. 23-24). The original document, recently uncovered by R. Limouzin-Lamothe ("La rétractation de Talleyrand: documents inédits," *Revue d'Histoire de l'Eglise de France,* XL [1954], 234) reveals an illuminating variation: "The direction which was imposed on my youth was absolutely opposed to a true vocation."

[22] J. E. Acton, "Talleyrand's Memoirs," *Historical Essays and Studies* (London, 1907), p. 402. Félix Dupanloup, Bishop of Orleans and one of the luminaries of the Church of the Second Empire, achieved his first fame as the young priest who returned Talleyrand to Catholicism before his death in 1838. Scarcely known is that the intimate of the aged Prince was also his biographer and that during various moments of his busy life, he was hard at work on a vast unpublished manuscript, "Monsieur de Talleyrand, histoire inconnu de Monsieur de Talleyrand, ou, Monsieur de Talleyrand, étude sur sa vie, son caractère, ses dernières années et sa fin" (deposited in the papers of Count Bernard de Lacombe), by which he hoped to rehabilitate the misunderstood victim of a system which reversed divine order. Sympathetic, yet critical and no fool, Dupanloup points out that Talleyrand long held that Fénelon's dictum that nothing could "force the impenetrable shelter of the liberty of the heart" applied particularly to himself. ("Livre premier, enfance, éducation, malheureux commencements de M. de Talleyrand," fols. 5-6). The Bishop of Autun actually used this expression officially in a letter to his Cathedral Chapter in May, 1790, after having refused to vote Catholicism as the official religion of the State (*La réponse de M. l'évêque d'Autun au chapitre de l'église cathédrale d'Autun, 29 mai, 1790* [Paris, 1790], p. 5).

[23] Portions of this chapter have appeared in L. S. Greenbaum, "Talleyrand and his Uncle: The Genesis of a Clerical Career," *Journal of Modern History,* XXIX (1957), pp. 226-236.

[24] L. Ducros, *La société française au XVIIIe siècle* (Paris, 1922), p. 248; L. Lévy-Schneider, "L'autonomie administrative de l'épiscopat français à la fin de l'ancien régime," *Revue Historique,* CLI (1926), 9. The requirements of the four quarterings of nobility exacted by royal statutes in 1781 and 1788 for places in the army and magistracy also had their influence upon the Church. (Cf. Sée, *France économique,* pp. 77-78; P. Sagnac, *La formation de la société française moderne, 1660-1789* [Paris, 1946] II, 217). To be a *roturier* was considered a second cardinal sin by the lower clergy who aspired to places in the episcopate. Gone were the days when Louis XIV had made cardinals and bishops of plebeians like Dubois, Bossuet, Mascaron, Massillon, Fléchier, and Huet. The low-born Bossuets of the latter eighteenth century, the Abbés Maury, Sieyès, Louis, Morellet, Grégoire, and others were justly bitter that under the dispensation of the *ancien régime* they were not "episcopable," that, regardless of their talents, they would never become bishops.

[25] Abbé A. de Morellet, *Mémoires sur le XVIIIe siècle et sur la Révolution,* (Paris, 1822) I, 18.

[26] A. Frézet, *Le Cardinal de Talleyrand-Périgord* (Reims, 1936), p. 14;

Précis de la vie du prélat d'Autun digne ministre de la fédération (Paris, 1790), p. 3. Two typical panegyrics of the prelate, Cardinal Bausset, *Notice historique sur S. E. Mgr. Alexandre-Angélique de Talleyrand-Périgord* (Versailles, 1821), and D. Frayssinous, *Oraison funèbre de S. E. Mgr. le Cardinal de Périgord* (Paris, 1822), make no mention whatever of consanguinity.

27 Among the better biographies of Talleyrand: G. Lacour-Gayet, *Talleyrand* (Paris, 1928) I, 28-30; C. Brinton, *Lives of Talleyrand* (New York, 1936), p. 37; B. de Lacombe, *Talleyrand, évêque d'Autun* (Paris, 1903), pp. 8-9; D. Cooper, *Talleyrand* (New York, 1932), p. 5; L. Madelin, *Talleyrand* (Paris, 1944), p. 17; E. de Saint-Aulaire, *Talleyrand* (Paris, 1936), pp. 29-30; E. Aujay, *Talleyrand* (Paris, 1946), p. 15; J. McCabe, *Talleyrand, A Biographical Study* (New York, 1906), pp. 10-11; A. B. Dodd, *Talleyrand: The Training of a Statesman, 1754-1838* (New York, 1927), p. 24.

28 *L'Almanach Royal de 1789* (Paris, n.d.), pp. 58-69; *La France Ecclésiastique pour l'Année 1789* (Paris, n.d.), pp. 15-21.

29 As for example the Richelieu in Luçon; the Gondi (Retz) in Paris; the Sourdis in Maillezais; the Bonzi in Béziers; and the Rohan in Strasbourg. (A. Sicard, *Les évêques pendant la Révolution* [*L'ancien clergé de France*, Paris, 1894, II] p. 12).

30 P. de La Gorce, *Histoire religieuse de la Révolution française* (Paris, 1921) I, 18-19; G. Desdevises du Dézert, *L'église et l'Etat en France depuis l'édit de Nantes jusqu'au concordat, 1598-1801* (Paris, 1907), I, 165; A. Sicard, *Les évêques avant la Révolution* (*L'ancien clergé de France*, [Paris, 1905] I), pp. 211, 224; L. Dollot, *La question des privilèges dans la seconde moitié du XVIIIe siècle* (Paris, 1941), 51; E. Hocquart de Turtot, *Le tiers état et les privilèges* (Paris, 1907), 52-59; A. Dubuc, "La gestion de la manse abbatiale de Fécamp à la fin du règne de Louis XV," *Actes du 84e congrès national des sociétés savantes, section d'histoire . . .* (Paris, 1960), 25.

31 Talleyrand, *Mémoires*, I, 117. Recent scholarship has revealed the same monopolistic, proprietary control of parishes among "family dynasties" of bourgeois lower clergy, who also aspired to substantial benefices which accorded higher social rank, and who, like the bishops, moved "always or nearly always to take a better-endowed benefice." (L. Perouas, "Le nombre des vocations sacerdotales, est-il un critère valable en sociologie religieuse historique aux 17e et 18e siècles?" *Actes du 87e congrès national des sociétés savantes, section d'histoire. . . .* [Paris, 1963], 36-38; P. Guillaume, *Essai sur la vie religieuse dans l'Orléanais de 1600 à 1789* [Orleans, 1957]; M. Join-Lambert, "La pratique religieuse dans le diocèse de Rouen de 1707 à 1789," *Annales de Normandie*, III [1953], 247-274; V [1955], 35-49).

32 M. Göhring, *Weg und Sieg der Staatsidee in Frankreich vom Mittelalter zu 1789* (Tübingen, 1946), p. 10.

33 J. Perrin, *Le Cardinal de Loménie de Brienne, archevêque de Sens* (Sens, 1896), p. 3; A. Jean, *Dictionnaire des évêques et archevêques en France, 1682-1801* (Paris, 1891), p. 292; Sicard, *Ancien clergé*, I, 51-52.

34 J. N. Duport de Cheverny, *Mémoires sur les règnes de Louis XV et Louis XVI et sur la Révolution, 1731-1802*, R. de Crèvecoeur, ed. (Paris, 1886) I, 42-43, 61.

35 Morellet, *Mémoires*, I, 11-13.

36 Sicard, *Ancien clergé*, I, 12-13, 88-90, 112-113.

37 Cited by Carré in Lavisse, *Histoire de France*, IX, Part 1, 157.

38 Archives de l'évêché d'Autun. "Registres des délibérations du conseil épiscopal d'Autun," February 3, 1789.

39 Sicard expressed this movement very well: "The prelates were tempted

to compose their ecclesiastical houses according to their tastes and the exigencies of kinship . . . This pride in the name, in the family . . . tended to transform the bishop into a brother or uncle devoted to his relative even to the pocketbook . . . The uncle-bishops were asked to use all their influence (and they did not lack it) to procure for their relatives advancement, positions, and pensions." (Sicard, *Ancien clergé*, I, 3, 24, 37-38, 378).

[40] Jean, *Evêques*, pp. 247-248; L. Lalanne, *Dictionnaire historique de la France* (Paris, 1872), p. 1574.

[41] Sicard, *Ancien clergé*, I, 209-211, 224; *Journal de l'abbé de Véri*, J. de Witte, ed., I (Paris, 1929), 198.

[42] J. Loth, *Histoire du Cardinal Dominique de La Rochefoucauld* (Evreux, 1892), p. 12; L. Audiat, *Deux victimes des septembriseurs, Pierre-Louis de La Rochefoucauld, dernier évêque de Saintes, et son frère, évêque de Beauvais* (Lille, 1897), pp. 1-25.

[43] F. Masson, *Le Cardinal de Bernis, depuis son ministère, 1758-1794* (Paris, 1884), p. 497; *Procès-verbal de l'assemblée générale du clergé de 1785* (Paris, 1788), p. 16. Sicard, *Ancien clergé*, I, 318; E. Lavaquery, *Le Cardinal de Boisgelin, 1732-1804* (Angers, 1920), I, 207; Perrin, *Loménie de Brienne*, pp. 28-29; L. d'Illiers, *Deux prélats d'ancien régime; les Jarente* (Monaco, 1948), p. 82; Jean, *Evêques*, pp. 235-236, 262-263, 377-378, 448; Duport de Cheverny, *Mémoires*, I, 42-43.

[44] L. Lévy-Schneider, *L'application du concordat par un prélat d'ancien régime, Mgr. Champion de Cicé* (Paris, 1921), p. 3.

[45] Sicard, *Ancien clergé*, I, 318.

[46] Talleyrand, *Mémoires*, I, 8.

[47] H. L. Bouquet, *L'ancien collège d'Harcourt et le lyceé Saint-Louis* (Paris, 1891), p. 418.

[48] Cf. P. de Crouzas-Crétet, *L'église et l'Etat, ou les deux puissances au XVIIIe siècle, 1715-1789* (Paris, 1893), pp. 339-349.

[49] Frézet, *Talleyrand-Périgord*, pp. 7-8.

[50] Talleyrand, *Mémoires*, I, 17-18.

[51] A. Sorel, "Talleyrand et ses mémoires," *Lectures historiques* (Paris, 1894), p. 10; R. Lévy, "Le renouveau de Talleyrand," *Grande Revue*, LXVII (1911), 755. As a young seminarist Talleyrand stole off frequently to the Sorbonne Chapel to dream in the shadows of Richelieu's mausoleum. Even in his late age, he admitted that his diplomatic heroes had been the great Cardinal-diplomats, Duprat, Ossat, and Polignac. (*Eloge de M. le comte Reinhard, prononcé à l'Académie des sciences morales et politiques par M. le prince de Talleyrand dans la séance du 3 mars, 1838* [Paris, 1838], pp. 7-9; C. A. Sainte-Beuve, *Monsieur de Talleyrand* [Paris, 1880], p. 6).

[52] *Lettres secretes* [sic] *sur l'état actuel de la religion et du clergé de France* (Paris, 1781), pp. 5-6, 79-81; D. de Pradt, *Les quatres concordats* (Paris, 1818), III, 4-9.

[53] Sicard, *Ancien clergé*, I, 36-39.

[54] A. Mathiez, "L'église de la Révolution: son organisation intérieure," *Revue des Cours et Conférences*, XXIII (1932), 200-203.

[55] E. Cauly, *Histoire du collège des bons-enfants de l'Université de Reims* (Paris, 1885), pp. 600-628; C. Loriquet, "Le bureau des incendies et les autres établissements de charité de M. de Talleyrand, Archevêque de Reims," *Travaux de l'Académie Nationale de Reims*, LV (1873-1874), 199-225; P. Denis, "Un projet de fondation de Mgr. de Talleyrand-Périgord, Archevêque de Reims en faveur des jeunes gentilhommes de sa province (1787)," *Travaux de l'Académie Nationale de Reims*, CXXVII (1909-1910), 259-267; A. Frézet,

"Mgr. de Talleyrand et les inondations de 1784," *Bulletin du Diocèse de Reims,* XLIII (1910), 638-640.

[56] A.N. T88[2]; T88[1]; *Almanach Royal de 1787* (Paris, n.d.), pp. 60, 74, 87. By order of the National Assembly of November 13, 1789, he listed his revenues as 218,251 *l.* (A.N. T 87, "Coppie [sic] de la déclaration des biens et revenues et des charges foncières et annuelles de l'archevêque de Reims et abbayes y réunies à perpetuité.")

[57] M. Hubert, "Les prétendues 'histoires scandaleuses' de Mgr. le Cardinal de Talleyrand-Périgord. La démolition de l'église abbatiale de Saint-Thierry, l'emplacement de l'édifice," *Revue de Champagne,* I-III (1908-1910), 3-8.

[58] A.N. T88[1]; "Alexandre-Angélique de Talleyrand-Périgord, Ex-archevêque de Reims, Emigré: Etat de mobilier et des réparations de l'hôtel de Gramont rue de Bourbon."

[59] Talleyrand, *Mémoires,* I, 19.

[60] *Mémoires de Talleyrand,* P. L. Couchoud, ed. (Paris, 1957) I, xi.

[61] Talleyrand, *Mémoires,* I, 18. He must have expressed this grievance often, for it appears frequently in the works of his friends. Cf. *Mémoires de Madame de Rémusat, 1802-1808* (Paris, 1880), III, 326; E. Dumont de Genève, *Souvenirs sur Mirabeau et sur les deux premières assemblées législatives* (Paris, 1832), p. 359; H. R. Lord Holland, *Foreign Reminiscences* (London, 1850), p. 34. His London secretary, H. Colmache (*Reminiscences of Prince Talleyrand* [London, 1850], p. 122), claimed that it was not until he was seventeen that he spent time at the home of his elders. Carré (*Noblesse de France,* pp. 195-196), on the contrary, reminds us that such practices were not atypical in the eighteenth century.

[62] Especially the fantastic allegations of hostile nineteenth-century biographers like Michaud, Bastide, Touchard-Lafosse, and Villemarest, who painted in lurid colors the desperate crises of conscience which supposedly afflicted Talleyrand along every step of his clerical career.

[63] N. P. Zacour, "Petrarch and Talleyrand," *Speculum,* XXXI (1956), 683-703.

[64] Perrin, *Loménie de Brienne,* pp. 4-8.

[65] This friendship was never forgotten by the later diplomat, who got Napoleon to appoint him Bishop of Evreux. (*Discours prononcé dans la séance du mardi 13 novembre, 1821 par M. le prince duc de Talleyrand à l'occasion du décès de M. le comte Bourlier, évêque d'Evreux* [Paris, 1821], pp. 5-9).

[66] J. Leflon, *Monsieur Emery: l'église d'ancien régime et la Révolution* (Paris, 1944), I, 83-87; E. Méric, *Histoire de Monsieur Emery et de l'église de France pendant la Révolution* (Paris, 1885), I, 74-80. There are, unfortunately, no histories of the famous seminary. The late E. Levesque, former archivist of the Seminary of Saint-Sulpice, has offered two studies on the physical development of the school in the eighteenth century, *L'ancien séminaire de Saint-Sulpice* (Limoges, 1922); "Le séminaire de Saint-Sulpice," *Revue du Clergé Français,* XCVII (1919), 49-54.

[67] V. de Broc, *Un évêque sous l'ancien régime: M. de Maillé de la Tour Landry* (Paris, 1894), p. 12.

[68] Leflon, *Emery,* pp. 83-87; C. G. Bowers (*Pierre Vergniaud, Voice of the French Revolution* [New York, 1954], p. 29) claimed that he "felt no call for the priestly life [and] terminated in time, like Turgot, all intentions of becoming a priest."

[69] Frézet, *Talleyrand-Périgord,* p. 14.

[70] Talleyrand, *Mémoires,* I, 33.

Notes   223

[71] This regulation had previously been subject to grievous abuse. Richelieu was named Bishop of Luçon not only without the subdiaconate, but without any theological study whatever. Cardinal Dubois had only the clerical tonsure at the time he was made Archbishop of Cambrai. Cardinal Bernis, favorite of Mme de Pompadour, received the subdiaconate in 1755 at the age of forty and was ordained priest in 1760, two years after he had been elevated to the cardinalate. Under reforms instituted by the Minister of the *feuille des bénéfices*, La Roche-Aymon, no offices, prebends, or benefices would be given to ecclesiastical personnel not in possession of the subdiaconate. (Sicard, *Ancien clergé*, II, 12, 29, 34).

[72] L. de Héricourt, *Les loix ecclésiastiques de France* (Paris, 1771), Part 4, 300.

[73] Archives épiscopales de Paris, "Registre des ordinations d'avril 1774 à septembre, 1777," fol. 34.

[74] Archives du Séminaire de Saint-Sulpice, "Papiers Emery: souvenirs de Mgr. Sausin," Vol. IV, fol. 47.

[75] Archives Municipales de Reims (hereafter cited as "Reims") G 235, fol. 41.

[76] Reims, G 246, fol. 289; G 235, fol. 79. It is further corroborated by the credentials which the deputy from Reims laid before the Assembly of 1775: "Charles-Maurice de Talleyrand-Périgord, sous-diacre et chapelain de la chapelle de la Sainte-Vierge, fondée en l'église paroissiale de Saint-Pierre de la ville de Reims" (*Procès-verbal de l'assemblée générale du clergé de France de 1775* [Paris, 1777], p. 7).

[77] *Ibid.*, pp. 17-18; Talleyrand, *Mémoires*, I, 32; cf. footnote #95.

[78] Published in *La Chronique de Champagne*, I (1837), 119.

[79] Reims, G 646, fol. 173.

[80] *La Chronique de Champagne*, I, 119-120.

[81] Reims, G 247, fol. 43. The Bull contains much interesting information regarding the duties, prerogatives, and pecuniary interests of the Abbot.

[82] Desdevises du Dézert, *Eglise et l'Etat*, I, 165.

[83] Reims, G 247, fol. 43.

[84] Reims, G 247, fol. 57.

[85] Cf. A. Cans, *L'organisation financière du clergé de France à l'époque de Louis XIV* (Paris, 1910), pp. 140-144; G. Lepointe, *L'organisation et la politique financières du clergé de France sous le règne de Louis XV* (Paris, 1923), pp. 56-57.

[86] Talleyrand, *Mémoires*, I, 32-33, 42.

[87] Page 66. The issue for 1781 (p. 22) named the appointees for 1785.

[88] *Mémoires de Talleyrand*, Couchoud ed., I, 23.

[89] "Quaenam est Scientia quam custodient Labia Sacerdotalis." The only extant copy is in the Dupanloup collection. This period was one of declining academic standards for the Sorbonne. A good share of the responsibility for this decline is attributable to the king, who with lavish hand accorded dispensations exempting noble students of degree requirements. Talleyrand was given royal permission to take his final examination despite the fact that he had not yet reached the canonically required age of twenty-two. (A.N., MM 258, "Conclusions de la faculté de théologie, 1759-1778," fol. 469). The best discussion of the Sorbonne's plight may be had in P. Feret, *La faculté de théologie à Paris, ses docteurs les plus célèbres* (Paris, 1909), VI, 44ff.

[90] Dupanloup MS, fol. 49.

[91] A.N., MM 277, fol. 149. A definition of these grades, together with a description of the requirements for the various degrees in theology, may be had

224   Talleyrand: Statesman Priest

in E. Méric, *Le clergé sous l'ancien régime* (Paris, 1890), pp. 486-497.

[92] Reims, G 247, fol. 43. A.N. S 4406 "Procès-verbal des Religieuses de Belle Chasse, 30 Août, 1790," "bail à Mgr. l'abbé de Périgord, . . . 8 juin, 1786."

[93] *A Catalogue of the Entire, Elegant, and Valuable Library (late the Property) of Mons. de Telleyrand* [sic] *Perigord, Bishop of Autun in France . . . sold by Auction by Leigh and Sotheby . . . Thursday, April 11, 1793 and the Nine Following Days . . .* (n.p., n.d.).

[94] Archives Départementales de la Seine et Archives de la Ville de Paris, Vente de mobilier d'émigrés (27 messidor, an III [July 15, 1795], DQ[10] 788.

[95] The deputy's salary was 15 *l.* per day during the several months of the Assembly. Salaries of the Promoter and Secretary, usually around 5000 *l.*, were accorded by special vote of the membership. Deputies not only were given travel expenses to and from the Assembly but were also permitted to retain their diocesan revenues. (*Recueil des actes, titres, et mémoires concernant les affaires du clergé de France* [Paris, 1769], VIII, 44, 718).

[96] A.N., MM 258, fols. 480, 527; Dupanloup MS, fol. 52. A royal dispensation dated March 15, 1777, admitted Talleyrand to the preliminary exams of the *licence*. A second, dated July 19, 1777, admitted him to the second large thesis "despite the fact that he has not yet received the order of the diaconate required by your statutes from whose vigor we authorize you to dispense him." (MM 258, "Conclusions de la faculté de théologie," fols. 480, 527).

[97] *Rapport sur l'instruction fait au nom du comité de Constitution à l'assemblée nationale les 10, 11, et 19 septembre, 1791 par M. de Talleyrand-Périgord, ancien évêque d'Autun* (Paris, 1791), pp. 37-40. D. Jourdain (*Histoire de l'université de Paris aux XVIIe et XVIIIe siècles* [Paris, 1888], II, 479) and Feret (*Faculté de théologie de Paris,* VI, 327) maintained that if the faculty of the Sorbonne, the old University, was to fall under the blows of the Revolution, it was made possible by this plan submitted by "one of its sons, one of its graduates, Talleyrand-Périgord."

[98] Morellet, *Mémoires,* I, 30.

[99] Talleyrand, *Mémoires,* I, 36-37; Duchesse d'Abrantes, *Histoire des salons de Paris, tableaux et portraits du grand monde* (Paris, 1838), VI, 2-5; *Mémoires de l'abbé de Baston, Chanoine de Rouen,* J. Loth and C. Verger, eds. (Paris, 1897), I, 116; H. Wendorff, "Die Ideenwelt des Fürsten Talleyrand: ein Versuch," *Historische Vierteljahrschrift,* XXVIII (1922), 344-348.

[100] A.N., G[8]* 792A, "Recueil concernant l'agence générale du clergé (1767)," fol. 218.

[101] Talleyrand, *Mémoires,* I, 23.

[102] Reims, G 240, fol. 129. The original records, which should have been in Paris, have been lost.

[103] Reims, G 240, fol. 129.

[104] *Ibid.*

[105] "Lettres d'excorporation accordées par Christophe de Beaumont," *ibid.*

[106] "Lettres d'incorporation au diocèse de Reims," *ibid.*

[107] *Ibid.,* fol. 130.

[108] Reims, G 248, fol. 23.

[109] Reims, G 240, fols. 131-132.

[110] Reims, G 248, fol. 31.

[111] *Nouvelles Ecclésiastiques de l'Année 1780* (n.p., n.d.), p. 110.

[112] There is a correspondence between Talleyrand and his uncle in the archives of the Broglie family (Eure) which confirms the feelings of mutual

Notes 225

respect and affection between nephew and uncle. Among the personal effects of Citizen Talleyrand *émigré* sold at public auction by order of the Republic in 1795 were several portraits of the Cathedral of Reims and his uncle. (Archives Départementales de la Seine et Archives de la Ville de Paris, Vente de mobilier d'émigrés [27 messidor, an III (July 15, 1795)], DQ¹⁰ 788.)

NOTES TO CHAPTER II

[1] Much of this chapter appeared in slightly altered form as an article, "The General Assembly of the Clergy of France and its Situation at the End of the *Ancien Régime*," *The Catholic Historical Review*, LIII (1967), 153-193. Useful bibliography on the origins of the Assembly may be had in A. Cauchie, "Les assemblées du clergé de France sous l'ancien régime: matériaux et origines," *Revue des Sciences Philosophiques et Théologiques*, II (1908), 74-95.

[2] A. Luchaire, *Louis VII, Philippe-Auguste, Louis VIII (Histoire de France,* ed. E. Lavisse, III, Part 1 [Paris, 1901]), p. 242ff; A. Cans, *L'organisation financière du clergé de France à l'époque de Louis XIV* (Paris, 1910), p. 14; C. V. Langlois, *Saint Louis, Philippe le bel, les derniers capétiens directs (Histoire de France,* ed. E. Lavisse, III Part 2 [Paris, 1901]), 69ff, 241ff.; A. Maury, "Les Assemblées générales du clergé sous l'ancienne monarchie," *Revue des Deux Mondes,* XXXI (1879), 758; L. Bourgain, "La contribution du clergé à l'impôt sous l'ancienne monarchie," *Revue des Questions Historiques,* XLVIII (1890), 65-80; E. Méric, *Le clergé sous l'ancien régime* (Paris, 1890), pp. 176-177.

[3] L. Serbat, *Les assemblées du clergé de France: origines, organisation, développement, 1561-1615* (Paris, 1906), pp. 31-36; I. Bourlon, *Les assemblées du clergé de France sous l'ancien régime* (Paris, 1907), p. 8.

[4] Reprinted in *Collection des procès-verbaux des assemblées générales du clergé de France depuis l'année 1560 jusqu'à présent* (Paris, 1767), I, 22-44.

[5] The monarchy was hard put at the outset to content itself with the modesty of the clergy's offerings. Regent Catherine de Médici actively opposed the clergy for this reason. G. Picot, *Histoire des états-généraux considérés au point de vue de leur influence sur le gouvernement et de la France de 1355 à 1614* (Paris, 1872), I, 9ff.

[6] P. Blet, *Le clergé de France et la monarchie: Étude sur les assemblées générales du clergé de 1615 à 1666,* I (Rome, 1959), 148-172. For a definition of the office of Agent-General in the eighteenth century see L. S. Greenbaum, "Talleyrand as Agent-General of the Clergy of France: A Study of Comparative Influence," *Catholic Historical Review,* XLVIII (January, 1963), 473-486.

[7] "Procès-Verbal de l'Assemblée du clergé de France de 1788," Bibliothèque Sainte-Geneviève (Paris), MS #109, fols. 57-58 (henceforth cited as "PV 1788").

[8] Cans, *op. cit.,* p. 38.

[9] Serbat, *op. cit.,* p. 356; Méric, *op. cit.,* p. 231.

[10] Paris was made an archbishopric in 1623; Albi, in 1678.

[11] P. Gagnol, *Les décimes et les dons gratuits* (Paris, 1911), pp. 68-69; M. Marion, *Histoire financière de la France depuis 1715* (Paris, 1914), I, 40.

[12] *Recueil des actes, titres, et mémoires concernant les affaires du clergé de France* (Paris, 1769), VIII, 103-105. (Cited hereafter as *Mémoires du clergé,* all quotations refer to Volume VIII, devoted exclusively to the General Assembly and the Agent-General); G. Lepointe, *L'organisation et la politique financières du clergé de France sous le règne de Louis XV* (Paris, 1923), p. 24.

[13] *Procès-verbal de l'assemblée générale extraordinaire du clergé de France tenue au couvent des Grands Augustins en l'année 1782* (Paris, 1783), p. 11 (henceforth cited as *PV 1782*).

[14] *Mémoires du clergé*, pp. 737-740; Archives Nationales de France (Paris) [henceforth cited as "A.N."], G[8]* 792A, "Recueil concernant l'agence générale du clergé (1767)," (henceforth cited as "Recueil: Agence Générale"), fols. 161-162.

[15] L. S. Greenbaum, "Talleyrand and the Temporal Problems of the French Church from 1780-1785," *French Historical Studies*, III (Spring, 1963), 50-53.

[16] *Mémoires du clergé*, p. 6; *Procès-verbal de l'assemblée du clergé de France tenue à Paris au couvent des Grands Augustins en l'année 1785 et continuée en l'année 1786* (Paris, 1789), p. 753 (henceforth cited as *PV 1785*).

[17] *Mémoires du clergé*, pp. 381-382.

[18] Lepointe, *op. cit.*, p. 29. The last *curé* with charge of souls seated in the Assembly was elected in 1680.

[19] *Procès-verbal de l'assemblée générale du clergé de France tenue à Paris au couvent des Grands Augustins en l'année 1780* (Paris, 1782), pp. 5-11 (henceforth cited as *PV 1780*); *PV 1782*, pp. 5-10.

[20] Lavisse, *Histoire de France*, IX, Part 1, 151.

[21] Alexandre-Angélique de Talleyrand-Périgord, Archbishop of Reims, was representative of his Province's first order, serving in the Assembly of 1780 as Chairman of the Committee for the Accounts of the Clergy's Loans at Four Per Cent. In 1785 he was Honorary President of the Assembly and chairman of the important Committee on the Tithes. Jean de Dieu-Raymond de Boisgelin, Archbishop of Aix and deputy of the first order of that province, was in 1780 and 1785 chairman of the key Committee on the Church Temporal. He was one of the ablest and most respected leaders of the clergy before the Revolution. See L. S. Greenbaum, "Talleyrand and his Uncle: The Genesis of a Clerical Career," *Journal of Modern History*, XXIX (September, 1957), 226-236.

[22] L. de Héricourt, *Les loix ecclésiastiques de France* (Paris, 1771), Part 4, p. 300; *Mémoires du clergé*, pp. 118, 403-405; model *procurations* are reproduced here.

[23] *Procès-verbal de l'assemblée générale du clergé de France tenue à Paris au couvent des Grands Augustins en l'année 1775* (Paris, 1777), p. 7 (henceforth cited as *PV 1775*).

[24] *PV 1780*, pp. 8-9.

[25] *Ibid.*, p. 6.

[26] Lepointe, *op. cit.*, p. 28.

[27] *Journal de l'abbé de Véri*, J. de Witte, ed. (Paris, n.d.), I, 268-269.

[28] Cans, *op. cit.*, pp. 49-58.

[29] N. Ravitch, *Sword and Mitre: Government and Episcopate in France and England in the Age of Aristocracy* (The Hague, 1966), pp. 159-160.

[30] *Mémoires du clergé*, pp. 39, 181-183; *PV 1780*, p. 1; *PV 1782*, p. 1.

[31] "Recueil: Agence Générale," fol. 39.

[32] *Mémoires du clergé*, p. 215. The Assembly honored First Ministers of the king who were also prelates, Richelieu, Dubois, and Fleury, with the titles "Président honoris causa." See G. Lepointe, article, "Assemblées du clergé de France," in *Dictionnaire de droit canonique* (Paris, 1935-1965), I, 1122. In the Assembly of 1780 there were five Honorary Presidents and in 1782, four (*PV 1780*, pp. 11-12; *PV 1782*, p. 10).

[33] *PV 1780*, p. 11; *PV 1782*, p. 10.

[34] Cans, *op. cit.*, pp. 68-69, 72. Similarly, the Honorary Presidents also

enjoyed the favor of the king. (Lepointe, *op. cit.,* pp. 34-35.)

[35] This was announced as early as July 1, 1784. L. P. de Bachaumont, *Mémoires secrets pour servir de l'histoire de la république des lettres en France depuis 1762 jusqu'à nos jours,* XXVI (Paris, 1786), 88.

[36] *PV 1780,* pp. 233, 261, 527, 687, 1010, 1023; *PV 1782,* pp. 126, 621.

[37] *PV 1780,* pp. 21, 183, 217, 1021; *PV 1782,* pp. 39, 48, 107, 109, 157, 212, 255, 352.

[38] Bourlon, *op. cit.,* 42.

[39] *Mémoires du clergé,* pp. 572-573; "Recueil: Agence Générale," fols. 245-246.

[40] *Ibid.,* fol. 70; *Mémoires du clergé,* p. 572; Cans, *op. cit.,* pp. 86-87; Serbat, *op. cit.,* pp. 248-258.

[41] *Mémoires du clergé,* p. 183.

[42] Bourlon, *op. cit.,* p. 43.

[43] *PV 1785,* pp. 30-32.

[44] Bourlon, *op. cit.,* p. 41; Lepointe, *op. cit.,* pp. 41-43.

[45] Bourlon, *op. cit.,* pp. 67-68.

[46] *PV 1780,* pp. 335-356; *PV 1782,* pp. 110-111, 166; Maury, *op. cit.,* p. 794.

[47] Cans, *op. cit.,* pp. 94-95.

[48] Lepointe, *op. cit.,* p. 41; Bourlon, *op. cit.,* pp. 69-70.

[49] *Mémoires du clergé,* p. 610; Lepointe, *op. cit.,* p. 70; Cans, *op. cit.,* pp. 20-32.

[50] *Collection des procès-verbaux,* VI, 1367-1375.

[51] A. Brette, "La dette du clergé de France en 1789," *La Révolution Française,* XLVI (1904), 416.

[52] *Documents relatifs aux rapports du clergé avec la royauté, 1705-1789,* ed. L. Mention, II (Paris, 1903), 104-105; *PV 1780,* pp. 1126-1128.

[53] P. J. Guyot, *Répertoire universel et raisonné de jurisprudence civile, criminelle, canonique et bénéficiale,* VI (Paris, 1781), 131.

[54] J. Egret, "La dernière assemblée du clergé de France," *Revue Historique,* CCXIX (1958), 8.

[55] Gagnol, *op. cit.,* pp. 40, 48.

[56] *PV 1780,* p. 1114.

[57] A. Rébillon, "La situation économique du clergé français à la fin de l'ancien régime," *La Révolution Française,* LXXXII (1929), 343.

[58] R. Chevaillier, "Les revenues des bénéfices ecclésiastiques au 18e siècle d'après les comptes de la régale et de la garde," *La Révolution Française,* LXXIV (1921), 113-115; Brette, *op. cit.,* p. 415; Rébillon, *op. cit.,* pp. 328-329, 343-348.

[59] *PV 1780,* pp. 100-107; *PV 1782,* pp. 122-125. *Rapport de l'agence contenant les principales affaires du clergé depuis 1780 jusqu'en 1785 par M. l'abbé de Périgord et M. l'abbé de Boisgelin, anciens agents généraux du clergé* (Paris, 1788), pp. 291-296, 303-307. M. G. Hutt, "The *Curés* and the Third Estate. The Ideas of Reform in the Pamphlets of the French Lower Clergy in the Period 1787-1789," *Journal of Ecclesiastical History,* VIII (April, 1957), 74-92. For a rebellion of *curés* in Angers, see John McManners, *French Ecclesiastical Society under the Ancien Régime: A Study of Angers in the Eighteenth Century* (Manchester, 1960), pp. 190-207.

[60] *Collection des procès-verbaux,* VIII, Part 2, 1790-1811; Lepointe, *op. cit.,* pp. 99-113.

[61] Brette, *op. cit.,* p. 415.

[62] Cited in Chevaillier, *op. cit.,* p. 132.

[63] F. A. de Voltaire, *Le Siècle de Louis XIV* (Flammarion edition; Paris,

n.d.), II, 96-102; H. A. Taine, *Les origines de la France contemporaine* (Paris, 1917), II, 100-101.

[64] C. Berthelot du Chesnay, "Le clergé séculier français du second ordre d'après les insinuations ecclésiastiques," *Bulletin de la Société d'Histoire Moderne*, LXII (1963), 3.

[65] "PV 1788," fol. 655.

[66] A. N., G⁸* 533, "Département général des décimes arrêté par l'assemblée du clergé de 1760."

[67] Egret, *op. cit.*, p. 10. Cf. Norman Ravitch, "The Taxing of the Clergy in Eighteenth Century France," *Church History*, XXXIII (June, 1964), 157-174.

[68] "PV 1788," fol. 653.

[69] M. Picot, *Mémoires pour servir à l'histoire ecclésiastique pendant le dix-huitième siècle* (Paris, 1855), V, 133; Bourgain, *op. cit.*, pp. 113-155.

[70] *PV 1780*, pp. 21-23; 261-321.

[71] I. Bourlon, *Les assemblées du clergé et le Protestantisme* (Paris, 1909), pp. 87-88; Bourlon, *Assemblées du clergé*, pp. 83-91; Serbat, *op. cit.*, pp. 325-329.

[72] Lavisse, *Histoire de France*, Vol. IX, Part 1, 160-161. Cf. David Bien, "Catholic Magistrates and Protestant Marriage in the French Enlightenment," *French Historical Studies*, II (Fall, 1962), 409-429; *PV 1780*, pp. 184-195; 342-350; Bourlon, *Les assemblées du clergé et le Protestantisme*, pp. 93-96.

[73] "PV 1788," fols. 141-169.

[74] A. Cans, "La caisse du clergé de France et les Protestants convertis (1598-1790)," *Bulletin de la Société d'Histoire du Protestantisme Français*, LI (1902), 237-243.

[75] Serbat, *op. cit.*, pp. 323-331.

[76] I. Bourlon, *Les assemblées du clergé et le Jansénisme* (Paris, 1911).

[77] *PV 1785*, p. 202.

[78] A. Monod, *De Pascal à Chateaubriand. Les défenseurs français du Christianisme de 1670 à 1802* (Paris, 1916), pp. 459-465.

[79] *PV 1775*, pp. 260-268; *PV 1780*, pp. 54-66, 335-356; *PV 1782*, pp. 167-170; *PV 1785*, pp. 65-71, 147-153, 188-204.

[80] *PV 1780*, p. 338. Cf. R. R. Palmer, *Catholics and Unbelievers in Eighteenth Century France* (Princeton, 1939), p. 17; P. Grosclaude, *Malesherbes, témoin et interprète de son temps* (Paris, n.d.), pp. 106-113.

[81] *PV 1782*, pp. 167, 258, 169, 170.

[82] *PV 1785*, pp. 69-71, 189.

[83] *PV 1780*, pp. 1006-1010; *PV 1782*, pp. 1227-1229, 301-303; *PV 1785*, pp. 148-149, 994.

[84] *PV 1782*, pp. 257-261; *PV 1785*, p. 1227.

[85] *PV 1780*, p. 1009; *PV 1782*, pp. 300-301.

[86] L. S. Greenbaum, "Ten Priests in Search of a Miter: How Talleyrand Became a Bishop," *Catholic Historical Review*, L (October, 1964), 307-331.

[87] Lavisse, *Histoire de France*, Vol. IX, Part 1, 162; note on page 17 bottom.

[88] *PV 1780*, pp. 277, 355.

[89] Lavisse, *Histoire de France*, Vol. VIII, Part 2, 327-332; *PV 1780*, p. 929.

[90] *PV 1782*, pp. 88-90, 187-191, 239, 415-418; *PV 1785*, pp. 471-472, 821.

[91] "Recueil: Agence Générale," fol. 30; *PV 1782*, p. 180. Cf. C. Florange, *Les assemblées du clergé de France avant 1789 at leurs jetons commémoratifs* (Paris, 1927).

[92] Bourlon, *Assemblées du clergé*, p. 97; Méric, *op. cit.*, p. 204.

[93] *Mémoires du clergé*, pp. 707-708; *PV 1780*, pp. 35-36, 1179-1192; *PV 1782*, p. 35.

Notes

[94] *PV 1780*, p. 548.
[95] *Ibid.*, pp. 662-664; *PV 1782*, p. 239; *PV 1785*, p. 477.
[96] *PV 1780*, p. 546.
[97] Bourlon, *Assemblées du clergé*, p. 103; *PV 1782*, pp. 171-175; E. Sol, *Le vénérable Alain de Solminihac, abbé de Chancelade et évêque de Cahors* (Cahors, 1928); H. Drouot, "Talleyrand et la béatification de Marie Alacoque," *Revue de Bourgogne*, VIII (1920), 398-400; E. Bougaud, *Histoire de la bienheureuse Marguérite-Marie et des origines de la dévotion au coeur de Jésus* (Paris, 1874).
[98] *Mémoires du clergé*, pp. 380-381; "Recueil: Agence Générale," fol. 309; Lepointe, article, "Assemblées du clergé de France," p. 1123.
[99] J. Le Gras, *Diderot et l'Encyclopédie* (Amiens, 1928), pp. 66-68.
[100] *PV 1785*, pp. 800-804.
[101] *Mémoires du clergé*, pp. 147-149.
[102] Bourlon, *Assemblées du clergé*, pp. 47-49; Méric, *op. cit.*, p. 234; "Recueil: Agence Générale," fols. 241-243.
[103] Cans, *Organisation financière*, p. 92; *Mémoires du clergé*, pp. 122-123; Bourlon, *Assemblées du clergé*, p. 51; Méric, *op. cit.*, p. 211; *Mémoires du clergé*, pp. 435-439 print the various versions of the oath.
[104] *Collection des procès-verbaux*, I, 665. The Assembly met only three Saturdays in 1780 and 1782.
[105] Cans, *Organisation financière*, pp. 87-90.
[106] *Mémoires du clergé*, pp. 610-611.
[107] A. N., G^8 152, "Rangs et préséances des archevêques, des évêques, et autres ecclésiastiques."
[108] A. N., G^{8*} 704, fols. 88-89.
[109] Bourlon, *Assemblées du clergé*, p. 63.
[110] *Mémoires du clergé*, pp. 463, 505-511, 546, 556-557.
[111] *PV 1780*, p. 993; Lepointe, *Organisation et la politique financières*, p. 47; *Mémoires du clergé*, p. 457.
[112] A. N., G^{8*} 777, "Comptes des frais communs de l'assemblée extraordinaire du clergé de 1782."
[113] Cans, *Organisation financière*, p. 104. A. N. S. 3632-3633: "Etat exact du revenu des grands augustins de Paris en maisons, boutiques ou échoppes, rentes, et fondations." H. Jaillot, *Recherches critiques, historiques, et topographiques sur la ville de Paris*, XVIII (Paris, 1774), 22. "Recueil: Agence Générale," fols. 29, 252.
[114] P. Hurtaut et J. Magny, *Dictionnaire historique de la ville de Paris et de ses environs*, I (Paris, 1779), 391-394; J. Hillairet, *Evocation du vieux Paris, vieux quartiers, vieilles rues, vielles demeures historiques, vestiges, annales et anecdotiques* (Paris, 1951), pp. 447-548. A. N., G^{8*} 2490, fols. 431-432. A. N., LL 1470, "Répertoire historique, instructif, et méthodique des titres et papiers contenus dans les archives du grand couvent royal et collège généralissime des révérends pères ermites de l'ordre de Saint Augustin au bout du pont neuf à Paris [1746]," fol. 249.
[115] A. N., LL 1470, "Carte topographique du couvent royal et collège généralissime des Grands Augustins de Paris au bout du pont neuf et dépendances [1746]."
[116] *PV 1780*, pp. 522-525, 879-885, 1159.
[117] A. Babeau, *Le château de Brienne* (Troyes, 1877).
[118] *PV 1785*, p. 1246.
[119] A. N., G^8 722, "Couvent des Grands Augustins à Paris. Dévis, plans et desseins de M. Antoine architecte pour l'établissement des salles d'assemblées,

et bureau d'Agence du clergé aux Grands Augustins [1785]."

[120] A. N., G[8] 772, "Dévis estimatif des ouvrages de toutes natures qu'il convient faire pour l'établissement de tous les lieux nécessaires aux assemblées du clergé dans les bâtiments du couvent des Grands Augustins."

[121] *PV 1785*, p. 827; G[8] 772.

[122] Hillairet, *op. cit.*, p. 548.

[123] "Recueil: Agence Générale," fols. 313-314; A. N., G[8] 107, "Comptes des frais communs des assemblées du clergé de 1775, de 1780, de 1782, et de 1785."

[124] "Recueil: Agence Générale," fols. 106, 313-314. Lepointe, *Organisation et la politique financières*, pp. 54-55. *PV 1785*, p. 1246.

[125] A. N., G[8]* 777, "Frais communs de l'assemblée de 1782"; G[8] 220-248, "Pensions des ministres convertis et autres gratifiés du clergé"; G[8] 249-254, "Subventions du clergé à des établissements religieux"; G[8] 255-261, "Pensions des ministres protestants et autres gratifiés du clergé." Cf. Cans, *Organisation financière*, pp. 105-109.

[126] G. Sénac de Meilhan, *Du gouvernement, des moeurs, et des conditions en France avant la Révolution* (Hambourg, 1795), p. 75.

NOTES TO CHAPTER III

[1] *Mémoires du clergé*, pp. 2377-2378.
[2] *Ibid.*, p. 2331.
[3] Bourlon, *Assemblées du clergé*, p. 116.
[4] *Mémoires du clergé*, pp. 1867-1869, 1877-1879.
[5] *Ibid.*, pp. 2331-2332, 2371-2372.
[6] Serbat, *Assemblées du clergé*, pp. 184-185.
[7] "Recueil: Agence Générale," fol. 218; *Mémoires du clergé*, p. 2355; Héricourt, *Loix ecclésiastiques*, pp. 303-305.
[8] *Mémoires de Talleyrand*, I, 32-33.
[9] *La France Ecclésiastique de 1779* (n.p., 1780), p. 66; *La France Ecclésiastique de 1781* (n.p., 1782), p. 22; *Précis des rapports de l'agence générale du clergé* (Paris, 1786), p. viii indicates the Agents for 1790.
[10] Archivio Vaticano Segreto, "Nunziature di Francia, 1780-1781," #571, fol. 123.
[11] *Mémoires du clergé*, 121; Lepointe, *Organisation et la politique financières*, p. 29.
[12] *Mémoires du clergé*, pp. 2334-2336; "Recueil: Agence Générale," fol. 220.
[13] *Ibid.*, fol. 231; *Précis des rapports de l'agence générale du clergé*, p. viii.
[14] *Mémoires du clergé*, p. 55.
[15] Héricourt, *Loix ecclésiastiques*, p. 305; "Recueil: Agence Générale," fols. 239-240, 251.
[16] *Ibid.*, fol. 251.
[17] *Mémoires du clergé*, pp. 13, 49, 2339, 2343-2345, 2393-2395; *Précis des rapports de l'agence générale du clergé*, pp. ii-iii.
[18] "Recueil: Agence Générale," fols. 238-240, 251; *Mémoires du clergé*, p. 2339.
[19] Méric, *Clergé sous l'ancien régime*, p. 191.
[20] J. Coudy, *Les moyens d'action de l'ordre du clergé au conseil du roi, 1561-1715* (Paris, n.d. [1954]), pp. 89, 141; Cans, *Organisation financière du clergé*, p. 135.
[21] G[8]* 2580, #52, 299, 310; G[8]* 2581, #15.
[22] G[8]* 2593, #15, 84.

Notes

23 G[8]* 2605, #305.
24 *PV 1780*, p. 609.
25 *Précis des rapports de l'agence générale du clergé*, pp. ii-iii.
26 *Mémoires du clergé*, p. 2345.
27 *Ibid.*, pp. 2393-2395.
28 *Ibid.*, pp. 12, 48; cf. *PV 1780*, p. 861.
29 *Mémoires du clergé*, pp. 12-13.
30 "Recueil: Agence Générale," fols. 120-124; *Mémoires du clergé*, p. 13.
31 *Ibid.*, pp. 13, 2379-2380.
32 "Recueil: Agence Générale," fol. 267; *Mémoires du clergé*, p. 2380.
33 "Recueil: Agence Générale," fols. 4-6.
34 *Ibid.*, fols. 8-11.
35 *Ibid.*, fols. 12-29.
36 *Ibid.*, fols. 43-45.
37 G[8]* 2620, #260, 262; "Recueil: Agence Générale," fols. 32-36, 46, 66-67.
38 *PV 1782*, p. 15; "Recueil: Agence Générale," fol. 48.
39 *PV 1780*, pp. 38, 41, 439, 861, 898; *PV 1782*, pp. 2, 20.
40 "Recueil: Agence Générale," fols. 48-56, 74-87, 89-95.
41 *Mémoires du clergé*, pp. 2391-2392; "Recueil: Agence Générale," fols. 134-139.
42 *Ibid.*, fols. 57-66, 112, 115, 120, 124.
43 *Ibid.*, fol. 140.
44 *Ibid.*, fols. 146-155, 187-212.
45 *Ibid.*, fol. 277.
46 *Précis des rapports de l'agence générale du clergé*, p. v. The Assembly suggested that reports follow this three-fold division.
47 *PV 1785*, pp. 872-873, 1451-1452; *PV 1780*, pp. 877-878.
48 Pp. 384-387, 227.
49 "Recueil: Agence Générale," fols. 245-247.
50 *Ibid.*, fol. 245. The Assembly of 1775 admitted the inadequacy of this sum and attempted to compensate the Agents by a larger bonus (*PV 1775*, p. 755).
51 All these *gratifications* were subject to the approval of the Assembly (*PV 1785*, p. 817).
52 Cf. G[8]* 777, "Frais communs de l'Assemblée de 1782."
53 *Mémoires du clergé*, pp. 2414-2415.
54 Lepointe, *Organisation et la politique financières*, p. 60.
55 L. S. Greenbaum, "Ten Priests in Search of a Mitre: How Talleyrand Became a Bishop," *Catholic Historical Review*, L (October, 1964), 328.
56 *PV 1780*, p. 16; *PV 1782*, p. 16.
57 "Recueil: Agence Générale," fol. 165; *PV 1780*, p. 19; *PV 1782*, p. 37.
58 Cans, *Organisation financière du clergé*, pp. 139-140.
59 *Almanach Royal de 1782* (Paris, n.d.), p. 67; *Almanach Royal de 1785* (Paris, n.d.), p. 70.
60 *Précis des rapports de l'agence générale du clergé*, p. viii.
61 The outstanding example was Jean-Marie Dulau, Agent between 1770 and 1775 and named Archbishop of Arles before the termination of his Agency. (*PV 1775*, p. 755).
62 *Mémoires du clergé*, p. 2363.
63 G[8]* 2618, #357; G[8] 682, July 9, 1783.
64 Bourlon, *Assemblées du clergé*, p. 127.
65 The substance of the remainder of this chapter appeared as an article "Talleyrand as Agent-General of the Clergy of France: A Study in Com-

parative Influence," *The Catholic Historical Review*, XLVIII (1963), 473-486.
   [66] "Recueil: Agence Générale," fol. 241.
   [67] Bourlon, *Assemblées du clergé*, pp. 115-127; Cans, *Organisation financière du clergé*, pp. 123-144; Serbat, *Assemblées du clergé*, pp. 178-189; Lepointe, *Organisation et la politique financières*, pp. 56-74; Méric, *Clergé sous l'ancien régime*, pp. 190-200.
   [68] G⁸ 701.
   [69] *PV 1780*, p. 6; L. S. Greenbaum, "Talleyrand and His Uncle: The Genesis of Clerical Career," *Journal of Modern History*, XXIX (1957), 226-236; cf. Cans, *Organisation financière du clergé*, pp. 140-144; Lepointe, *Organisation et la politique financières*, pp. 56-57.
   [70] Published in L. Larchey, "Nouveautés anecdotiques," *Le Bibliophile Français*, I, (1868), p. 272.
   [71] Talleyrand, *Mémoires*, I, 50.
   [72] A. J. Valynseele, *Les enfants naturels de Louis XV* (Paris, 1953), p. 183.
   [73] Talleyrand, *Mémoires*, I, 50.
   [74] *Mémoires secrets pour servir à l'histoire de la république des lettres en France depuis 1772 jusqu'à nos jours* (London, 1782), XVII, 58-59; *Correspondance secrète inédite sur Louis XVI, Marie-Antoinette, la cour et la ville de 1777 à 1792, publiée d'après les manuscrits de la bibliothèque impériale de Saint Pétersbourg*, M. de Lescure, ed. (Paris, 1866), I, 365.
   [75] *Mémoires secrets*, pp. 78-79; Valynseele, *Les enfants naturels de Louis XV*, p. 193.
   [76] A. N., M. 788.
   [77] *Ibid.*
   [78] *Ibid., #223.*
   [79] *Ibid.*, letter of February 13, 1781 and #223.
   [80] *Correspondance secrète inédite sur Louis XVI*, I, 378.
   [81] P. Caron, *Les massacres de Septembre* (Paris, 1935), p .482.
   [82] G. Lacour-Gayet, *Talleyrand* (Paris, 1928), I, 61-64; C. Brinton, *Lives of Talleyrand* (New York, 1936), p. 64; B. de Lacombe, *Talleyrand, évêque d'Autun* (Paris, 1903), pp. 38-45; A. Marcade, *Talleyrand, prêtre et évêque* (Paris, 1883), pp. 54-59; D. Cooper, *Talleyrand* (New York, 1932), pp. 25-27; L. Madelin, *Talleyrand* (Paris, 1944), pp. 26-28; J. McCabe, *Talleyrand, A Biographical Sketch* (London, 1906), pp. 40-44; A. B. Dodd, *Talleyrand: The Training of a Statesman* (New York, 1928), pp. 107-110.
   [83] A. Leroy, *Talleyrand économiste et financier* (Paris, 1907), p. 10.
   [84] E. Beurlier, "L'épiscopat de Talleyrand," *Revue du Clergé Français*, XXXV (1903), 116.
   [85] L. Bastide, Vie religieuse et politique de Talleyrand-Périgord (Paris, 1838); L. G. Michaud, *Histoire de Talleyrand, ancien évêque d'Autun* (Paris, 1853); Stewarton [L. Goldsmith, pseud.], *Memoirs of C. M. Talleyrand, Containing the Particulars of his Private and Public Life, of his Intrigues in Boudoires as well as in Cabinets* (London, 1806, 2 vols.); G. Touchard-Lafosse, *Histoire politique et vie intime de Charles-Maurice de Talleyrand, Prince de Bénévent* (Paris, 1848); C. M. Villemarest, *Monsieur de Talleyrand, Mémoires pour servir à l'histoire de France* (Bruxelles, 1834, 4 vols.)
   [86] Among the most important are: *La vie laïque et ecclésiastique de monseigneur l'évêque d'Autun* (Paris, 1789); *Le diable boiteux révolutionnaire* (Paris, n.d.); *Les miracles carnales de St. Charles, évêque d'Autun et patriarche de la révolution* (Paris, 1792); *Confession de l'évêque d'Autun* (n.p., n.d.); *La vérité à l'évêque d'Autun* (n.p., n.d.); *Précis de la vie du prélat d'Autun, digne ministre de la fédération* (Paris, 1790); *Dialogue entre M. l'évêque*

d'Autun et M. l'abbé Maury (n.p., n.d.); *Observations réfléchies sur différentes motions de M. l'évêque d'Autun et sur la conduite de ses confrères dans l'assemblée par Rougane, ancien curé d'Auvergne* (n.p., 1790); *Réponse à la lettre de M. l'évêque d'Autun* (n.p., n.d.); *Le décret du 13 avril mal justifié par M. l'évêque d'Autun* (Paris, n.d.); *Lettre à M. de Talleyrand, ancien évêque d'Autun, chef de la communion des Talleyrandistes* (Paris, 1791); *Le triumvirat redévoilé* (n.p., n.d.). A large number of pamphlets published in Autun and other places is listed in P. Montarlot, "L'épiscopat de Talleyrand," *Mémoires de la Société Eduenne*, XXII (1894), 83-157. An enormous anonymous and pseudonymous ecclesiastical pamphlet literature in which Talleyrand figures prominently is to be had in the Aulard and Boulay de la Meurthe Collections in Widener Library, Harvard University.

[87] *Précis de la vie du prélat d'Autun, digne ministre de la fédération* (Paris, 1790), pp. 5-6.

[8b] A. F. Allonville, *Mémoires tirés des papiers d'un homme d'Etat* (Paris, 1834), VIII, 110.

[89] The Abbé Montesquiou was named Agent by the Ecclesiastical Province of Paris for the term 1785-1790. (*L'Almanach Royal, Année Commune 1789* [Paris, n.d.], p. 70).

[90] Especially typical are: Bastide, *Vie religieuse et politique de Talleyrand*, pp. 111-112, 462; Stewarton, *Memoirs of C. M. Talleyrand*, II, 362-366; Villemarest, *Monsieur de Talleyrand* (American edn., Philadelphia, 1834), p. 40.

[91] J. McCabe, *Talleyrand, a Biographical Sketch*, p. 44.

[92] 1780-1781, G8* 2617; 1782-1783, G8* 2618; 1784, G8* 2619; 1785, G8* 2620.

[93] The addenda are published in volume G8* 2620 (1785).

[94] 1780-1781, 186; 1782-1783, 378; 1784, 382; 1785, 144; 1781-1785, 21.

[95] *Précis des rapports de l'agence générale du clergé de France*, p. 1, Talleyrand personally recognized the importance of signing his correspondence for the diocesan ecclesiastics in order that they might have in their archives a full and permanent record of their contact with the Agents for their successors, and in order that they might themselves more easily refer their case to the Agent involved. In a note to M. Duchesne, Talleyrand confessed having signed some correspondence for the Diocese of Vienne, and he requested that the letters not be mailed before he signed the rest. May 6, 1784, G8 683.

[96] 1780-1781, 135; 1782-1783, 258; 1784, 223; 1785, 82; 1781-1785, 12.

[97] 1780-1781, 114; 1782-1783, 222; 1784, 183; 1785, 71; 1781-1785, 12.

[98] 1780-1781, 19; 1782-1783, 36; 1784, 40; 1785, 11.

[99] 1780-1781, #352, 425; 1782-1783, #10, 188, 215, 216, 325bis, 328, 329, 335bis, 345, 346, 378, 390, 391, 392, 482, 483, 486, 489, 508, 509, 542, 558, 568; 1784, #6 15, 79, 80, 82, 84, 88, 90, 91, 92, 99, 100, 118, 119, 128, 190, 191, 219, 220, 221, 268, 277, 278, 357, 358, 369, 388, 389, 395, 485, 486; 1785, #86, 87, 88, 106, 122, 123, 164, 181, 463.

[100] In A.N., G8* 2631, "Lettres originales des secrétaires d'Etat, intendants des finances et autres magistrats aux Agents Généraux du clergé," Vol. V, 1780-1782; A.N., G8 624; G8 632; G8 638; G8 640; G8 659, "Correspondance des Agents Généraux du clergé: lettres reçues, XVIIIe siècle"; A.N., G8 663; G8 664, "Correspondance des Agents Généraux et autres officiers du clergé: XVIIIe siècle"; A.N., G8 686, "Lettres d'Agence générale du clergé, 1727-1787: lettres envoyées."

[101] G8* 2631; G8* 2632, "Lettres originales des secrétaires d'État, intendants des finances et autres magistrats aux Agents Généraux du clergé," Vol. VI,

1725-1784; A.N., G⁸ 139, "Frais de sommation et d'impression, 1726-1788," "Feuilles de délibérations des Assemblées du clergé"; A.N., G⁸ 623; G⁸ 627; G⁸ 648; G⁸ 659, "Correspondance des Agents Généraux du clergé: Lettres reçues, XVIIIe siècle"; A.N., G⁸ 663; G⁸ 665; G⁸ 666; G⁸ 668; G⁸ 669; G⁸ 670, "Correspondance des Agents Généraux et autres officiers du clergé; XVIIIe siècle"; G⁸ 682; G⁸ 759; G⁸ 770, "Lettres d'Agence générale du clergé, 1727-1787: Lettres envoyées."

[102] G⁸* 2632; G⁸ 625, "Correspondance des Agents Généraux du clergé: Lettres reçues, XVIIIe siècle"; A.N., G⁸ 682; G⁸ 683; G⁸ 684, "Lettres d'Agence générale du clergé, 1727-1787: Lettres envoyées."

[103] G⁸ 685.

[104] 1780-1781, 29; 1782-1783, 26; 1784, 52; 1785, 18.

[105] G⁸ 682.

[106] *Ibid.*

[107] *Ibid.*

[108] G⁸* 2619, #88, 164, 395.

[109] 1780-1781, #439bis, 439ter.

[110] G⁸ 683, #425.

[111] G⁸ 683, #7, 389, 390.

[112] G⁸ 625; G⁸ 659.

[113] 1782-1783, #325bis.

[114] G⁸* 2619, #138-186, 1784. It is interesting that when the originals of these letters, unsigned in the official transcript, but of certain Talleyrand composition, touching his correspondence with the episcopate over legislation which he introduced, were found in G⁸ 684, they were all of Talleyrand's composition.

[115] G⁸ 627; G⁸ 638; G⁸ 663; G⁸ 666; G⁸ 682; G⁸ 683; G⁸ 684; G⁸ 685.

[116] G⁸* 777, "Frais communs de l'assemblée de 1782"; G⁸ 107, "Comptes des frais communs des assemblées du clergé de 1775, de 1780, de 1782, et de 1785"; G⁸ 139, "Frais de sommation et d'impression; feuilles de délibérations des assemblées du clergé (1726-1788)."

[117] G⁸* 2617, #190, 354; G⁸* 2618, #291, 474, 483, 487, 499, 552, 667; G⁸* 2620, #74, 181.

[118] G⁸* 2619, #613.

[119] G⁸* 2617, #381; G⁸* 2618, #117; G⁸* 2619, #218; G⁸* 2620, #130.

[120] *PV 1782*, p. 156.

[121] *PV 1785*, p. 761.

[122] G⁸ 627; G⁸ 693; G⁸* 2828.

[123] G⁸* 2618, #225, September 14, 1782; G⁸* 2620, #106; G⁸* 2828, fols. 459-460; G⁸ 139.

[124] 1780-1781, 28; 1782-1783, 128; 1784, 102; 1785, 53.

[125] 1780-1781, 17; 1782-1783, 75; 1784, 44; 1785, 25.

[126] G⁸* 2631; G⁸ 139; G⁸ 625; G⁸ 648; G⁸ 659; G⁸ 663; G⁸ 668; G⁸ 670; G⁸ 682; G⁸ 683; G⁸ 684; G⁸ 685.

[127] 1780-1781, 2; 1782-1783, 7; 1784, 17; 1785, 4.

[128] Talleyrand, *Mémoires*, I, 42-43. Talleyrand did not name in his memoirs Vergennes, Ségur, and Necker, but we have letters and many indirect interchanges between these men and Talleyrand as Agent.

[129] G⁸* 2631, #351, 439, 463, 474, 478-480, 481.

[130] A.N., G⁸* 2827, "Consultations et délibérations du Conseil du clergé, 1727-1788."

[131] 1780-1781, 31; 1782-1783, 90; 1784, 40; 1785, 26.

Notes

[132] G⁸* 2631; G⁸* 2632; G⁸ 663; G⁸ 668; G⁸ 670; G⁸ 682; G⁸ 683; G⁸ 684; G⁸ 685.
[133] 1780-1781, 4; 1782-1783, 18; 1784, 6; 1785, 9.
[134] G⁸* 2618, #131.
[135] G⁸* 2618, #103.
[136] G⁸ 663.
[137] Cf. Louis S. Greenbaum, "Talleyrand and the Temporal Problems of the French Church from 1780 to 1785," *French Historical Studies*, III (Spring, 1963), pp. 41-71.
[138] E. Préclin, *Les Jansénistes du 18e siècle et la constitution civile du clergé* (Paris, 1929), p. 227.

NOTES TO CHAPTER IV

[1] These are handily summarized in M. Marion, *Histoire financière de la France depuis 1715*, (Paris, 1914), I, 374ff; Lavisse, *Histoire de France*, IX, Part 1, 319-320. Cf. M. G. Hutt, "The Curés and the Third Estate: the Ideas of Reform in the Pamphlets of the French Lower Clergy in the period 1787-1789," *Journal of Ecclesiastical History*, VIII (1957), 74-92; B. C. Schafer, "Quelques jugements de pamphlétaires sur le clergé à la veille de la Révolution," *Annales Historiques de la Révolution Française*, XVI (1939), 110 ff; G. Schelle, *Du Pont de Nemours et l'école physiocratique* (Paris, 1888), pp. 295-300; C. Bloch, *L'assistance et l'Etat en France à la veille de la Révolution (1764-1790)* (Paris, 1908), pp. 372-373.

[2] A statement by the moderate and circumspect Boisgelin on July 18, 1780, is typical. He urged the Assembly "to place directly under the eyes of His Majesty a striking picture of the present position of the clergy of His kingdom, anxious about its possessions, tormented in their use, and troubled on all points in the usage and exercise of its rights, privileges and franchises . . . [and] the infractions . . . of the clauses and stipulations of its contracts." (*PV 1780*, p. 243).

[3] Cf. the important work of G. Lefebvre, "La répartition de la propriété et de l'exploitation foncière à la fin de l'ancien régime," *Revue d'Histoire Moderne*, III (March-April, 1928), 110-111.

[4] A. Latreille, E. Delaruelle, J. R. Palanque, *Histoire du catholicisme en France*, (Paris, 1960), II, 389.

[5] *Journal et mémoires du marquis d'Argenson*, E. J. B. Rathéry, ed., (Paris, 1864), VI, 162-164, VIII, 241-242; *Journal historique et anecdotique du règne de Louis XV par E. J. F. Barbier, avocat du parlement de Paris*, A. de la Villegelle, ed. (Paris, 1851), III, 170-171; *Lettres secretes [sic] sur l'état actuel de la religion et du clergé de France* (Paris, 1781), pp. 1-5; Soulavie, *Mémoires*, I, 199-210; VI, 103-110.

[6] *PV 1780*, pp. 762-765; G⁸* 2620, #52: Cf. A. Monod, *De Pascal à Chateaubriand: Les défenseurs du christianisme de 1670 à 1802* (Paris, 1916), p. 463.

[7] D. Mornet, "Les enseignements des bibliothèques privées, 1750-1780," *Revue d'Histoire Littéraire de la France*, XVII (1910), 449-496.

[8] R. R. Palmer, *Catholics and Unbelievers in Eighteenth Century France* (Princeton, 1939), pp. 117-131.

[9] M. Cheke, *The Cardinal de Bernis* (London, 1958), pp. 29-31, 198-199; L. Lévy-Schneider, "Un prélat très représentatif du haut clergé de la fin de l'ancien régime, le Cardinal de Boisgelin," *Revue d'Histoire de l'Eglise en*

France, VIII (1922), 170-181; J. Laurentie, "Trois archevêques de Sens, membres de l'académie française, Mgr. Languet de Gergy, le Cardinal Albert de Luynes, le Cardinal Loménie de Brienne," *Bulletin de la Société Archaéologique de Sens*, XXXVI (1927-1928), 62-115.

[10] Talleyrand, *Mémoires*, I, 24-25.

[11] In his edict of 24 May, 1766, reprinted in L. de Héricourt, *Les loix ecclésiastiques de France* (Paris, 1771), Part E, pp. 399-400.

[12] M. Bloch, *Les rois thaumaturges, étude sur le caractère surnaturel attribué à la puissance royale* (Strasbourg, 1924), pp. 186-215; A. Lemaire, *Les lois fondamentales de la monarchie française d'après les théoriciens de l'ancien régime* (Paris, 1907), pp. 289-290; P. Sagnac, *La formation de la société française moderne, 1660-1789* (Paris, 1946), I, 90-95; II (Paris, 1946), 132-135; W. Gurian, *Die politischen und sozialischen Ideen des französischen Katholizismus, 1789-1914* (Gladbach, 1929), pp. 4-7; J. Declareuil, *Histoire générale du droit français des origines à 1789* (Paris, 1929), pp. 943-953.

[13] *Mémoires de Louis XIV*, D. Dreyss, ed. (Paris, 1860), I, 209.

[14] *Documents relatifs aux rapports du clergé avec la royauté de 1682 à 1789*, L. Mention, ed., (Paris, 1903), II, 104-105; Marion, *Histoire financière de France* I, 130. The details of these struggles may be found in M. Marion, *L'impôt sur le revenu au XVIIIe siècle* (Paris, 1901), pp. 109-145, and *Impôts directs sous l'ancien régime, principalement au XVIIIe siècle* (Paris, 1910), pp. 74-81.

[15] J. J. Clageran, *Histoire de l'impôt en France*, III (Paris, 1876), 310 ff; Mention, *Documents*, II, 105-124; Marion, *Histoire financière*, I, 170-176; G. Lepointe, *L'organisation et la politique financières* pp. 224-225; P. de Crousaz-Crétet, *L'église et l'Etat ou les deux puissances au XVIIIe siècle, 1715-1789* (Paris, 1893), pp. 72-81. The Church-State conflict is expertly handled by M. Marion, *Machault d'Arnouville* (Paris, 1891), pp. 239-260. Colonne's memorandum, "Le remboursement des dettes du clergé," is printed in *Collection des mémoires présentées à l'assemblée des Notables: première et seconde division* (Versailles, 1787), pp. 23-29. See also J. Wallon, *Le clergé de quatre-vingt-neuf* (Paris, 1876), pp. 24, 111; A. Goodwin, "Calonne and the Assembly of French Notables of 1787 and the Origins of the 'Révolte Nobiliare'," *English Historical Review*, LXI (1946), 213ff; and P. Chevallier, *Journal de l'assemblée des notables de 1787* (Paris, 1960), Introduction.

[16] *Journal et mémoires du marquis d'Argenson*, VI, 318-319.

[17] Talleyrand, *Mémoires*, I, 24.

[18] *Gazette de France du vendredi 28 juin, 1782*, #52, p. 249.

[19] M. C. Goodwin, *The Papal Conflict with Josephinism* (New York, 1939), p. 69-77.

[20] This was reported to Joseph as late as April 12, by the Austrian Ambassador in Paris. (*Correspondance secrète du comte de Mercy-Argenteau avec Joseph II et le prince de Kaunitz*, E. Geffroy, ed., [Paris, 1889]), I, 93-94.

[21] G8* 2618, #131, "M. le comte de Vergennes ministre et secrétaire d'état par M. l'ab. de Périgord."

[22] G8* 2631 ("Lettres originales des secrétaires d'Etat, Intendants des finances et autres magistrats aux Agents Généraux du clergé"), V [1750-1782], #426.

[23] *PV 1780*, p. 40; For the clergy's taxes of 1780 and contribution to the success of the American Revolution cf. Sister M. Ceslas (Normand), "Financial Contribution of the French Clergy to American Independence, June 12-26, 1780," *United States Catholic Historical Society, Historical Records and Studies*, XXV (1935), 163-208

[24] *PV 1782*, pp. 26-31.

25 In each of these crises, the clergy compensated the crown with a higher extraordinary free gift. It was precisely this same hope of incurring a monetary sacrifice to protect its property and privileges that prompted Archbishop Boisgelin to offer the nation 400 millions on April 12, 1790, to stave off sequestration. *Archives parlementaires,* XII, 691-698.

26 *PV 1782,* p. 31.

27 Latreille, Delaruelle, Palanque, *Histoire du catholicisme en France,* II, 389.

28 *Recueil général des anciennes lois françaises,* J. Isambert, A. Jourdan, O. Décrusy, eds. (Paris, n.d.), XXII, 236-238; *Règlement du 5 août 1787 sur les fonctions des assemblées provinciales* (Versailles, 1787), #LV, article 82.

29 *Journal de l'abbé de Véri,* I, 344-346.

30 *Anciennes lois françaises,* XIX, 151; XXI, 296.

31 *Mémoires du clergé,* pp. 1626-1631; "PV 1788," fols. 299-300.

32 *PV 1775,* p. 258.

33 *PV 1785,* p. 1195 and *passim.*

34 *PV 1782,* p. 273.

35 Marion, *Machault,* p. 218ff.

36 *PV 1780,* p. 772.

37 *PV 1782,* pp. 279-281.

38 "Mémoire de M. l'abbé Bouquet sur l'origine et la nature de l'ancienne et de la nouvelle allodialité des seigneuries temporelles et ecclésiastiques (1780)"; "Clauses tirés sur Dom Bouquet pour la preuve des fiefs en bénéfices, des alleus, et distraction du ressort des biens du clergé de France"; "Mémoire sur les foy et hommages par M. l'Abbé Parent"; "Exemption des foi et hommage." G^8 167, G^8 168.

39 "Réfutation du mémoire de l'Inspecteur des domaines où il pretend prouver que les églises doivent foy-hommage et dénombrement à cause des fiefs qu'elles possedent dans la mouvance du Roy," and "Réplique pour le clergé de France à la réponse du défenseur du domaine (ce mémoire a été remis par MM les Agens Généraux à M. le Garde des Sceaux le 5 May, 1784)." G^8 168.

40 G^8 167; G^8 107.

41 G^8 107; G^8 167; *PV 1785,* p. 798.

42 *PV 1782,* pp. 282-283.

43 *PV 1785,* p. 996.

44 *Ibid.,* p. 1203.

45 *Précis des conférences des commissaires du clergé avec les commissaires du conseil concernant la demande faite aux bénéficiers de la prestation des foi et hommages, aveux et dénombrement, pour les fiefs dépendants des bénéfices dans la mouvance du Roi.* G^8 167.

46 Talleyrand warned the clergy to reveal nothing of its wealth. His admonition to the Bishop of Tarbes in January, 1783, is typical: "En un mot, user [sic] de toutes les précautions possible pour mettre à couvert les deniers du clergé et prevenir un dérangement qui tournait nécessairement au préjudice du clergé." G^{8*} 2618, #302.

47 *PV 1775,* pp. 191-227.

48 *Ibid.,* p. 222.

49 B. F. Hyslop, *L'Apanage de Philippe-Egalité, duc d'Orléans, (1785-1791)* (Paris, 1965), p. 104.

50 A. Britsch, *La jeunesse de Philippe-Egalité (1747-1785)* (Paris, 1926), pp. 308-309.

51 *Ibid.,* pp. 309-314.

52 G^8 167.

53 *PV 1782*, pp. 146-153; G⁸* 2617, #220; Talleyrand, *Mémoires*, I, 26.

54 *Rapport de l'agence contenant les principales affaires du clergé depuis 1780 jusqu'en 1785 par M. l'abbé de Périgord, et M. l'abbé de Boisgelin, anciens agents généraux du clergé* (Paris, 1788), pp. 61-74. (Henceforth cited as *Rapport de l'agence*).

55 Talleyrand, *Mémoires*, I, 26. Cf. article "Foi et hommage" in M. Marion, *Dictionaire des institutions de la France aux XVIIe et XVIIIe siècles* (Paris, 1923), pp. 239-240.

56 *Rapport de l'agence*, p. 75.

57 *PV 1780*, p. 1022; *PV 1782*, pp. 270-271.

58 G⁸ 158, "Exemptions des aveux et dénombrement, foi et hommages, 1574-1780."

59 Cf. Marion, article "Dîme" in *Dictionnaire des institutions*, pp. 172-176.

60 H. Marion, *La dîme ecclésiastique au XVIIIe siècle et sa suppression* (Paris, 1912), p. 111.

61 *L'administration de l'agriculture au contrôle général des finances (1785-1787), procès-verbaux et rapports*, H. Pigeonneau and A. de Foville, eds. (Paris, 1882), pp. 224-231; 331-333, and *passim;* cf. Schelle, *Du Pont de Nemours et l'école physiocratique*, pp. 296-300.

62 *Ibid.*, pp. 2, 173-184, 188-214; E. Champion, *La France d'après les cahiers de 1789* (Paris, 1897), pp. 182-185; A. Denys-Buirette, *Les questions religieuses dans les cahiers de 1789* (Paris, 1919), pp. 241-254.

63 "PV 1788," fol. 284; cf. Egret, "Dernière assemblée du clergé," p. 10.

64 Marion, *Dîme ecclésiastique*, pp. 163-164; A. Laveille, "Les revenus du clergé breton avant la Révolution," *Revue des Questions Historiques*, XLVIII (1912), 466-467; A. Rébillon, *La situation économique du clergé à la veille de la Révolution dans les districts de Rennes, de Fougères et de Vitré* (Rennes, 1913), pp. XLIII-XLV, XCVIII-CIV, CXXIII; C. Porée, *Cahiers des curés et des communautés ecclésiastiques du baillage d'Auxerre pour les Etats-Généraux de 1789* (Auxerre, 1927), pp. XCII-CVIII, 202-212.

65 Marion, *Dîme ecclésiastique*, pp. 20-21; P. Gagnol, *La dîme ecclésiastique en France* (Paris, 1911), p. 94.

66 Marion, *Dîme ecclésiastique*, pp. 162-166.

67 *PV 1780*, pp. 942-951.

68 E. Sevestre, *L'organisation du clergé paroissial à la veille de la Révolution* (Paris, 1911), p. 15.

69 *PV 1780*, pp. 443-450, 528-544; *PV 1782*, pp. 31-33.

70 Marion, *Dîme ecclésiastique*, pp. 46-47; *Rapport de l'agence*, pp. 186-203.

71 A. Floquet, *Histoire du parlement de Normandie* (Rouen, 1842), VI, 411-431.

72 G⁸* 2619, #427, 338; cf. Marion, *Dîme ecclésiastique*, pp. 45-48.

73 *Rapport de l'agence*, pp. 219-228; G⁸* 2617, #143bis; G⁸* 2618, #581.

74 *PV 1780*, pp. 503-505.

75 *Ibid.*, pp. 940-943.

76 *Rapport de l'Agence*, pp. 206-208.

77 Gagnol, *Dîme ecclésiastique*, pp. 98-99. From 1571 to 1686 it had been 120.

78 *Annales politiques, civiles et littéraires du dix-huitième siècle, ouvrage périodique par M. Linguet*, Vol. IX (Londres, 1780), pp. 119-124; C. Beaurin, "Les curés de campagne au XVIII siècle," *Correspondant*, CXLVIII (1887), 1102-1133; CXLIX (1887), 151-172; C. Meignan, "Le clergé des campagnes avant la Révolution," *Correspondant*, CXII (1878), 418-432; A Babeau, *Le village sous l'ancien régime* (Paris, 1884), pp. 144-169; L. Chassin, *Les*

cahiers des curés en 1789 (Paris, 1882), pp. 62-65; Denys-Buirette, *Les questions religieuses dans les cahiers,* pp. 268-271, 283-287; E. Sevestre, *L'organisation du clergé paroissial à la veille de la Révolution* (Paris, 1911), pp. 18-32.

[79] P. de Vaissière, *Curés de campagne de l'ancienne France* (Paris, 1932), pp. 202-204. Cf. N. Ravitch, "The Taxing of the Clergy in Eighteenth Century France," *Church History,* XXXIII (1964), 168-172; Lavisse, *Histoire de France,* IX, Part 1, p. 171.

[80] *Rapport de l'agence,* pp. 8-11.

[81] Marion, *Dîme ecclésiastique,* p. 165.

[82] Lavisse, *Histoire de France,* IX, Part 1, 172.

[83] Gagnol, *Dîme ecclésiastique,* pp. 105-117.

[84] G^{8*} 2618, #612; G^{8*} 2619; #57; G^{8*} 621. The Agent brought this matter before the Assembly of 1785. (*Rapport de l'agence,* pp. 267-268). A letter from Calonne in March, 1784 promised payment. (*Rapport de l'agence.* pièces justificatives, DXIV). This problem was not new. Minister of Finances, Joly de Fleury, consented to give orders on October 25, 1782, that the king's *curés à portion congrue* "would be paid each three months." (G^{8*} 2631, #464).

[85] G^{8*} 2826.

[86] C. E. Labrousse, *Esquisse du mouvement des prix et des revenues en France au XVIIIe siècle* (Paris, 1933); G. Lefebvre, "Le mouvement des prix et les origines de la Révolution française," *Annales d'Histoire Economique et Sociale,* IX (1937), 156-163, and his "Le mouvement des prix et les origines de la Révolution française," *Annales Historiques de la Révolution Française,* XIV (1937), 311-316.

[87] *PV 1782,* pp. 122-125; *Rapport de l'agence,* pp. 291-296, 303-307.

[88] G. Sénac de Meilhan, *Du gouvernment, des moeurs, et des conditions en France avant la Révolution* (Hambourg, 1795), p. 75.

[89] N. Ravitch, *Sword and Mitre: Government and Episcopate in France and England in the Age of Aristocracy* (The Hague, 1966), p. 180.

[90] Chassin, *Les Cahiers des curés en 1789,* pp. 57-65; Denys-Buirette, *Les questions religieuses dans les cahiers,* pp. 267-287; A. Rébillon, "La situation économique du clergé français à la fin de l'ancien régime," *La Révolution Française,* LXXXII (1929), 343-350; Marion, *Dîme ecclésiastique,* pp. 72-73; Gagnol, *La Dîme ecclésiastique,* p. 94.

[91] Préclin, *Jansénistes du 18e siècle,* p. 254.

[92] Mathiez, "L'église de France en 1789," p. 208.

[93] E. Préclin, "Les conséquences sociales de Jansénisme," *Revue d'Histoire de l'Eglise de France,* XXI (1935), 385-391; Sicard, *Ancien clergé de France,* I, 456; Lavisse, *Histoire de France,* IX, Part 1, 174.

[94] Préclin, *Jansénistes du 18e siècle,* p. 253.

[95] G^{8*} 2617, #457, 350, 353; G^{8*} 2618, #224.

[96] *Anciennes lois françaises,* XXVII, 15.

[97] *Ibid.,* XXVII, 167. Talleyrand reported this law to the Assembly of 1782 (*PV 1782,* pp. 123-125). There is an interesting exchange between Talleyrand and the *Garde des sceaux,* Miromesnil, on this subject. (G^{8*} 2618, #63, 213; G^{8*} 2631, fol. 403.)

[98] *PV 1775,* pp. 69-86; 757-763; *PV 1780,* p. 654.

[99] *Rapport de l'agence,* pp. 8-22.

[100] *PV 1780,* p. 982; *PV 1782,* pp. 144-145, 242-245, 459.

[101] *PV 1785,* pp. 107-108.

[102] *Ibid.,* pp. 12, 21.

103 Talleyrand, *Mémoires,* I, 53. Cf. J. Egret, *La pré-Révolution française, 1787-1788.* (Paris, 1962), p. 133.
104 *Anciennes lois françaises,* XXVIII, 232.
105 Vaissière, *Curés de campagne,* p. 174.
106 "PV 1788" fol. 455; Marion, *Dîme ecclésiastique,* p. 28.
107 *Motion de M. l'Evêque d'Autun sur les biens ecclésiastiques du 10 Octobre, 1789,* (Versailles, 1789) pp. 6-8; A. Latreille, *L'église catholique et la Révolution française* (Paris, 1946), I, 88.
108 *Anciennes lois françaises,* XVIII, 94-99; 226-235.
109 *PV 1780,* pp. 129; *PV 1782,* p. 197.
110 D. Boiteau, *Etat de France en 1789* (Paris, 1861), pp. 13-50; C. Raudot, *La France avant la Révolution* (Paris, 1847), pp. 120-121; J. Wallon, *Le clergé de quatre-vingt-neuf,* pp. 149-156, 176-197, 76-86; P. de la Gorce, *Histoire religieuse de la Révolution française* (Paris, 1917), I, 133-134; A. Sicard, *Le clergé de France pendant la Révolution* (Paris, 1912), I, 177-182: *Journal et mémoires du marquis d'Argenson,* VI, 46.
111 L. de Héricourt, *Les loix ecclésiastiques de France* (Paris, 1771), Part H, VII, 309ff.
112 G. de la Véronne, "Contribution à l'étude de la propriété foncière sous l'ancien régime," *Revue des Questions Historiques,* LII (1914), pp. 490-495; Wallon, *Clergé de quatre-vingt-neuf,* pp. 77-80.
113 Héricourt, *Les loix ecclésiastiques,* H, pp. 190-191; C. Fleury, *Discours sur l'histoire ecclésiastique* (Paris, 1763), pp. 83-86, 95-108, 125-129, 154-157; *De l'état religieux . . . par M. l'abbé de B.* [de Bernard] *et M. l'abbé B. de B.* [Bonnefoy de Bonyon], *avocat en Parlement* (Paris, 1784), p. 285; [B. Feron], *Vues d'un solitaire patriote* (Paris, 1784), *passim;* L. S. Mercier, *Tableau de Paris* (Amsterdam, 1783), IV, 142-145.
114 P. Chevallier, *Loménie de Brienne et l'ordre monastique* (Paris, 1959), I, 119-124.
115 The Assemblies of 1775, 1780, 1785, 1786, and 1788 petitioned the king for the enforcement of this legislation. "PV 1788," fol. 299, and *passim.*
116 G8* 2620, #49, 89; G8* 2619, #245, 441; *Rapport de l'agence,* pp. 248-254, pièces justificatives, CCCCLXXI.
117 *Rapport de l'agence,* pp. 255-265; G8* 2619, #135.
118 *Rapport de l'agence,* pp. 236-241, 248-254, 265-267, 268-277; G8* 2619, #245, 441; G8* 2620, #56.
119 G8* 2619, #135.
120 This argument was particularly invoked by Talleyrand in claiming ecclesiastical exemption from feudal duties *(droit de feu, droit d'amortissement, foi et hommage)* which implied subservience and obligations which the Church considered onerous and incompatible with its dignity *(PV 1780,*. pp. 328-329, 619-621, 884-886, 896, 1022; *PV 1782,* pp. 298-299; *Rapport de l'agence,* pp. 285-289; pièces justificatives, DXXIII; G8* 2618, #208; G8 107; G8* 2617, #365).
121 *Rapport de l'agence,* pp. 57-58.
122 *PV 1785,* p. 817.
123 *Rapport de l'agence,* pp. 248-254; G8* 2619, #245, 441.
124 *Rapport de l'agence,* pièces justificatives, CCCLXXI.
125 *Motion de M. l'Évêque d'Autun sur les biens ecclésiastiques,* pp. 5-6.
126 A. Pericauld, *Les célestins de Lyon* (Lyon, 1840), pp. 30-31.
127 *Rapport de l'agence,* pp. 242-248.
128 *Motion de M. l'Évêque d'Autun sur les biens ecclésiastiques,* p. 5.
129 X. Raduget, "La carrière politique de l'abbé Maury de 1786 à 1791,"

Revue d'Histoire de l'Eglise de France, III (1912), 505-511, 631-643; J. Godechot, *La contre-révolution: doctrine et action, 1789-1804* (Paris, 1961), pp. 33-34.

[130] *Opinion de M. l'abbé Maury, député de Picardie, sur la propriété des biens ecclésiastiques prononcée dans l'assemblée nationale le mardi, 13 octobre, 1789* (Paris, 1789), pp. 30-32; A. Ricard, *L'abbé Maury, 1746-1791* (Paris, 1887), pp. 186-189.

NOTES TO CHAPTER V

[1] *Mémoires du clergé,* p. 2339. *Précis des rapports de l'agence générale du clergé* (p. ii) repeats much the same: "to oppose the decrees of Parlements and the other sovereign courts of the kingdom which might be rendered as an encroachment on ecclesiastical jurisdiction."

[2] *Mémoires du clergé,* pp. 2344-2345.

[3] *Ibid.,* p. 2343.

[4] E. Glasson, *Histoire du droit et des institutions de la France,* VIII (Paris, 1903), 221-225.

[5] L. de Héricourt, *Les loix ecclésiastiques de France* (Paris, 1771), Part E, pp. 312-315; *Recueil des actes, titres, et mémoires concernant les affaires du clergé de France,* VII (Paris, 1769), 390-399. The whole question of jurisdiction is superbly summarized in Héricourt, chapter XIX, "Des affaires qui sont de la compétence du juge ecclésiastique," pp. 304-317.

[6] Abbé C. Fleury, *Institution au droit ecclésiastique,* II (Paris, 1767), pp. 35, 41-50, 72-73, 103-112, 134-135; Héricourt, *Loix ecclésiastiques,* E, pp. 308-309; *Mémoires du Clergé,* VII, 583-587.

[7] Héricourt, *Loix ecclésiastiques,* Part F, 605-607.

[8] *Recueil général des anciennes lois françaises,* J. Isambert, A. Jourdan, O. Décrusy, eds., XX (Paris, 1830), 243-257.

[9] Article "Appel comme d'abus" in M. Marion, *Dictionnaire des institutions de la France aux 17e et 18e siècles* (Paris, 1923), pp. 21-22.

[10] Fleury, *Droit ecclésiastique,* II, 213.

[11] These may be read in L. Cahen, *Les querelles religieuses et parlementaires sous Louis XV* (Paris, 1913); P. de Crousaz-Crétet, *L'église et l'Etat ou les deux puissances au 18e siècle, 1715-1789* (Paris, 1893), pp. 94-161, 217-238; E. Préclin and E. Jarry, *Les luttes politiques et doctrinales aux 17e et 18e siècles,* I (Paris, 1955), 228-230; W. Henley Jervis, *The Gallican Church: A History of the Church of France from the Concordat of Bologna, A.D. 1516 to the Revolution,* II (London, 1872), 310-323; E. Fayard, *Aperçu historique sur le parlement de Paris,* III (Paris, 1878), 89-119.

[12] E. Glasson, *Le parlement de Paris, son rôle politique depuis le règne de Charles VII jusqu'à la Révolution,* II (Paris, 1901), 156; cf. L. Gottshalk, "The French Parlements and Judicial Review," *Journal of the History of Ideas,* V (1944), 105-112.

[13] R. Bickart, *Les parlements et la notion de souveraineté nationale au 18e siècle* (Paris, 1932), p. 279; cf. R. R. Palmer, "The National Idea in France Before the Revolution," *Journal of the History of Ideas,* I (1940), 103-105.

[14] Bickart, *Les parlements,* pp. 273-277.

[15] F. Bassieux, "Théorie des libertés gallicanes du parlement de Paris au 18e siècle. *Nouvelle Revue Historique de Droit Français et Etranger,* XXX (1906), 333-335.

[16] I. Bourlon, *Les assemblées du clergé et le Jansénisme* (Paris, 1909), p. 315.

[17] *Collection des procès-verbaux des assemblees générales du clergé de France depuis l'année 1560 jusqu'à présent*, VIII, Part 2, (Paris, 1778), pièces justificatives, pp. 417-452; cf. J. Picot, *Mémoires pour servir à l'histoire ecclésiastique pendant le 18e siècle*, IV (Paris, 1855), 180-193.

[18] "Remonstrances sur les actes de l'assemblée du clergé en 1765," in *Remonstrances du parlement de Paris au 18e siècle*, J. Flammermont and M. Tourneux, eds., II (Paris, 1895), 596-656.

[19] P. Nau, "A l'origine des encycliques modernes, un épisode de la lutte des évêques et des parlements, 1755-1756," *Revue Historique de Droit Français et Etranger*, 4th series, XXIV (1956), 228.

[20] *PV 1780*, pp. 662-664; *PV 1782*, p. 239; *PV 1785*, p. 477.

[21] Marion, *Dictionnaire des institutions*, p. 108.

[22] P. Affre, *L'appel comme d'abus* (Paris, 1845), pp. 208-225.

[23] This paragraph leans heavily on J. Coudy, *Les moyens d'action de l'ordre du clergé au conseil du roi, 1561-1715* (Paris, n.d. [1954]) which, despite its title is applicable to the period up to the Revolution, and J. M. Aucoc, *Le conseil d'Etat avant et depuis 1789. Ses transformations, ses travaux, et son personnel* (Paris, 1876), pp. 41, 56-57.

[24] H. de Luçay, *Les secrétaires d'Etat depuis leur institution jusqu'à la mort de Louis XV* (Paris, 1881), pp. 422-425.

[25] G^8 712.

[26] *Mémoires du clergé*, pp. 2346-2349.

[27] P. Viollet, *Le roi et ses ministres pendant les trois derniers siècles de la monarchie* (Paris, 1912), pp. 261, 264.

[28] F. Olivier-Martin, *Histoire du droit français des origines à la Révolution* (Paris, 1951), p. 445.

[29] Luçay, *Secrétaires d'Etat*, pp. 512-513.

[30] G^8 107.

[31] Coudy, *Les moyens d'action de l'ordre du clergé au conseil du roi, 1561-1715*, p. 179.

[32] *PV 1780*, pp. 871-875.

[33] *Ibid.*, pp. 874-875.

[34] *Rapport de l'agence*, pp. 297-299.

[35] G^{8*} 2619, #117.

[36] Reprinted in *Rapport de l'agence*, pièces justificatives, p. DXXXIV.

[37] *PV 1780*, pp. 951-952.

[38] *Ibid.*, 953-954.

[39] *Ibid.*, 956.

[40] G^{8*} 2618, #107.

[41] *PV 1782*, pp. 119-157.

[42] Talleyrand, *Mémoires*, I, 32.

[43] Champion de Cicé, Agent from 1765 to 1770, delivered a similar report to the Extraordinary Assembly of 1766. Dulau, Agent from 1770 to 1775, delivered his report to the Extraordinary Assembly of 1772. Of Dulau he noted, "To cite an example of this prelate to justify a usage is almost to erect a law." Of Champion de Cicé, Talleyrand remarked that his "clarity of expression, his order of reasoning, and his abundance of resources, which combined constitute real eloquence in these matters," was already apparent in 1766. Talleyrand had a third model, Pierre-Louis de Leyssin (1724-1801), Archbishop of Embrun, and former Agent. He wrote of him in 1785: "My wish for the longest time, Monseigneur, is to follow the steps you left behind in your career as Agent." (*PV 1782*, p. 120; G^{8*} 2620, #106.)

Notes 243

44 G⁸* 2619, #393.
45 G⁸* 2619, #254.
46 G⁸* 2617, #288.
47 G⁸* 2618, #122.
48 G⁸* 2618, #95.
49 G⁸* 2619, #498.
50 G⁸* 2619, #179 bis.
51 G⁸* 2618, #572.
52 G⁸* 2618, #239.
53 G⁸* 2619, #566.
54 G⁸* 2619, #526.
55 G⁸* 2619, #206.
56 G⁸* 2620, #110.
57 G⁸* 2617, #312, 406.
58 G⁸* 2620, #65.
59 G⁸* 2618, #103.
60 "Recueil: Agence Générale," fols. 161-162; *Mémoires du clergé*, p. 737.
61 "Recueil: Agence Générale," fols. 162-163.
62 G⁸* 2617, #157.
63 G⁸* 2631, #320.
64 G⁸* 2618, #291. It is significant that this letter, like so many of Talleyrand's, carried no name of author and used the first person plural, "nous." The original manuscript in G⁸ 670 confirms his authorship. It is not surprising, however, that Cardinal Rochefoucauld should have detected the unmistakable hand of Talleyrand and wrote him personally as other bishops and ministers had, as official replies "to the Agents-General."
65 G⁸ 623.
66 G⁸* 2618, #118.
67 G⁸* 2620, #38.
68 P. Delannoy, *La juridiction ecclésiastique en matière bénéficiale sous l'ancien régime en France* (Bruxelles, 1910), pp. 155-159.
69 G⁸* 2620, #56.
70 E. Glasson, *Histoire du droit et des institutions de la France*, VIII (Paris, 1903), 221.
71 G⁸* 2619, #536.
72 *Rapport de l'agence*, pp. 77-89.
73 Delannoy, *Juridiction ecclésiastique*, p. 204.
74 *Rapport de l'agence*, pp. 95-106; Cf. Delannoy, *Juridiction ecclésiastique*, pp. 5-10.
75 Glasson, *Histoire du droit*, VIII, 228; F. Bassieux, "Théorie des libertés gallicanes du parlement de Paris au 18e siècle," *Nouvelle Revue Historique de Droit Français et Etranger*, XXX (1906), 348.
76 *Rapport de l'agence*, p. 102.
77 *Ibid.*, p. 57.
78 *Ibid.*, pp. 180-185.
79 G⁸ 47.
80 *Rapport de l'agence*, pp. 107-116; G⁸* 2618, #325bis.
81 G⁸* 2618, #168.
82 Louis XIV granted this power as a reward for the bishop's approval of the *capitation*. (Préclin, *Jansenistes du 18e siècle*, p. 28.)
83 R. Suaudeau, *L'évêque inspecteur administratif sous la monarchie absolue* (Paris, 1940), pp. 20-21; 35-61.
84 *Recueil général des anciennes lois françaises*, **XX**, 243-257.

[85] D. Jousse, *Commentaire sur l'édit du mois d'avril 1695 concernant la juridiction ecclésiastique* (Paris, 1764), I, 297.
[86] G8* 2827.
[87] Berthelot du Chesnay, "Le clergé séculier français du second ordre d'après les insinuations ecclésiastiques," p. 2; E. Appolis, "Le droit de nomination aux cures dans l'ancien diocèse de Lodève," *Actes du 80e congrès des sociétés savantes, section d'histoire* . . . (Paris, 1955), pp. 11-13.
[89] G8* 2620, #87.
[90] G8 47; *Rapport de l'agence*, pp. 138-146
[91] *Ibid.*, pp. 161-166.
[92] G8* 2618, #299, #350.
[93] G8* 2618, #351.
[94] *Rapport de l'agence*, p. 166.
[95] G8* 2618, #297bis.
[96] *Rapport de l'agence*, pp. 167-180; G8* 2618, #364; G8 745.
[97] *Rapport de l'agence*, pp. 291-296; *PV 1782*, pp. 122-125.
[98] *Rapport de l'agence*, pp. 303-307.
[99] *PV 1782*, p. 124.
[100] *Rapport de l'agence*, pp. 303-304.
[101] *PV 1780*, pp. 100-107.
[102] *Ibid.*, p. 107.
[103] N. Ravitch, "The Taxing of the Clergy in Eighteenth Century France," *Church History*, XXXIII (1964), 168-172.
[104] G. R. Cragg, *The Church of the Age of Reason (1648-1789)* (n.p., 1960), p. 206.
[105] Lavisse, *Histoire de France*, IX, Part 1, 172.
[106] *Ibid.*, p. 171.
[107] L. Lévy-Schneider, "L'autonomie administrative de l'épiscopat français à la fin de l'ancien régime," *Revue Historique*, CLI (1926), 4.
[108] *Ibid.*, p. 3.
[109] A summary of *curé* grievances may be sampled in M. G. Hutt, "The *Curés* and the Third Estate: The Ideas of Reform in the Pamphlets of the French Lower Clergy in the Period 1787-1789," *Journal of Ecclesiastical History*, VIII (1957), 74-92.
[110] P. Sagnac, *La formation de la société française moderne*, II (Paris, 1946), 215.
[111] *PV 1782*, p. 125.
[112] *Ibid.*
[113] *Ibid.*
[114] *PV 1780*, pp. 359-364.
[115] *Recueil général des anciennes lois françaises*, XXVII, 15.
[116] G8* 2631, #403.
[117] G8* 2618, #63.
[118] G8* 2618, #213.
[119] G8* 2619, #497.
[120] G8* 2619, #568.
[121] P. d'Avenel, "Le clergé français et la liberté de conscience sous Louis XIII," *Revue Historique*, XXXIII (1887), 3.
[122] *PV 1780*, pp. 548-557; *PV 1785*, pp. 157-168.
[123] G8* 2620, #48.
[124] This long letter was incompletely transcribed in G8* 2620, #49. The manuscript is in G8 685.
[125] *Rapport de l'agence*, pp. 57-58; *PV 1785*, p. 817.

Notes   245

[126] G. de la Véronne, "Contribution à l'étude de la propriété foncière sous l'ancien régime," *Revue des Questions Historiques*, LII (1914), 490-495; Wallon, *Clergé de quatre-vingt-neuf*, pp. 77-80; Soulavie (*Mémoires*, II, 19) claimed that "Lomenie seized one-hundred thousand *écus* in property of the clergy"; cf. Archives Départementales de la Haute-Garonne (Toulouse) B 1721, C 964, B 1757; Archives Départementales des Bouches-du-Rhone (Marseilles) G 116.

[127] G8* 2618, #143.

[128] Abbé E. Allain, *L'instruction primaire en France avant la Révolution* (Paris, 1881), pp. 242-274. This section also provides an excellent summary of the teaching orders; cf., Lavisse, *Histoire de France*, IX, Part 1, 163-164; Suaudeau, *Evêque inspecteur administratif*, pp. 55-61.

[129] G8* 2617, #273.

[130] *Rapport de l'agence*, pp. 89-93; *PV 1782*, pp. 133-137.

[131] *Rapport de l'agence*, p. 94.

[132] G8* 2617, #409.

[133] G8* 2618, #68.

[134] G8* 2617, #442.

[135] G8* 2619, #571.

[136] G8* 2617, #379.

[137] G8* 2618, #112.

[138] G8* 2617, #63.

[139] G8* 2822, "Consultations et délibérations du conseil de clergé, 1727-1788," fols. 374-375.

[140] G8* 2620, #109.

[141] G8* 2619, #545.

[142] "Recueil: Agence Générale," fol. iii. "Le clergé ennemi de toutes novations. . . ."

NOTES TO CHAPTER VI

[1] *PV 1780*, pp. 31-33, 74; *Recueil des anciennes lois françaises*, XXVI, 375.

[2] "Recueil: Agence Générale," fols. 100-101.

[3] *PV 1780*, pp. 216-217.

[4] *Ibid.*, p. 428.

[5] *Recueil des anciennes lois françaises*, XXVI, 417.

[6] *PV 1780*, p. 990.

[7] *Ibid.*, pp. 866-867.

[8] *Rapport de l'agence*, p. 56; cf. article "Gradué" in Marion, *Dictionnaire des institutions*, p. 262.

[9] *PV 1780*, p. 609.

[10] *PV 1782*, pp. 326-330.

[11] *Ibid.*, pp. 292-294.

[12] *PV 1775*, pp. 259-268; *PV 1780*, pp. 54-66, 662-663; *PV 1782*, pp. 88-90, 166-170, 300.

[13] "Recueil: Agence Générale," fol. 112.

[14] *PV 1780*, pp. 547-548.

[15] *PV 1785*, pp. 1179-1204.

[16] He listed these under "déclarations à solliciter," *Rapport de l'agence*, pp. 46-60.

[17] *PV 1785*, pp. 917-927, 1069.

[18] *Ibid.*, p. 817.

[19] *PV 1782*, pp. 187-191; *Recueil des anciennes lois françaises*, XXI, p. 407.

Actually the article in question accorded no such power at all. It merely stipulated that the priest would be responsible for entering data of parents or godparents who, required to sign the registry, "did not know how or could not sign." Cf. I. Bourlon, *Les assemblées du clergé et le Protestantisme* (Paris, 1909), pp. 102-108; E. Préclin and E. Jarry, *Les luttes politiques et doctrinales aux 17e et 18e siècles,* I (Paris, 1955), 146-148.

[20] B. C. Poland, *French Protestantism and the French Revolution* (Princeton, 1957), pp. 22-23.

[21] G⁸ 707; G⁸* 2822, "Consultations et délibérations du conseil du clergé (1780)," fol. 346.

[22] *Recueil des anciennes lois françaises,* XXVII, 190-191; G⁸ 707.

[23] *PV 1782,* p. 191.

[24] *Rapport de l'agence,* pp. 41-43.

[25] G⁸* 2619, #458. M. Beaurin who studied the registers in provincial archives found that many were not kept up regularly, that important information was frequently omitted, and inaccuracies were rife. ("Les curés de campagne au XVIIIe siècle," *Correspondant,* CXLVIII [1887], 160-161). Another authority found them interlarded with all manner of irrelevant, though oftentimes valuable local, literary, political, or social information. (T. Meignan, "Les anciens registres paroissiaux de l'état civil," *Revue des Questions Historiques,* XXV (1879), 131-172).

[26] G⁸* 2822, fols. 346-347.

[27] G⁸* 2619, #70; cf. A. Lods, "L'attitude du clergé Catholique à l'égard des Protestants en 1789," *La Révolution Française,* XXXIII (1897), 129-130.

[28] *Recueil des anciennes lois françaises,* XXVIII, 394.

[29] E. C. F. Bonifas, *Le mariage des Protestants depuis la réforme jusqu'à 1789* (Paris, 1901), 117-147.

[30] *Journal de l'abbé de Véri,* I, 255; P. Taillandier, *Le mariage des Protestants français sous l'ancien régime* (Clermont-Ferrand, 1919), p. 89; Bonifas, *Le mariage des Protestants,* p. 148.

[31] "PV 1788", fol. 199 ff; cf. A. Lods, "Le clergé Catholique et les Protestants français: 1775, 1780, 1788," *Bulletin de la Société de l'Histoire du Protestantisme Français,* XXXV (1887), 539.

[32] "Recueil: Agence Générale," fol. 271.

[33] *Mémoires du clergé,* pp. 13, 2380.

[34] "Recueil: Agence Générale," fols. 271-275.

[35] These circulars are housed in the Archives Nationales and the Bibliothèque Nationale in Paris. In the former, they are scattered in uneven chronological order in the correspondence of the Agents (G⁸* 2617-2620) and various cartons (G⁸ 166, 181, 270, 741, 755, 756). A large portion is available in the Bibliothèque Nationale as "Collection des circulaires de l'agence générale du clergé de France," Ld⁵ 41-50. Certain circulars are also reprinted in the proceedings of the Assemblies and in the Report of the Agency.

[36] "Recueil: Agence Générale," fol. 271.

[37] G⁸* 2617, #180.

[38] "Recueil: Agence Générale," fol. 112.

[39] G⁸* 2617; reprinted in *PV 1780,* pp. 1100, 1141.

[40] Ld⁵ 49, reprinted in *PV 1780,* pp. 1157-1160.

[41] G⁸* 2617, reprinted in *PV 1780,* pp. 1136-1137.

[42] G⁸* 2618.

[43] *Ibid.*

[44] "Recueil: Agence Générale," fols. 278-279.

45 G⁸* 2618, #535; G⁸* 2617.
46 G⁸ 756.
47 "Recueil: Agence Générale," fols. 4-6.
48 G⁸* 2618, #130.
49 G⁸* 2619, #483.
50 *PV 1780*, p. 10.
51 "Recueil: Agence Générale," fol. 163.
52 G⁸* 2617; G⁸* 2618; G⁸* 2620.
53 *Mémoires du clergé*, pp. 2392-2393.
54 "Recueil: Agence Générale," fol. 183. Circulars sent out for deceased prelates for 1780: June 27, former Bishop of Léon; August 5, former Bishop of Troyes. For 1781: January 23, Archbishop of Cambrai; October 7, Bishop of Saintes; December 13, Archbishop of Paris. (G⁸* 2617, Ld⁵ 45). For 1782: July 26, Bishop of Angers; September 29, Bishop of Nevers. For 1783: May 9, Bishop of Oleron; May 30, Archbishop of Auch; October 13, former Bishop of Viviers; October 15, Bishop of Vence; November 16, Bishop of Aire. (G⁸* 2618). For 1784: January 29, Bishop of Saint-Papoul; February 12, Bishop of Nîmes; March 24, former Bishop of Limoges; October 14, former Bishop of Glandève. (G⁸* 2619). For 1785: March 30, Bishop of Saint-Claude; April 22, former Archbishop of Embrun; May 9, former Bishop of Acqs. (G⁸* 2620). The Secretariat apparently did not always have a sufficient number of printed circulars to announce the death of each prelate. Several specimens reveal the name of a deceased bishop crossed out from the printed form and another substituted in its place. (G⁸ 686).
55 "Recueil: Agence Générale," fols. 187-194.
56 G⁸* 2617.
57 "Recueil: Agence Générale," fols. 153, 212.
58 *PV 1780*, pp. 772-775; 1098.
59 G⁸* 2617, #107; Ld⁵ 49.
60 G⁸* 2617, #180; reprinted in *PV 1780*, p. 1155.
61 *PV 1782*, p. 154.
62 *Ibid.*, pp. 242-244.
63 G⁸* 2618, #461.
64 *PV 1780*, pp. 792-795.
65 *Ibid.*, p. 875; G⁸* 2617, #181. Reprinted in *PV 1780*, pp. 1151-1152.
66 *Rapport sur l'instruction publique fait au nom du comité de constitution à l'assemblée nationale les 10, 11 & 19 septembre, 1791, par M. de Talleyrand-Périgord, ancien évêque d'Autun* (Paris, 1791).
67 *PV 1782*, p. 155.
68 *Ibid.*, pp. 217-218.
69 G⁸* 2618, #450.
70 *PV 1782*, pp. 256-259.
71 G⁸* 2618, #450.
72 G⁸* 2619, #179.
73 G⁸* 2618, #522 bis. The manuscripts of most of the circulars were unfortunately not kept. It is therefore virtually impossible to guess their authorship, save from internal evidence: typical ideas, recurrent idioms, and stylistic peculiarities. Of the two manuscript circulars in the records (G⁸ 685) both are autographs of Talleyrand.
74 G⁸* 2826; G⁸ 566; G⁸ 758; G⁸ 765.
75 *Mémoires du clergé*, p. 13.
76 G⁸* 2618, #235, 237, 264, 281, 324.
77 G⁸* 2618, #1.

[78] *Ibid.*, #84 bis.
[79] *Ibid.*, #625.
[80] *Ibid.*, #14 bis.
[81] *Ibid.*, #2.
[82] G^8* 2617, #135.
[83] *Ibid.*, #392.
[84] G^8* 2618, #12 bis.
[85] G^8* 2619, #105.
[86] An interesting discussion of the importance of church bells both to community and clergy is available in A. Babeau, *Le village sous l'ancien régime* (Paris, 1883), pp. 117-120.
[87] G^8* 2618, #631.
[88] E. Sevestre, *L'organisation du clergé paroissial à la veille de la Révolution* (Paris, 1911), pp. 5-8.
[89] G^8* 2618, #623.
[90] G^8* 2617, #345.
[91] *Ibid.*, #153.
[92] *Ibid.*, #371.
[93] *Ibid.*, #407; cf. M. Marion, *Les impôts directs sous l'ancien régime, principalement au XVIIIe siècle* (Paris, 1910), pp. 49-61.
[94] G^8* 2617, #136.
[95] G^8* 2619, #78; cf. M. Marion, *L'impôt sur le revenu au dix-huitième siècle, principalement en Guyenne* (Paris, 1901), pp. 1-33.
[96] G^8* 2617, #223; cf. Marion, *Impôts directs*, pp. 90-91.
[97] G^8* 2617, #313.
[98] G^8* 2619, #196.
[99] Article "Franc-fief" in Marion, *Dictionnaire des institutions*, p. 244.
[100] G^8* 2617, #255, 400, 178.
[101] *Recueil des anciennes lois françaises*, XX, 249.
[102] Cited in H. Marion, *Dîme ecclésiastique*, pp. 150-159, 171-172.
[103] *PV 1785*, pp. 388-403; cf. *PV 1780*, pp. 410-422; *PV 1782*, pp. 251-254.
[104] G^8* 2618, #334.
[105] G^8* 2617, #249.
[106] *Ibid.*, #398.
[107] *Ibid.*, #402.
[108] *Ibid.*, #210; G^8* 2618, #208.
[109] G^8* 2618, #349.
[110] G^8* 2619, #80.
[111] G^8* 2617, #221. Cf. article "Amortissement" in Marion, *Dictionnaire des institutions*, pp. 18-19.
[112] G^8* 2618, #83.
[113] G^8* 2617, #215.
[114] G^8* 2618, #155.
[115] G^8* 2619, #232.
[116] G^8* 2617, #295.
[117] G^8* 2618, #619.
[118] G^8* 2619, #96.
[119] G^8* 2617, September 12, 1780.
[120] G^8* 2619, #206.
[121] *Ibid.*, #668.
[122] G^8* 2620, #45.
[123] G^8* 2619, #668.
[124] G^8* 2618, #354.

125 G⁸* 2619, #449.
126 G⁸* 2620, #126.
127 *Ibid.*, #9.
128 G⁸* 2617, #356.
129 *Ibid.*, #361.
130 *Ibid.*, #224.
131 G⁸* 2619, #463.
132 G⁸* 2617, #245
133 G⁸* 2618, #439.
134 *Ibid.*, #28.
135 G⁸* 2617, #150.
136 G⁸* 2619, #536.
137 G⁸* 2617, #376.
138 Cf. "Necker's Reforms" in P. Renouvin, *Les assemblées provinciales de 1787, origines, développement, résultats* (Paris, 1921), pp. 46-78.
139 G⁸* 2617, #290.
140 G⁸* 2618, #30.
141 G⁸* 2620, #20. To another cleric he wrote in December, 1784, "It is almost five years now that MM. de La Rochefoucauld and de Jarente are no longer Agents-General of the Clergy." (G⁸* 2619, #620)
142 G⁸* 2617, #302.
143 G⁸* 2619, #619.
144 *Ibid.*, #620.
145 *Ibid.*, #631.
146 *Ibid.*, #271 bis.
147 *Ibid.*, #633.
148 G. Lepointe, *L'organisation et la politique financières du clergé de France sous le règne de Louis XV* (Paris, 1923), pp. 61-62.
149 G⁸* 2617, #127.
150 G⁸* 2618, #63; *PV 1780*, pp. 893-895.
151 *Rapport de l'agence*, pp. 277-278; G⁸* 2619, #23, 121, 122; Marion, *Impôt sur le revenu*, pp. 10-11.
152 Reprinted in *Rapport de l'agence*, pièces justificatives, DXV.
153 *Rapport de l'agence*, p. 278.
154 G⁸* 2618, p. 196; reprinted in *Rapport de l'agence*, pièces justificatives, DXVI.
155 G⁸* 2617, #213.
156 *Ibid.*, #153, 407; cf. Marion, *Impôts directs*, pp. 50-51.
157 G⁸ 746; *PV 1780*, pp. 847-848; *Rapport de l'agence*, pp. 278-280, pièces justificatives, DXVI; Marion, *Impôt sur le revenu*, pp. 148-149; Marion, *Impôts directs*, pp. 90-91.
158 G⁸* 2619, #118.
159 *PV 1780*, pp. 406-408.
160 Reprinted in *Rapport de l'agence*, pièces justificatives, DXVIII.
161 G⁸* 2619, #368. However important a source of clerical revenue, the *casuel* was abhorred by the laity and disliked by the lower clergy as "degrading, odious, and onerous." (C. Porée, *Cahiers des curés et des communautés du baillage d'Auxerre pour les Etats-Généraux de 1789* [Auxerre, 1927], p. XCIV, p. 22; A. Laveille, "Les revenus du clergé breton avant la Révolution," *Revue des Questions Historiques*, XLVIII [1912], 467).
162 Marion, *Dictionnaire des institutions*, pp. 247-250.
163 P.-T. Durand de Maillane, *Dictionnaire de droit canonique et de pratique bénéficiale* (Lyons, 1770), II, 636.

250   *Talleyrand: Statesman Priest*

[164] *PV 1782*, pp. 141-146, 292-293.
[165] *Ibid.*, pp. 305-307.
[166] G[8] 746; G[8]* 2617, #398; *Rapport de l'agence*, pp. 282-285, pièces justificatives, DXXI.
[167] Reprinted in *Rapport de l'agence*, pièces justificatives, DXXIII. Cf. G. Constant, "Les registres de marguilliers," *Revue d'Histoire de l'Eglise de France*, XXIV (1938), 170-183.
[168] G[8]* 2618, #113. Talleyrand, not averse to displaying his zeal for the affairs of the prelacy, whose ranks he was anxious to enter, often communicated with the local bishop at the same time he announced a favorable decision to one of his diocesan priests. He wrote to the Bishop of Nantes informing him of the favorable decision received for one of his priests, adding, "I really sincerely wish that my interventions are favorably received." (G[8]* 2618, #114)
[169] Coudy, *Les Moyens d'action de l'ordre du clergé au conseil du roi*, p. 86.
[170] *Rapport de l'agence*, pp. 232-235, pièces justificatives, CCCXXXVIII-CCCXXXIX; G[8]* 2618, #37.
[171] G[8]* 2618, #9; Marion, *Impôts directs*, pp. 113-119.
[172] G[8]* 2617, #257.
[173] *Ibid.*, #241.
[174] *Ibid.*, #191.
[175] *Ibid.*, #424; G[8]* 2618, #508; G[8]* 2619, #441.
[176] G[8]* 2618, #508.
[177] *Ibid.*, #349.
[178] G[8]* 2619, #572. This item did not appear in the final report, however. The inability to secure in time the notarized documents applicable to this case for presentation to the Assembly was the probable cause for its exclusion.
[179] G[8]* 2617, #405; *Rapport de l'agence*, pièces justificatives, CCCCXXX-VIII; Marion, *Dîme ecclésiastique*, p. 155. Marion reviews geographical differences which accounted for variations in the interpretation of the 1695 law which assigned responsibility for church repairs (pp. 150-159).
[180] G[8] 745.
[181] *PV 1780*, pp. 849-851; *Rapport de l'agence*, pp. 210-212, pièces justificatives, CCCLXXVIII.
[182] *PV 1782*, pp. 251-252.
[183] G[8]* 2617, #375; G[8]* 2619, #15.

NOTES TO CHAPTER VII

[1] *Mémoires du clergé*, p. 2438ff; "Recueil: Agence Générale," fols. 252-254; *PV 1748*, pp. 55-59.
[2] These were collected in eighty-nine volumes, G[8]* 2468-2556.
[3] "Recueil: Agence Générale," fols. 254-256, 264-265.
[4] G[8]* 700, fol. 1526; "Recueil: Agence Générale," fol. 260; *Almanach Royal de 1775*, p. 64; *La France Ecclésiastique de 1780*, p. 23; cf. Lepointe, *Organisation et la politique financières*, p. 71. M. de Beauvais, uncle of the famous sermonizer and notorious sole non-noble member of the episcopate in the reign of Louis XVI, the Bishop of Senez, adopted and educated the boy after the death of his father, tried without success to induce him to forego entering the priesthood, to remain instead in the service of the Bureau, to marry his daughter, and to succeed him as Director. (H. Moulin, *Monseigneur de Beauvais, évêque de Senez* [Cherbourg, 1879], p. 3; A. de Sambucy, *Vie de Monseigneur de Beauvais, ancien évêque de Senez* [Paris, 1842], p. 9; A.

Rosne, M. de Beauvais, Évêque de Senez 1731-1790 [Paris, 1887], pp. 15-16; Dictionnaire de biographie française, M. Prevost and R. d'Amat, eds., V [Paris, 1951], 1189-1190). There are suggestions that the eminent Jesuit writer and royal preacher, Gilles-François Beauvais (d. 1773) was related to the two Beauvais and may also have served the Bureau as editor of *La France Ecclésiastique,* between 1764 and 1768. (L. Lebreton, *Biographie Normande,* I (Rouen, 1957), 81-83; R. Kerviler, *Répertoire général de Bio-bibliographie bretonne,* II (Rennes, 1888), 284.

[5] "Recueil: Agence générale," fols. 267-268.
[6] G^{8*} 777; G^{8*} 2620, #241.
[7] G^8 694; G^{8*} 2828.
[8] These might vary from the notation and underlining of important items of current business (G^8 625) to his personal composition of lengthy memoirs in reply to individual questions or requests. (G^8 682).
[9] G^8 682.
[10] G^{8*} 2628.
[11] For example, G^{8*} 2827, #137.
[12] G^8 663; G^8 694; G^8 701.
[13] G^8 668; cf. G^{8*} 2829, #248.
[14] *PV 1748,* pp. 57-59.
[15] G^8 682, obv. May 31, 1781; cf. G^8 763; receipts to Mannay as secretary were found in Talleyrand's papers sequestered in 1794. (A. N. T 1668, #44, "Charles-Maurice de Talleyrand Périgord, ex-Evêque d'Autun, Emigré demeurant ci devant Rue de l'Université No. 900 sec. de la fontaine de Grenelle.")
[16] G^{8*} 2828, fol. 492; G^8 701.
[17] Letters of September, 1781, in the Broglie Papers (Eure); G^8 107, "Comptes des frais communs des assemblées du clergé de 1775, 1780, de 1782 et de 1785."
[18] G^{8*} 2620, #29.
[19] In referring to those loose leaves in various cartons, we have quoted the date appearing on the Agent's letters on the obverse side. This device is helpful in more readily identifying the letters chronologically.
[20] G^8 682, obv. #247, February 14, 1781.
[21] *Ibid.,* obv. #233, February 8, 1781.
[22] *Ibid.,* obv. #235, February 8, 1781; cf. G^8 158.
[23] G^8 684, obv. December 16, 1784.
[24] *Ibid.,* obv. #103, March 18, 1784.
[25] *Ibid.,* obv. #96, March 18, 1784; obv. #423, July 28, 1784; G^8 682, #269.
[26] G^{8*} 2619, #297; G^{8*} 2617, #406; G^{8*} 2619, #307; G^{8*} 2620, #88, 164.
[27] G^{8*} 2618, #155.
[28] G^{8*} 2618, #227.
[29] G^{8*} 2619, #583. It should be noted that Talleyrand was not absent without authorization. This date fell between September 7 and November 12, the official vacation of the Agents. ("Recueil: Agence Générale," fols. 269-270).
[30] G^{8*} 2619, #593.
[31] *Ibid.,* #582.
[32] G^{8*} 2617, #288, 289; G^{8*} 2619, #393, 426.
[33] G^8 666; G^8 627; G^{8*} 2618, #297 bis.; G^{8*} 2828, fol. 492.
[34] G^8 684, obv. #613, Nov. 30, 1784.
[35] *Mémoires du clergé,* p. 2438 *et seq.*
[36] "Recueil: Agence Générale," fol. 1.

[37] *PV 1748*, p. 56; "Recueil: Agence Générale," fol. 1.
[38] *Mémoires du clergé*, p. 2456.
[39] *PV 1748*, p. 59.
[40] G^{8*} 2490, fol. 442.
[41] "Recueil: Agence Générale," fols. 256-260.
[42] *PV 1748*, p. 55.
[43] G^{8*} 2468-2556; G^{8*} 2556, frontispiece. The last two volumes provide the alphabetical tables in this series.
[44] G^{8*} 2781-2834. The register for these volumes is in G^{8*} 2832.
[45] G^{8*} 2451-2467.
[46] G^{8*} 2633-2780.
[47] G^{8*} 2557-2834. The index for this series is in five additional volumes.
[48] "Mémoire sur l'Etat actuel des archives du clergé (1785)," G^8 95.
[49] He crossed out a less modest first version of this sentence: "Tables were necessary. I offered myself. I executed."
[50] "Procès-verbal de l'assemblée générale du clergé de France tenue à Paris au couvent des Grands Augustins en l'année 1775," G^{8*} 699, fols. 1138-1147.
[51] While this collection was never brought together and bound, a manuscript in the archives reveals its title ("Recueil des édits, ordonnances, déclarations, lettres patentes, arrêts, jugements, sentences, et décisions concernant le clergé général, les diocèses, sièges, bénéfices, corps, et communautés ecclésiastiques du Royaume de France") and that its materials ranging from 1057 to 1769 were to be prepared in ten volumes." (G^{8*} 585, "Modèles de differentes pièces imprimées par ordre des Agents généraux").
[52] *PV 1780*, pp. 929-930.
[53] *PV 1785*, p. 1226.
[54] *PV 1748*, p. 59.
[55] "Recueil: Agence Générale," fol. 245.
[56] G^8 107.
[57] G^8 95, "Mémoire sur l'Etat actuel des archives du clergé."
[58] "Recueil: Agence Générale," fol. 266.
[59] *Ibid.*, fol. 252.
[60] *Mémoires du clergé*, p. 2439.
[61] G^{8*} 707K. "Table générale des procès-verbaux des assemblées générales du clergé de France, 1561-1748," Vol. I, fol. 205.
[62] "Recueil: Agence Générale," fols. 31, 253.
[63] *Mémoires du clergé*, pp. 2438-2439.
[64] *Ibid.*, pp. 2444-2445. Talleyrand's five year supervision of the Agency's papers was submitted to the inspection of the Committee on the Archives of the Assembly of 1785 under the chairmanship of the Bishop of Grenoble. (*PV 1785*, p. 33).
[65] "Recueil: Agence Générale," fol. 30.
[66] *PV 1715*, pp. 120-121.
[67] Lepointe, *Organisation*, p. 68.
[68] Cans, *Organisation financière*, p. 131.
[69] G^{8*} 707K, Vol. I, fols. 204-205.
[70] *Mémoires du clergé*, pp. 2438-2450.
[71] G^{8*} 2490, fol. 432.
[72] G^{8*} 2619, #593.
[73] *Ibid.*, #583.
[74] *PV 1780*, pp. 522-526.
[75] *Ibid.*, pp. 918-930, 1154.
[76] *PV 1785*, pp. 824-829.

Notes 253

[77] "Recueil: Agence Générale," fol. 256.
[78] *PV 1715*, pp. 228-231.
[79] *PV 1780*, pp. 926-929.
[80] G^8 95.
[81] *Ibid.*
[82] G^8* 2617, #175.
[83] *PV 1785*, pp. 824-825.
[84] Coudy, *Les moyens d'action de l'ordre du clergé au conseil du roi, 1561-1715*, pp. 133-134.
[85] Lepointe, *Organisation*, p. 74.
[86] *La France Ecclésiastique de 1780*, p. 22.
[87] "Recueil: Agence Générale," fol. 325; G^8* 700, fols. 1524-25; *Almanach Royal de 1777* (Paris, n.d.), p. 66.
[88] *PV 1785*, p. 319.
[89] "Recueil: Agence Générale," fol. 128.
[90] *PV 1785*, p. 764.
[91] "Recueil: Agence Générale," fols. 268-269.
[92] Lepointe, *Organisation*, p. 75.
[93] "Recueil: Agence Générale," fols. 267-270, 273.
[94] G^8* 2827, fols. 451-452; G^8* 2828, fol. 143.
[95] G^8* 2464, fols. 395, 686.
[96] G^8* 2464, fols. 485, 518, 560, 665.
[97] G^8* 2465, fol. 109 ter.
[98] G^8* 2827, #519.
[99] G^8* 2464, fol. 718.
[100] G^8* 2834, fol. 2.
[101] G^8* 2781-2803.
[102] G^8 682, 683, 684.
[103] G^8 683, obv. #79, March 12, 1784.
[104] *Ibid.*, obv. #444, August 8, 1784.
[105] G^8 685, obv. #6, January 12, 1785.
[106] G^8 683, obv. #550, September 11, 1783.
[107] G^8 683, obv. #551, September 13, 1783; *ibid.*, obv. #204, April 8, 1784.
[108] *Ibid.*, obv. #62, March 5, 1784.
[109] *Ibid.*, obv. #303, May 27, 1784; *ibid.*, obv. #251, dated "lundy 9 fév., 1784," by Talleyrand.
[110] *Ibid.*, dated "ce lundy 9 fév., 1784," by Talleyrand; dated "28 fév., 1784," by Talleyrand.
[111] *Ibid.*, obv. #288, May 13, 1784; G^8 685, dated "ce mardy ler mars, 1785," by Talleyrand, obv. #104, March 3, 1785.
[112] G^8 683, obv. #345, June 24, 1784.
[113] *Ibid.*
[114] G^8 685, obvs. #135, March 31, 1785.
[115] G^8* 2619, #323.
[116] G^8* 2827, #451.
[117] *Ibid.*, #188.
[118] G^8* 2617.
[119] G^8 682. He was in contact with the Abbé de Barral, his second successor, even earlier. A communication in Talleyrand's hand is dated February, 1783. (G^8* 2618, #357.)
[120] *Mémoires du clergé*, p. 2379.
[121] Lepointe, *Organisation*, pp. 85-87.
[122] *PV 1770*, pp. 626-635.

123 *Journal et mémoires du marquis d'Argenson*, I, 293; and II, 103, cited in Lepointe, *Organisation et politique financières*, p. 86. Cf. J. F. Bluche, *L'origine des magistrats du parlement de Paris au 18e siècle, 1715-1771* (Paris, 1956), p. 331.
124 *PV 1785*, pp. 84-87.
125 *Mémoires du clergé*, pp. 12, 49; Héricourt, *Les loix ecclésiastiques de France*, p. 264; cf. Gagnol, *Les décimes et dons gratuits*, p. 40ff.
126 I. Bourlon, "La caisse du clergé avant '89," *Revue du Clergé Français*, LIV (1908), 404-405.
127 *Mémoires du clergé*, p. 1419.
128 *Ibid.*, p. 1447; cf. Cans, *Organisation*, p. 257.
129 "Recueil: Agence Générale," fol. 257.
130 Bourlon, "La caisse du clergé avant '89," pp. 411-413.
131 "Recueil: Agence Générale," fol. 257.
132 G^8 756; G^8* 777, "Comptes des frais communs de l'assemblée extraordinaire du clergé de 1782."
133 G^8 107; G^8 139, "Frais de sommation et d'impression. Feuilles de délibérations des assemblées du clergé (1726-1788)."
134 G^8 220-248, "Pensions des ministres convertis et autres gratifiés du clergé"; G^8 255-261, "Pensions des ministres protestants et autres gratifiés du clergé."
135 *Mémoires du clergé*, p. 2380; "Recueil: Agence Générale," fol. 245.
136 *Mémoires du clergé*, pp. 2382-2384; G^8 81^9, "Diocèses spoliés."
137 *PV 1780*, p. 990.
138 *PV 1782*, pp. 69-70.
139 G^8 682, obv. #248, February 15, 1781.
140 G^8* 585.
141 G^8 158; G^8 691, "Consultations du Conseil du clergé."
142 G^8* 2621, #34; J. M. Quérard, *La France littéraire, ou dictionnaire bibliographique des savants, historiens et gens de lettres de France*, II (Paris, 1828), 625-626; J. F. Michaud, *Bibliographie universelle ancienne et moderne*, XI (Paris, n.d.), 405-406; J.-C. F. Hoefer, *Nouvelle biographie générale depuis les temps les plus reculés jusqu'à nos jours*, XIV (Paris, 1868), 949-950; F.-X. Feller, *Dictionnaire historique*, IV (Lille, 1832), 562-563.
143 *Mémoires du clergé*, pp. 1894-1895; G. Lepointe, article "Bureau diocésain," in *Dictionnaire de droit canonique contenant tous les termes de droit canonique avec un sommaire de l'histoire et des institutions et de l'état actuel de la discipline . . . publié sous la direction de R. Naz* (Paris, 1935), II, 1157-1167.
144 *Mémoires du clergé*, p. 1893; Serbat, *Assemblées*, pp. 190-191.
145 Lepointe, *Organisation*, pp. 97-98.
146 *PV 1770*, pp. 301-306; the Assembly of 1780 acknowledged that new upheavals in the Diocesan Chambers of Poitiers, Vence, and Apt were due to *curés* who demanded representation. (*PV 1780*, pp. 359-364).
147 *Mémoires du clergé*, pp. 1262-1270, 1309-1312; Méric, *Clergé sous l'ancien régime*, p. 180.
148 *Mémoires du clergé*, pp. 1312-1342, 1358, 1382-90; Maury, "Assemblées générales du clergé," p. 779; Cans, *Organisation*, pp. 215-227.
149 *PV 1770*, pp. 536-545, 823-826; reprinted in *Collection des procès-verbaux des assemblées générales du clergé de France*, VIII (Paris, 1780), Part I, appendices, pp. 267-268.
150 Brette, "La dette du clergé de France en 1789," p. 415.

151 G. Lepointe, Article "Assemblées générales du clergé," *Dictionnaire de droit canonique*, R. Naz, ed., I, 1134.
152 G^8* 706, fols. 652-736.
153 Lepointe, article, "Assemblées générales du clergé," p. 1125.
154 *Mémoires du clergé*, pp. 93-94.
155 *Ibid.*, p. 12; Méric, *Clergé sous l'ancien régime*, pp. 179-181, 187.
156 Bourlon, *Assemblées du clergé*, p. 15.
157 *Mémoires du clergé*, pp. 93-94, 238.
158 *Ibid.*, pp. 1663-1668.
159 Méric, *Clergé sous l'ancien régime*, p. 188.
160 *Mémoires du clergé*, p. 97; Lepointe, *Organisation*, p. 114; Méric, *Clergé sous l'ancien régime*, p. 188.
161 *Mémoires du clergé*, p. 1447; Bourlon, "Caisse du clergé," pp. 410-411.
162 "Recueil: Agence Générale," fol. 257.
163 G. Lepointe, article, "Chambres supérieures des décimes," in *Dictionnaire de droit canonique*, III, 431-454.
164 *Mémoires du clergé*, pp. 2177-2180; *Précis des rapports de l'agence générale du clergé de France*, p. 1.
165 G. Lepointe, "La composition et l'organisation intérieure de la chambre supérieure des décimes de Paris au XVIIIe siècle," *Revue Historique de Droit Français et Etranger*, 4th ser., XVI (1936), 302-336, 315; "Le rôle des chambres supérieures des décimes et leur situation juridique," *Revue Historique de Droit Français et Etranger*, 4th ser., XVII (1938), 71-91.
166 G. Lepointe, "La chambre ecclésiastique de Strasbourg," *Revue Historique de Droit Français et Etranger*, 4th ser., XXIX (1951), 522-559.
167 Bourlon, "La caisse du clergé avant '89," pp. 160-164.
168 Lepointe, article, "Assemblées générales," p. 1128.

NOTES TO CHAPTER VIII

1 That the plan was entirely of Talleyrand's inspiration is evidenced by his personal correspondence with clerical personnel between 1782 and 1785 to solicit its adoption and by statements such as the following to the Bishop of Châlons-sur-Marne: "Comme le projet est de moy . . . comme les motifs qui l'ont déterminé m'appartiennent . . . si le projet présent des inconvénients, c'est à moy à les détruire ou à en avoir le tort." G^8* 2619, #179.
2 *Rapport de l'agence*, pp. 308-317; G^8* 2618, #675; G^8* 2620, #470.
3 *PV 1782*, p. 154.
4 G^8* 2617, #260; G^8* 2619, #102, 315; *Rapport de l'agence*, pièces justificatives, DLXX, DLXIX.
5 *Rapport de l'agence*, p. 309.
6 *Ibid.*, pp. 77-130, 161-166, 297-299, 300-301; pièces justificatives, DXXXIV. Cf. P. Delannoy, *La juridiction ecclésiastique en matière bénéficiale sous l'ancien régime en France* (Bruxelles, 1910), pp. 155-159.
7 *Rapport de l'agence*, pp. 311-312; pièces justificatives, DLXXIII-DLXXIV.
8 *Ibid.*, pièces justificatives, DLXXIII-DLXXIV.
9 *Ibid.*, p. 313.
10 *PV 1782*, pp. 141-146.
11 *PV 1782*, p. 146.
12 *Rapport de l'agence*, pièces justificatives, DLXXI.
13 *PV 1782*, p. 146.

[14] *Rapport de l'agence,* pièces justificatives, DLXX.
[15] Reprinted in *Rapport de l'agence,* pièces justificatives, DLXVI-DLXXVIII; DLXXIX-DLXXXIII.
[16] G^8* 2619, #218.
[17] G^8 623; G^8* 2618, #667.
[18] G^8* 2619, #186.
[19] *Rapport de l'agence,* pp. 308, 312.
[20] *Rapport de l'agence,* pièces justificatives, DLXVIII.
[21] G^8* 2620, #470.
[22] *PV 1785,* 764; J. L. Soulavie, *Mémoires historiques du règne de Louis XVI depuis son mariage jusqu'à sa mort,* III (Paris, 1803), 5.
[23] Talleyrand gave his circulars the gloss of approved precedent by subtitling them "Lettre circulaire . . . conformément aux vues de l'assemblée de Melun."
[24] This correspondence may be found in G^8* 2617-2620.
[25] In a letter of January, 1784, to Marbeuf, influential Minister of the *feuille des bénéfices,* and his predecessor as Bishop of Autun, Talleyrand requested his approval (which was almost immediately given) "in order that the most perfect unity may preside over all our operations." (G^8* 2619, #150, 158, 169). In a letter to the Bishop of Dijon the following December he observed that "the plan had been adopted by the greatest number of the dioceses." (G^8* 2620, #468).
[26] *Rapport de l'agence,* pièces justificatives, DLXXIX-DLXXXII.
[27] Talleyrand summarized these grievances to the Assembly of 1785. *Rapport de l'agence,* p. 311.
[28] *Rapport de l'agence,* p. 313; G^8* 2618, #676, 677, 678, 679, 699; G^8* 2619, #90, 157, 166, 168, 179 bis; G^8* 2620, #177, 470.
[29] G^8* 2618, #699.
[30] *PV 1785,* pp. 762-764.
[31] "Recueil des conférences du conseil du clergé," A. N., G.^{8}* 2464, 2465, 2466, 2467; "Table alphabétique at raisonnée des lettres d'agence rédigée par M. Duchesne chef du bureau de l'agence générale et garde des archives du clergé de France et par luy présentée à l'assemblée générale du clergé en 1785," G^8* 2622; G^8* 2620, #40, 177.
[32] G^8* 2620, #468.
[33] G^8* 705, fol. 1231.
[34] *PV 1785,* p. 764.
[35] *Rapport de l'agence,* pièces justificatives, DLXXXIII.
[36] V. Crabbe, "Entretien sur Talleyrand, sur l'esprit de l'administration, ainsi que sur les conditions et les motifs d'un statut du personnel," *Revue Internationale des Sciences Administratives,* XXII (1956), 138.
[37] Bachaumont, *Mémoires secrets,* XXIII (London, 1784), 270-271. These securities were not illicitly entered into the clergy's treasury. Before the fall of Law sixty-five years before, the First Estate held two millions in notes of his bank. (Lepointe, *Organisation,* pp. 86-87).
[38] G^8* 2621, #197.
[39] Published in P. L. Roederer, *Mémoires d'économie publique, de morale, et de politique* (Paris, An VIII), p. 148 *et seq.,* and reprinted in Crabbe, *op. cit.,* pp. 163-166.
[40] Talleyrand, *Mémoires,* I, 52-57.
[41] P. Renouvin, *L'assemblée des notables, conférence du 2 mars* (Paris, 1920); H. Glagau, *Reformsversuche und Sturz des Absolutismus in Frankreich* (Munich, 1938); W. Struck, "Die Notabelnversammlung von 1787", *Historische Vierteljahrschrift,* VIII (1905), 362-420.

[42] P. Mautouchet, "Les questions politiques à l'assemblée du clergé de 1788," *La Révolution Française,* XLII (1902), 5-44; A. Chérest, *La chute de l'ancien régime, 1787-1789* (Paris, 1887), pp. 44-46 *et seq.;* J. Egret, *La pré-Révolution française, 1787-1788* (Paris, 1962), pp. 290-295.

Bibliography

A. ARCHIVES

1. Archives Nationales de France (Paris)

I. Unpublished Primary Sources:

G^{8*} 2557-2626 Lettres d'agence: bureau de l'agence générale du clergé de France, 1721-1787.
G^{8*} 2622 Table alphabétique et raisonnée des lettres d'agence rédigée par M. Duchesne chef du bureau de l'agence générale et garde des archives du clergé de France et par luy présentée à l'assemblée générale du clergé en 1785.
G^{8*} 792A Recueil concernant l'agence générale du clergé, 1767.
G^{8*} 671-686; 747; 757; 758; 762; 763; 764; 765; 767; 771; 775; 776; 779: Lettres d'agence générale du clergé, 1727-1787: lettres envoyées.
G^8 662-670 Correspondance des agents généraux et autres officiers du clergé: XVIIIe siècle.
G^8 619-661; 620; 623; 624; 625; 627; 628; 630; 632; 633; 634; 638; 640; 648; 659; 757; 758; 759; 760; 762; 763; 764; 765; 766; 767; 768; 770; 771; 775; 776; 779: Correspondance des agents généraux du clergé: lettres reçues, XVIIIe siècle.
G^8 745, 746 Rapports des agents généraux du clergé de 1750, de 1775, et de 1785.
G^{8*} 2631 Lettres originales des secrétaires d'état intendants des finances et autres magistrats aux agents généraux du clergé: Vol. V, 1750-1782.
G^{8*} 2632 Lettres originales des secrétaires d'état intendants des finances et autres magistrats aux agents généraux du clergé: Vol. VI, 1725-1784.
G^{8*} 687 Procès-verbal de l'assemblée générale du clergé de 1748.
G^{8*} 699-700 Procès-verbal de l'assemblée générale du clergé de 1775.
G^{8*} 701-702 Procès-verbal de l'assemblée générale du clergé de 1780.
G^{8*} 703 Procès-verbal de l'assemblée générale du clergé de 1782.
G^{8*} 704-705 Procès-verbal de l'assemblée générale du clergé de 1785-1786.
G^{8*} 706 Procès-verbal de l'assemblée générale extraordinaire du clergé de France tenue à Paris au couvent des Grands-Augustins en l'année 1788.
G^{8*} 707k Table générale des procès-verbaux des assemblées générales du clergé de France depuis 1560 jusqu'en 1748.
G^8 84-85 Extraits des procès-verbaux des assemblées du clergé de 1780 et de 1785.
G^8 124 Procès-verbaux, 1750-1785.
G^{8*} 569-70-71-72 Table générale des matières, ordre et pouvoir des assemblées du clergé de France contenues dans les procès-verbaux dudit clergé—tant manuscrits qu'imprimés.
G^{8*} 2781-2834 Consultations et délibérations du conseil du clergé, 1727-1788. 2822: 1780.

258

2825: 1760-1780.
2826: 1749-1781.
2827: 1676-1782.
2828: 1783-1784.
2829: 1785.
2830: 1764-1786.
2834: Table alphabétique.
G8* 2451-2467 Recueil des conférences du conseil du clergé, par M. Duchesne, chef du bureau de l'agence générale et garde des archives du clergé de France, 1766-1788.
2462: 1779-1780.
2463: 1781-1782.
2464: 1783-1784.
2465: 1785-1786.
2467: Table.
G8* 2468-2556 Mémoires et requêtes du clergé de France.
2555: Table alphabétique.
G8 129 Appointements des agents généraux du clergé: XVIIe-XVIIIe siècles.
G8 118 Cahiers du clergé présentés au roi par les assemblées générales, 1775-1780.
G8 47 Conseil du roi.
G8 121 (*Mémoires* on the Assembly of 1780 on the Philosophes, Protestants, and Provincial Councils).
G8 95 Mémoire sur l'état des archives du clergé après 1780, rattaché à la vérification de l'inventaire des titres et papiers du clergé de France conservées dans la chambre des archives dudit clergé estant dans le cloistre de l'église de Paris. (1785)
G8* 549 Plan de distribution des archives du clergé de France, présenté à l'assemblée de 1780.
G8 756 Archives du clergé de France: détails de l'armoire des assemblées du clergé et des contrats de l' "armoire" des rentes et pensions du clergé.
G8* 2846-2856 Anciens inventaires des archives du clergé de France, 1579-1788.
LL. 1470 fol. 249 Répertoire historique, instructif, et méthodique des lettres et papiers contenus dans les archives du grand couvent royal et collège généralissime des révérends pères ermites de l'ordre de Saint Augustin au bout du pont neuf à Paris. (1746)
G8 95 Procès-verbaux d'assemblées provinciales.
——— Procès-verbaux d'assemblées particulières de prélats.
——— Procès-verbaux des cérémonies.
G8 152 Rangs et préséances des archevêques, des évêques, et autres ecclésiastiques. (1752)
G8 29 Actes du conseil.
G8 709-720 Délibérations du conseil du clergé.
G8 687-702; 704-707: Mémoires, requêtes, consultations du clergé.
G8 120 Délibérations de l'assemblée.
G8* 47 Don Gratuit, 1780-1785.
G8 111 Contrats avec le roi et l'hôtel de ville, 1580 à 1788.
G8 114 Contrats passés entre le roi et le clergé de France pour le paiement des dons gratuits accordés au roi par le clergé en 1775 et en 1785.
G8 27 Comptes des décimes ordinaires de 1781 à 1785.
G8 67 Nouveau département général de 1755 rectifié en 1760 et en 1765.
G8 126 Comptes des décimes.

G⁸* 250-465 Départements des décimes extraordinaires, dons gratuits: 1621-1788.
G⁸* 466-498 Comptes des décimes extraordinaires, 1568-1782: Quittances.
G⁸* 499-515 Département général des décimes arrêté par l'assemblée du clergé de 1755.
G⁸* 516-547 Département général des décimes arrêté par l'assemblée du clergé de 1760.
G⁸* 553 Département général des dîmes arrêté par l'assemblée du clergé de 1760.
G⁸ 506-534 Rentes constituées sur le clergé en 1780, 1781, 1782, en conséquence de l'emprunt fait pour le paiement du don gratuit accordé au roi.
G⁸ 106 Comptes des frais communs des assemblées du clergé de 1775.
G⁸ 107 Comptes des frais communs des assemblées du clergé de 1780, 1782, 1785-1786.
G⁸* 777 Comptes des frais communs de l'assemblée extraordinaire du clergé de 1782.
G⁸ 128 Pièces justificatives du compte des frais communs des assemblées du clergé.
G⁸ 220-248 Pensions des ministres convertis et autres gratifiés du clergé.
G⁸ 249-254 Subventions du clergé et des établissements religieux.
G⁸ 255-261 Pensions des ministres protestants et autres gratifiés du clergé.
G⁸ 604-618 Quittances de pensions tirées par ordre alphabétique des titulaires de pensions.
G⁸ 115 François-Ollivier de Senozan; François-David Bollioud de St. Jullien. (1785)
G⁸ 120 Avocats du clergé, 1669-1778.
G⁸ 130 Gages des autres officiers du clergé: états de ce qui est dû par le clergé à divers.
G⁸ 127; 128; 129; 130; 139: (Furnishings, wages, costs of printing, wages of officers of the clergy).
G⁸ 139 Frais de sommation et d'impression, 1726-1788. Feuilles de délibérations des assemblées du clergé.
G⁸ 177 Privilèges pour l'impression des mémoires, actes, et titres divers du clergé.
G⁸* 585 Modèles de différentes pièces imprimées par ordre des agents généraux.
G⁸ 756 Quittances du receveur général du clergé, 1780-1785.
G⁸ 2462-2465 Immunités du clergé sur l'administration de ses finances et sur la juridiction ecclésiastique, 1779-1786.
G⁸ 164 Exemptions et immunités: arrêts du conseil, ordonnances des intendants des généralites et des provinces, mémoires et lettres classés par ordre alphabétique de bénéfices.
G⁸ 167-168; 187: Exemption des foi et hommage.
G⁸ 169 Mémoire de M. l'abbé Bouquet sur l'origine et la nature de l'ancienne et de la nouvelle allodialité des seigneuries temporelles et ecclésiastiques. (1780)
G⁸ 744 Droits et privilèges du clergé des bénéfices et des bénéficiers.
G⁸* 799-801 Défense des pouvoirs légitimes des évêques dans l'église contre le livre intitulé *Des pouvoirs légitimes du premier et du second ordre dans l'administration des sacrements et le gouvernement de l'église en France.*
G⁸ 149 Bénéfices et bénéficiers.
G⁸ 158 Exemptions des aveux et dénombrement, foi et hommages, 1574-1780.
G⁸ 110 Circulaires concernant le foi et hommage.

G^8 155 Dîmes de Normandy.
G^8 156 Réparations des églises et des presbytères.
G^8 81 Diocèses spoliés.
G^8 94 Procès-verbaux des assemblées provinciales ecclésiastiques.
G^8 94 Procurations des députés. Assemblées de 1782, de 1785, et de 1788.
MM258 Conclusions de la faculté de théologie, 1759-1778.
MM257 Extractum e registris priorum sorbona ex comitis generalibus in vigilio annuntiationes beata Maria virginis.
G^8 772 Couvent des grands-augustins à Paris. Devis, plans et dessins de M. Antoine, architecte pour l'établissement des salles d'assemblées, d'archives et bureaux d'agence du clergé aux grands-augustins. (1785)
S 3632-33 Etat exact du revenu des grands-augustins de Paris en maisons, boutiques ou échoppes, rentes et fondations.
S 4406 Domaines ecclésiastiques. Procès-verbal des religieuses de Belle-Chasse, 30 août, 1790.
T82-89; T92: Emigrés: papiers séquestrés.
T1668, T1685 Charles-Maurice de Talleyrand Périgord, ex-évêque d'Autun, émigré demeurant ci devant Rue de l'Université No. 900 sec. de la fontaine de Grenelle.

2. Archives du Ministère des Affaires Etrangères (Paris)

Res. 35, 1884, 1786-1787: Correspondance secrète de Mirabeau. Papiers entrés aux archives des affaires étrangères après la mort de A. de Bacourt, 1865, qui les tenait du prince d'Aremberg, auquel Mirabeau les avait légués.

3. Archives Départementales de la Seine et Archives de la Ville de Paris

DQ^{10} 788 Vente de mobilier d'émigrés: Tailleyrand [sic] Périgord, émigré.

4. Archives Départementales, Saône-et-Loire (Macon)

G^3 Evêché d'Autun, 1758-1790, #27. Déclaration des revenus ecclésiastiques dont jouit Mr. Charles Maurice de Talleyrand-Perrigord [sic], évêque d'Autun, membre de l'assemblée nationale et des charges affectées sur ses bénéfices.
1 L^8 107 Département des cultes. Précis relatives au district d'Autun: M. de Périgord. Anc. év. d'Autun. Traitement. Arrêté le 22 avril, 1791.
2 L^8 71 District d'Autun, cultes.
2 L 3* Registre des délibérations du directoire d'Autun, 18 juin, 1790—13 Mai, 1791. (16 Décembre, 1791)
2 G 348 Chambre ecclésiastique du diocèse d'Autun.
2 G 351 Compte qui rend par devant Mons. Mgr. l'évêque d'Autun et MM. les députés en chambre du clergé du diocèse d'Autun.
2 G 352 Diocèse d'Autun: Rolle pour le don gratuit de 1789 que doit fournir le diocèse d'Autun.
2 G 353 Diocèse d'Autun: registre pour inscrire les pensions que Mgr. accorde aux pauvres prêtres, 1775-1789.
2 G 347 Registre contenant les délibérations de la chambre ecclésiastique du diocèse d'Autun à commencer le trente-unième jour du mois de Mai, Mil Sept Cent Quatre-Vingt Un.
Série B. Supplément Baillage d'Autun: insinuations, 1775-1790.

3 L Autun: rôle et réparation.
G 845; 853; 862; 863; 867; 868; 869; 872: Présentations aux bénéfices, nominations, etc.
1 B Registre du procureur du roi au baillage d'Autun, 1787-1790.

5. Archives Départementales de la Haute-Garonne (Toulouse)

B 1721; B 1757; C 964: (Papers of Loménie de Brienne, Archbishop of Toulouse.)

6. Archives Départmentales des Bouches-du-Rhône (Marseilles)

G 116 (Papers of Jean de Dieu-Raymond de Boisgelin, Archbishop of Aix.)

7. Archives Communales: Autun

B B 78 Archives du conseil muncipal d'Autun 22 Décembre, 1788 au 16 Janvier, 1790.

8. Archives Muncipales: Reims

G 235, fol. 41 Collation de la chapelle de la Sainte-Vierge en l'église paroissiale de Saint Pierre de Reims à Charles Maurice de Talleyrand-Périgord, acolyte du diocèse de Paris, 16 Janvier, 1775: provisions de bénéfices et autres expéditions de l'archevêché, 1773-1779.

G 235, fol. 79 Provisions de la chapelle de la Sainte Vierge en l'église paroissiale de Saint Pierre de Reims, vacante par la démission de Charles-Maurice de Talleyrand, 15 Mars, 1776.

G 240, fol. 129 Requête adressé par Charles-Maurice de Talleyrand-Périgord sous diacre du diocèse de Paris, abbé commendataire de l'abbaye de Saint Denis de Reims, à Alexandre Angélique de Talleyrand, archevêque de Reims, son oncle, pour être incorporé dans son diocèse: registre des ordinations, 1763-1782.

——————— Consentement donné par le dit archevêque, 14 Septembre.

——————— Lettres d'excorporation accordées par Christophe de Beaumont, archevêque de Paris, 16 Septembre.

G 240, fols. 130-131 Lettres démissoriales autorisant Charles-Maurice de Talleyrand à être ordonné diacre par l'évêque de Beauvais, 17 Septembre.

G 240, fol. 131-132 Ordinations faites dans la chapelle de l'archevêque par Louis-André de Grimaldi, évêque de Noyon, 18 Décembre: promotion à la prêtrise de Charles-Maurice de Talleyrand-Périgord diacre du diocèse de Paris.

G246, fol. 289 Prise de possession de la chapelle de la Sainte Vierge en l'église paroissiale de Saint Pierre de Reims au nom de C.M. de Talleyrand-Périgord: registre des insinuations ecclésiastiques du diocèse de Reims, 1771-1775.

G247, fol. 42 Bulle de Pie VI instituant Charles-Maurice de Talleyrand-Périgord, clerc du diocèse de Paris, abbé commendataire de l'abbaye de Saint Denis, 3 Octobre, 1775.

G247, fol. 43 Prise de possession par François-Louis de Coppy d'Oisy, prieur de cette abbaye au nom de Charles-Maurice de Talleyrand, 4 Décembre: registre des insinuations ecclésiastiques du diocèse de Reims: 1775-1779.

——————— Procuration donnée par celui-ci à Antoine Pierre de la Condamine

de Lescure, vicaire-général du diocèse de Reims, pour nommer aux bénéfices dépendant de l'abbaye de St. Denis, 24 janvier, 1776.
G248, fol. 23 Lettres de prêtrise de Charles-Maurice de Talleyrand Périgord, abbé commendataire de Saint Denis de Reims: registre des insinuations ecclésiastiques du diocèse de Reims.
G248, fol. 31 Lettre du grand vicaire: nomination de Talleyrand à la charge de l'archevêque, 19 Décembre, 1780.
G249, fol. 82-83 Collation d'un canonicat de l'église métropolitaine pour M. Pierret: registre des insinuations ecclésiastiques du diocèse de Reims, 1783-1787.
G249bis, fol. 133 Brevet du roi, sur la réquisition de Charles-Maurice de Talleyrand Périgord, nommé à l'évêché d'Autun, abbé de Saint Denis de Reims, consent à la création d'une pension annuelle et viagère de douze cents livres sur les revenus de ladite abbaye de Saint Denis, au profit de Louis Théodore Angard, prêtre du diocèse de Paris, 30 Novembre, 1788: registre des insinuations ecclésiastiques du diocèse de Reims.
G646 (Records of Cathedral Chapter) Registre des actes capitulaires de l'abbaye de Saint Denis, commençant, en l'année 1766.

9. Bibliothèque de la Ville d'Arles

La vie et le martyre de Mgr. Jean-Marie du Lau, archevêque de la Sainte église de la ville d'Arles. Le tout recueilli par Les. Pierre Veran de ladite ville. (1803)

10. Bibliothèque Sainte-Geneviève de Paris

MS# 199 1) Procès-verbal de l'assemblée générale du clergé de 1788.

B. CHURCH ARCHIVES

1. Archivio Segreto Vaticano (Rome)

Nunziature di Francia.

570-571: Cifre de Mr. Doria, Nun. in Francia, 1781.
553: 1780.
554: 1781.
555: 1782.
556: 1783.
557: 1784.
558: 1785.
463: A. Mons. Nunzio dal 1785 a tutto 1790 e parte del 1791.
463A: Min. di Biglietti della Segreteria all 'ambasciatori di Francia dal 31 marzo, 1775 al 23 sett., 1794.
579: Minuti di C. Pieracchi alla Segreteria, dal 7 luglio, 1783 al febb., 1793.
573: Dispacci di Mons. Nunzio 1789: Lett. Originali del Nunzio alla Segreteria dal 5 gennaio, 1789, al 15 giunio, 1789.
574: Dispacci di Mons. Nunzio 1789: 9 febbraio, 1789 al 28 decembre, 1789.
580: Minuti di P. Pieracchi a diversi dal 21 febb., 1785 al 4 agosto, 1792.
596: Lettere e carte diversi dal 27 agosto, 1788 al 30 gennaio 1805.

529D: Biglietti del sig. Ambasciatori dell'anno 1788 e 1794. Big. dell 'Ambasciatori di Francia alla Segreteria dal 9 febb., 1788 al 28 dec., 1791.
Processus Consistorialis, #189.
(Nomination of Talleyrand to the bishopric of Autun by Louis XVI) Nov 2, 1788.
(Profession of faith: Oath and signature of Talleyrand) Nov. 2, 1788.
(Testimony of Antonio Dugnani, Papal nuncio) Nov. 2, 1788.
(Testimony of Thémines de Lozières [sic], Bishop of Blois) Nov. 2, 1788.
(Testimony of Barral, Bishop of Troyes) Nov. 2, 1788.

2. Archives du Séminaire de Saint-Sulpice de Paris

Matériaux pour la vie de M. Emery, Saint Sulpice: 13 volumes.
Mémoires de Mgr. Sausin évêque de Blois, IV, fol. 43-47.
Mémoires de M. de Courtade, XII, fol. 10,084-10,085.
Mémoires de M. Caron, XII, fol. 10,153.
Mémoires de M. Le Surre, XII, fol. 10,155.
Mémoires de M. Migneaux, IV, fol. 485.
Mémoires de M. Terrasse, XII, fol. 10,167-10,169.
Mémoires de M. Le Tourneur, évêque de Verdun, IV, fol. 212.
Mémoires de M. Bodé, IV, fol. 289.
Registre des naissances et baptêmes (1754).

3. Archives Archiépiscopales de Paris

0³ Registre des ordinations d'Avril 1774 à Septembre, 1777.

4. Archives Archiépiscopales de Reims

Registre ambulant des provisions de bénéfices et autres expéditions du secrétariat de l'archevêque, 1783-1799.

5. Archives de l'Evêché d'Autun

Registre des délibérations du conseil épiscopal d'Autun, 1788-1799.
Lenoble, Récit des actes de l'épiscopat de Mr. de Périgord.
Project de réponse à la lettre de Mgr. l'évêque d'Autun.
Letters of Talleyrand to his chapter.
Mémoire à consulter pour le diocèse d'Autun.

C. PRIVATE ARCHIVES

1. Papers of Count Bernard de Lacombe containing the documents of Félix Dupanloup, Bishop of Orleans

Monsieur de Talleyrand, histoire inconnue de Monsieur de Talleyrand, ou Monsieur de Talleyrand, études sur sa vie; son caractère, ses dernières années et sa fin. (18 MS. volumes).
I. Monsieur de Talleyrand: premier manuscrit.
II. Monsieur de Talleyrand: second manuscrit.
III. Monsieur de Talleyrand: opus jam absolutum.
IV. Manuscrit radical, I: (Acts, correspondence, sources up to 1791.)

V. Manuscrit radical, II: (Concordats, Consulate.)
VI. Manuscrit radical, III: (Monsieur de Talleyrand et l'église, 1814-1815.)
VII. Manuscrit radical, IV: (Dernières années de Talleyrand.)
VIII. Manuscrit radical, V: (Fin Chrétien de Talleyrand.)
IX. Manuscrit radical, VI: (Reports, Journals till 1838.)
X. Manuscrit radical: supplément (Copies of letters, correspondence and writings of Talleyrand.)
XI. Précis: tome I: (Original documents, copied in Manus. Rad.)
XII. Précis: tome II.
XIII. Précis: tome III: (Original documents copied in Manus. Rad.)
XIV. Précis: (Third Copy: Correspondence on Concordat and Consulate.)
XV. Précis: (Fourth Copy.)
XVI. Précis: (Fifth Copy: Correspondence of Dupanloup and the Archbishop of Paris, 1836-1838.)
XVII. Fragments du quatrième et du cinquième livre.
XVIII. Pièces importantes: supplément. (Thesis of Talleyrand, 1774; correspondence of Talleyrand, Mme de Dino, Dupanloup, Colmache; clippings).

2. Archives of Duke Louis de Broglie (Broglie, [Eure])

Ecrits politiques de Talleyrand.
Manuscripts of Political Discourses.
Pensées et maximes.
Contributions on Talleyrand by Dino and Bacourt.
Letters to Talleyrand.
Letters of Talleyrand.
Correspondence of Bacourt.

3. Papers of Georges Lacour-Gayet (Paris)

Correspondence transcriptions.
Letters of Maurice Dumolin.
Letters of Countess Arthur de Voguë.
Archives of Commarin: Papers of Countess d'Antigny and Mme. Charlemagne.

II. Printed Primary Sources

A. *Official Documents and Proceedings of Church and State*

Archives parlementaires de 1787 à 1860, recueil complet des débats législatifs et politiques des chambres françaises, J. Mavidal et E. Laurent, eds., 1ère série (1787-1799), 33 vols. Paris, 1864-1889.
Collection des circulaires de l'agence générale du clergé de France. (Bibliothèque Nationale Ld^5 41-50).
Collection des procès-verbaux des assemblées générales du clergé de France, depuis l'année 1560, jusqu'à présent, rédigés par ordre des matières, et réduits à ce qu'ils ont d'essentiel, R. Duranthon, A. Desaulzet, R. Gandin, eds., Paris, 1767-1780, 9 vols.
Collection des mémoires présentées à l'assemblée des notables, première et seconde division, Versailles, 1787.

Collection des mémoires présentées à l'assemblée des notables, troisième et quatrième division, Versailles, 1787.
Documents relatifs aux rapports du clergé avec la royauté de 1688 à 1789, L. Mention, ed., 2 vols., Paris, 1903.
L'administration de l'agriculture au contrôle général des finances (1785-1787), procès-verbaux et rapports. H. Pigeonneau and A. de Foville, eds., Paris, 1882.
Les loix ecclésiastiques de France, L. de Héricourt, ed., Paris 1771.
Liste des députés aux assemblées générales du clergé de France. (Bibliothèque Nationale, Ld⁵ 36).
Précis des rapports de l'agence du clergé de France par ordre matières ou extraits raisonnés desdits rapports concernant les principales affaires du clergé qui se sont passées depuis l'année 1660 jusqu'en l'année 1780. (Paris, 1786).
Procès-verbal de l'assemblée générale du clergé de France tenue à Paris au couvent des Grands-Augustins en l'année 1715. (Paris, 1723).
Procès-verbal de l'assemblée générale du clergé de France tenue à Paris au couvent des Grands-Augustins en l'année 1748. (Paris, 1750).
Procès-verbal de l'assemblée générale du clergé de France tenue à Paris au couvent des Grands-Augustins en l'année 1770. (Paris, 1776).
Procès-verbal de l'assemblée générale du clergé de France tenue à Paris au couvent des Grands-Augustins en l'année 1775, l'abbé du Lau, ancien agent général, secrétaire de l'assemblée, depuis archevêque d'Arles (Paris, 1777).
Procès-verbal de l'assemblée générale du clergé de France tenue à Paris au couvent des Grands-Augustins en l'année 1780. (Paris, 1782).
Procès-verbal de l'assemblée générale du clergé de France extraordinaire du clergé de France tenue à Paris au couvent des Grands-Augustins en l'année 1782. (Paris, 1783).
Procès-verbal de l'assemblée générale du clergé de France tenue à Paris au couvent des Grands-Augustins en l'année 1786. M. l'abbé de Périgord, ancien agent général, secrétaire de l'assemblée. (Paris, 1789).
Rapport de l'agence, contenant les principales affaires du clergé depuis 1780 jusqu'en 1785 par M. l'abbé de Périgord et M. l'abbé de Boisgelin, anciens agents généraux du clergé. (Paris, 1788).
Recueil des actes, titres et mémoires concernant les affaires du clergé de France, 13 vols., Paris, 1757-1769.
Recueil général des anciennes lois françaises. J. Isambert, A. Jourdan, O. Décrusy, eds., 29 vols., Paris, 1823-1833.
Remonstrances du clergé, présentées au roi le 15 Juin, 1788. Paris, 1788.
Remonstrances du clergé, présentées au roi le Dimanche 15 Juin, 1788 sur les droits, franchises, et immunités du clergé. Paris 1788.
Remonstrances du parlement de Paris au 18e siècle. J. Flammermont, ed., Paris, 1888-1898, 3 vols.

B. *Contemporary Journals and Periodicals*

Almanach Royal, 1775-1789.
La France Ecclésiastique, 1775-1789.
La Gazette de France, 1780-1785.
Mercure de France, 1775-1789.
Nouvelles Ecclésiastiques, 1780-1789.

C. Dictionaries and Collections

Chéruel, A., *Dictionnaire historique des institutions, moeurs et coutumes de la France*, 2 vols., Paris, 1874.
Durand de Maillane, P. T., *Dictionnaire de droit canonique et de pratique bénéficiale*, 3 vols., Lyon, 1769-1772.
Expilly, F., *Dictionnaire géographique, historique, et politique des Gaules et de la France*, Paris, 1762.
de Feller, F.-X., *Biographie universelle*. 13 vols. Besançon, 1844.
Fleury, C., *Institution au droit ecclésiastique*. (Paris, 1767), 2 vols.
Hurbaut, J. et Magny, A., *Dictionnaire historique de la ville de Paris et de ses environs*, 4 vols. Paris, 1779.
Guyot, R. J., *Répertoire universel et raisonné de jurisprudence civile, criminelle, canonique et bénéficiale*, 36 vols., Paris, 1780-1788.
Hoefer, J.-C., *Nouvelle biographie générale depuis les temps les plus reculés jusqu'à nos jours*. (Paris, 1862-1870), 46 vols.
Jean, A., *Dictionnaire des évêques et archevêques en France, 1682-1801*, Paris, 1891.
Lalanne, L., *Dictionnaire historique de la France*, 1871.
Marion, M., *Dictionnaire des institutions de la France aux XVIIe et XVIIIe siècles*, Paris, 1923.
Michaud, J.-F., *Biographie universelle, ancienne et moderne*. (Paris, n.d. [1843-1865]), 45 vols.
Quérard, J.-M., *La France littéraire, ou dictionnaire bibliographique des savants, historiens et gens de lettres de la France*. (Paris, 1827-1864), 12 vols.

D. Select Writings of Talleyrand

L' ancien évêque d'Autun à ses concitoyens, London, 1792.
Discours prononcé dans la séance du mardi 13 Novembre, 1821 par M. le prince duc de Talleyrand à l'occasion du décès de M. le comte Bourlier, évêque d'Evreux, Paris, 1821.
Eclaircissements donnés par le citoyen Talleyrand à ses concitoyens, Paris, le 25 Messidor, an VII, Paris, 1799.
Eloge de M. le comte Reinhart prononcé à l'académie des sciences morales et politiques par M. le prince de Talleyrand dans la séance du 3 Mars, 1838, Paris, 1838.
Extrait du cahier des délibérations du clergé assemblé à Autun, n.d.o.p.
Larchey, L., "Nouveautés anecdotiques," *Le Bibliophile Français*, I (1868), 271-274. (Letters to Choiseul-Gouffier).
"Lettres de Mgr. de Talleyrand et son neveu à MM les chanoines de Notre Dame de Reims," *Chronique de Champagne*, I (1834), 119-120.
Mémoires de Talleyrand, P. L. and J. P. Couchoud, 2 vols., Paris, 1957.
Mémoires du Prince de Talleyrand, publiés avec une préface et des notes par le Duc de Broglie, 5 vols., Paris, 1891-1892.
Mémoires du Prince de Talleyrand, et ce qu'ils n'ont pas dit, P. Léon, ed., 8 vols., Paris, 1952-1958.
Mémoires, lettres inédites et papiers secrets, J. Gorsas, ed., Paris, 1891.
Motion de M. l'évêque d'Autun sur les biens ecclésiastiques du 10 Octobre, 1789, Versailles, 1789.
Motion de M. l'évêque d'Autun sur les loteries, 12 Décembre, 1789, Paris, 1789.

Motion de M. l'évêque d'Autun tendant à l'appuie de l'amendement de Chasset, relatif aux dîmes, Paris, 1789.

Opinion de M. l'évêque d'Autun non prononcée sur les biens ecclésiastiques, annexe de la séance de l'assemblée nationale du 2 Novembre, 1789, Paris, 1789.

Rapport sur l'instruction publique, fait au nom du comité de constitution, à l'assemblée nationale les 10, 11 et 19 Septembre, 1791, par M. de Talleyrand-Périgord, ancien évêque d'Autun, imprimé par ordre de l'assemblée, Paris, 1791.

E. Memoirs and Correspondence

Bachaumont, L.-P., *Mémoires secrets pour servir à l'histoire de la république des lettres en France depuis 1762 jusqu'à nos jours*, 36 vols., London, 1780-1789.

Barruel, Abbé, *Mémoires pour servir à l'histoire du Jacobinisme*, 5 vols., Hambourg, 1799.

Bernis, Cardinal F.-J., *Mémoires et lettres*, F. Masson, ed., 2 vols., Paris, 1878.

de Biron, A.-L., duc de Lauzun, *Mémoires*, Paris, 1880.

Correspondance secrète du comte de Mercy-Argenteau avec Joseph II et le prince de Kaunitz, E. Geffroy, ed., 2 vols., Paris, 1889-1891.

Correspondance secrète inédite sur Louis XVI, Marie-Antoinette, la cour et la ville de 1777 à 1792. Publiée d'après les manuscrits de la Bibliothèque impériale de Saint Pétersbourg, M. de Lescure, ed. (Paris, 1866) 2 vols.

Creuze-Latouche, J.-A., *Journal des états généraux et du début de l'assemblée nationale, 18 Mai-29 Juillet, 1789, publié par Jean Marchand*, Paris, 1946.

Duchesse de Dino, chronique de 1831 à 1862, P. de Radziwill, ed., 4 vols., Paris, 1910.

de Dino, D., *Notice sur Valençay*, Paris, 1848.

Dumont de Genève, E., *Souvenirs sur Mirabeau et sur les deux premières assemblées législatives, ouvrage posthume publié par M. J. L. Duval*, Paris, 1832.

Féron, B., *Vues d'un solitaire patriote*, Paris, 1784.

Georgel, Abbé R., *Mémoires pour servir à l'histoire des événemens de la fin du dix-huitième siècle, depuis 1760 jusqu'en 1806-1810, par un contemporain impartial*, 6 vols., Paris, 1817.

d'Hérisson, C. H., *Autour d'une Révolution, 1788-1799*, Paris, 1888.

H. R. Lord Holland, *Foreign Reminiscences, Edited by his Son, H. E. Lord Holland*, London, 1850.

I Dispacci degli ambasciatori Veneti alla Corte di Francia durante la Rivoluzione, H. Kovalevsky, ed., Torino, 1895.

Journal d'Adrien Duquesnoy sur l'assemblée constituante, R. de Crèvecoeur, ed., Paris, 1894.

Journal de l'abbé de Véri, J. de Witte, ed., 2 vols., Paris, n.d.

Journal de l'assemblée des notables de 1787, P. Chevallier, ed., Paris, 1960.

Journal et mémoires du marquis d'Argenson, E. J. B. Rathéry, ed., 9 vols., Paris, 1859-1864.

Journal historique et anecdotique du règne de Louis XV par E. J. F. Barbier, avocat du parlement de Paris, A. de la Villegelle, ed., 6 vols., Paris, 1851.

Journal inédit de Jallot, curé de Cherigne, député du clergé de Poitou, aux états généraux de 1789, J. J. Brethé, ed., Fontenay-le-Comte, 1871.

Mémoires, correspondance et manuscrits du Général Lafayette, publiés par sa famille, 6 vols., Paris, 1837.
Mémoires de l'abbé Baston, Chanoine, de Rouen, J. Loth, ed., 2 vols., Paris, 1897.
Mémoires de Louis XIV, D. Dreyss, ed., Paris, 1860.
Mémoires de Mme. la duchesse d'Abrantes, 18 vols., Paris, 1835-1838.
Mémoires inédits de Madame la comtesse de Genlis sur le dix-huitième siècle et la Révolution française, 8 vols., Paris, 1825.
Mémoires sur les règnes de Louis XV et Louis XVI et sur la Révolution par J. N. Duport, comte de Cheverny, 1731-1802, R. de Crèvecoeur, ed., 2 vols., Paris, 1886.
Comte de Mirabeau, histoire secrète de la cour de Berlin, 2 vols., Paris, 1788.
Morellet, Abbé A., *Mémoires·inédits sur le dix-huitième siècle*, N. Lemontey, ed., 2 vols., Paris, 1822.
Morris, A. C., *Diary and Letters of Gouverneur Morris*, 2 vols., New York, 1888.
Opinion de M. l'abbé Maury député de Picardie sur la propriété des biens ecclésiastiques prononcée dans l'assemblée nationale le Mardi 13 Octobre, Paris, 1789.
Panchaud, A., *Reflexions sur l'état actuel du crédit publique de l'Angleterre et de la France*, Paris, 1781.
Raikes, T., *Portion of a Journal Kept by Thomas Raikes*, 2 vols., London, 1831-1847.
J. Rangéard, *député du clergé d'Angers, procès-verbal historique des actes du clergé à l'assemblée des états-généraux des années 1789 et 1790*, Paris, 1791.
Mémoires et correspondance du cardinal Maury, C. de Ricard, ed., 2 vols., Lille, 1891.
Roederer, P. L., *Mémoires d'économie publique, de morale, et de politique*, Paris, An. VIII.
Les séances des députés du clergé aux états-généraux de 1789 journaux du curé Thibault et du chanoine Coster, A. Houtin, ed., Paris, 1917.
Soulavie, Jean Louis, *Mémoires historiques du règne de Louis XVI depuis son mariage jusqu'à sa mort*, 6 vols., Paris, An. X.
Les souvenirs de Jacob Nicolas Moreau, C. Hermelin, ed., 2 vols., Paris, 1898.
Souvenirs de la marquise de Créquy, 1710 à 1800, 7 vols., Paris, 1834.
Vallet, M., *Récit des principaux faits qui se sont passés dans la salle de l'ordre du clergé depuis le commencement des états généraux, le 4 mai, 1789, jusqu'à la réunion des trois ordres dans la salle commune de l'assemblée nationale*, Paris, 1790.
Weber, J., *Mémoires concernant Marie-Antoinette, archiduchesse d'Autriche, reine de France*, 2 vols., London, 1804.

III. Secondary Sources

A. WORKS ON THE GENERAL ASSEMBLY AND THE CLERGY IN THE LATTER OLD REGIME

Affre, P. *L'appel comme d'abus*, Paris, 1845.
Appolis, E. "Le droit de nomination aux curcs dans l'ancien diocèse de Lodève," *Actes du 80e congrès des sociétes savantes, section d'histoire . . .* (Paris, 1955), pp. 11-13.

d'Avenel, P. "Le clergé français et la liberté de conscience sous Louis XIII." *Revue Historique,* XXXIII (1887), 1-24.
Audiat, L. *Deux victimes des septembriseurs, Pierre-Louis de La Rochefoucauld, dernier évêque de Saintes et son frère, évêque de Beauvais.* Lille, 1897.
Auguste, Abbé. "Lettres inédites de Loménie de Brienne." *Bulletin de la société archéologique du midi de la France,* second series, XLII-XLIII (1912-1914), 245-250.
Aulard, F. V. A. *Christianity and the French Revolution,* Trans. Boston, 1927.
Bausset, Cardinal. *Notice historique sur S. E. Mgr. Alexandre-Angélique de Talleyrand-Périgord, archevêque de Paris, pair et grand aumônier de France.* Versailles, 1821.
Beaurin, C. "Les curés de Campagne au XVIIIe siècle." *Correspondant,* CXLVIII (1887), 1102-1133; CXLIX (1887), 151-172.
Berthelot du Chesnay, C. "Le clergé séculier français du second ordre d'après les insinuations ecclésiastiques." *Bulletin de la Société d'Histoire Moderne,* LXII (1963), 2-5.
Besnier, E. *Les agents généraux du clergé de France.* Paris, 1939.
Bien, D. "Catholic Magistrates and Protestant Marriage in the French Enlightenment." *French Historical Studies,* II (1962), 409-429.
Blet, P. *Le clergé de France et la monarchie: Etude sur les assemblées générales du clergé de 1615 à 1666.* 2 vols., Rome, 1959.
Bloch, C. *L'assistance et l'Etat en France à la veille de la Révolution.* Paris, 1908.
Bonifas, E. C. F. *Le mariage des Protestants depuis la réforme jusqu'à 1789.* Paris, 1901.
Bougaud, E. *Histoire de la bienheureuse Marguérite-Marie et des origines de la dévotion au coeur de Jésus.* Paris, 1874.
Bourgain, L. "Contributions du clergé à l'impôt sous la monarchie française." *Revue des Questions Historiques,* XLVIII (1890), 62-132.
Bourlon, I. "La caisse du clergé avant '89." *Revue du Clergé Français,* LIV (1908), 150-167; 403-23; 654-77.
——————. *Les assemblées du clergé et le Protestantisme.* Paris, 1909.
——————. *Les assemblées du clergé et le Jansénisme.* Paris, 1911.
——————. *Les assemblées du clergé sous l'ancien régime.* Paris, 1907.
Bowers, C. G. *Pierre Vergniaud, Voice of the French Revolution.* New York, 1954.
Brette, A. "La dette du clergé de France en 1789." *La Révolution Française,* XLVI (1904), 412-423.
de Broc, V. *Un évêque sous l'ancien régime: M. de Maillé la Tour Landry.* Paris, 1894.
Cahen, L. *Les querelles religieuses et parlementaires sous Louis XV.* Paris, 1913.
Caillet, M. "Le livre des dépenses de la maison de l'archevêque Loménie de Brienne." *L'Auta* [Toulouse], #273 (1958), 51-57.
Cans, A. "La caisse du clergé de France et les Protestants convertis (1598-1790)." *Bulletin de la Société d'Histoire du Protestantisme Français,* LI (1902), 225-43.
——————. *La contribution du clergé de France à l'impôt pendant la seconde moitié du règne de Louis XIV (1689-1715).* Paris, 1910.
——————. "Lettres de M. de Boisgelin, archevêque d'Aix à la comtesse de Gramont, 1776-1789." *Revue Historique,* LXXIX (1902), 316-323; LXXX (1902), 65-77; 301-317.

――――. *L'organisation financière du clergé de France à l'époque de Louis XIV.* Paris, 1910.
Caron, P. *Les massacres de Septembre.* Paris, 1935.
Carrière, V., *Introduction aux études d'histoire ecclésiastique locale.* 3 vols., Paris, 1934-1935.
Cauchie, A. "Les assemblées du clergé sous l'ancien régime: matériaux et origines." *Revue des Sciences Philosophiques et Théologiques,* II (1908), 74-95.
Cauly, E. *Histoire du collège des bons enfants de l'Université de Reims.* Paris, 1885.
Ceslas, M. (Normand), Sister. "Financial Contribution of the French Clergy to American Independence, June 12-26, 1780." *United States Catholic Historical Soc., Hist. Records and Studies,* XXV (1935), 163-208.
Champion, E. *La France en 1789 d'après les cahiers.* Paris, 1897.
――――. "Les biens du clergé et la Révolution." *La Révolution Française,* XXVI (1894), 431-502.
Charles-Billet, L. "Un portrait du cardinal de Bernis." *Revue du Tarn,* I (1935), 232-6.
Chassin, L. *Les cahiers des curés en 1789.* Paris, 1882.
――――. *Les élections et les cahiers de Paris en 1789.* 4 vols., Paris, 1888-1889.
Cheke, M. *The Cardinal de Bernis.* London, 1958.
Chevaillier, R. "Les revenus des bénéfices ecclésiastiques au 18e siècle d'après les comptes de la régale et de la garde." *La Révolution Française, LXXIV* (Apr., 1921), 113-149.
Chevallier, P. *Loménie de Brienne et l'ordre monastique.* 2 vols., Paris, 1959.
Constant, G. "Les registres des marguilliers." *Revue d'Histoire de l'Eglise de France,* XXIV (1938), 170-183.
Cormary, A. *Loménie de Brienne à Toulouse, 1763-1788.* Albi, 1935.
Coudy, J. *Les moyens d'action de l'ordre du clergé au conseil du roi (1561-1715).* Paris, n.d., [1954].
de Coulanges, A. *La chaire française au XVIIIe siècle,* Paris, 1901.
Cragg, G. *The Church and the Age of Reason (1648-1789).* (n.p., 1960).
Crousaz-Crétet, P. de. *L'église et l'Etat ou les deux puissances au XVIIIe siècle, 1715-1789.* Paris, 1892.
Dansette, A. *Histoire religieuse de la France contemporaine, 1780-1870.* I, Paris, 1948.
Debidour, A. *Histoire des rapports de l'église et l'Etat en France de 1789 à 1870,* Paris, 1911.
Delannoy, P. *La juridiction ecclésiastique en matière bénéficiale sous l'ancien régime en France.* Bruxelles, 1910.
De l'état religieux . . . par M. l'abbé de B. [de Bernard] *et M. l'abbé B. de B.* [Bonnefoy de Bonyon], *avocat en Parlement.* Paris, 1784.
Denis, P. "Un projet de fondation de Mgr. de Talleyrand-Périgord, archevêque de Reims en faveur des jeunes gentilhommes de sa province en 1787." *Travaux de l'Académie Nationale de Reims,* CXXVII (1909-10), 259-267.
Denys-Buirette, A. *Les questions religieuses dans les cahiers de 1789.* Paris, 1919.
Desdevises du Dézert, G. *L'église et l'Etat en France, 1598-1906,* 2 vols., Paris, 1907.
Dessalles, L. *Histoire du Périgord.* 3 vols. Périgueux, 1883-1885.
Dollot, L. *La question des privilèges dans la seconde moitié du XVIIIe siècle.* Paris, 1941.

Dubuc, A. "La gestion de la manse abbatiale de Fécamp à la fin du règne de Louis XV," *Actes du 84e congrès national des sociétés savantes, section d'histoire* . . . Paris, 1960, pp. 9-30.
Ducros, L. *La société française au XVIIIe siècle.* Paris, 1922.
Dutil, L. "Philosophie ou religion, Loménie de Brienne, archevêque de Toulouse." *Annales du Midi,* LXI (1948), 33-70.
Dutilleul, E. *Histoire des corporations religieuses en France.* Paris, 1864.
Egret, J. "La dernière assemblée du clergé de France." *Revue Historique,* CCXIX (1958), 1-15.
Feret, P. *La faculté de théologie de Paris, ses docteurs les plus célèbres.* 7 vols., Paris, 1894-1910.
Flammermont, J. *Les jésuites et les parlements au 18e siècle,* Paris, 1885.
Fleury, C. *Discours sur l'histoire ecclésiastique.* Paris, 1763.
Florange, C. *Les assemblées du clergé de France avant 1789 et leurs jetons commémoratifs.* Paris, 1927.
Frayssinous, D. *Oraison funèbre de S. E. Mgr. le cardinal de Périgord,* Paris, 1822.
Frézet, A. *Le cardinal de Talleyrand-Périgord.* Reims, 1936.
—————. "Mgr. de Talleyrand et les inondations de 1784." *Bulletin du Diocèse de Reims,* XLIII (1910), 638-640.
Gagnol, P. *La dîme ecclésiastique.* Paris, 1911.
—————. *Les décimes et les dons gratuits.* Paris, 1911.
Galton, A. H. *Church and State in France, 1300-1907.* London, 1907.
Garrett, M. B. "A Critical Bibliography of the Pamphlet Literature published in France between 5 July and 27 December, 1788." *Howard College Bulletin,* LXXXIII (1925), 1-45.
Gazier, A. *Etudes sur l'histoire religieuse de la Révolution française.* Paris, 1887.
Gendry, G. *Pie VI.* 2 vols., Paris, 1906.
Gerin, C. "Les augustins et les dominicains en France avant la Révolution." *Revue des Questions Historiques,* XXI (1877), 35-99.
—————. "Les bénédictins français avant 1789 d'après les papiers de la commission des réguliers." *Revue des Questions Historiques,* XIX (1876), 449-512.
—————. "Les monastères franciscains et la commission des réguliers, 1766-1789." *Revue des Questions Historiques,* XVII (1875), 76-135.
Goodwin, M. C. *The Papal Conflict with Josephinism.* New York, 1938.
Goyau, G. *Histoire religieuse de la France.* Vol. VI of G. Hanotaux, *L'histoire de la nation française.* Paris 1922.
Greenbaum, L. S. "The General Assembly of the Clergy of France and its Situation at the End of the *Ancien Régime.*" *The Catholic Historical Review,* LIII (1967), 153-193.
Greenlaw, R. W. "Pamphlet literature in France during the Period of the Aristocratic Revolt (1787-1788)." *Journal of Modern History,* XXIX (1957), 349-54.
Gurian, W. *Die politischen und sozialen Ideen des franzoesischen Katholizismus 1789-1914.* Gladbach, 1929.
Heinrich, H. *Die politische Ideologie des französischen Klerus bei Beginn der grossen Revolution.* Berlin, 1934.
Hubert, M. "Les prétendues histoires scandaleuses de Mgr. le cardinal de Talleyrand-Périgord. La démolition de l'église abbatiale de Saint-Thierry —l'emplacement de l'édifice." *Revue de Champagne,* I-III (1908-10), 3-8.
Hutt, M. G. "The Curés and the Third Estate: The Ideas of Reform in the

Pamphlets of the French Lower Clergy in the period 1787-1789." *The Journal of Ecclesiastical History,* VIII (1957), 74-92.
d'Illiers, L. *Deux prélats d'ancien régime: les Jarente.* Monaco, 1948.
Jervis, W. H. *The Gallican Church: A History of the Church of France from the Concordat of Bologna, A.D. 1516 to the Revolution.* 2 vols., London, 1872.
Jourdain, C. *Histoire de l'université de Paris aux XVIIe et XVIIIe siècles.* 2 vols., Paris, 1888.
Jousse, D. *Commentaire sur l'édit du mois d'avril 1695 concernant la juridiction ecclésiastique.* 2 vols., Paris, 1764.
Lacouture, J. *La politique religieuse de la Révolution.* Paris, 1919.
de la Gorce, P. *Histoire religieuse de la Révolution française.* 5 vols., 1909-1923.
Lagrange, F. *Vie de Monseigneur Dupanloup.* 3 vols., 1883-1884.
Latreille, A. Delaruelle, E. Palanque, J. R. *Histoire du catholicisme en France,* 2 vols., Paris, 1960.
Latreille, A. *L'église Catholique et la Révolution française, le pontificat de Pie VI et la crise religieuse,* 1776-1799. 2 vols., Paris, 1946-1950.
Laurentie, J. "Trois archevêques de Sens membres de l'académie française, Mgr. Languet de Gergy, le cardinal Albert de Luynes, le cardinal Loménie de Brienne." *Bulletin de la Société Archéologique de Sens,* XXXVI (1927-28), 62-115.
Lavaquery, E. *Le cardinal de Boisgelin, 1732-1804.* 2 vols., Angers, 1920.
——————. "L'histoire religieuse de la Révolution française dans le cadre diocésain." *Revue d'Histoire de l'Église de France,* XX (1934), 216-230.
Laveille, A. "Les revenus du clergé breton avant la Révolution," *Revue des Questions Historiques,* XLVIII (1912), 461-471.
Lecarpentier, P. *La propriété foncière du clergé sous l'ancien régime.* Paris, 1902.
Lecomte, E. "Exercises pratiqués sur les sources à la faculté de théologie." *Annuaire de l'Université Catholique de Louvain,* LXIX (1905), 421-437.
Lefebvre G. "Les recherches relatives à la répartition de la propriété et de l'exploitation foncières à la fin de l'ancien régime." *Revue d'Histoire Moderne,* III (1928), 103-130.
Leflon, J. *La crise révolutionnaire, 1789-1846, Histoire de l'église.* A. Fliche, V. Martin, eds. Vol. XX. Paris, 1949.
——————. *Monsieur Emery: l'église de l'ancien régime et la Révolution.* 2 vols., Paris, 1944-1946.
Lemaire, A. *Les lois fondamentales de la monarchie française d'après les théoreticiens de l'ancien régime.* Paris, 1907.
Lepointe, G. "Assemblées du clergé de France." *Dictionnaire de droit canonique contenant tous les termes de droit canonique avec un sommaire de l'histoire et des institutions et de l'état actuel de la discipline,* I (Paris, 1935), 1107-1142.
——————. "Assemblées des paroisses." I, 1179-1187.
——————. "Bureaux diocésains." II, 1157-67.
——————. "Chambres supérieures des décimes." III, 431-54.
——————. "La chambre ecclésiastique de Strasbourg." *Revue Historique de Droit Français et Etranger,* 4th ser., XXIX (1951), 522-559.
——————. "La composition et l'organisation intérieure de la chambre supérieure des décimes de Paris au XVIIIe siècle." *Revue Historique de Droit Français et Etranger,* 4th ser., XVI (1936), 302-336.
——————. "Le rôle des chambres supérieures des décimes et leur situation

juridique." *Revue Historique de Droit Français et Etranger,* 4th ser., XVII (1938), 71-91.

―――――. *L'organisation et la politique financières du clergé sous le règne de Louis XV.* Paris, 1923.

Lettres secrettes [sic] sur l'état actuel de la religion et du clergé de France, à M. le Marquis de. . ., ancien mestre de camp de cavalerie, retiré dans ses terres. n.p., n.d. [1781].

Levack, A. P. *Principal, Immediate, Non-Parliamentary Origins of the Civil Constitution of the Clergy.* Cambridge, Mass., 1941.

Levesque, E. *L'ancien séminaire de Saint Sulpice.* Limoges, 1922.

―――――. "Le séminaire de Saint Sulpice." *Revue du Clergé Français,* XCVII (1919), 49-54.

Levy-Schneider, L. *L'application du concordat par un prélat d'ancien régime, Monseigneur Champion de Cicé, archevêque d'Aix et d'Arles (1802-1810).* Paris, 1921.

―――――. "L'autonomie administrative de l'épiscopat français à la fin de l'ancien régime." *Revue Historique,* CLI (1926), 1-33.

―――――. "Un prélat très représentatif du haut clergé de la fin de l'ancien régime, le cardinal de Boisgelin." *Revue Historique de l'Eglise de France,* VIII (1922), 170-181.

Lods, A. "L'attitude du clergé Catholique à l'égard des Protestants en 1789." *La Révolution Française,* XXXIII (1897), 128-37.

―――――. "Le clergé Catholique et les Protestants français: 1775, 1780, 1788." *Bulletin de la Société de l'Histoire du Protestantisme français,* XXXVI (1887), 531-39.

Loriquet, C. "Le bureau des incendies et les autres établissements de charité de M. de Talleyrand, archevêque de Reims." *Travaux de l'Académie Nationale de Reims,* LV (1873-4), 199-225.

Loth, J. *Histoire du cardinal de La Rochefoucauld,* Evreux, 1893.

Marchal, J. *Le "droit d'oblat" essai sur une variété de pensionnés monastiques.* Poitiers, 1955.

Marion, H. *La dîme ecclésiastique en France au XVIIIe siècle et sa suppression.* Bordeaux, 1912.

Martin, V. *Le Gallicanisme politique et le clergé de France.* Paris, 1929.

Masson, F. *Le cardinal de Bernis, depuis son ministère, 1758-1794.* Paris, 1884.

Mathiez, A. *Contributions à l'histoire religieuse de la Révolution française.* Paris, 1907.

―――――. *La question religieuse sous la Révolution.* Paris, 1930.

―――――. *La Révolution et l'église: études critiques et documentaires.* Paris, 1910.

―――――. "L'église de France en 1789: Son organisation intérieure." *Revue des Cours et Conférences,* XXXIII (1932), 201-212; "Le programme des philosophes et des révolutionnaires," 327-336; "Le mariage de l'église et l'Etat," 448-459; "Les causes de l'échec de la constitution civile du clergé," 579-592.

―――――. *Rome et le clergé français sous la constituante: la constitution civile du clergé: l'affaire d'Avignon.* Paris, 1911.

Maury, A. "Les assemblées générales du clergé sous l'ancienne monarchie." *Revue des Deux Mondes,* XXXI (1879), 754-796; XXXII (1879), 509-555; XXXV (1879), 265-300; XL (1880), 621-667.

Mautouchet, P. *De ultimo generali conventu cleri Gallicani anno MDCCLXXXVIII Habito.* Le Mans, 1900.

―――――. "Les questions politiques à l'assemblée du clergé de 1788." *La Révolution Française*, XLII (1902), 5-44.
Maynard, E. *Monseigneur de Dupanloup et son historien.* Paris, 1887.
McManners, J. *French Ecclesiastical Society under the Ancien Régime: A Study of Angers in the Eighteenth Century.* Manchester, 1960.
Meignan, C. "Le clergé des campagnes avant la Révolution." *Correspondant*, CXII (1878), 418-432.
Meignan, T. "Les anciens registres paroissiaux de l'état civil." *Revue des Questions Historiques*, XXV (1879), 131-172.
Méric, E. *Histoire de M. Emery et de l'église de France pendant la Révolution.* 2 vols., Paris, 1885.
―――――. *Le clergé sous l'ancien régime.* Paris, 1890.
Monod, A. *De Pascal à Chateaubriand, les défenseurs français du Christianisme de 1670 à 1802.* Paris, 1916.
Monternot, C. *Yves-Alexandre de Marbeuf, Ministre de la feuille des bénéfices, archevêque de Lyon (1734-1799).* Lyon, 1911.
Mourret, F. *Histoire de l'église; VI, L'ancien régime.* Paris, 1917.
Opinion de M. l'abbé Maury, député de Picardie, sur la propriété des biens ecclésiastiques prononcée dans l'assemblée nationale le mardi, 13 octobre, 1789. Paris, 1789.
Nau, P. "L'origine des encycliques modernes, un épisode de la lutte des évêques et des parlements, 1755-1756." *Revue Historique de Droit Français et Etranger*, 4th ser., XXIV (1956), 225-267.
Palmer, R. R. *Catholics and Unbelievers in Eighteenth Century France.* Princeton, 1939.
Pericauld, A. *Les céléstins de Lyon.* Lyon, 1840.
Peronnet, M. "Les assemblées du clergé de France sous le règne de Louis XVI (1775-1788)." *Annales Historiques de la Révolution Française* (1962), pp. 8-35.
Perouas, L. "Le nombre des vocations sacerdotales, est-il un critère valable en sociologie religieuse historique aux 17e et 18e siècles?" *Actes du 87e congrès national des sociétés savantes, section d'histoire. . .* (Paris, 1963), pp. 35-40.
Perrin, J. *Le cardinal de Loménie de Brienne, archevêque de Sens.* Sens, 1896.
Picot, G. *Histoire des états-généraux considérés au point de vue de leur influence sur le gouvernement et de la France de 1355 à 1614.* 6 vols., Paris, 1872.
Picot, J. *Mémoires pour servir à l'histoire ecclésiastique pendant le 18e siècle.* 7 vols., Paris, 1853-1857.
Pisani, P. *L'église de Paris pendant la Révolution.* 4 vols., Paris, 1909-1912.
Poland, B. C. *French Protestantism and the French Revolution.* Princeton, 1957.
de Pradt, D. *Les quatres concordats.* 3 vols., Paris, 1818.
Porée, C. *Cahiers des curés et des communautés ecclésiastiques du baillage d'Auxerre pour les Etats-Généraux de 1789,* Auxerre, 1927.
Préclin, E. "Les conséquences sociales de Jansénisme." *Revue d'Histoire de l'Eglise de France*, XXI (1935), 385-391.
―――――. *Les Jansénistes du XVIIIe siècle et la constitution civile du clergé.* Paris, 1929.
Préclin, E. and Jarry, E. *Les luttres politiques et doctrinales aux XVIIe et XVIIIe siècles, Histoire de l'Eglise.* A. Fliche, V. Martin, eds. Vol. XIX, 2 vols., Paris, 1955-57.

Raduget, X. "La carrière politique de l'abbé Maury de 1786 à 1791." *Revue d'Histoire de l'Eglise de France,* III (1912), 505-11; 631-43.

Raudot, C. *La France avant la Révolution.* Paris, 1847.

Ravitch, N. *Sword and Mitre: Government and Episcopate in France and England in the Age of Aristocracy.* The Hague, 1966.

——————. "The Taxing of the Clergy in Eighteenth Century France." *Church History,* XXXIII (1964), 157-174.

Rébillon, A. *La situation économique du clergé à la veille de la Révolution dans les districts de Rennes, de Fougères et de Vitré,* Rennes, 1913.

——————. "La situation économique du clergé français à la fin de l'ancien régime," *La Révolution Française,* LXXXII (1929), pp. 326-350.

de Ricard C. *L'abbé Maury, 1746-1791.* Paris, 1887.

Rist, C. "Les procès-verbaux des assemblées générales du clergé." *La Révolution Française,* XXVI (1894), 548-555.

Rosne, A. M. *de Beauvais, évêque de Senez, 1731-1790, étude biographique et littéraire.* Paris, 1887.

Sagnac, P. "Les cahiers de 1789 et leur valeur." *Revue d'Histoire Moderne,* VIII (1906-1907), 329-349.

de Sambucy, M. *Vie de Mgr. de Beauvais, ancien évêque de Senez.* Paris, 1842.

Shafer, B. C. "Quelques jugements de pamphlétaires sur le clergé à la veille de la Révolution." *Annales Historiques de la Révolution Française,* XVI (1939), 102-113.

Sciout, L. *Histoire de la constitution civile du clergé.* 4 vols., 1872-1881.

Sée, H. *La France économique et sociale de France au XVIIIe siècle.* Paris, 1925.

——————. "La rédaction et la valeur des cahiers des paroisses." *Revue Historique,* CIII (1910), 292-306.

Sénac de Meilhan, G. *Du gouvernement, des moeurs, et des conditions en France avant la Révolution.* Hambourg, 1795.

Sevestre, E. *L'organisation du clergé paroissial à la veille de la Révolution.* Paris, 1912.

Serbat, L. *Les assemblées du clergé de France: origines, organisation, développement, 1561-1615.* Paris, 1906.

Sicard, A. *L'ancien clergé de France: I. Les évêques avant la Révolution.* 4th ed., Paris, 1905.

——————. *II. Les évêques pendant la Révolution.* 2nd ed., Paris, 1894.

Sol, E. *Le vénérable Alain de Solminihac abbé de Chancelade et évêque de Cahors.* Cahors, 1928.

Suaudeau, R. *L'évêque inspecteur administratif sous la monarchie absolue d'après les archives du centre de la France,* Paris, 1940.

Sykes, N. *Church and State in the Eighteenth Century.* Cambridge, 1934; reprinted, Hamden, Connecticut, 1962.

Taillandier, R. *Le mariage des Protestants français sous l'ancien régime.* Clermont-Ferrand, 1919.

Taylor, W. W. *Confiscation of Church Property in France in 1789.* Iowa City, Iowa, 1942.

Hocquart de Turtot, E. *Le tiers état et les privilèges.* Paris, 1907.

de Vaissière, P. *Curés de campagne de l'ancienne France.* Paris, 1932.

de la Véronne, G. "Contribution à l'étude de la propriété foncière sous l'ancien régime." *Revue des Questions Historiques,* LII (1914), 490-95.

Wallon, J. *Le clergé de quatre-vingt-neuf: le pape, le roi, la nation fin de l'ancien régime.* Paris, 1876.

Willaert, P. "Exercises pratiqués sur les sources à la faculté de théologie." *Annuaire de l'Université Catholique de Louvain*, LXX (1906), 499-519.

Winter, E. *Der Josephinismus und seine Geschichte: Beitraege zur Geistesgeschichte Oesterreichs, 1740-1848.* Bruenn, 1943.

B. POLITICAL, SOCIAL AND ECONOMIC WORKS RELEVANT TO THE CHURCH

d'Abrantes, D. *Histoire des salons de Paris: tableaux et portraits du grand monde.* 2 ed., 6 vols., Paris, 1838.

Allain, E. *L'instruction primaire en France avant la Révolution.* Paris, 1881.

Artaud de Montor, F. *Histoire de la vie et des travaux politiques du comte d'Hauterive.* Paris, 1839.

Aucoc, J. M. *Le conseil d'Etat avant et depuis 1789. Ses transformations, ses travaux, et son personnel.* Paris, 1876.

Babeau, A. *La province sous l'ancien régime.* 2 vols., Paris, 1894.

──────. *L'assemblée d'élection et le bureau intermédiaire de Bar-sur-Aube.* Troyes, 1873.

──────. *L'assemblée d'élection et le bureau intermédiare de Troyes.* Troyes, 1873.

──────. *La vie rurale dans l'ancienne France.* Paris, 1883.

──────. *La ville sous l'ancien régime.* Paris, 1880.

──────. *Le château de Brienne.* Troyes, 1877.

──────. *Le village sous l'ancien régime.* Paris, 1883.

Barthou, L. *Mirabeau.* Paris, 1920.

Bassieux, F. "Théorie des libertés gallicanes du parlement de Paris au 18e siècle." *Nouvelle Revue Historique de Droit Français et Etranger,* XXX (1906), 330-350.

Belin, J. *Le mouvement philosophique de 1748 à 1799.* Paris, 1913.

Bickart, R. *Les parlements et la notion de souveraineté nationale au 18e siècle.* Paris, 1932.

Bigo, R. *La caisse d'escompte (1776-1793) et les origines de la banque de France.* Paris, 1927.

Bloch, M. *Les rois thaumaturges, étude sur le caractère surnaturel attribué à la puissance royale.* Strasbourg, 1924.

Bluche, J. F. *L'origine des magistrats du parlement de Paris au 18e siècle (1715-1771).* Paris, 1956.

Boiteau, P. *Etat de la France en 1789.* Paris, 1861.

Bord, G. *La franc maçonnerie en France, des origines à 1815.* Paris, 1908.

Bouchary, J. *Les manieurs d'argent à Paris à la fin du XVIIIe siècle.* 3 vols., Paris, 1939-1943.

Bouquet, H. L. *L'ancien collège d'Harcourt et le lycée Saint Louis.* Paris, 1891.

Britsch, A. *La maison d'Orléans à la fin de l'ancien régime: la jeunesse de Philippe Egalité, 1747-1785, d'après des documents inédits.* Paris, 1926.

Cabanes, A. *Le cabinet secret de l'histoire.* 4 vols., Paris, 1912-1920.

Carré, H. *La fin des parlements, 1788-1790.* Paris, 1912.

──────. *La noblesse de France et l'opinion au XVIIIe siècle.* Paris, 1920.

Carré, H. Sagnac, P., Lavisse, E. *Louis XVI, 1774-1789; Histoire de France,* Vol. IX, Part I. E. Lavisse, ed., Paris, 1911.

Challamel, A. *Les clubs contre-révolutionnaires, cercles coites, sociétés, salons, réunions, cafés, restaurants, et libraires,* Paris, 1895.

Cherest, A. *La chute de l'ancien régime, 1787-1789.* 3 vols., Paris, 1884-1886.

Clamageran, J. J. *Histoire de l'impôt en France.* 3 vols., Paris, 1876.

Declareuil, J. *Histoire général du droit français des origines à 1789.* Paris, 1929.
Deschamps, G. "Les portraits de M. de Calonne." *Revue de Paris,* 1926, pp. 364-389.
Dupont, de Nemours P. S. *Mémoires sur la vie et les ouvrages de Turgot, ministre de l'état.* Philadelphie, 1782.
Egret, J. *La pré-Révolution française, 1787-1788.* Paris, 1962.
Fayard, E. *Aperçu historique sur le parlement de Paris.* 3 vols., Paris, 1878.
Fling, F. M. "Mirabeau and Calonne in 1785." *Annual Report of the American Historical Society.* Washington, D.C., 1897, pp. 133-147.
Funck-Brentano, F. *L'affaire du collier.* Paris, 1903.
Glagau, H. *Reformsversuche und Sturz des Absolutismus in Frankreich (1774-1788).* Munich, 1938.
Glasson, E. *Histoire du droit et des institutions de la France.* Vol. VIII. Paris, 1903.
―――――. *Le parlement de Paris, son rôle politique depuis le règne de Charles VII jusqu'à la Révolution.* 2 vols., Paris, 1901.
Godechot, J. *La contre-Révolution: doctrine et action, 1789-1804.* Paris, 1961.
Göhring, M. *Weg und Sieg der Staatsidee in Frankreich vom Mittelalter zu 1796.* Tübingen, 1946.
Goodwin, A. "Calonne, the Assembly of French Notables of 1787 and the Origins of the 'Révolte Nobiliaire.'" *English Historical Review,* LXI (1946), 202-234; 329-377.
Gottschalk, L. "The French Parlements and Judicial Review." *Journal of the History of Ideas,* V (1944), 105-112.
Grérard, C. *Nos adieux à la vieille Sorbonne.* Paris, 1893.
de Guilbourne Anselme de Sainte-Marie, P. *Histoire généalogigue et chronologique de la maison royale de France, des pairs, grands officiers de la couronne et de la maison du roi.* M. Pol Potier de Courcy, ed. 9 vols., Paris, 1873-1881.
Hillairet, J. *Evocation du vieux Paris, vieux quartiers, vieilles rues, vieilles demeures historiques, vestiges, annales et anecdotiques.* Paris, 1951.
Hyslop, B. F. *L'apanage de Philippe-Egalité, duc d'Orléans (1785-1791).* Paris, 1965.
Jaillot, H. *Recherches critiques, historiques et topographiques sur la ville de Paris.* 20 vols., Paris, 1774.
Jolly, P. *Calonne, 1734-1802.* Paris, 1949.
Labrousse, E. *Esquisse du mouvement des prix et des revenus en France au XVIIIe siècle.* Paris, 1933.
―――――. *La crise de l'économie française à la fin de l'ancien régime et au début de la Révolution.* I, Paris, 1944.
Lefebvre, G. *La Révolution française.* Vol. XIII of *Peuples et civilisations.* L. Halphen, Philippe Sagnac, eds. Paris, 1951.
―――――. "Le mouvement des prix et les origines de la Révolution française." *Annales d'Histoire Economique et Sociale,* IX (1937), 139-170.
―――――. "Le mouvement des prix et les origines de la Révolution française." *Annales Historiques de la Révolution Française,* XIV (1937), 289-327.
―――――. *Les paysans du nord pendant la Révolution française.* 2 vols., Lille, 1924.
Le Forestier, R. *Les illuminés de Bavière et la franc maçonnerie Allemande.* Paris, 1914.

Léonce de Lavergne, L. G. *Les assemblées provinciales sous Louis XVI.* Paris, 1864.
Letourneau, G. *Histoire du séminaire d'Angers depuis son union avec Saint Sulpice en 1695 jusqu'à nos jours.* Angers, 1895.
Loliée, F. *La comédie française, histoire de la maison de Molière de 1658 à 1907.* Paris, 1907.
de Loménie, L. *Les Mirabeau.* 5 vols., Paris, 1885-1889.
de Luçay, H. *Les secrétaires d'Etat depuis leur institution jusqu'à la mort de Louis XV.* Paris, 1881.
Luchaire, A. *Louis VII, Philippe-Auguste, Louis VIII.* E. Lavisse, ed., *Histoire de France,* Vol. III, Part 1, Paris, 1901.
Marion, M. *Histoire financière de France.* Vol. I, Paris, 1914.
——————. *Le garde des sceaux Lamoignon et la réforme judiciaire de 1788.* Paris, 1905.
——————. *Les impôts directs sous l'ancien régime, principalement au XVIIIe siècle.* Paris, 1910.
——————. *L'impôt sur le revenu au dix-huitième siècle principalement en Guyenne.* Paris, 1901.
——————. *Machault d'Arnouville, étude sur l'histoire du contrôle général des finances de 1749 à 1754.* Paris, 1891.
Martin, G. *La franc maçonnerie française et la préparation de la Révolution.* Paris, 1926.
——————. *Manuel d'histoire de la franc maçonnerie française.* Paris, 1932.
Mathiez, A. *La Révolution française,* 3 vols., Paris, 1922-1923.
Mercier, L. S. *Tableau de Paris.* 20 vols., Amsterdam, 1783-1789.
Mornet, D. "Les enseignements des bibliothèques privées, 1750-1780." *Revue d'Histoire Littéraire de la France,* XVII (1910), 449-496.
——————. *Les origines intellectuelles de la Révolution,* Paris, 1947.
Necker, J. *De l'administration des finances de France.* 3 vols., n.p., 1784.
Olivier-Martin, F. *Histoire du droit français des origines à la Révolution.* Paris, 1951.
Palmer, R. R. *The Age of Democratic Revolution, A Political History of Europe and America, 1760-1800: The Challenge.* Princeton, 1959.
——————. "The National Idea in France before the Revolution." *Journal of the History of Ideas,* I (1940), 95-111.
Pugh, W. J. "Calonne's New Deal." *Journal of Modern History,* XI (1939), 289-312.
Regnier, J. "Notice historique sur l'assemblée provinciale de Champagne de Louis XVI." *Revue de Champagne et Brie,* L (1893), 1-19.
Remacle, C. *Les relations secrètes des agents de Louis XVIII.* Paris, 1899.
Renouvin, P. *L'assemblée des notables, la conférence du 2 Mars.* Paris, 1920.
——————. *Les assemblées provinciales de 1787, origines, développement, résultats.* Paris, 1921.
Rocquain, F. *L'esprit révolutionnaire avant la Révolution.* Paris, 1874.
Roustan, M. *Les philosophes et la société française au XVIIIe siècle.* Paris, 1911.
Sagnac, P. *La fin de l'ancien régime et la révolution américaine (1763-1789).* Vol. XII of *Peuples et civilisations.* L. Halphen, P. Sagnac, eds., Paris, 1952.
——————. *La formation de la société française moderne, 1660-1789.* 2 vols., Paris, 1945-1946.
——————. *La législation civile de la Révolution française 1789-1804.* Paris, 1898.

Schelle, G. *Dupont de Nemours et l'école physiocratique.* Paris, 1888.
Sée, H. *L'évolution de la pensée politique en France au XVIIIe siècle.* Paris, 1925.
———. *Les idées philosophiques en France au XVIIIe siècle.* Paris, 1920.
Sénac du Meilhan, G. *Du gouvernement, des moeurs, et des conditions en France avant la Révolution.* Hambourg, 1795.
Sicard, A. *L'éducation morale et civique avant et pendant la Révolution, 1700-1808.* Paris, 1913.
Stern, A. *Vie de Mirabeau.* 2 vols., Paris, 1895.
Struck, W. "Die Notabelnversammlung von 1787." *Historische Vierteljahrschrift,* VIII (1905), 362-420.
Susane, G. *La tactique financière de Calonne.* Paris, 1901.
Valynseele, J. *Les enfants naturels de Louis XV.* Paris, 1953.
Viollet, P. *Le roi et ses ministres pendant les trois derniers siècles de la monarchie.* Paris, 1912.
Wahl, A. *Studien zur Vorgeschichte der franzoesischen Revolution.* 2 vols., Tuebingen, 1908.
Welschinger, H. *La mission secrète de Mirabeau à Berlin, 1786-1787 d'après des documents originaux des archives des affaires étrangères.* Paris, 1900.

C. SELECT WORKS ON TALLEYRAND

Acton, J. "Talleyrand's Memoirs." *Historical Essays and Studies,* London, 1907.
Arrigon, L. J. "Autour de Talleyrand: années d'apprentissage." *Revue des Deux Mondes* (December, 1957), 652-67.
Aujay, E. *Talleyrand.* Paris, 1946.
Aulard, F. "Talleyrand et ses mémoires." *Etudes et leçons sur la Révolution française,* VIII, Paris, 1924.
Barante, A. *Discours prononcé à la chambre des pairs, le 8 Juin 1838 à l'occasion du décès de M. de Talleyrand.* Paris, 1838.
Bastgen, H. "Talleyrands Aussoehnung mit der Kirche, Nach Vatikanischen Aktenstuecken." *Historisches Jahrbuch,* XLVIII (1928), 42-85.
Bastide, L. *Vie religieuse et politique de Talleyrand-Périgord.* Paris, 1838.
Bergler, E. *Psychoanalytische-biographische Essays.* Vienna, 1935.
Bertaut, J. *Talleyrand.* Paris, 1946.
Beurlier, E. "L'épiscopat de Talleyrand." *Revue du Clergé Français,* XXXV (1903), 113-134.
Blei, F. *Talleyrand.* Berlin, 1932.
Blennerhasset, C. J. *Talleyrand.* Trans. 2 vols., Chicago, 1894.
Brinton, C. *Lives of Talleyrand.* New York, 1936.
Brougham, H. *Historical Sketches of Statesmen who Flourished in the Time of George III.* 2 vols., London, 1842-1844.
Cabanes, A. "Conversations avec M. le Docteur Luys, les lésions cérébrales et les pieds bots, le cerveau de Talleyrand." *La Chronique Médicale,* I (1894), 35-38.
de Castellane, J. *Talleyrand.* Paris, 1934.
A Catalogue of the Entire, Elegant and Valuable Library (late the Property) of Mons. de Telleyrand [sic] Perigord, Bishop of Autun in France . . . sold by Auction by Leigh and Sotheby . . . Thursday, April 11, 1793, and the Nine Following Days . . . (n.p.,n.d.)
Colmache, M. *Reminiscences of Prince de Talleyrand.* London, 1850.
Cooper, D. *Talleyrand.* London, 1932.

Crabbe, V. "Entretien sur Talleyrand, sur l'esprit de l'administration, ainsi que sur les conditions et les motifs d'un statut du personnel." *Revue Internationale des Sciences Administratives,* XXII (1956), 125-39; 163-66.
Danrit, R., Desvergnes, L., et al. "Enfants naturels de Talleyrand." *Chercheurs et Curieux,* X (Jan., 1960), 467-74.
Dennehy, W. F. "Talleyrand's Conversion." *American Catholic Quarterly,* XXXVI (1911), 354-373; 493-516.
Devoucoux, A "Monsieur le prince de Talleyrand." *Annales de la Société d'Eduenne* (1853-1857), 115-144.
Dodd, A. B. *Talleyrand: The Training of a Statesman, 1754-1838.* New York, 1927.
Drouot, H. "Talleyrand et la béatification de Marie Alacoque." *Revue de Bourgogne,* VIII (1920), 398-400.
Dumolin, M. "La maison natale de Talleyrand." *Bulletin de la Société Historique du VIème Arrondissement de Paris,* XXX (1929), 44-46.
Ferrero, G. *Reconstruction of Europe: Talleyrand and the Congress of Vienna.* Trans. New York, 1941.
Fleury, S. *Talleyrand: maître souverain de la diplomatie.* Montreal, 1942.
Greenbaum, L. S. "Talleyrand and his Uncle: The Genesis of a Clerical Career." *Journal of Modern History,* XXIX (1957), 226-236.
―――――. "Talleyrand and the Temporal Problems of the French Church from 1780 to 1785." *French Historical Studies* (Spring, 1963), 41-71.
―――――. "Talleyrand as Agent-General of the Clergy of France: A Study in Comparative Influence." *Catholic Historical Review,* XLVIII (1963), 473-486.
―――――. "Ten Priests in Search of a Miter: How Talleyrand Became a Bishop." *Catholic Historical Review,* L (1964), 307-331.
Huth, H., Pugh, W. *Talleyrand in America as a Financial Promoter.* Washington, 1942.
Kipling, R. "The Priest in Spite of Himself," in *Rewards and Fairies. Complete Works,* 36 vols., London, 1897-1937, Vol. XXV.
Lacombe, B. *La vie privée de Talleyrand.* Paris, 1910.
―――――. *Talleyrand, évêque d'Autun.* Paris, 1903.
Lacomme, L. *Les élections et les représentants de Saône-et-Loire depuis 1789.* Paris, 1885.
Lacour-Gayet, G. "L'enfance de Talleyrand, 1754-1770." *Revue de Paris* (1926), pp. 799-815.
―――――. *Talleyrand, 1754-1838.* 4 vols., Paris, 1928-1932.
Lagrange, A. "Monseigneur Dupanloup et M. de Talleyrand." *Correspondant,* CXXXI (1883), 623-651.
LaForgue, R. *Talleyrand, l'homme de la France: Essai psychoanalytique.* Lausanne, n.d.
de Latouche, H. *Album perdu, pensées et maximes de Talleyrand.* Paris, 1829.
Leroy, A. *Talleyrand économiste et financier.* Paris, 1907.
Lesourd, P. "Plaidoyer pour Talleyrand." *Revue Générale Belge,* XCI (1954), 427-439.
Lévy, R. "Le renouveau de Talleyrand." *Grande Revue,* LXVIII (1911).
Limouzin-Lamothe, R. "La rétractation de Talleyrand: documents inédits." *Revue d'Histoire de l'Eglise de France,* XL (1954), 220-244.
Loliée, F. *Talleyrand et la société française depuis la fin du règne de Louis XV jusqu'aux approches du second empire.* Paris, 1910.
Loth, A. "Talleyrand et l'église constitutionnelle de France." *Revue Anglo-Romaine,* III (1896), 481-501; 594-602.

Lytton-Bulwer, G. *Historical Characters: Talleyrand.* London, 1868.
Madelin, L. *Talleyrand.* Paris, 1942.
―――――. "Talleyrand préhistorique." *Revue des Etudes Historiques,* LXIX (1903), 147-155.
Marcade, A. *Talleyrand prêtre et évêque.* Paris, 1883.
McCabe, J. *Talleyrand, A Biographical Study.* New York, 1906.
McHarg, C. K. *Life of Prince Talleyrand with Extracts from his Speeches and Writings.* New York, 1857.
Michaud, L. G. *Histoire de Talleyrand, ancien évêque d'Autun.* Paris, 1853.
Mignet, A. *Notice Historique sur Talleyrand.* Paris, 1846.
Missoffe, M. *Le coeur secret de Talleyrand.* Paris, 1956.
―――――. "Les livres de Talleyrand." *Mercure de France,* CCCXXIII (Jan.-Apr. 1955), 165-68.
Montarlot, P. "L'épiscopat de Talleyrand." *Mémoires de la Sociéte d'Eduenne,* XXII (1894), 83-157.
―――――. "Les députés de Saône-et-Loire aux assemblées de la Révolution, 1789-1799." *Mémoires de la Société d'Eduenne,* XXX (1902), 281-365.
Muguet, P. *Recherches historiques sur la persécution religieuse dans le département de Saône-et-Loire pendant la Révolution, 1789-1803.* 2 vols., Chalon, 1896-1897.
Nervo, B. *La conversion et la mort de M. de Talleyrand: récit de cinq témoins.* Paris, 1910.
Paléologue, G. *Romantisme et diplomatie: Talleyrand.* Paris, 1926.
Pichot, A. *Souvenirs intimes de Monsieur de Talleyrand.* Paris, 1870.
Place, C., Florens, J. *Mémoire sur Monsieur de Talleyrand, sa vie politique et sa vie intime.* Paris, 1838.
Précis de la vie du prélat d'Autun, digne ministre de la Fédération. Paris, 1791.
Rahn, R. *Charles-Maurice, Prince de Talleyrand, Portrait und Dokumente,* Tuebingen, 1949.
Rose, J. H. "Talleyrand's Protest at his Expulsion from England." *English Historical Review,* XXI (1906), 330-332.
Roux, E. "Le collège d'Autun sous les Oratoriens, 1786-1792." *Mémoires de la Société d'Eduenne,* VI (1877), 1-82.
de Saint-Aulaire, C. *Talleyrand.* Paris, 1936.
Saint-Beuve, C. A. *Monsieur de Talleyrand.* Paris, 1880.
Salle, A. *Vie politique de Charles-Maurice de Talleyrand.* Berlin, 1834.
Sindral, J. *Talleyrand.* Paris, 1926.
Sorel, A. "Talleyrand et ses mémoires." *Lectures Historiques,* Paris, 1894.
Stewarton (pseudonym L. Goldsmith). *Memoirs of C. M. Talleyrand, Containing the Particulars of his Private and Public Life, of his Intrigues in Boudoires* [sic] *as well as in Cabinets.* 2 vols., London, 1805.
Touchard-Lafosse, G. *Histoire politique et vie intime de Charles-Maurice de Talleyrand, Prince de Bénévent.* Paris, 1848.
de Vars, A. *Les femmes de Talleyrand.* Paris, 1891.
Villemarest, C. M. *Monsieur de Talleyrand, mémoires pour servir à l'histoire de France.* 4 vols., Bruxelles, 1834.
Vivent, J. *La vie privée de Talleyrand.* Paris, 1940.
Wendorff, H. "Die Ideenwelt des Fuersten Talleyrands, ein Versuch." *Historische Vierteljahrschrift,* XXVIII (1933), 335-384.
Zacour, N. P. "Petrarch and Talleyrand." *Speculum,* XXXI (1956), 683-703.
―――――. *Talleyrand: The Cardinal of Périgord (1301-1364).* Philadelphia, 1960.

Index

Abbés, 51, 68, 98, 130
Acton, Lord, 10
"Acts of the Clergy," 112, 113
Agen, *curés* of, 173
AGENTS-GENERAL OF THE CLERGY,
  Accepted by General Assembly, 60
  Advisers of clergy, 158
  Arbitrators of clergy, 167
  And Archives of the Clergy, 175, 178, 179, 181, 183, 184, 186, 188
  And Assembly of Prelates or Private Assembly, 28, 62, 115, 171
  And attorneys of clergy, 188, 189, 190
  Audit *décime* receipts, 196
  Authorized to convoke meetings of prelates, 123
  In Bureau of Ecclesiastical Affairs, 115
  And the central administrative agencies of the clergy, 66
  As Church's first-ministers, 57
  And Committee on Ecclesiastical Affairs, 63
  Conditions requiring legal intervention of Agents, 120
  And Council of Clergy, 174, 188, 190, 191
  As Counsellors of State, 63, 67
  As couriers of the clergy, 151
  And Diocesan Syndics, 200
  Duties within the General Assembly, 64, 65
  And ecclesiastical jurisdiction, 108
  Election of, 59, 60
  Established by the Assembly of Melun, 58, 73, 74
  As executives and spokesmen of the clergy, 57, 61
  Financial duties, 64, 174
  And the Guardian of the Archives, 176, 178, 179, 190
  Initiate successors, 68
  Intervention before the State, 168
  Intervention on behalf of clergy, 62
  Introduced to king and ministers, 63
  And inviolability of the clergy's temporal, 82
  And King's Council, 63, 115
  As legal advisers of the clergy, 157
  Office considered property of higher nobility, 59
  Origins of, 57
  Powers and duties, 60, 61
  Powers of presenting remonstrances, 108
  Prestige of office, 68
  As printers of the clergy, 184
  And promulgation of new laws, 148
  Protect episcopal jurisdiction, 125
  Qualifications needed for the office, 60
  And Receiver-General of the Clergy, 194
  In the "Recueil concernant l'agence générale du clergé," 61, 67, 124
  Registration and enforcement of laws, 145
  Relations to King, 59
  Relations with the dioceses, 63, 175
  Replace Syndics-General, 58
  And Report of the Agency, 65, 115
  Reprove clergy, 165
  Requirements for election, 58
  Responsibilities to parish clergy, 145
  And right of *committimus*, 63
  Salary of, 67
  And Secretariat, 175, 180, 191
  As Secretary and Promoter in the General Assembly of the Clergy, 66, 67

Index

Aides, 38
Aix, 14, 31, 53, 59, 69, 70, 133, 173, 201
Albi, 14, 15, 53, 59
Alençon, 169
Alienations, 102, 137
Almanach Royal, 15, 40, 68
Alsace, 27
Amadeus VIII, Count of Savoy, 104
Amelot, Antoine-Jean, 124, 187
American War of Independence, 86
Amiens, 40, 169
Anjou, 97
Antibes, 97
Antigny, d', 7
Antilles, 101
Antoine, Pierre-Joseph, 54
Appel comme d'abus, 110, 111, 113, 114, 129, 141
Aquin, Bishop d', 187
Archives of the Clergy, 36, 53, 54, 55, 60, 61, 72, 89, 97, 175, 178, 179, 181, 183, 184, 186, 188
Argenson, Marquis d', 79
Arles, 53, 59
Armagnac, Count d', 127
Arnaud, 98
Arrêt de surséance, 88
Artois, 27
Artois, Count of, 91
Assembly of Municipal Notables, 159
Assembly of Notables, 36, 215
Assignats, 55
Athanasius, 143
Attorneys of the Clergy, 188, 190, 192
Auch, 53, 59, 127
Audra, Abbé, 5
Auger, Abbé, 44
Austria, 86
Autun, 2, 12, 14, 15, 17, 66, 69, 72, 106, 140
Auxerre, 162, 169
Aveu et dénombrement, 88
Avranches, 159

Bachaumont, 69, 213
Baillages, 63
Bailly, Abbé, 187
Ballard, *Curé,* 135
Baptismal registry, 148, 149, 193

Bargemond, *Curé,* 159
Barnabites, 139
Barral, 11
Barral, de, Bishop of Troyes, 11, 13, 30
Barrère, 17
Bayeux, 165, 166, 172
Béarn, 42, 199
Beaumarchais, 213
Beaumont, de, Archbishop of Paris, 21, 22, 28
Beauvais, M. de, 176, 181, 197
Beauvillier, Duke of, 12
Beccaria, 21
Bellechasse, 20, 178, 181
Belley, 40, 158
Benedictine nuns, 160
Benefice holders, 25, 28, 29, 152
Bernis, 11, 23
Bernis, de, Cardinal-Archbishop of Albi, 13, 14, 15, 75, 81, 207
Berry, 97
Berthier, Abbé, 44
Besançon, 27
Beurlier, Emile, 71
Bickart, Roger, 112
Bishops, 16, 17, 22, 28, 29, 31, 33, 47, 48, 51, 54, 67, 70, 81, 84, 89, 97, 101, 103, 107, 108, 109, 112, 114, 116, 121, 125, 126, 127, 128, 129, 130, 131, 133, 134, 135, 138, 140, 141, 143, 148, 151, 152, 153, 154, 155, 156, 158, 181, 196, 202, 204, 206, 214
Blaize, *Curé* of, 164
Blancmesnil-Lamoignon, Guillaume de, 195
Blois, 17
Boisgelin, 23
Boisgelin de Cucé, Archbishop of Aix, 12, 13, 31, 33, 36, 68, 69, 70, 81, 93, 101, 134, 139, 154
Boisgelin de Kerdu, Abbé, Agent-General of the Clergy, 30, 31, 69, 71, 76, 78, 180
Bollioud de Saint-Julien, 195, 197, 213
Bonac, de, Bishop of Clermont, 185
Bordeaux, 14, 59, 97, 132, 201
Bossuet, 3, 44, 83
Boulogne, 140

Index 285

Bouquet, Abbé, 89
Bourbon, Abbé de, 69, 70
Bourganeuf, Canon of, 166
Bourg-en-Bresse, 177
Bourges, 59, 140, 170, 201
Bourlier, M., 17
Breteuil, Louis-Auguste Le Tonnelier de, 130, 150
Brette, Armand, 37
Bridelle, 30
Brignolles, *Curé* of, 173
Brittany, 94, 97, 100, 161, 171
Broglie, 68
Brougham, Lord 7
Budget for New Converts, 44, 156
Buffon, 197
Buisonnier, 130
Bureau de l'agence générale du clergé, 175, 178, 181
Bureau of Ecclesiastical Affairs, 115
Bureaux des finances, 90
Burgundy, 15

Caen, 122
Cahiers de doléances of the clergy, 25, 29, 32, 45, 47, 48, 49, 52, 58, 63, 65, 96, 115, 147, 151, 161
Cahors, 121, 170
Calas Affair, 42
Calonne, Charles-Alexandre de, 40, 76, 83, 84, 97, 170, 210, 215
Cambrai, 27
Camus, 188
Cans, Albert, 33, 42
Capet, Hugh, 7
Capetians, 16, 91
Capitation, 27, 83, 93, 160, 169, 170, 194
Carré, Henri, 45
Castellane, 11
Castries, 76
Casuel, 170
Cavanac, M. de, 70
Cavanac, Mme. de, 69
Celestines, 55, 104, 105, 106, 210
Censure of the clergy, 43, 165
Cercamp, Abbey of, 15
Chaalis, Abbey of, 102
Chalais, Princes of, 7, 13
Chalcedon, Council of, 126
Châlons-sur-Marne, 122, 156, 161, 163, 165

Chambre des comptes, 38, 90, 178
Chambres supérieures des décimes, 197, 201
Champagne, 15, 17, 161, 173
Champion de Cicé, 11
Champion de Cicé, Archbishop of Bordeaux, 12, 13, 15, 33, 36, 66, 68, 75, 101, 120, 154
Champion de Cicé, Bishop of Auxerre, 13
Champmotteux, *Curé* of, 165
Chancellor, 37, 114, 115, 116
Charlemagne, 95, 97
Charles IX, 58
Charlin, *Curé,* 159
Chartres, 91, 163, 166
Chastenet de Puységur, 30
Chateaubriand, 12, 16
Chatre, Abbé de, 137, 142
Choiseul, 76
Choiseul-Gouffier, 69
Cinquantième, 37, 83
Circular letters, 151
Cistercian, 118
Civil Constitutional Church, 12, 98, 100
Civil Constitutional clergy, 6
Civil register, 3, 45, 96, 148
Clément, Abbé, 44
Clergy of France, 27
Clermont, 95, 121, 132
Colbert, 114
Collection des procès-verbaux des assemblées générales du clergé de France, 50
Colloquy of Poissy, 24, 26, 58, 181, 195
Commendatory abbots, 22, 93
Commission du domaine, 90
Commission of Regulars, 102
Committee on the Administration of Agriculture, 93
Committimus, 63, 119
Concordat of Bologna, 109
Condillac, Abbé, 5
Condom, 169
Confession certificates, 111
Congregation of the Oratory of Orleans, 167, 168
Conseil du clergé, 36, 181, 182, 188, 190, 191, 209, 213
Controller-General of Finances, 125, 170, 171
Conversion treasury, 42

286 Index

Conzié, 11
Corbeau de Saint-Albin, 30
Corbeille, Canon of, 159
Cordon bleu (knights of the holy spirit), 8, 53
Corsica, 27, 67
Cortois de Pressigny, Bishop of Belley, 11, 13, 30
Cortois de Pressigny, Bishop of Nîmes, 13, 30
Cortois de Pressigny, Bishop of Saint-Malo, 13, 30
Corvée, 165, 172
Council of the Clergy, 174, 188, 209, 213
Council of Dispatches, 104, 132
Council of State, 114
Counsellors of State, 115
Cour des aides, 38, 114, 164, 171, 192
Cour des comptes, 197
Curés, 29, 39, 40, 59, 81, 93, 95, 96, 97, 98, 99, 100, 119, 129, 130, 132, 133, 134, 136, 137, 140, 141, 143, 161, 166, 172, 181, 198, 203, 211
Curés à portion congrue, 93, 95, 96, 97, 99, 134, 140, 154, 211
Curia Regis, 116

Dauphin, 153
Dauphiné, 39, 67, 92, 97, 133, 172
Debt of clergy, 56
Décime, 27, 30, 38, 39, 47, 67, 96, 117, 119, 136, 152, 170, 195, 198, 199, 200, 201
Deism, 80
Département général des décimes, 40-1
Diatribe à l' auteur des Ephémérides, 80
Dillon, 23
Dillon, Archbishop of Narbonne and President of the Assemblies of 1785 & 1788, 13, 30, 33, 36, 52, 66, 75, 141
Diocesan Assembly, 28
Diocesan Bureaus, 31, 39, 40, 83, 97, 107, 117, 118, 134, 136, 186, 198, 201, 202, 203, 204, 205, 212
Diocesan Receiver, 195, 199, 200, 201

Diocesan Syndic, 60, 61, 137, 151, 152, 156, 159, 164, 178, 200, 201, 204, 205, 206, 207, 209
"Diocesan Syndic Plan," 78, 157, 171, 203, 210, 211
Diocletian, 84
Discount Bank, 213
Dixième, 37, 83
Dominican Islands, 86
Dons gratuits, 3, 24, 27, 28, 37, 40, 46, 52, 53, 56, 63, 65, 67, 81, 82, 83, 86, 88, 115, 116, 136, 145, 147, 152, 170, 199, 200, 201, 212
Droit d'amortissement, 38, 41, 162, 164, 167
Droit de contrôle, 164, 171
Droit de feu, 161
Droit de gros, 171
Droit de l'huile, 171
Dubois, Cardinal-Minister, 14
Duchesne, Henri-Gabriel, 175, 176, 177, 178, 179, 180, 182, 183, 185, 186, 190, 196, 197
Dulau, Archbishop of Arles, 13, 30, 33, 36, 41, 44, 45, 47, 68, 75, 120, 154, 156, 207
Dunolé, 213
Dupanloup, Bishop of Orleans, 20
Du Plessis d'Argentré, 11
Du Plessis d'Argentré, Bishop of Limoges, 13
Du Plessis d'Argentré, Bishop of Tulle, 13
Dupont de Nemours, 93
Duranthon, Abbé, 50, 197

Ecclesiastical jurisdiction, 108
Ecclesiastical tribunals, 109-110
Economists, 78
Edict of Nantes, 41, 42
Edict of 1695, 128, 129, 130, 131, 132, 134, 172, 173
Education, 45, 47, 139, 154, 155
Embrun, 53, 59, 113
Encyclopédie, 50
Enlightenment, 44, 81
Estates-General, 26, 82, 109, 215
Estates-General of 1560, 2, 24
Estates-General of 1614, 53
Estates-General of 1789, 135
"Evil books," 43, 47
Evreux, *Curé* of, 165

Fénelon, 17, 44
Feuille des bénéfices, Minister of, 14, 66, 71, 89
First Estate, 1, 4, 25, 42, 49, 58, 61, 62, 80, 83, 89, 101, 105, 107, 109, 110, 116, 121, 134, 136, 147, 168, 209, 212
Flanders, 27, 94, 97, 161
Foi et hommage, 28, 38, 88, 89, 90, 91, 92, 145, 151, 153, 154, 160, 162, 163, 166, 186, 210
Fontenay, *Curé* of, 140
"Foreign clergy," 27
Fouché, 16
Franc fief, 38, 160
Franche Comté, 27
Fréjus, 159

Gabelle, 146, 170, 171
Gaignant, 188
Gallia Christiana, 157
Gallicanism, 32, 111, 81, 129
Gandin, Abbé, 44
Garancière, rue (Paris), 8
Garde des archives, 175, 181
Gaunot, 164
Gazette de France, 52, 84, 85, 86
GENERAL ASSEMBLY OF THE CLERGY,
"Accounts" or "Small" Assembly, 27, 34
Acts, ceremonies, etiquette, 50-2
Agent-General in, 24
Assembly of Prelates or Private Assembly, 28, 62, 115, 123, 171
Assembly of 1670, 48
Assembly of 1715, 123, 184, 187
Assembly of 1748, 177
Assembly of 1770, 39, 40
Assembly of 1775, 108
Assembly of 1780, 36, 183, 196
Assembly of 1782, 155, 196
Assembly of 1785, 28, 207, 209
Assembly of 1788, 41, 150
Cahier of clergy, compilation of, 46
Cahier of clergy, king's response to, 47, 65
Committee on Affairs of Church and Doctrine, 41
Committee on the Archives, 46, 181, 184, 185
Committee on Coins, 46
Committee for the *Don Gratuit,* 37
Committee on Ecclesiastical Affairs, 63
Committee on the *Foi et Hommage,* 89
Committee for the *Portion Congrue,* 35
Committee on Religion and Jurisdiction, 41, 42, 44, 48, 90, 99, 147, 154
Committee on the Revision of the Minutes, 46, 48, 65
Committee for the Servants, 46
Committee for the Temporal, 36, 154
Committee of the Ten Year Contract, 37
Committee for the Tithes, 35
Committee to visit prisons, hospitals and the poor, 46
Committees *Pour les comptes des rentes,* 41
"Contract" or "Large" Assembly, 27, 34
Contracts with the king, 24
Convocation of, 28
Cost of sessions, 55
Curés in, 29
Disputes in, 50
Election to, 28
Enacts Talleyrand's "Diocesan Syndic Plan," 209
Extraordinary Assembly, 26, 28, 55, 67, 153
Extraordinary Assembly of 1782, 120, 153, 187, 206
Gifts, gratuities, bonuses, and pensions of, 55
Honorary Presidents, 32
Luncheonette of, 46, 53
Meeting rooms and quarters, 53, 54
Meets as committee of the whole, 35
Ordinary Assembly, 26
President in, 33, 34, 52, 53
Proceedings, 50
Procurations (credentials) of deputies, 30
Promoter in, 18, 24, 33, 34, 66, 67
Provisional President in, 32, 64

288   Index

Recommendations for the canonization of French saints, 46
Royal audiences, 51-2
Salaries of delegates, 52
Secretary in, 24, 33, 34, 66, 67
As supreme court of clergy, 119
Suspension of Assembly of 1785, 28
Voting, 51
Généralités, 201
Gérard, Abbé, 44
Germigny, *Curé* of, 169
Glandève, 40
Glasson, Ernest, 126
Gourcy, Abbé, 44
Gouttes, *Curé*, 135
Gradué benefices, 146, 147
Gramont, Countess de, 70
Gramont, Hôtel de, 15
Grand Almoner of France, 12, 14
Grand Council, 168
Grands Augustins Convent (Paris), 46, 51, 52, 53, 54, 55, 64, 182, 184, 185, 189
Grasse, Count de, 86
Great Council, 127
Great Seal, 63
Grégoire, *Curé*, 135
Grenoble, 128, 130, 133
Grimaldi, de, Bishop of Noyon, 23, 30
Guardian of the Archives, 54, 175, 176, 178, 179, 183, 189, 190
Guénée, Abbé, 44
Guyenne, 100
Guyot, Pierre, 38

Hainaut, 27
Harcourt, Collège d', 13
Harlay, Archbishop of Paris, 33
Haute-Guyenne, 15
Hautvilliers, Abbey of, 162
Henrietta of England, 42
Henry III, 3
Henry IV, 42, 53
Heresy, 47
Hervé, 188
Hincmar of Reims, 14
Holbach, 80
Homme aux quarante écus, 80
Hospitals, 47, 146
Hôtel de Ville of Paris, 24
Houbigant, Abbé, 44

Impôt territorial, 83, 166

Innocent III, 95
Insolites, 94
Inspector of the Domain, 88, 89
Intendants, 129, 169, 171, 172, 173

Jallet, *Curé*, 135
James II, 42
Jansenism, 1, 13, 26, 31, 32, 42, 80, 81, 98, 111, 112, 113
Jarente, de, 23
Jarente, de, Bishop of Orleans, 12, 13, 68
Jesuits, 1, 26, 32, 45, 80, 101, 109, 127, 128, 148, 154, 155, 169, 199
Jesus Christ, 80
Joinville, Chapter of, 173
Joly de Fleury, Jean-François, 14, 37, 125, 131, 170, 171, 172, 173
Joseph II of Austria, 84, 85, 87
Jouques, 139
Jousse, 129
Judas, 215
July Monarchy, 72

Keeper of Seals, 44, 63, 76, 90, 136, 137, 147
Kehl edition of the Works of Voltaire, 43, 47
King's Council, 38, 62, 63, 95, 103, 104, 109, 114, 115, 116, 118, 119, 124, 136, 139, 168, 169, 192, 194
King's Great and Private Councils, 115

La Fare, 30
Lafayette, 150
Lafont de Savines, 12
La France Ecclésiastique, 19, 40, 59, 197
Laget Bardelin, 188, 193
Lamoignon de Malesherbes, Chrétien-Guillaume de, 43, 76, 100, 150
Langres, 164
Languedoc, 14, 94, 97
Laon, 161
La Roche-Aymon, de, Cardinal-Archbishop of Reims, President of the Assembly of 1775, 14, 15, 18, 19, 33
La Rochefoucauld, Abbé de, 166

Index 289

La Rochefoucauld, de, 11
La Rochefoucauld, de, Bishop of Beauvais, 13, 23
La Rochefoucauld, de, Bishop of Saintes, 13
La Rochefoucauld, de, Cardinal-Archbishop of Bourges, 13
La Rochefoucauld, de, Cardinal-Archbishop of Rouen, President of the Assemblies of 1780 and 1782, 13, 32, 33, 36, 68, 75, 89, 124, 207
La Rochelle, 150, 158
Lastic, 11
Latour d'Auvergne Lauragais, 12
Launday, Abbé de, 167
Lavoisier, 93
La voix du sage et du peuple, 80
Law, John, 28
Lazarists, 95
Le Cesve, *Curé,* 135
Le christianisme dévoilé, 80
Leclerc de Juigné, Archbishop of Paris, 36, 68, 123
Leflon, J., 17
Lefranc de Pompignan, Archbishop of Vienne, 36, 75, 128
Le Mans, 40, 137, 138, 142, 158, 164
Lepointe, Gabriel, 29, 202
Leroy, André, 71
Lescure, 19
Les prêtres démasqués, 80
Lettre de cachet, 70
Lettres d'encadrement, 187
Lettres d'Etat, 64
Letters patent, 38, 63, 100, 102, 104, 146
Le vicaire savoyard, 80
Leyssin, de, Archbishop of Embrun, 76
Licet, 64
Limoges, 121, 128, 166
Lisieux, 131, 140, 165
Loans of clergy, 38
Locke, 210
Lods-et-ventes, 159
Loire, 199
Lombez, 118, 119
Loménie de Brienne, 11, 17, 23, 53
Loménie de Brienne, Archbishop of Toulouse, later of Sens, 12, 13, 15, 16, 17, 20, 30, 33, 36, 41, 53, 54, 81, 101, 146, 185, 207, 208
Lorraine, 27, 92
Louis XIII, 52, 53
Louis XIV, 32, 33, 42, 83, 100, 111, 113
Louis XV, 8, 69, 111, 113
Louis XVI, 8, 20, 42, 47, 48, 84, 85, 86-7, 90, 104, 147, 148
Lubersac, de, Bishop of Chartres, 13
Luçon, 142
Luynes, de, Cardinal-Archbishop of Sens, 32, 75
Luzerne, 68
Lyon, 59, 104, 172, 177, 201

Mably, Abbé, 5
Machault, Jean-Baptiste, 28, 83, 84, 88, 91, 111
Macon, 97
Mallet, Abbé, 5
Malta, Knights of, 93, 95, 199
Mannay, Bishop of Trèves, 177
Marc d'or, 38, 171
Marguillier, 171
Maria-Theresa of Austria, 126, 153
Marie de Médicis, 53
Marion, Henri, 93
Marion, Marcel, 114
Marmontel, Abbé, 5
Marolles, *Curé* of, 137
Maurepas, 70, 76
Maury, 131
Maury, Abbé, 105, 106
Mazarin, 14
Meaux, 131
Melun, Assembly of, 58, 73, 74, 184, 196, 198, 200, 207, 208
Meslier, Abbé, 5
Metropolitan Syndics, 151, 201, 207
Metz, 169
Mignet, François, 8, 10
Military service, 47
Miromesnil, Armand-Thomas Hue de, 137
Montalet-Alais, 30
Montazet, de, Archbishop of Lyon, 30, 32
Montesquieu, 55, 95, 109, 215
Montesquiou, Abbé de, 72, 194
Montigny, 160
Montmorency, de, 23

Montmorency, de, Cardinal-Bishop of Metz, 13
Montpellier, 126, 165
Morainville, *Curé* of, 121
Morellet, Abbé, 5, 10, 12, 21, 45
Mortmain, 100

Napoleon, 214
Narbonne, 14, 53, 59, 141
National Assembly, 2, 105
Necker, 76, 166, 171, 172, 210
Necklace Affair, 28, 29, 89
Nevers, 169
Nicolaï, 11
Noailles, de, Cardinal-Archbishop of Paris, 14, 33
Nogent-le-Rotrou, *Curé* of, 121, 122
Normandy, 94
Normandy, Duke of, 153
Novales, 94

Ogier, M., 195
Oleron, 139
Orleans, 91, 97, 160, 166, 169
Orleans, Duke of, 90, 91, 92, 151, 166
Ormesson, Président d', 123, 131
Osmond de Médavy, Bishop of Comminges, 12, 13, 30

Pamiers, 117
Panchaud, 213
Papal Nuncio, 59
Parent, Abbé, 89
Paris, 21, 28, 40, 53, 59, 64, 67, 91, 101, 112, 113, 115, 118, 121, 123, 127, 128, 131, 137, 146, 153, 159, 166, 168, 169, 172, 201
Parlementaires, 81, 109, 111, 112
Parlements, 1, 10, 28, 32, 33, 63, 76, 82, 93, 94, 100, 101, 110, 111, 112, 113, 115, 118, 121, 125, 127, 128, 130, 131, 132, 133, 137, 139, 143, 146, 150, 159, 161, 168, 173, 186, 189, 201, 210, 212, 215
Parthenay, 127
Patrimony of the clergy, 71, 92, 138, 148, 215
Patrouille, 162
Pau, 139
Périgord, 15

Périgord and Grignols, Counts of, 7
Petrarch, 16
Pey, Abbé, 44
Philip-Augustus, 24, 108
Philosophers, 1, 36, 41, 43, 44, 79, 81, 93, 109, 150, 156
Philosophical Dictionary, 80
Physiocrats, 93
Picardy, 102
Pius VI, 84, 104
Poitiers, 127, 159
Pommeraye, *Curé* of, 122
Pont de Lodi, rue du (Paris), 55
Pont Neuf (Paris), 53
Pontoise, Assembly of, 41
Portion congrue, 77, 93, 96, 97, 98, 100, 134, 140, 154, 157, 160, 199, 203, 212
Prades, Abbé de, 5, 20, 81
Praemonstratensians, 127
Précis des rapports de l'agence générale du clergé de France, 49
Préclin, Edmond, 66, 78, 98
Presbyterianism, 98
Presbytery repairs, 161, 173
Prévost, Abbé, 5
Protestant civil legislation of 1787, 42, 150
Protestants, 19, 26, 41, 42, 47, 100, 109, 128, 148, 150, 166, 189
Provence, 14, 39, 67, 92, 93, 97, 133, 161
Provence, Count of, 90, 91
Provincial Assemblies, 29, 44, 59, 64, 83, 152, 154, 156, 166, 184
Provincial Councils, 36, 47, 113, 114
Provincial Estates, 2
Provincial Receiver, 152, 201

Quesnel, 98
Quimper, 141
Quinson, M. de, 195

Rabaut de Saint-Etienne, 150
Raforin, Abbé, 164
Rastignac, Abbé de, 103, 104, 124
Rat de Mondon, Abbé, 188
Raynal, Abbé, 5

Receiver-General of the Clergy, 36, 51, 53, 152, 174, 182, 183, 186, 189, 194, 195, 196, 200, 201, 213
"Recueil concernant l'agence générale du clergé," 61, 124, 181
Recueil des actes, titres, et mémoires concernant les affaires du clergé de France, 50, 152, 183
Reformation, 108
Refusal of sacraments, 111
Reims, 14, 21, 22, 40, 59, 162
Relecq, Abbey of, 118
Rennes, 118
Reports of the Agency-General of the Clergy, 49, 65, 115, 120
Resignation *in favorem,* 130, 147
Retz, Cardinal de, 14, 16
Reymond, Henri, 132
Ribeaucourt, *Curé,* 118
Richelieu, 14, 114
Richerism, 98, 129, 132
Rieux, 164
Rigault, 188, 192
Rodney, Admiral, 86
Rohan, 11, 23, 54
Rohan, Cardinal-Bishop of Strasbourg, 28, 29, 89, 101
Rouen, 33, 40, 59, 131, 132, 159, 160, 201
Rousseau, 80
Roussillon, 27
Rulhière, 100, 150

Sagnac, Philippe, 161
Saint Bertin, Abbey of, 126
Saint Brieuc, 31
Saint Brieuc, Collège de, 165
Saint Brunet, *Curé* of, 132
Saint Claude, 164
Saint Cyran, 98
Saint Denis, Abbey of, 9
Saint Dié, 130
Saint François de Sales, 48
Saint François Régis, 48
Saint Germain, Faubourg (Paris), 20, 21
Saint Leger, 161
Saint Louis, 210
Saint Pierre de Mailloc, *Curé* of, 165
Saint Quentin, Abbey of, 15
Saint Quentin, *Curé* of, 161
Saint Remy, 23
Saint Sulpice, Church of, 8

Saint Sulpice, *Curé* of, 53, 54, 185
Saint Sulpice, Seminary of, 15, 177
Saint Vaast, Abbey of, 126
Saint Valusien, Abbey of, 117
Saint Vincent de Paul, 48
Sainte Agnès de Jésus, 48
Sainte Jeanne de Chantal, 48
Sainte Madeleine de Saint Joseph, 48
Sainte Marie de l'Incarnation, 48
Saintes, 132
Saints, *Curé* of, 162
Saints Pères, rue des (Paris), 32
Sanson du Peronnet, 188
Sarlat, 122, 162
Sarlat, Chapter of, 166
Saunay, *Curés* of, 170
Sausin, Bishop of Blois, 17
Scholastics, 19
Second Estate, 2, 7, 37
Secretariat of the Clergy, 36, 53, 73, 74, 174, 175, 180, 184, 191, 204, 213
Secretaries of State, 115
Secretary of State for Ecclesiastical Affairs, 115, 187
Sedan, Collège de, 169
Séez, 121, 142, 179, 187
Ségur, Philippe-Henri, 76, 172
Seignelay de Colbert, 30
Seminaries, 146
Sénéchaussées, 63
Seneschal, 140
Senez, 113
Senozan, M., 195, 197
Sens, 40, 59, 165
Servandoni, 8
Sieyès, 17
Sillards, *Curé* of, 159
Sirven Affair, 42
Soanen, Bishop of Senez, 113
Solites, 94
Solminiac, de, Bishop of Cahors, 48
Sorbonne, 8, 43, 52
Strasbourg, 12
Styx, 17
Syndics-General of the Clergy, 25, 58, 133, 207

Taille, 2, 27, 37, 93, 160, 165, 169, 189
Taine, 40
Talleyrand-Périgord, 11
Talleyrand-Périgord, Alexandre-Angélique de, Archbishop of

Reims, later Cardinal-Archbishop of Paris, 9, 10, 11, 15, 17, 18, 19, 33, 36, 177
Talleyrand-Périgord, Archambault de, 7, 9
Talleyrand-Périgord, Count Charles-Daniel de, 8, 9
Talleyrand-Périgord, Countess Charles-Daniel de, 8
Talleyrand-Périgord, Hélie de, Cardinal, 16
TALLEYRAND-PERIGORD, CHARLES-MAURICE DE,
And the Abbé de Chatre, 137, 142
And the Abbé Maury, 105, 106, 131
As the Abbé de Périgord, 17, 20, 74, 105, 177, 179
And the Abbé de Rastignac, 103, 104, 124
Abbé de Saint-Denis, 9, 18, 22
And Abbey of Chaalis, 102
Agent-General of the Clergy, 1, 2, 6, 68, 69
And Archbishop Dulau, 207
And Archbishop Leclerc de Juigné, 123
Author of correspondence of the Agency, 73
Author of "Diocesan Syndic Plan," 78, 157, 171
Author of plan to prohibit alienations, 103
Author of "Report of the Agency," 78
And the baptismal registry, 149, 193
As Bishop of Autun, 2, 12, 15, 17, 66, 69, 72, 106
And Cardinal de Bernis, 207
And Cardinal de La Rochefoucauld, 124, 207
And the Celestines of Lyon, 104, 210
And the Chapel of Saint John the Evangelist of Tours, 31
As Chaplain of the Chapel of the Virgin Mary of Reims, 18
Collection of furniture, 20
Collections of books, 20
As commendatory abbot, 19, 22
And Committee for Religion and Jurisdiction in the Assembly of 1775, 90, 99
On complexity of the office of Agent-General, 120
And *curés*, 96, 97, 98, 99, 100, 119, 129, 130, 132, 133, 136, 137, 140, 141, 143, 159, 161, 162, 163, 164, 165, 166, 170, 171, 172, 173, 181, 211
Defines complexity of the Agency, 120
Defines conditions of Agents' legal intervention, 120
Deputy to General Assembly of the Clergy, 1775, 20, 108
And Diaconate, 23
And "Diocesan Syndic Plan," 203, 210, 211
And Duchesne, 176, 177, 178, 179, 180, 189, 190, 196
And educational reform, 155
Elected Agent-General from the Province of Tours, 30
And Episcopal Council of Autun, 12
Excorporation from Archdiocese of Paris, 21
Wins favor of ministers and political leaders as Agent-General, 76, 83, 84, 90, 96, 97, 100, 125, 131, 136, 137, 147, 150, 166, 169, 170, 171, 172, 173, 177
Foe of alienations, 102-3, 137
And *foi et hommage*, 91, 92, 145, 151, 153, 154, 160, 162, 163, 166, 210
Founding bishop of Civil Constitutional Church, 12
Handwriting, 178
As *hospes* and *socius* at the Sorbonne, 20
Incorporation into Archdiocese of Reims, 22
And lawyers of the clergy, 192
And Loménie de Brienne's "Syndic-General" plan, 207, 208
And Louis XVI, 86-7, 90, 104, 147, 148
And Mannay, Bishop of Trèves, 177
Ordained priest, 23
And the *portion congrue*, 100, 134, 140, 154, 157, 160, 212

As Prince de Bénévent, 7
On principles of property ownership, 102-106
Promoter of the General Assembly, 18, 20
Report of the Agency praised by Assembly of 1785, 65
Responsible for most of the work of the Agency, 72-78
And scheme of hierarchical authority, 107
At Seminary of Saint Sulpice, 17, 19, 20
At the Sorbonne, 19
Statesmanlike qualities as Agent-General, 214
As Subdeacon of Paris, 20, 21
And Subdiaconate, 17, 18, 19
Thesis for baccalaureate in theology, 19
Ties to bishops and cardinals, 75
And tithes of Normandy, 94
And Vergennes, 84, 85, 87, 124, 153, 169, 210
Vicar-General of Reims, 23
Views on sovereignty of the General Assembly, 117
Tarbes, 139
Tax farmers, 206
Te Deum, 52, 153, 159
Temple, 5
Tencin, Cardinal-Minister, 14
Terrasson, Abbé, 5
Third Estate, 5, 37
Tithe-owners, 39, 93, 96, 99, 160, 163
Tithes, 25, 82, 92, 97, 110, 146, 159, 189, 203
Toulon, 13, 113, 122, 169
Toulouse, 53, 59, 140, 173, 201
Tours, 31, 59, 131, 158, 179, 201

Trannes, *Curé* of, 163
Tréguier, 156
Trent, Council of, 126
Troyes, 163, 198
Turgot, 12, 16, 17, 20, 52, 76, 96

Ultramontanism, 26, 31
Unigenitus, Bull, 32, 111, 112
Ursulines, 122, 169

Vaison, 40
Valence, 128
Verdun, 167
Vergennes, 76, 77, 84, 85, 87, 93, 124, 153, 169, 210
Vergniaud, 17
Versailles, 52, 58, 213
Vicars, 96, 97
Victor-Amadeus III, King of Sardinia, 104
Vienna, 84
Vienne, 59, 128, 133
Villiers, Canon de, 131
Vingtième, 27, 28, 37, 83, 88, 93, 111, 160, 169, 170, 189
Vintimille, de, Bishop of Toulon, 13
Virgin, the, 20
Visa, 128, 130, 131, 147, 189, 193
Visitandines, 199
Voguë, 68
Voisin, Abbé, 44
Voltaire, 40, 44, 45, 80, 146, 210
Vulpian, 188

Wars of Religion, 1, 2, 24, 41

Ximenès, 14

Yvon, Abbé, 5